Jay G. Will

HAMILTON COLL

UNDERSTANDING THE OLD TESTAMENT

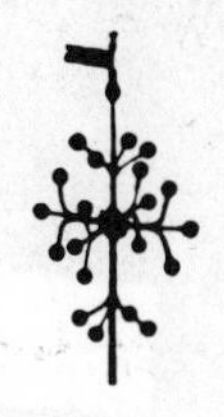

EDUCATIONAL SERIES, INC.
New York • London • Toronto • Sydney

All inquiries should be addressed to:
Barron's Educational Series, Inc.
250 Wireless Boulevard
Hauppauge, New York 11788

Library of Congress Catalog Card No. 74-162825

International Standard Book No. 0-8120-0424-8

PRINTED IN THE UNITED STATES OF AMERICA

012 500 11 10 9

Gloria M. Barron Editions.
Books bearing this imprint represent a distinguished contribution to scholarship and to world understanding. Their purpose is to help people learn to live together in peace.

To my children

Jay, Lynn, Daryl, and Ruth

Preface

This book has been written to serve as a guide for reading in that rich but sometimes confusing library of books which is often called the Old Testament. Because it is meant for the general reader rather than the specialist, primary emphasis has been placed upon the central ideas and motifs of these thirty-nine books rather than upon technical literary criticism. For those who wish to pursue questions of source, form, and tradition criticism further, a selected bibliography of more specialized books is provided.

It cannot be emphasized too vigorously that this volume is designed as a guide to the Old Testament rather than as a substitute for it. Nothing can replace the reading of the text itself. Although nearly every translation has its value, quotations in this volume are taken from the Revised Standard Version. The serious student, however, may wish to consult several modern translations to savor the variety of ways in which the Hebrew may be rendered.

Perhaps the best way to use this book in connection with the study of the Old Testament is to begin by reading the introductory chapters found in Part I, for these provide essential textual, geographical, and historical information. Then one can turn to one or another of the Biblical books for further study. Although it is probably *not* best to read the Old Testament the way one reads a novel, i.e., from cover to cover, it may be helpful to start with Genesis and Exodus which tell of the origins of Israel's Holy History and set forth the basic motifs of the Bible as a whole. After these have been studied, the reader may then wish to turn to a book of prophecy or to one of the Writings. The Chapters V, XI, and XX provide general introductions to the major sections of the Old Testament and ought to be read before proceeding to the individual books.

In this volume each book of the Bible is introduced and summarized briefly. Needless to say, the summaries provided are by no means exhaustive. They are meant simply as an indication to the reader of what the book contains and of how some of the central passages may be interpreted. Like any road map, they indicate the main curves in the route but seldom deal with the many jogs and bumps along the way.

In general there has been no attempt in this book to set forth new or radical theories concerning the Old Testament. My aim is not to resolve difficult issues once and for all, but to provide a well-informed interpretation which can be used as a starting point for further investigation. Still, no author can quite resist the temptation to express his own, particular opinions concerning the interpretation of the text. The reader ought to be warned, then, that this volume by no means contains the "last word" about any of the topics discussed. Anyone who reads further in the critical literature will surely discover many opinions which contradict what is said herein. That is inevitable, for no issue of interpretation is ever quite settled permanently.

Furthermore, the reader ought to be cognizant of the fact that because the author is particularly interested in Near Eastern archaeology and in the nature of Biblical mythology, these subjects receive special emphasis. Basically, however, the impetus which has led to the writing of this book has been my own delight in and admiration of the Old Testament as an expression of the grandeur and the misery of the human spirit. If the reader comes, through a reading of this book, to a fuller appreciation of why the Old Testament has served mankind so long as a source of inspiration and self-awareness, I shall be more than satisfied.

Acknowledgment

The author and publisher, *Barron's Educational Series, Inc.*, acknowledges with thanks permission by the National Council of the Churches of Christ in the U.S.A. to quote from the following book:

The Scripture quotations in this publication are from the *Revised Standard Version of the Bible,* © 1946 and 1952 by the Division of Christian Education of the National Council of the Churches of Christ in the U.S.A., and used by permission.

Contents

PREFACE iv

CHAPTER I: SOME PROBLEMS OF INTERPRETATION 1

CHAPTER II: INTERPRETING THE BIBLE: SOME CLASSIC CONSIDERATIONS 7

The Question of Text, p. 7

The Question of Canon, p. 9

The Question of Historiography, p. 12

Myth and History, p. 19

CHAPTER III: THE GEOGRAPHY OF THE LAND OF ISRAEL 23

The Setting, p. 23

The Geography of Israel: Unity and Diversity, p. 25

CHAPTER IV: A BRIEF HISTORY OF ISRAEL 31

The Major periods of Israel's History, p. 31

From Before the Hebrews, p. 32

To the End of the Old Testament Period, p. 62

CHAPTER V: THE TORAH: AN INTRODUCTION 66

The Argument, p. 67

The Composition of the Torah, p. 69

CHAPTER VI: GENESIS: INTRODUCTION AND ANALYSIS 74

The Origin of the World and of Man and His Families, p. 76

The Sagas of Abraham and Isaac, p. 84

The Jacob Sagas, p. 90

The Saga of Joseph, p. 93

CHAPTER VII: EXODUS: INTRODUCTION AND ANALYSIS 96

The Composition of Exodus, p. 96

The Date of the Exodus, p. 99

Analysis, p. 101

CHAPTER VIII: LEVITICUS: INTRODUCTION AND ANALYSIS 114

The Date of Composition, p. *116*

Laws for the Cult, p. *118*

The Holiness Code, p. *121*

CHAPTER IX: NUMBERS: INTRODUCTION AND ANALYSIS 124

Israel at Sinai, p. *125*

From Sinai to Moab, p. *127*

Israel in Moab, p. *130*

CHAPTER X: DEUTERONOMY: INTRODUCTION AND ANALYSIS 133

The Contents of Deuteronomy, p. *133*

The Uniqueness of Deuteronomy, p. *136*

Conclusion, p. *142*

CHAPTER XI: THE PROPHETS, A GENERAL INTRODUCTION 144

CHAPTER XII: JOSHUA: INTRODUCTION AND ANALYSIS 149

The Entering of the Promised Land, p. *151*

The Conquest of the Land, p. *152*

The Division of the land and the affirmation of the Covenant, p. *155*

CHAPTER XIII: JUDGES: INTRODUCTION AND ANALYSIS 157

CHAPTER XIV: I AND II SAMUEL: INTRODUCTION AND ANALYSIS 167

I. The birth and judgeship of Samuel, p. *169*

II. The reigns of Saul and David, p. *170*

CHAPTER XV: I AND II KINGS: INTRODUCTION AND ANALYSIS 177

From Solomon until the Fall of Jerusalem, p. *180*

CHAPTER XVI: ISAIAH: INTRODUCTION AND ANALYSIS 193

The Life and Times of Isaiah, p. *195*

PART I: *Isaiah 1-39,* p. *195*

PART II: *Isaiah 40-66,* p. *204*

CHAPTER XVII: JEREMIAH: INTRODUCTION AND ANALYSIS 212

The Nature of the Book, p. *213*

Jeremiah's Life and Times, p. *215*

Analysis, p. *219*

CHAPTER XVIII: EZEKIEL: INTRODUCTION AND ANALYSIS 224

The Life and Times of Ezekiel, p. *226*

Analysis, p. *227*

CHAPTER XIX: The Minor Prophets: Introduction and Analysis 234

Hosea, p. 235
Joel, p. 239
Amos, p. 241
Obadiah, p. 245
Jonah, p. 245
Micah, p. 248
Nahum, p. 250
Habakkuk, p. 251
Zephaniah, p. 253
Haggai, p. 255
Zechariah, p. 256
Malachi, p. 260

CHAPTER XX: The Writings 262

CHAPTER XXI: The Book of Job: Introduction and Analysis 266

Job and Wisdom, p. 267
Analysis, p. 269
Conclusion, p. 274

CHAPTER XXII: The Psalms: Introduction and Analysis 276

CHAPTER XXIII: The Book of Proverbs: Introduction and Analysis 286

Some General Considerations, p. 286
Analysis, p. 288

CHAPTER XXIV: The Megillot 292

Ruth, p. 294
The Song of Songs, p. 295
Ecclesiastes, p. 297
Lamentations, p. 301
Esther, p. 303

CHAPTER XXV: Daniel 307

CHAPTER XXVI: Ezra and Nehemiah: Introduction and Analysis 317

The Composition of the Books, p. 317
Analysis, p. 320
Ezra, p. 320
Nehemiah, p. 321
Conclusion, p. 323

CHAPTER XXVII: Chronicles I and II: Introduction and Analysis 324

Date of Authorship, p. 325
Sources for Chronicles, p. 325
I Chronicles, p. 327
II Chronicles, p. 328

SUGGESTED READINGS 331

CHAPTER I

Some Problems of Interpretation

ESPITE the many new translations of the Bible which have appeared in recent years, most laymen still find the Bible difficult to read. Its very size makes it seem unapproachable to those of us who do our reading in bits and snatches. Even when one takes a deep breath and decides to plunge in, one finds himself very soon in a forest of names and strange customs where there seems to be very little light. More than one reader has started Genesis with the most pious hopes only to put the Book of Books down a few Patriarchs later in bewilderment.

This book is written to make the Old Testament more available for the modern reader, but it should be cautioned at the outset that this is no easy task. Not only does the Bible presuppose a knowledge of Palestinian geography and history which is foreign to most of us, the world-view of the Bible is so different from ours that it is sometimes difficult to ascertain what truths it is attempting to proclaim. In order to enter into the world of the Bible one must be prepared for the cultural and intellectual shock which it presents.

The intention of this volume is not to make the difficult appear superficially easy but to set forth, in as simple a manner as possible, what problems do in fact face the reader of Scripture and to offer some guidelines and information for setting about the absorbing task of understanding the text before us. Before we can look at the text itself, certain basic problems of interpretation must be discussed and the outlines of a methodology must be developed. It is to be hoped that the reader will not skip over this opening discussion to the main body of the book, for much which is said later depends, at least in part, upon the recognition of the various problems which are now to be discussed.

One of the first problems which the reader of Scripture must face is raised by the title "the Old Testament." Quite clearly this phrase is of Christian origin, for it implies the existence of another, "New" Testament, which, in some sense, supercedes the "Old." A Jew, when speaking of the same set of books, ought to call them "the Hebrew Scriptures" or, to use the Hebrew word, the *Tanak*. This difference is more than a matter of nomenclature, for it indicates that Jews and Christians, as believing men, approach the Scriptures in different ways. The Christian, as a Christian, interprets what he reads from the vantage point of the New Testament and of his own theological and ecclesiastical tradition. The Jew, as an heir of a rich and distinctive Rabbinical tradition, inevitably reads the same text from that perspective.

This is as it should be, for, as a part of a living religious tradition the Hebrew Scriptures must be understood in the light of the other aspects of that tradition. Thus it is quite appropriate for a Christian, when stating the theological position of his Church, to interpret the Old Testament in terms of the truths developed later in the New Testament and in the Creeds of the Church. In so doing, he is not so much interested in what the Old Testament meant to the original authors as in what it means to the Christian today and how it coheres with the faith of the Church as a whole. The theologian, of course, may also study the Old Testament simply as a product of the past and may concentrate upon its original meaning. In doing so, however, he is acting not so much as a theologian as an objective historian.

Needless to say, I do not mean to imply that the theologian ought to avoid acting as an objective historian. Such objectivity may, in fact, sometimes help him to understand the Bible better. A theologian, however, quite appropriately understands the tradition of his Church as a unity and reads the Old Testament with "Christian eyes." Only when he does so can the Hebrew Scriptures be considered a "living tradition" for him.

Within the Jewish and Christian communities there are many "sub-communities," each with its own particular identity and view-point. A Roman Catholic may well read the Old Testament with somewhat different "eyes" than a member of the Greek Orthodox or Presbyterian communion. Reformed and Orthodox Jews will certainly disagree about the interpretation of many passages of the *Tanak*. A student of Scripture, then, is confronted by a plethora of interpretations which emphasize different meanings to be found in the text. Nor is it possible to distinguish easily between correct interpretations and wrong ones. If one begins with the assumption that the task of the theological interpreter is carried on within the circle of his own tradition and is to "break open" Scripture so that it will speak to his particular community in his particular age, then obviously interpretations must vary according to the community and age which is addressed.

Such a fact should not seem strange to anyone acquainted with the interpretation of other works of art. The meaning of a work of art is not simply lodged immutably in the work itself. Meaning springs from the interaction of, for instance, the poem as an objective work of art and the interpreter who brings to the poem his own set of questions and presuppositions. Thus *Hamlet* will mean quite different things to a Freudian, a Marxist, and an Existentialist. The fact that Shakespeare himself had neither the Oedipus complex nor dialectical materialism nor the nausea of absurdity in mind when he wrote the drama is beside the point. As an artist he created an objective work of art which transcends his own interpretation of it. *Hamlet* is a great art because countless generations have found and will find it to be a source of meaning and insight for them.

This is not to say that the interpretation of art is purely subjective. There is a "giveness" to art which defies pure subjectivity and which may, indeed, convert the observer to a new point of view. Still, the interpreter brings himself to the dialogue with the work, and that self, with all its predispositions, needs, and preconceptions, inevitably shapes the interpretation which results.

There are, of course, many scholars who disagree with this point of view. The only way to read the Bible correctly, they say, is to rid oneself of all dogmatic presuppositions and analyze the text "objectively." Instead of reading into the Bible what is not there, let us, through the use of anthropological, archaeological, and philological findings, discover what the Bible meant to those who wrote it. Only when one does this, can one discover *the* meaning of the Bible.

There is, of course, something admirable and appealing about this approach. For those who are bewildered and alienated by the variety of interpretations offered by different sects and traditions, modern scientific scholarship comes as a breath of fresh air. It must be admitted that such an approach does have much to offer, not only to those outside the "circle of faith," but to all the groups which have for so long taken the Bible as their holy book. It is important for all to know that some passages of the Bible are historically inaccurate and that others are highly reliable. It is interesting to recognize what Israel borrowed from her neighbors and how she transformed the myths of Mesopotamia and Canaan to suit her own ends. Certainly one ought not to be willing to interpret a text without having thoroughly examined the original meanings of the words involved. Still, it would be illusory to think that scientific scholarship circumvents the problems of interpretation which have been raised or that it can bring us to *the* meaning of the text. In the first place, the decision to approach Scripture with pure objectivity is, in itself, subjective. It is an expression of our age. The academic scholar who puts aside any dogmatic consideration or "faith commitment" to study the text "objectively" is, as a matter of fact, expressing the faith of the academic community in which he lives and works. It may well be that his methodology can shed a certain kind of light upon the meaning of the text which other types of interpreters have missed, but it must also be recognized that scientific objectivity has certain important limitations which ought not to be overlooked.

The truth of the matter—and this is the second point—is that the Bible was not meant to be read "objectively." It was written to be read with faith, as a witness to the power and mercy of God in the life of Israel. The scholar who eschews faith for the sake of objectivity in order to recover the "original meaning of the text" may then miss that meaning precisely because of his objectivity. In his quest for "the facts" the personal and communal meaning of scripture may well elude him.

Furthermore, the objective historian does not really put away all dogmatic considerations. Rather, he replaces the presuppositions of faith with the presuppositions of modern science and historiography. Hence, he reads Scripture with eyes already preconditioned to accept certain assertions and reject certain others. For instance, when it is claimed that a miracle occurred, he is compelled to reject that assertion on the grounds that such an event could not happen. That is to say, there is no room in his world-view for the possibility of miracles. When it is claimed that someone saw a vision about the future, he explains this as a later addition to the text "after the fact." In his world-view, predicting the future is not a possibility. This is not the place to challenge some of the presuppositions which shape modern historiography. It may well be, in fact, that in many instances, the scientific historian is correct. My only point is that scientific interpretation, like every other type, involves the interaction of the text and the individual. It is the interpretation of Scripture for a particular community, the community of objective scholarship.

This leads us to a third point. There seems to be an underlying assumption among both religious and non-religious academic scholars that there is, finally, one meaning for each text under consideration. The question is, however, whether great art ever contains but *one* meaning. My contention is that the search for one meaning is illusory. Rather than asking for the one immutable truth lodged in the passage which holds true for all men at all times, one ought to ask, "What does this story or commandment or parable mean today, for my community and for me?"

How then can anyone write a book about the Old Testament, meant for a wide variety of readers, without simply offering a personal confession or engaging surreptitiously in interpretation from a particular theological or academic perspective? In one sense, it is clear that one cannot, for every approach to the Hebrew Scriptures inevitably must imply certain presuppositions which will not be accepted by all. The most that can be done is to indicate the biases and limitations of the interpretation given, with the hope that the reader will take them into account while reading it.

The aim of this book is to provide some basic historical, philological, and textual facts so that the reader may interpret the text for himself more intelligently. My primary assumption is that in the twentieth century most people want to approach the Bible from an historical point of view. Our whole educational system teaches the religious and the non-religious alike to ask of the text a series of factual questions: Did the events described really happen? Who wrote this book? When and for what purposes was it written? What does this word mean? These, therefore, are the primary questions to which we will address ourselves in this book.

It should be underlined, however, that the answers to these questions provide only a prolegomena to real interpretation. Unless one uses them carefully, the facts may be of little use to the interpreter. For instance, the scholar who studies *Macbeth* may well find it important to ascertain whether or not Shakespeare really wrote the play or to compare Shakepeare's account of the life of Macbeth with what we know historically about that Scottish king. It certainly will be important to examine the meaning of certain words which the author uses which now are archaic or of different import. All these facts, however, will hardly bring the scholar to an understanding of murder, the theme of the drama. To find meaning in the play the scholar must put aside his pure objectivity and enter into the drama itself. Only in the interaction of the Dramatis Personnae and the person who "actively sees and hears" will meaning be born. Only then can the scholar engage in the high art of interpretation.

The phrase *The Old Testament* also implicitly raises other problems which must be dealt with at the outset, for it implies that there is one "thing" which can be designated by that name. The truth is, however, that there is no one absolutely fixed text or canon of the Old Testament which is accepted by all. In order to elucidate this statement, let us first look briefly at the question of text and then at the question of canon.

CHAPTER II

Interpreting the Bible: Some Classic Considerations

The Question of Text
The Question of Canon
The Question of Historiography
Myth and History

OST TRANSLATIONS of the Old Testament are based primarily upon the Masoretic text (MT), a Hebrew text prepared by a group of Jewish scholars called the Masoretes who flourished from about the sixth century to the twelfth century A.D. in Palestine and Babylonia. Before the time of the Masoretes, the basic consonantal text of the *Tanak* had already become fairly well standardized, but, because in ancient Hebrew the vowels were not written, the text could be pronounced and, hence, interpreted in a variety of ways. The Masoretes worked out a system of marks indicating how the vowels should be pronounced, standardized the division of words in the text, and decided among variant readings extant at the time. Thus they produced for Judaism and, ultimately for Christianity, a standardized text of the Hebrew Scriptures.

The Question of Text

The question is, how well did the Masoretes do their work? Did they always find the best reading for a particular text or were they sometimes led to select one because of their own particular prejudices? Unfortunately we do not have enough manuscripts which antedate their work really to tell. Furthermore, even if we uncovered a full text of the Bible from earlier times, we could not be sure exactly how it was pronounced. The discovery of the great Isaiah scroll among the so-called Dead Sea scrolls shows that the consonantal text of the Masoretes did not differ much from consonantal texts of much earlier times, but whether the pronunciation and, hence, the meaning of the text was sometimes changed we do not know. On the whole it would appear, however, that the Masoretes would note the peculiarity of a reading, but seldom tampered with it. Thus we can conclude that they have delivered to us the Jewish text of the *Tanak* as it was known and read during their era.

There is another text (or series of texts) which does raise some doubts, however, concerning the complete accuracy of the MT. The Greek translation of the Old Testament, usually called the Septuagint (LXX), which was prepared during the third century B.C. for use by Greek-speaking Jews, differs from the Masoretic text in many ways. Particularly in the prophetic books there are many textual variations to be found. Is this so because the LXX was a rather free translation? Certainly this is true in many cases. There are times, however, when the LXX may contain earlier readings which were lost in the Hebrew text itself.

Thus it is not always possible to say, "This is what the Old Testament says." The student must be aware that there sometimes are variations in the text which make considerable difference. Let me give one, rather crucial, example. In Isaiah 7:14 the prophet predicts that "someone" shall conceive and bear a son and shall call his name Immanuel. The word used for that "someone" in the Hebrew text is *almah*, which is best translated "young woman." In the Greek translation the word used is *parthenos* or virgin. During much of its history the Christian Church, following Matthew 2:23, accepted the Greek reading and took this passage to be a prediction of the Virgin Birth. Modern translators, however, argue that the Hebrew text contains a better (older) reading and thus have translated the text, "A young woman shall conceive . . . ," much to the consternation of many conservative Christians. I believe the modern translators to have made a sound choice, for the Isaiah scroll of Qumran proves *almah* to be an ancient Hebrew reading. Probably the Septuagint contains a mistranslation of the original. Because the Church has never settled upon a standardized text, however, the question remains open. One must ask not only, "Is the text translated correctly?" but also "Which Old Testament is being translated?"

The reader of an English version also ought to be aware of some other problems which face the translator which tend to be obscured by the translation. Although most of the Hebrew text is reasonably clear, there are many words and sentences which are not. Sometimes a word or words seem to have been omitted due to some scribal error. Sometimes a word or phrase appears which makes no sense at all, either because the meaning of the words is unknown or because the word has somehow become garbled in transmission. The translator must compare various early texts and versions and must use his knowledge of comparative linguistics as best he can. Often the translation which he offers can be no more than a calculated guess. The person who then quotes such a translation as the supreme authority is doing something very risky. He may be, in effect, substituting the guess of some translator for what he believes to be the authority of God.

One can make too much of these problems. On the whole, the Hebrew Scriptures are reasonably plain and understandable. Nevertheless, the person who can only use a translation rather than the original languages must be wary. Even the specialist equipped to deal with the complicated textual and linguistic problems raised must seek to understand the spirit of the work under consideration rather than depend too much on a single word or sentence. Anyone who rests his interpretation upon a single proof text is likely to discover, if he is honest, that his whole case is supported by very shaky evidence.

The Question of Canon

THE WORD *canon* is derived from a Semitic root meaning "reed or measuring stick." Within a religious context it is used to refer to the norm according to which faith is measured. The canon for both Christians and Jews is the Holy Scripture, though, of course, the Christian canon includes the New Testament, while the Jewish canon does not. Unfortunately, there are also differences among Christians and Jews concerning precisely what constitutes the Old Testament canon. That is to say, not only has there been no universal agreement about the text of the Old Testament; there also has been no absolute agreement about what books should be included among the Scriptures.

This lack of agreement is due in large measure to the fact that at the time when the Christian Church began, the Hebrew canon was not complete. We know little about the early formation of the Hebrew canon, but most scholars agree that the first part of it, i.e., the Pentateuch or *Torah*, gained official authoritative status about 400 B.C. Since that time, these five books (Genesis, Exodus, Leviticus, Numbers, and Deuteronomy) have been regarded by Jews as the most sacred of all their canonical writings. In about 200 B.C. the Jews added to their canon the former prophets (Joshua, Judges, Samuel, and Kings) and latter prophets (Isaiah, Jeremiah, Ezekiel, and a scroll containing the twelve "minor" prophets). The Samaritans, a group of believers in the God of Israel inhabiting the north-central region of Israel around Samaria, did not concur in this addition. Hence, to this day their canon consists of only the Torah.

At the time of Jesus, the Jews regarded only the Law and the Prophets as canonical, though other books were becoming increasingly thought of as authoritative works. It was not until 90 A.D. at the Council of Jamnia, however, that a final decision was reached concerning the last section of the canon. At that time a group of distinguished Rabbis, meeting in the wake of the destruction of Jerusalem by the Romans in 70 A.D. and the rise of a new "sect" called "the Nazareans" which regarded Jesus as the Messiah, decided upon the books to be included in and excluded from the third section of the canon which is now called "the Writings" or, in Hebrew, the *Kethuvim*. After much debate they decided upon the following books: Psalms, Proverbs, Job, the five scrolls to be read on major holy days (Song of Songs, Ruth, Lamentation, Ecclesiastes, and Esther), Daniel, and the history of the Chronicler (I and II Chronicles, Ezra, and Nehemiah).

In the meantime, however, editions of the Septuagint which contained not only the Law and the Prophets but other works as well had been circulating widely among Greek-speaking Jews and Christians. These editions of the Greek translation apparently included not only many of the works finally accepted by the council of Jamnia but also several works later excluded from the canon by the Rabbis. Hence the Christian Church, which grew rapidly among Greek-speaking peoples, used from the beginning a canon which was somewhat different from the canon finally settled upon by Judaism. Included among those "extra" books accepted by Christianity but rejected by Judaism were: the first and second books of Esdras, Tobit, Judith, the Wisdom of Solomon, the Wisdom of Jesus ben-Sirach, Baruch, Susanna, the Prayer of Manasseh, and the first and second books of Maccabees. The Septuagint version also included certain additions to both Esther and Daniel. These works are together designated as the *Apocrypha.*

This difference between the Christian and Jewish canons continued until the time of the Protestant Reformation. At that time, some of the Protestant Reformers argued that since the Old Testament is meant to represent the faith of Pre-Christian Israel, the Old Testament canon ought to be that of the Jews. Some Protestant Churches (particularly Calvinistic ones) therefore excluded the Apocrypha from the canon completely. Others, like the Anglican and Lutheran Churches, retained the Apocrypha as "edifying" but without the full canonical status of the Law, Prophets, and Writings. The Roman Catholic Church, on the other hand, decided to retain the Apocrypha as canonical.

To add even more confusion to an already confusing situation, both Protestants and Roman Catholics retained the basic order of the Septuagint, an order which differs somewhat from the Hebrew order. The Hebrew Bible is divided into three parts: the Law, the Prophets, and the Writings. In the Greek Bible, however, the books of the Writings are mixed together with the prophetic books. Since the story of Ruth, for instance, is set "in the time of the Judges," it is placed, in the Greek canon, immediately after the book of Judges. I and II Chronicles, Ezra, Nehemiah, and Esther, as historical works, are placed immediately after the historical books of Samuel and Kings. In other words, in Christian Bibles the distinction between the Prophets and the Writings is thoroughly blurred. Although this may seem a minor matter, the position of the book in the order of the canon can be very important. For instance, in interpreting Ruth it is significant to remember that it was included in the canon as the scroll to be read at Pentecost rather than as simply another historical work. In Christian Bibles the festival scrolls are separated one from the other and their cultic significance is consequently obscured.

When one speaks of "the Old Testament," then, one must specify not only what text is referred to but which canon is to be used. In this book, we shall use the text, contents, and order of the Jewish canon as a basis for discussion. It must be recognized, however, that a decision to proceed in this way is somewhat arbitrary. One could, just as easily, use the Roman Catholic or Protestant canon.

The discussion of the Old Testament contained in this volume will proceed, then, according to the Jewish canonical order and will be based primarily, though not exclusively, on the Masoretic text. The treatment, however, will not be from a Jewish point of view. Rather, we will approach the Old Testament by asking of it the questions usually raised by an "objective" historian. Hopefully, this approach will serve as a useful basis for interpretation, but it ought not to be considered an end in itself. Ultimately, though an interpreter must use the objective facts in his analysis of the text, he must confront the text as a "person" in order to hear what it says to his time, his community, his situation.

The Question of Historiography

ALTHOUGH IT IS appropriate to approach the Bible and its history with a modicum of objectivity, the attempt to do so raises certain historiographical problems which ought not to be lightly dismissed. Quite obviously much of the Bible is, in itself, historical; yet it is also apparent that Biblical historiography differs in many important respects from the kind of history that modern scholars write. It is important, therefore, to characterize the difference between these types of historiography so that the aims and limitations of both modern objective scholarship and Biblical historiography may be better appreciated and understood.

The task of the modern historian can be described quite simply as an objective and unbiased attempt to discover and relate what "really happened." That is to say, the historian must put aside his own "dogmatic" assumptions and, through an analysis of the data available, determine what can be known about the past. Such data, for an historian of ancient Israel, comes from a variety of sources.

First of all, the Biblical historian has been greatly aided in recent years by the work of the archaeologists who have excavated many of the ancient Biblical sites and have, through painstakingly careful work, developed a fairly accurate method for dating the strata which they have uncovered. The key to dating a site is, in most cases, the pottery. Carbon 14 dating may be useful for the very early pre-pottery periods, but is much too inexact for the later, historical era. Basically, it is the potsherd which tells the story of a city's development and demise. One of the major tasks of the archaeologist has been to work out in detail a careful chronology of pottery types and styles and to correlate this chronology with the history of Israel which we know. This chronology is now well-developed and the archaeologist, by examining pottery remains of a given stratum in an excavation, can usually date that stratum rather exactly. Archaeologists have also studied carefully the development of architecture and city planning and now know how men built buildings in most periods and to what uses they were put. Epigraphists have, at the same time, studied the development of writing and can write at least an outline history of the development of the alphabet and the formation of various letters during Israel's long history. This area of archaeology needs much more exploration and development, for, as a matter of fact, the number of written documents from Israel during the Biblical period is quite limited. Nevertheless, enough fragments have been found to give some clues as to the development of writing.

As a result of long and careful work, the archaeologist can tell the Biblical historian a great deal about the history of the material culture of the land. Not only can he describe to the historian how ancient Canaanites and Israelites made pottery and built buildings; he can provide essential information about the time and extent of invasions by foreign peoples, when a city came into existence and passed out of existence, and what the social and political structure of a given community, as it is revealed in its public and private buildings and artifacts, was like. Occasionally an ostracon (a bit of pottery with writing on it) will give insight into the way business was conducted or justice meted out.

The reconstruction of the development of material culture, however, is hardly enough to constitute a history of a people. In order to write a full history of Israel there must be written documents which do more than record some business transaction. Unfortunately, the documents from Israel are very few in number and are limited in scope and significance. Most of the writings from the land of the Book have simply perished with the passing of time. There are, however, many documents from neighboring countries which help to illumine the world in which Israel and the Bible were born.

Thousands of cuneiform tablets containing myths, codes of law, business transactions, and historical material have been recovered from the southern Mesopotamian region and from Asshurbanipal's library at Ninevah. Egyptian tombs have also been a great source for ancient documents, inscriptions, and paintings. The cultures of both of Israel's great neighbors, therefore, can be described in some detail. The recovery of the Ras Shamra tablets at Ugarit has greatly enhanced our knowledge of the Phoenecian-Canaanite culture so that we can now form a much clearer picture of Israel's antagonists. Tablets from Mari and Nuzi help us to understand the culture of the northern Mesopotamian region from which Abraham's family is said to have come.

Sometimes these documents not only help us to describe the cultures surrounding Israel; they also shed direct light on the Bible itself. The Nuzi tablets, for instance, mention customs of that people which parallel quite exactly customs described in the book of Genesis. The myths of Mesopotamia are remarkably similar in many respects to some in the first chapters of Genesis. King-lists from Assyria and Babylonia and Pharaoh-lists from Egypt help us to correlate the history of Israel with the histories of those lands.

The discovery of all of these documents, however, should not blind us to the fact that the major source for understanding Israel's history is the Bible itself. Without the Bible little could be known about Israel at all. Therefore, the historian of Israel must depend heavily upon the Bible if he is to write a history of that people. Herein lies one of the major problems for the historian of Israel, for it is quite apparent that although the Bible is an "historical" work, its historiography is by no means modern. If a modern historian uses the Bible as an historical "source book" for writing a history of Israel, he must be very careful to observe and take into account the type of history which the Bible includes.

What are some of these differences between Biblical and modern historiography? The first, and perhaps most important, difference involves the purpose of the writer. The modern historian claims to want to reconstruct what happened in the past "objectively," without any motivation beside pure intellectual interest. The Biblical writers, on the other hand, wrote what German scholars have called *Heilsgeschichte*, or holy history. Their intent was to reveal and proclaim how God acted in the life of their people and how his promises and judgments shaped their destiny. Hence, those events chosen for retelling were, in some way, "revelatory" for Israel. This means, of course, that many other events which, from a secular view, might seem very important, were not even mentioned. Other occurrences of seeming insignificance were described at length, because they "contain a message" for the people of Israel.

Actually, Biblical and modern historians do not differ so much concerning this matter as may at first seem. No historian can mention all the events which have occurred, since the number of events is inexhaustible. This means that all historians must pick and choose carefully what they are going to include. In this sense, the modern historian is not purely "objective," for he employs his own personal or cultural norms for determining the importance of events. Nevertheless, it is also clear that the criterion for selection is quite different for modern historians. While the writers of the Bible chose for retelling events which revealed to Israel something of the will of God, the modern historian tends to concentrate upon political, social, and economic facts—facts which are of paramount importance for modern, secular society. The historian of Israel who simply "takes over" the facts recorded in the Bible to write a history of Israel, therefore, may employ a criterion for relevance which is not really his own.

Second, while the modern historian tries to write objectively and thus thinks of history "in the third person," Biblical writers conceived of history as "their own." The exodus, they proclaim, is something which happened to us. This was not just an event which happened to our fore-fathers; we all were there; we all have been freed from bondage; we all have made a covenant with the "freeing God" at Sinai. In other words, the Biblical writer thinks of the past, not as immutable and dead, but as alive and, in a sense, changeable. Not that the "fact" of the Exodus can ever be erased or cancelled, but because the writer of the Bible recited a living memory, he told of events which recur over and over again in the life of Israel. Each generation must return in memory to those days when God led Israel out of Egypt and relive that event once more. And when each generation returns it experiences this event in a somewhat new way.

Because the Biblical writers recognized that they dealt with a living memory they treated the question "What really happened?" quite differently than would a modern historian. That is to say, the Biblical writers felt no compunctions about adding to the story the experiences and feelings of later Israelites. The account of the Exodus, for instance, is a mixture of the experiences of many generations of Israelites who escaped from Egypt in their memory. For the modern historian this attitude is very frustrating. He wishes to describe the event "as it occurred" once and for all. He wishes to strip away all later, and therefore superfluous, additions to get to the event itself. Although this is a worthwhile and, for us, necessary task, it must be recognized that it is not the way the Biblical writers intended their works to be read. Rather than simply giving us the facts, they ask us to relive the events ourselves and experience their meaning for us. The anonymous writer of the Negro spiritual "Go Down Moses," therefore, probably understood far more deeply the meaning of the Exodus, which the writers wished to convey, than the host of Biblical scholars who pick apart the text trying to deal with it objectively.

Furthermore, although we shall take the opportunity in Chapter Three to discuss what "really happened" from a modern historical point of view, it must be noted that this modern quest is ultimately self-defeating. The modern historian wants to describe the events themselves; he wants to rid himself of subjective accretions and get to the facts. The truth of the matter is, however, *that events always happen to someone.* Indeed, an event becomes such only when it is experienced by an observer. Nor is a human observer simply a passive recipient of sensations. Rather, he perceives as he does and what he does according to his own world-view, interests, and predispositions.

A tragi-comic example of this fact was given in a recent newspaper article. It seems that to "entertain" refugees in some of the camps in Vietnam, American movies, with appropriate Vietnamese subtitles, were shown. Among the films were a number of "Cowboy and Indian" movies. For the average GI these were rather light-hearted "romps" in which the "good guys" defeated the "bad guys" and the right triumphed. The Vietnamese, however, so identified with the Indians that, for them, these movies were tragedies of the first order; they left with tears running down their faces. Thus, although the same film was projected on the screen, the GI's and the Vietnamese saw quite different dramas.

Not only may the same event engender different emotional responses. Because different people see the world quite differently, there ultimately may be no agreement among men as to what really happened. This fact is somewhat blurred for us because we live in a community of people who share a common world view and language. When we try to understand what happened to the ancient Israelites and Egyptians, however, we must be careful not to read into the events our own preconceptions about what they "ought" to have seen. Events undoubtedly happened to the ancient Israelite quite differently than they happen to us.

When a modern scientific historian says that he is studying the past "objectively" and will tell us what "really happened," what he is often actually saying is that he is going to describe the events as they would have happened to us had we been there. In other words, he describes the world as it is seen according to a modern secular-scientific world view. Such a description is interesting, and perhaps informative, but it tells us little about the events which actually occurred to people. The ancient Israelite perceived certain happenings as signs of God's action; he heard God speak in the events of his life; he saw visions of the future and lived by those visions. One can hardly describe Biblical events without taking this way of looking at life into account.

The modern historian, of course, might well respond by saying, "Of course, the Israelite *thought* he saw visions and signs and wonders, but we know better. He was simply deluded." This approach is so prevalent today that it is virtually impossible to argue cogently against it. "Obviously," says modern man, "science is right and mythology is wrong; there's no doubt about that." The truth is, however, that there *is* doubt about such an assertion of scientific dogmatism. Although it is impossible within the scope of this work to develop the arguments fully, it is important to examine the truth-claims which both "science" and "religion" make.

The conflict between these two approaches to reality does not involve a difference of opinion concerning whether the universe operates consistently. Both modern science and the Bible agree that it does. The question is whether, to use the language of Martin Buber, one ought to address the universe as "Thou" or regard it only as "It." The scientist begins with the assumption that he will, as a scientist, deal with the observable phenomena "objectively." That is, he will treat all reality as an "It" which can be understood in terms of the laws of cause and effect. Such a working hypothesis has borne great fruit, for the scientist has been able to chart the consistencies of the universe and, as a result predict and control the phenomena around him.

Just because the scientist as a scientist assumes that all reality should be treated as "It," however, says nothing about the possibility of responding to the world as "Thou." Indeed, unless man can say "Thou," even the personhood of man evaporates before the objective scrutiny of the behavioral psychologist. Man becomes a thing among things and as such is seen merely as the effect of certain causes. Much of the anguish of modern man stems from the fact that in his quest for objectivity he has lost any sense of purpose in being objective. What value is there in going farther faster if there is no ultimate meaning for man's life, if man is but the effect of certain natural causes? If science is justified by its ability to control man's environment, religion is justified by its ability to provide some purpose for man's existence. I speak here, not just in defense of Biblical religion, but of any which provides personal insight into the meaning of existence. Whether or not Biblical religion provides the profoundest means for discovering man's nature and destiny is a question to be left for the reader to answer. My only point here is that although scientific "It-saying" works quite well within a limited sphere, it hardly provides man with any ultimate sense of purpose or destiny. Without such a sense, life can only be meaningless and nihilism is the inevitable result. The answer of the nihilist *may*, of course, be correct. There may not be any meaning in life at all; all values and purposes may be ephemeral and illusory. That, however, hardly provides a possible basis for living in the world and really makes the whole scientific enterprise useless. The scientific control of environment is only "useful" when it can be employed to advance toward some ultimate end about which science itself cannot rightfully speak.

Science, then, may provide a correct understanding of the nature of certain phenomena, but it is a partial understanding. If man is to find meaning and purpose in existence, he must somehow transcend the It-saying of the scientist to confront the world as Thou. This is the secret of all of the ancient religions of man. The difference between the Biblical religion and the polytheisms of Israel's neighbors is that while the latter saw the world as a multiplicity of Thous who often warred against one another, Israel saw the universe as ultimately united by the one Thou who is the source of all being. And it was in listening to that Thou who speaks in both the natural order and history that Israel found purpose and destiny for herself and mankind.

One may, of course, reject Israel's vision of God and the world as wrong-headed or misleading. Nevertheless, if one wishes to describe the events as they were experienced, one must acknowledge that Israel "heard" and "saw" certain events as revelations of meaning for her. Hence the Bible comes closer to describing the events of history as they were perceived than does the objective historian who substitutes his own world-view for the world-view of the original observers. This does not mean that the modern historian ought to give up his objective quest and simply repeat the Biblical story. There is some value in determining how certain events might have appeared to us had we been there. I am only arguing that the historian ought to be aware of the limitations placed upon him by his own world-view. Inevitably a history tells the reader as much about the historian as it does about the events he describes.

Myth and History

ULTIMATELY, THEN, history and mythology cannot be distinguished sharply. All history is, in a sense, mythological, for all history reflects the under-girding world-view of a particular age. Nevertheless, some provisional distinctions between history and mythology ought to be made, for surely ancient mythology and modern history are different.

The English word *myth* is derived from the Greek word *mythos* which means, quite simply, story or tale. Most, if not all, ancient myths had some basis in historical fact. The myth of Demeter recorded in the Homeric Hymns, for instance, tells of the coming of the goddess Demeter to Eleusis at a particular time. Archaeological evidence has now confirmed that the cult of Demeter did begin during the era mentioned in the myth. The story itself, however, transcends history, for it is an attempt to describe in "Thou" language the recurrent autumnal departure of Persephone, the goddess of flowers and vegetative life, and her return each spring. As in all myths what the scientist would regard as an "It," the mythologizer describes as "Thou." When the flowers begin to bloom once more, Persephone has returned from the underworld. Because we modern men have seemingly lost our ability to say "Thou" to nature, we consider such myths as false and superstitious. But is this not simply because we have forgotten how to think poetically? The scientist may study the effects of winter upon plant life in temperate regions and may give a description of the consistencies with which nature operates, but surely he does not prove the myth false. The fact that he says "It" to the natural order doesn't preclude the possibility of saying "Thou." Nor does the poetry of myth deny the possibility of scientific agriculture. Each expresses a way of looking at life; each records a partial truth which needs the supplementation of the other.

All true art, is, in a sense, mythological. For the sake of clarity, however, we ought to distinguish between the creative work of an individual artist and those more basic myths which form the spiritual foundation of a society's life. A myth, in this latter sense, provides an archetypal pattern and cohesive vision of the world which binds a culture together. It gives to society a common ground for feeling, thinking, and speaking about the world. In a real sense, the culture is born from the myth rather than the myth from the culture. The individual artist may offer his own interpretation and elaboration of the myth. He may sculpt a statue of Demeter or compose an Ode to Persephone or write a drama which reflects the archetypal pattern of the myth. But he does not, in this sense, create a myth. On the contrary, the myth creates his art. Even the author of the Homeric hymn to Demeter did not create the myth but simply retold in a poetic way a myth which had for a long time been a part of the Greek vision and experience. Real myths, then, are not created by individuals but arise out of the depth of a people's experience of life. They are not "true," but provide for a culture a basis for determining truth.

Several Biblical stories, contained particularly in the Torah, provide the basic archetypal patterns for Israel and hence can be considered Israel's myths. At the same time, Biblical myths must be distinguished sharply from the myths of the Greeks and other "pagans." When one opens the Bible, one enters a world populated not by gods and goddesses but by real, historical men. God is the chief character of the drama, but his actions take place in this world, in the world of population movements and bloody wars and historical action. Gone are the personifications of the recurrent forces of nature. God is in charge of the natural order, but he reveals himself most fully in unique historical events. Reality is no longer thought of in terms of cyclical return but in terms of historical particularity and uniqueness. Time marches on rather than around and around. Israel may live out her life according to the archetypal patterns set forth in the Torah and thus may experience the exodus over and over again, but these archetypal patterns always point forward to a destiny set before her. The difference between the Greek and the Hebrews (if I may be permitted to caricature each) is the difference between the return of Persephone and the entrance into the Promised Land.

This emphasis upon historical fact constitutes both the greatness and, perhaps, the Achilles' heel of Biblical religion. It constitutes its greatness, for through these myths Israel was freed from the cyclical process of nature to live out her destiny historically. One of the chief bases for the dynamic development of Western culture has been this vision of time and history as moving forward toward a goal. At the same time, it may well be the Achilles' heel of Biblical religion because it prompts men to ask whether or not the story is historically accurate. As long as springtime follows winter, the myth of the return of Persephone can be understood and believed. But did Moses really lead the people of Israel out of Egypt? Will God send a new Moses the next time his people are in bondage? Clearly, belief in the Biblical faith involves the taking of a risk which the believer in Demeter and Persephone did not have to take. The question which the reader of Scripture must ask himself repeatedly is, "Is the risk worth taking?"

The historian can, at times, provide answers to the questions raised by the historical "factuality" of the Biblical myths. He can, on the basis of archaeological evidence, show that the walls of Jericho did not fall down when Joshua marched into the land in the thirteenth century B.C., for archaeological evidence indicates that the walls of Jericho collapsed much earlier. He can prove that Abraham and Isaac did not deal with the Philistines, for the Philistines did not invade the land until much later. The question is, however, what does such proof of factual inaccuracy say about the myths themselves? Does proof that the Bible is sometimes historically wrong constitute a demonstration of the inadequacy of the Biblical faith?

This is by no means a simple question to answer. If one gives an unequivocal "Yes," then one makes the truth of the Biblical myths depend entirely upon the factual details of the story. Such an answer is clearly inadequate because the writers of the Bible surely wished to convey far more than factual historical information. Faith in the God of Israel certainly transcends the acceptance or rejection of some historical facts. This would make religious faith depend upon human historiographical skill. On the other hand, if one separates too decisively the myth and the historical event, one threatens the very essence of the Biblical myth, for the point of the Bible is that the archetypal patterns of Israel's existence were revealed in and through actual events. The God of the Bible was not encountered through abstract speculation but through the experience of meaningful occurrences which were regarded as revelatory. Without the exodus, the God of the exodus would remain unknown.

The answer to the question posed can then be neither an absolute yes nor an absolute no. Rather, the reader of Scripture must recognize that the events which are recorded in the Bible are the result of the experience of many generations of Israelites who returned to these events as revelatory. Some initial event prompted each memory in the first place, but as Israel remembered it she added to it her own insights and experiences. In so doing, she transformed the simple happening into a myth of her own destiny. Ultimately the question, then, is not whether the event initially happened as the Bible records it, but whether the reader can find in the event meaning similar to that discovered by generations of Israelites. The question is not so much "Did the exodus take place exactly as it is recorded in the Torah?" but rather "Can we still sing 'Go down Moses' with conviction?" The religious man cannot neglect the historical question entirely, for his myths are, to some extent, historical, but ultimately it is the acceptance or rejection of the archetypal myth which is crucial.

An historical analysis of the Bible, then, can only take us so far in the study of Scripture. It can help us to distinguish fiction from fact and can show us how the Israelites used their historical memories for mythological purposes. Historical study, however, can say little about the truth or falsity of the myth itself. In fact, as I have already indicated, it really makes no sense to speak about the truth of a myth. Truth can be ascertained only when a world-view or myth of reality is accepted. When people say that science has proved the Bible false, what they really mean is that the world-view of science and the world-view of the Bible are incompatible. If one accepts the vision of a mechanistic and essentially impersonal universe as adequate, then the ability to say "Thou" to reality is excluded. Contrariwise, if one conceives of the source of all reality as "Thou," then a purely mechanistic view must be rejected. Acceptance or rejection of a world-view cannot be made on the basis of some standard of truth which is foreign to it. Entrance into a world-view and the acceptance of myth are a matter of conversion.

CHAPTER III

The Geography of The Land of Israel

The Setting
The Geography of Israel: Unity and Diversity

LTHOUGH THE BIBLE is regarded by many people as containing "eternal truths" which are relevant for all people at all times, it was written by and for a particular people who lived in a particular place during a particular historical period. In searching for the meaning of Scripture this fact must not be glossed over or forgotten. Indeed, it is not too much to say that an understanding of the geographical and historical situation in which Israel found herself is essential for the comprehension of meaning which the text conveys.

The purpose of this brief chapter is not to provide an exhaustive geographical study of the land under consideration but only to give an elementary description of the "cradle" in which the Bible was born. For more complete surveys the reader is advised to consult the supplementary bibliography provided at the conclusion of this volume.

The Setting

THE LAND of Israel, located on the same latitude as Georgia and Spain, is a small country, about the size of the state of Vermont. The distance from Dan to Beersheba, its traditional northern and southern limits, is only about 150 miles as the crow flies. From the Mediterranean Sea in the west to Ramoth-Gilead in the east is about 70 miles. Therefore, even in ancient times, the length and breadth of the country could be traversed in only a few days. The size of the land, however, is by no means commensurate with its significance, for it forms the keystone in the arch of fertile land which stretches from the Nile valley in the west to the rich alluvial plain created by the Tigris and Euphrates rivers in the east. Since the desert to the south was (and is) forbidding to the traveler, all caravans, migrations, and armies proceeding to or from Egypt had to pass through the land of Israel. Even in pre-historic times, this area, which Israel eventually inhabited, was a center for trade, cultural interchange, and conflict.

Because of its position in the center of the ancient world, this land inevitably supported a population which was culturally and, perhaps, racially mixed. Wave upon wave of foreign invaders settled in Palestine; traders who passed through left behind new ideas and new types of artifacts; immigrants brought with them their own traditions and beliefs. Thus the land became a melting pot where the best (and sometimes the worst) of many cultures were mixed together and developed in a distinctive manner. This fact should be borne in mind when reading the Bible. The Bible did not develop in a vacuum, but in the very vortex of ancient culture. Therefore, one should not be surprised that within its pages the influence of many different cultures is in evidence. At the same time, these many signs of foreign influence should not blind the reader to the fact that from this melting-pot there came forth something highly distinctive and new. Israel may have used the myths and laws and customs of others, but in her hands this ancient lore took on radically new meaning and significance.

Not only did the land of Israel receive many foreign influences. She was also continually threatened by her larger and more powerful neighbors. Invariably, the strong Egyptian Pharaohs sought to control this land in order to protect Egypt from foreign invaders. The peoples of Mesopotamia (the Sumerians, Assyrians, and Babylonians) looked to Syria-Palestine as an area for expansion and pushed to the west in search of raw materials, slaves, and political power. The bedouin tribes from the desert and the migrating peoples of the north eyed the region as ripe for plunder and occasionally for settlement. Thus the people who inhabited the land of Israel were constantly under the threat of invasion and foreign domination. In fact, only for brief periods of time was this land completely free from foreign control.

The land of Israel, therefore, was and is a land of crisis. As a consequence, it is not surprising that the writers of the Bible turned from the rhythmic cycles of nature to historical events to find meaning for their existence. The Bible is a resounding proclamation that Israel *did* decipher the script of history and found meaning in the critical events which shaped her destiny. While other peoples worshipped the gods who bring fertility to the soil, Israel praised the God who brings enslaved people out of slavery. This, in essence, is what the Bible is about.

The Geography of Israel: Unity and Diversity

THE UNITY of the land of Israel is to be found in the fact that on all sides it is surrounded by relatively impassable natural barriers. On the west, of course, is the Mediterranean Sea. For the Greeks and Phoenecians this same Sea served not as a barrier but as a great highway for commerce, travel, and colonization, but, because Israel's coastline (when she controlled the coastline) had no natural harbors, she never became a maritime nation of note. In Old Testament times Israel's major port was not on the Mediterranean but on the Gulf of Aqaba. When the "Great Sea" is mentioned, it is usually used as a symbol for mystery or evil.

To the south and east Israel was bordered by the Negev and Arabian deserts. Although some bedouins did inhabit these sandy and rocky wastes and occasionally more permanent settlements were established through painstaking water control and irrigation, these deserts, in general, served both as a natural fortification against enemies and as a barrier to expansion. To the north, on the other hand, the high mountains of Lebanon and anti-Lebanon rise, precluding easy travel in that direction except through the "Great Rift," which will be discussed later, and a few mountain passes. Thus the land of Israel was relatively self-contained and naturally protected. Only in the southwest and northeast (i.e., from Egypt and Damascus) were there easy accesses to it.

At the same time, however, one should not think of Palestine as a geographically cohesive region. Although small, this country contains a wide variety of terrains and climates. As one travels about Israel one moves quickly from desert to tropical valley to rugged hill country to fertile plain. This diversity of landscape is one of the reasons why, for centuries, the land of Israel was neither politically nor culturally united. Of course, the fact that Egypt continually tried to keep Syria-Palestine politically weak also had much to do with the land's political diversity. Egypt's strategy was successful for so long, however, because it was based upon the fact of geographical and cultural disunity.

When one approaches Palestine from the sea, one encounters first a rather broad and relatively fertile plain stretching from the brook Besor in the south to Mount Carmel in the north. North of the Carmel range, which extends laterally across the country until it juts out into the Mediterranean, this plain, now called the plain of Acco, continues until it reaches the Ladder of Tyre where the limestone hills of central Palestine meet the Sea. This coastal plain, created in pre-historic times by the receding Mediterranean Sea, is dotted with sand dunes and some marshy areas, but still contains much fertile soil. Because the main trade route into Egypt ran along this plain, it supported, from early times, several fairly large settlements such as Gaza, Askelon, Ashdod, and Joppa. When Israel first entered the land, Egypt continued to control these cities. Later, however, the invading Philistines settled in the southern plain and retained hegemony over it during most of Israel's history.

The coastal plain varies, of course, in width, but is roughly about 20 miles across. Then the terrain becomes rockier and hillier as one enters the central hill country, characterized by a limestone ridge of low mountains which extends from the valley of Beersheba in the south to the mountains of Lebanon in the north. The highest of the peaks is scarcely more than 3,000 feet in elevation and hence can hardly compare to the mountains of Lebanon in majesty. Still, there is a rugged beauty about them which cannot be denied. The many mountain streams which flow toward the Mediterranean and the Jordan have cut deep valleys in the rock and these afford splendid panoramic views of the terraced slopes and villages which dot the land.

The Bible calls this a land flowing with milk and honey, but one should not think of Israel's homeland as a great agricultural region. Fertile land there is, but much of the country yields crops only when careful agricultural techniques are employed. In the south the hills are quite dry, receiving little more than 10-15 inches of rainfall a year, but as one proceeds north the rainfall is heavier and the land, when not too rocky, is suitable for some agriculture. For centuries farmers have eked out a living by painstakingly terracing the hill-sides and conserving every inch of fertile land possible.

It is not surprising, then, that in ancient times this hill country was somewhat less heavily populated than the coastal plain. Some modest-sized settlements there were at Jerusalem, Shechem, and Hebron, but on the whole, this was an area for shepherds and small farms, not for major cities. Those cities which did exist generally either sat astride one of the trade routes which crisscrossed the hills or served as fortress cities to protect the land and its people from invaders.

In the south the limestone hills gradually taper off into the Negev, a barren steppe with the desert encroaching upon it. Although the Negev was, at many times, dotted by some small settlements, inhabitants must have worked with special care to wring a living from it. The remains of ancient cisterns and dams in the desert, designed to preserve the little rain which does fall, are a testimony to the ingenuity of the inhabitants of the land. Unfortunately, however, such agricultural methods can only be effective when peaceful conditions prevail. One invading army could soon destroy the work of generations. And this is precisely what happened. Thus, although the Negev was inhabited during the Early and Middle Bronze periods, the population dwindled away because the rigorously exact methods of preserving water could not be maintained.

During much of Israel's history the Negev remained in Edomite hands. When Israel did control the territory, however, she took full advantage of the copper mines which exist in the region and the access which the Negev offers to the Red Sea through the Gulf of Aqaba. Since Israel's land was distinctly lacking in minerals and ores, these copper mines were particularly important. So too, the port at Ezion-geber allowed Israel to develop modestly as a maritime nation. The periodic recovery of the Negev by Edom, however, prevented Israel's full utilization of these assets.

In the north-central region the limestone ridge is broken decisively by the great plain of Megiddo or Esdraelon, formed by the Kishon River which flows in a northwesterly direction to the sea just north of the Carmel range. This plain joins with the Valley of Jezreel near Mount Gilboa and with it forms a green and fertile strip running laterally across the land. Here the rainfall is modestly heavy and the soil fairly rich. This is, indeed, the most fertile region in the whole of Palestine. Because of its fertility and because major trade routes ran through the broad valley, it was an area of fairly concentrated population and heavy fortification. The eastern end of the Vale of Jezreel was guarded by Beth-shan; the western entry to the plain, by Megiddo. Apparently, much of this area was controlled by the Canaanites long after Israel had conquered the hill country.

Eventually Israel took control of the plain—Judges 5 tells of one defeat of the Canaanites by Deborah—but the area remained a center of conflict. Inevitably, the invading armies of the foreign nations sought to dominate this prized region. And it is here where Israel often offered her stiffest defense. It is not strange, then, that the writer of Revelation foresaw that the last great battle of history would be fought at Armageddon, that is, at the hill of Megiddo.

North of the plain the limestone hills rise again rather sharply to form the foothills of the Lebanon and anti-Lebanon ranges of mountains. Here again the population was less concentrated, though there were fortified cities such as Hazor, which guarded the trade routes coming from the north. Most of the settlements were of very modest size and can be described even today as sleepy hill-country villages. In one of these little hamlets, Nazareth, it is said that Jesus lived as a boy. If that is true, he undoubtedly grew up among the rural poor whose only riches lay in their beautiful view of the Plain of Megiddo to the south.

The limestone hills which form the backbone of Palestine are separated from the Transjordanian hills to the east by a Great Rift extending from north to south created, in part, by the Jordon River. In the northern section of the rift lie the Leontes and Orontes Rivers which create a plain between the Lebanon and Anti-Lebanon mountains. Dan, the northernmost limit of ancient Israel, was located on the southern fringe of this plain. The waters from this southern section, however, drain not into the Leontes but into Lake Huleh, which is today only a marshy area. From Huleh the Jordan River (whose name means "that which goes down") descends rapidly to Lake Chinnereth, better known as the Sea of Galilee, which is 695 feet below sea level. From this lovely fresh water lake, the Jordan again winds its way southward through the rather barren Arabah to the Dead Sea. This famous sea, which is at the lowest point on the face of the earth, is more than 1200 feet below sea level. In prehistoric times this sea was connected with the Red Sea in the south, but geological disturbances cut it off from this original exit. Into the Dead Sea the water of the Jordan flows, but it can escape only through evaporation. Therefore, over the centuries this large lake has grown saltier and saltier and has become a depository for the many minerals brought by the Jordan from the north. There is evidence that even in very ancient times men used the Sea as a source for salt, bitumen, and other minerals. Today, "miners" have found the Dead Sea to be a great source for various minerals useful in a modern industrial society.

The climate around the Dead Sea is very dry and tropical. In the summer, temperatures are almost unbearable during the day, but in the winter the climate makes the shores of the Sea suitable as a resort area. While snow is falling a few miles away in Jerusalem, bathers can here relax in comfort under a date palm tree. The most ancient city known to man, Jericho, was located a few miles north of this Sea. Also near the northern end of the Sea an Essenic sect of Judaism built a monastery from which came the famous Dead Sea scrolls. Further south one finds the lovely oasis of Ein Geddi, created by a swiftly flowing mountain stream, where David hid from Saul. Still further south one finds the fortress of Masada, built on top of a butte by King Herod as a royal retreat. Because the limestone hills descend quite sharply to the sea, however, much of the western coastline is quite uninhabitable. The southern end of the sea is surrounded by a relatively flat plain and it is here that Sodom and Gomorrah were probably built. Since the Sea today is somewhat longer than in ancient times, the remains of those cities are now undoubtedly under water.

South of the Dead Sea the Arabah continues to the Gulf of Akabah. This dry rift, once a finger of the ocean extending into the heartland of Palestine, is arid and sun-baked. Only the rugged vegetation and animal life of the desert can survive long in its blistering heat. Springs of water there are, but the traveler must be well acquainted with the desert in order to find them. Nevertheless, a trip through the region is well worth the effort, for the desert with its rocky brilliance has a beauty all of its own.

On the eastern side of the Great Rift the trans-Jordanian hills rise rather abruptly. Through this tableland flow four important rivers: the Yarmuk, the Jabbok, the Arnon, and the Zered. In the north the land receives considerable rain and thus Bashan and Gilead are agriculturally productive. As one moves to the south or to the east the rainfall decreases and the land is less fruitful. In ancient times the southern hills were divided among the kingdoms of Ammon, Moab, and Edom and later served as the homeland for the surprising Nabateans. One can only stand in awe of this industry of these peoples who carved for themselves in this semi-wilderness a living space and, at times, even prospered in so doing. Through irrigation and much back-breaking labor they were able to survive quite successfully where now only bedouin shepherds graze their flocks.

In conclusion, then, the land of the Bible is one which fosters and supports a variety of "cultural types." It is the land of the merchant, the farmer, the miner, and the bedouin. It is not surprising, therefore, that in ancient times this was often a politically and socially divided country. Even today the merchant of Jerusalem and the farmer of Afula have little in common with the nomad of the Negev. Still, there is a unity to the people of the land which transcends this diversity, for all who inhabit the region are bound together by a common destiny shaped by Palestine's position in "the center of the world." Even the nomadic shepherd has played his part in the critical and sometimes tragic history of this ancient land.

CHAPTER IV

A Brief History of Israel

The Major periods of Israel's History
From Before the Hebrews
To the End of the Old Testament Period.

MANY LARGE VOLUMES and countless monographs have been written about the intricate developments of the history of Israel. Needless to say, there is neither space nor reason to offer a full and documented history of the land and its people in this brief survey. Rather, what will be presented is a synopsis of the major periods of that history as it can be pieced together by the objective historian. The major source for our understanding of Israel's development is, of course, the Bible. Because the Scriptures are obviously shaped by certain theological and national predilections, however, the historian must be circumspect in his use of them. Therefore, particular attention will be paid to the many non-Biblical sources which shed light upon the subject at hand. What will be offered to the reader are not "final answers" but clues for his own further research into this exceedingly complicated and absorbing subject.

The Major Periods of Israel's History

Before launching directly into the history of Israel a word must be said first about the question of chronology. The student of modern history is, of course, required to be very precise about the dating of the events which he studies and since innumerable records are available concerning the past few centuries the historian can usually speak about the recent past with great precision. Such, however, is not the case with much ancient history. We date events according to the B.C. (or B.C.E.)

and A.D. format; yet obviously ancient records used no such dating system. In order to develop a chronology of pre-Christian times scholars have had to work backward, piecing together the various king-lists, fragmentary histories, and genealogies in order to arrive at some relatively firm dates. Unfortunately, not all of the ancient records are accurate, but the extent of their unreliability is often difficult to determine. Then too, ancient calendars were arranged differently from ours. Some peoples celebrated the New Year in the spring, others, in the fall. Some used two or more calendars simultaneously. In any event, the further one recedes in history, the more difficult it is to date events with great precision.

All dates given in this chapter, therefore, should be taken with a grain of salt. If the student consults several different histories, he will find equally competent scholars giving different dates for the same event. For the person who likes chronological exactness, this may seem very frustrating. Nevertheless, it is one of the perils and the joys of studying the subject. Nothing in ancient history is really cut and dry. Virtually everything is subject to reevaluation and reinterpretation. Therefore, the student of the history of Israel must employ both exacting precision and a vivid imagination in piecing together the fragments of the past. As a consequence, no history of Israel is definitive or final. As new information is uncovered and as the subject is approached from new perspectives, many so-called facts must be discarded. Even in a brief chapter such as this many "facts" will be presented which may be disputed by others. My only hope is that what is presented generally represents what is agreed upon by several competent scholars and is the "best we can determine" at present.

For students who wish to pursue various questions further, the following histories are the most widely used and up to date:

John Bright; *A History of Israel*
Martin Noth; *The History of Israel*

A good example of the differences among scholars concerning the history of Israel can be found by reading the respective discussions of these two authors concerning the Patriarchal period.

From Before the Hebrews

FROM OUR perspective the Bible seems to be a very ancient book; 2,000 B.C., for instance, seems a long time ago. When seen from the perspective of the total length of time than man has lived on earth, however, the Bible is very modern. For instance, the earliest anthropoid remains thus far discovered in Palestine date somewhere between 300,000 to 600,000 years ago. Therefore, the length of time during which men lived in Palestine before the time of Abraham was at least 75 times as long as the time from Abraham to the present! Probably the pre-historic period was much, much longer than that.

During this exceedingly long time man evolved both physically and culturally a great deal. He learned to make increasingly complicated tools; he organized himself socially; he even learned to create art of high quality. By 2,000 B.C. he had developed most of the basic forms of life and thought which still characterize human culture. From our lofty "scientific perspective" the Patriarchs may appear as "primitive" and extraordinarily ancient. In truth, however, Abraham, if there was such a person, was doubtless much closer to us culturally than to those men of Pebble culture who inhabited Palestine in dim prehistoric times. From the vantage point of the anthropologist, at least, Abraham appears as a very modern man.

Although it is a fascinating story, there is no need, in this brief synopsis, to describe in any detail the arduous journey of man from Paleolithic times to the Middle Bronze Age when our story of Israel begins. Those who are interested should consult Emmanuel Anati's very readable book on the subject (see bibliography).[1] It suffices to say that archaeological excavations all over Palestine at such places as Atlit, Shaar Hagolan, Jericho, Teleilat Ghassul, Bir es Safedi, and Arad have revealed a variety of prehistoric cultures and peoples undreamed of before this century. Perhaps the most remarkable discovery was made at Jericho where the remains of a sizeable tower and fortification have been uncovered which date from about 7,000 B.C.! We call the area we are considering the land of Israel or Palestine (i.e., the land of the Philistines), but quite clearly people had lived in the area for millenia before either the Israelites or the Philistines appeared on the scene. Even the Canaanites were relatively late-comers to the land.

Perhaps the best place to begin our discussion of the history of Israel *per se* is with a brief review of the development of human civilization in the third and second Millenia B.C. Although we now know that men did build fairly sizeable cities at such places as Jericho as long ago as 7,000 B.C., the Age of the City did not really begin until the period

[1] Anati, Emmanuel. *Palestine Before the Hebrews*. New York: Alfred Knopf, 1963.

from 3,000 to 2,000 B.C. During this thousand-year period, "high" civilizations developed in Sumer in lower Mesopotamia, and along the banks of the Nile in Egypt. In both, the impulse to create an urban civilization may well have come from the necessity for cooperation in irrigation.

In Sumer, where, according to Samuel Kramer, history began, a whole host of advances were made. Not only did the Sumerians refine the technological skills of their ancestors in agriculture, metal-working, and the like. They also produced, under Sargon I, the first important "world" empire. Even more important for the history of the ancient Near East was their development of a great literature and religion, which were to dominate in various ways the thinking of many Mesopotamian peoples who were to follow them. Sumerian became the language of learning and religion so that even in such far away places as Ugarit, on the Syrian coast, and Hatti, in Anatolia, Sumerian texts have been found. To be sure, the ancient myths and legends of the Sumerians were radically revised and embellished by other peoples. Still, not very far beneath the surface of such works as the *Epic of Gilgamesh* and the *Enuma Elish* glows the spark of Sumerian inspiration. Even the Bible—particularly the book of Genesis—contains reminiscences of the beliefs of this ancient land. Thus the Sumerian city, dominated by its ziggurat but characterized by rather mean and cramped dwellings, produced cultural achievements whose impact has not yet been wholly dissipated.

Egypt, also, after the unification of Upper and Lower Egypt by Menes in about 2900 B.B., developed an extraordinary, if puzzling, civilization. The Great Pyramids which were built during this period stand as lofty monuments to the genius and brutality of the ancient Pharaohs. Too much, perhaps, has been made of the brutality. Egypt produced, not just massive structures built by thousands of slaves, but a refinement of art and culture which has seldom been matched. The Egyptians, however, were from the beginning a rather insular people who took great pride in their civilization and looked condescendingly upon foreigners. Partly for this reason and partly because of the esoteric nature of their thought they never influenced the whole of the Near East as much as Mesopotamia did. To this day, Egyptian religion remains something of an enigma to the scholar. Even a modern American can read the *Epic of Gilgamesh* with some appreciation. Egyptian mythology, on the other hand, seems so strange, so tied to the geographical conditions produced by the Nile, that it is difficult to read it with more than antiquarian interest. Among the more interesting documents from this time are the *Memphite Theology*, which contains a significant "doctrine of creation," and the *Pyramid Texts*, which are compiled in the so-called *Egyptian Book of the Dead.*

By the end of the third millenium both of these civilizations had run their course and a dark age overtook them for a while. With the death of Piopi II, a long-lived but weak ruler, Egypt was plunged into civil strife and anarchy. Historical sources are few, but it would appear that from about 2200 until 2000 B.C. Egyptian civilization was in turmoil. Sumerian civilization lasted somewhat longer, but in about 1950 B.C. the third dynasty of Ur fell before the invading Elamites. Even before that time waves of invading Amorites (the Westerners) had spread across the Near East, disrupting the *Pax Sumeria* which had existed under the aegis of Ur. Where these Amorites came from is not clear. Some scholars guess Arabia; others, from the north. At any rate, these Semitic peoples, who spread across the whole of the Near East, were to play a decisive political and cultural role in the area for many generations.

While the city-states of lower Mesopotamia quarreled with each other and sought vainly to keep back the power-hungry Elamites, the Amorites established themselves at Babylon, a previously unimportant town, and gradually gained power over the whole region. Under the famous Hammurabi Babylon flourished both culturally and politically. From this era come versions of the ancient Babylon accounts of creation, grammatical and mathematical texts, and, of course, the famous Hammurabic Code. Hammurabi did not, it is true, create this code of laws (which now can be viewed in the Louvre in Paris) *de novo*. Rather, it appears to be a synthesis and reorganization of a legal tradition reaching back into third millenium Sumer. Quite clearly the codes of Ur-nammu, of Lipit-Ishtar, and the Eshnunna laws are its ancestors. Nevertheless, the Hammurabic Code is significant as an expression of the ideals and practical realities of this Semitic Empire and as an eastern counterpart to the legal tradition represented in the Bible.

In the northern Mesopotamian region the Amorites established themselves at Mari and built a splendid, if ephemeral kingdom there. The great palace of Mari was, in many respects, comparable to the better known palace at Knossos in Crete, which, parenthetically, came into existence about this time. While the Minoan kings established their hegemony over much of the Aegean and laid foundations for the Hellenic society which was eventually to develop, the Amorite kings lived in equal splendor at Mari. East of them lay their great rivals, the Assyrians, who were not, for the moment, yet under the control of the Amorites. For a time, the Assyrians gained the upper hand, but under Zimri-lim Mari triumphed and enjoyed a few years of monumental brilliance before succumbing before the armies of Hammurabi.

Meanwhile, Egypt had recovered from the momentary dark age engendered by the collapse of the Old Kingdom and had entered a new period of prosperity and expansion. Under the dynasties of the Middle Kingdom Egypt exerted control over much of the Palestinian corridor and over southern, African provinces. Egyptian power could not prevent the immigration of Semites into Palestine, but it did prevent the immediate rise of a new Amorite kingdom on her northeastern border. Both Phoenecia and the land of Israel became, to a large extent, Amorite (Canaanite), but the newcomers had to submit to the suzerainty of the Egyptian Pharaohs.

During this time, the arts, literature, and "science" flourished in Egypt. Among the most interesting documents from the time are the Tale of Sinuhe and the Tale of the Shipwrecked Sailor. For the historian, the Execration texts are of great importance, for they reveal much about the distribution of population in Palestine at the time. The Coffin Texts imply that the hope for immortality, once reserved for the Pharaohs was now extended to anyone who could pay the price for the proper funerary rites.

After this era of brilliance, a new dark age fell across the Near East, again caused by foreign invasions. Among the new intruders into the fertile crescent were the Hurrians (the Biblical Horites) who settled in the upper Mesopotamian region, near Haran and Mari, but who spread out all over the Near East. Apparently there were sizeable settlements of Hurrians in Palestine at, for instance, Jerusalem and Shechem. These Hurrians spoke neither a Semitic nor an Indo-Aryan tongue, but rather used a language whose affinities were with that of the people of Urartu. Both linguistically and culturally the Hurrians were to influence strongly the Israelites.

At the same time, the Hittites of Anatolia also began to extend their influence southward and, for a time, were a major power with which to be dealt. This was also the era of the Indo-Aryan invasions of India, Iran, and along the fringes of the fertile crescent. Among the Hurrians we find certain Indo-Aryan rulers. In Greece the Mycenaeans came to power after the demise of Knossos.

By 1750 B.C. Egypt also experienced the beginning of a period of decline. The Eighteenth Dynasty finally met defeat at the hands of Asiatic invaders known as the Hyksos (i.e., the foreign rulers). Where the Hyksos came from we do not know, but it is clear that they were Semites who brought with them to Egypt gods similar to those worshipped in Canaan. From the Indo-Aryans they had apparently learned how to use the horse chariot, which they employed with great effectiveness. Although these invaders obviously had some affinities with the more settled inhabitants of Syria-Palestine and indeed controlled much of this region as well as Egypt, both their pottery styles and their methods of fortification were quite distinctive. From Avaris, their capital city in the northeast corner of Egypt, they ruled both Palestine and Egypt until they were driven out by the native Egyptians.

The Age of the Patriarchs

THE EARLY Middle Bronze Age which has been describe briefly in the preceding section was the era of the Patriarchs, In the midst of this time of population movement, upheaval, and change, the Bible says that a Semitic family from Ur returned to its "family land" in Haran, in the northwestern Mesopotamian region, and then traveled on to find a new home in the west. We do not know, of course, whether Abraham, Isaac, and Jacob were in any sense historical figures. There is no proof that any of these fathers of Israel did what the Bible claims they did. Only the roughest sort of dating for any of them can be given. Still, their sagas contain a surprisingly large number of authentic memories of that age, memories which simply could not have been concocted at a later time. For instance, Genesis describes quite accurately where the major settlements in Canaan were during the early Bronze Age. The population was, as Genesis suggests, culturally mixed; the Negev did support settled communities; much of the hill country was open for settlement. Several customs alluded to in the text (such as the adoption of an heir, the relation of concubines and wives, the sale of a birthright) find parallels in Hurrian texts from Nuzi. Biblical names find counterparts in texts from Haran and Mari.

In Genesis 14:13 Abram is described as a Hebrew. It is still not entirely clear what relation the Hebrews had to the *'apiru* mentioned in Egyptian and Mesopotamian texts, but it is likely that Hebrew and *'apiru* are synonymous. If so, Abram was a part of a culturally distinctive group of people who lived on the fringes of the civilized world and who made their living as donkey caravaners and seasonal laborers. In that case Hebrew designates Abram's cultural, but not his "racial" background.

The Bible also indicates that the Patriarchs were related to the Arameans of Haran. Deuteronomy 26 speaks of Israel's father as a "wandering Aramean." In Genesis Jacob returns to Haran and takes a wife. Isaac's wife, too, comes from Haran. If this relationship can be assumed, the Patriarchs, then were a part of still another group of Semitic intruders into the fertile crescent who eventually established themselves in what is now Syria. The Arameans never developed a very coordinated Empire, but their influence was so great that Aramaic eventually became the *lingua franca* of the ancient world. Since, at a later time, the Arameans were one of the chief enemies of Israel, it is highly unlikely that the writers of the Bible would have fabricated this relationship. In all probability Genesis describes quite accurately the cultural and racial stock from which Israel sprang.

Doubtless the Patriarchal stories were thoroughly revised and embellished in order to make certain theological points and to bring the early beliefs in line with later conceptions. Still, not all of the pagan roots of Israelite religion are totally hidden. Abraham seems on quite good terms with the Hurrian priest-king of Jerusalem, Melchizedek, and never questions his "orthodoxy." Jacob sets up a "massebah" as the Canaanites might have done. God is, at times called "El," a Canaanite name for the chief deity. One may surmise, therefore, that these early ancestors were culturally and religiously much closer to the peoples who surrounded them than later believers cared to admit. Only gradually did Israel develop a distinctive faith of its own.

Assessing the historicity of these Patriarchal narratives is, at best, a very difficult task. Certainly there are many anachronisms in the text which cannot be overlooked. For instance, Abraham is said to sojourn with the Philistines when no Philistines were yet in the land. Nevertheless, it is no longer possible to dismiss the authenticity of the Genesis account with a wave of the hand. It is probable that much of the material concerning the Patriarchs is based upon memories of the period, preserved orally by the story-tellers of Israel. Although it is impossible to corroborate any of the specific incidents recorded, it surely is not too much to say that the people of Israel were descendants of some early

Hebrew "sheiks" whose family center was in Haran, who settled in Canaan during the Middle Bronze Age, and who eventually went to Egypt in search of food, found a favorable situation, and stayed there.

Israel in Egypt

The story of Joseph sounds so much like an Horatio Alger, rags-to-riches tale that it is a little difficult to take it seriously as an historical account. Still, this story, like the sagas of Abraham, Isaac, and Jacob, contains a number of authentic touches which indicate that a kernel of historical truth underlies it. The very fact that the Semitic Hyksos overwhelmed Egypt in the late Eighteenth century B.C. makes more plausible the rapid rise to power of a Hebrew slave. One can well imagine that a Hyksos Pharaoh might have trusted a fellow foreigner more than the native Egyptians. So, too, it is quite conceivable that when the Hyksos were driven out, the Israelites might have been looked upon with suspicion.

Furthermore, there are a number of details in the story which cohere with what we know about Egypt at the time. The titles of chief butler and chief baker were used in Egypt to designate household officers. Joseph's title, "One who rules over the House," is an exact translation of an Egyptian title. From non-Biblical sources it has been learned that the Egyptians allowed bedouins to graze their flocks in the area east of the Delta which the Bible called Goshen. Genesis 47:20 says that Joseph bought all the land of Egypt for the Pharoah. Although there is no record of this, we do know that while before the coming of the Hyksos the land was in the hands of many landlords, after their expulsion all land was owned by the state.

Egyptian influence upon the tale is also in evidence. The story of Joseph and Potiphar's wife finds a parallel in the Egyptian "Tale of Two Brothers." Joseph is said to have lived for what the Egyptians considered a perfect length of time, 110 years. The interest in dream interpretation manifested in the text was very common among Egyptians. Even the tradition of seven lean years finds its counterpart in Egyptian literature.

None of these facts, of course, proves the story of Joseph to be historical. The most that can be said is that many of the features of the story do seem plausible and that the whole saga *may* have its basis in historical fact. The final decision concerning its historicity, however, rests as much upon the skeptical or believing penchant of the reader as it does upon the facts available.

After the death of Joseph a curtain falls upon the history of the Israelites, for the Bible tells us little more than that the Israelites were in Egypt for four hundred years and that they were enslaved by the Egyptians. At the same time, however, we do have considerable information about Egypt during the period following the expulsion of the Hyksos, that is, the period of the New Kingdom. Ancient documents reveal that this was a time for renewed prosperity and expansion for the Egyptians. Under Tutmosis I (1525-1494) and even more under Tutmosis III (1490-1435) Egypt expanded her control over her neighbors to the northeast until she gained hegemony over much of the land west of the Euphrates. Although impeded in her conquests first by Mitanni (the Hurrian kingdom) and then by the Hittites, she was, nevertheless, the most powerful nation of the time.

Perhaps the best-known Pharaoh of the Eighteenth Dynasty is Amenhophis IV (1370-1353) who, as a result of his own theological opinions, changed his name to Akhenaton. Although famous because of his attempts to introduce "solar monotheism" as the established religion of Egypt, Akhenaton was not a very effective ruler. In fact, his theological and cultic reforms turned the established priesthood against him just at a time when he could scarcely afford disunity at home. The Tell Amarna letters, which have been unearthed from the mound of his capital city, reveal that Egyptian hegemony over the Palestinian strip was threatened by invading *'apiru* and by the disloyalty of various local princes. Had Akhenaton come to their aid with force, most of these princes would probably have remained faithful to Egypt. The Amarna letters reveal, however, that the Pharaoh sent little support and as a result his foreign "Empire" collapsed.

There has been great speculation, of course, concerning the influence of Akhenaton's monotheism upon Israelite religion. Although some historical influence is not out of the question, it is also clear that such is not likely. In the first place, his "monotheism" was hardly similar to that of the Israelites. Akhenaton worshipped the sun god, Aton Re, as the one true god, but as Pharaoh still demanded that his subjects regard him also as a deity. Furthermore, Akhenaton's monotheism seems to have had few ethical implications; no ten commandments or other moral imperatives were derived from his teachings. His religious it is probable that his attempted reforms had little long-lasting effect upon anyone. Since traditional Egyptian religion was restored to favor shortly after his death, there is little possibility that his ideas would have had any influence upon Moses who probably was born at least two generations later.

reforms left Egyptian cultural and ethical norms unchanged. Finally,

We do not know, of course, precisely when Moses was born. The clues which we do have, however, point to the first half of the thirteenth century as the time of the exodus and to Ramesses II as the Pharaoh who would not let Israel go. According to the Bible, the conquest of the promised land began some forty-odd years after the escape from Egypt. Archaeologists have discovered that an invasion of Canaan did take place in the late thirteenth century and that a number of cities, such as Lachish, Debir, and Hazor, were taken, as the Bible maintains. If the remains discovered are of the Israelite conquest—which seem probable—then the exodus must have occurred earlier in that century. Moreover, since Seti I and Ramesses II did build (or rather rebuild) cities which may be identified as Pithim and Ramesses of the Bible, using *'apiru* as workers, it is likely that Seti is the Pharaoh from whom Moses fled and Ramesses the Pharaoh of the exodus.

According to the book of Exodus, Moses was an Israelite of Levite parentage who was brought up in the royal household. Certainly his name indicates a connection with the Egyptians, for Moses was a common Egyptian name. Moses, however, got into trouble with the Egyptians by killing a foreman who was maltreating the Israelites and was forced to flee to the land of Midian. Much has been made about Moses' connection with the Midianites, a semi-nomadic people. Theophile Meek, for instance, has argued that in fact Moses adopted a Midianite mountain god as his own. All of this, however, is a matter of unsubstantiated speculation, for we know virtually nothing about either the Midianites or Israelite religion at the time.

In due time, Moses felt himself called by the God of his fathers, who met him at a desert mountain called Sinai, to return to set his people free. According to the Bible, Moses returned and, despite the intransigence of the Pharaoh, finally succeeded in his task. Jack Finegan, among others, has argued at length to show that the story of the ten plagues that fell upon Egypt as a result of the Pharaoh's refusal is both believable and authentic. Although he argues his case with passion, there is little proof one way or the other. Since there are, unfortunately but not surprisingly, no non-Biblical records of the exodus, it is virtually impossible to separate fact and embellishment in the Biblical account. There is, indeed, no fool-proof evidence that the exodus occurred at all. Because it is not usual for a people to trace their origins to slavery and because the general outline of the exodus appears plausible, however, all but the most hardened skeptics affirm at the very least that some tribes of people who were later to inhabit the land of Canaan escaped from Egypt, made their way across the desert, and eventually invaded certain portions of the promised land.

One of the greatest stumbling blocks to the acceptance of the story is the account of the "miraculous" parting of the Red Sea. The Hebrew text is quite clear, however, that the Sea crossed was not the Red Sea but the Sea of Reeds. Although this does not verify the event, it is far more plausible to imagine the Israelites finding their way across a marshy area east of the Delta by dint of a strong wind that blew the water enough to show where the high spots were. In any case, later Israelites looked back upon this crossing as the turning-point in their life and as a sign that the power of the universe was watching over them.

Virtually nothing is known for certain about Israel's sojourn in the desert. Kadesh-barnea, one of the chief stops on route has been identified, but the location of most of the other places mentioned, including Mount Sinai, remains undetermined. Some of the strange events recorded in Exodus can now be "explained," but this hardly assures the historicity of the account. For instance, we now know that because the limestone rocks of the Sinai often contain pockets of water, thirsty travelers can, if they are lucky, find relief by striking a rock. Migratory quail do fly over the Sinai Peninsula and sometimes drop on the desert floor due to sheer exhaustion. There they lie, as though lifeless, and can be picked up easily. Manna, a sweet substance secreted by certain insects of the desert, can be, and still is, gathered and eaten.

According to the Bible, Moses led the people of Israel out of Egypt to the famous mountain where he had originally received his theophany. There, Israel too heard God's voice, this time in the thunder and earth tremors, and decided to make a new covenant with him. The basis of this covenant was the well-known Ten Commandments which have served generations of believers as a guide to proper conduct. As a result, Israel came to address God with a new covenantal name, Yahweh, and believed herself destined for a peculiarly important role among the nations of men.

Scholars disagree decisively about the historicity of this Biblical account. Some maintain that the events occurred about as the Bible describes them. Others argue that much of the account is a later fabrication. Even the most skeptical scholar, however, must admit that something happened in the desert which bound Israelites together and gave them a new sense of destiny. The religion of the Patriarchs may not have been very different from that of the surrounding pagans. When Israel emerged from the desert to enter the land of her hopes, however, she went forward with a new spirit and faith which she maintained had its origins on the slopes of Sinai. Doubtless the original story may have been embellished in many ways by later believers. Nevertheless, somehow, out of the memories of this desert experience was born a unique faith in a choosing God which was to shape the world.

The Conquest of the Promised Land

THE CANAAN which Israel attacked in the late thirteenth century was composed of a large number of small city-states, each with its own ruler. This political disunity, which was of great benefit to the Israelites, was in part the result of the geographical disunity of the land and in part the result of Egyptian attempts to keep the area politically and militarily weak and subservient. The organization of these states in which an elite ruled the masses may have been a legacy left by the Hyksos invasions.

The population of the land was composed in part of the Canaanites who were descendants of the Amorites who invaded the land about 2000 B.C. and who were related to their fellow Amorites to the north, the Phoenicians. These groups had absorbed the indigenous population of the land and had developed a fairly homogeneous Amorite civilization which stretched from the Negev to the upper reaches of the Syrian coast. Despite the fact that the Phoenicians were traders and seamen while their compatriots, the Canaanites, were largely agriculturalists, they shared a common set of values and myths.

The discovery of the Ras Shamra tablets at Ugarit on the Syrian coast has brought us a much fuller knowledge of the religion and culture of this whole region. Unfortunately, many of the tablets discovered are fragmentary or defective so it is difficult to piece together some of the myths there recorded. Still, the over-all sense of many of the texts comes through quite clearly. In the *Tale of Aqhat* King Dan'el is promised and receives a son (a prominent theme in the Old Testament). Because his son Aqhat will not give to the warrior-goddess Anath his bow, he is killed and the whole world mourns and becomes lifeless. The conclusion of the tale is lost, but surely, like the myths of Adonis and Tammuz, it ended with the restoration of Aqhat to life for a part of the year. Another important myth concerns the great god Ba'al, one of the sons of El, the father God. Ba'al defeats his brother Yamm, the sea, but is in turn defeated by Mot, death. This time it is Anath who kills Mot and restores Ba'al the Lord of the earth to life. Thus, in both of these two central myths the emphasis is upon the natural death and resurrection of vegetative life.

Because the documents are so few, it is difficult to say much about the historical development of Canaanite religion. Apparently, however, some changes did take place during the late Middle and early Late Bronze periods. Archaeologists have discovered that from the former few figurines of the goddess Ashtorah have been found; in the Late Bronze Age, they are very plentiful. This would seem to indicate a growing interest in this Mother Goddess who was so hated by the Israelites. It *may* be that during the Patriarchal Age the religion of the Canaanites and the religion of the predecessors of Israel were not so different. While Israel in Egypt moved toward a high ethical monotheism which stressed the oneness of God, the Canaanites began to emphasize more and more the Mother Goddess and the fertility cult.

The Bible, of course, repeatedly denounces Canaanite religion in the most vitriolic terms. Surely, one ought not to minimize the differences between these two world-views. On the other hand, it is also clear that Israelite religion shared much in common with its hated enemy. Both Canaanites and Israelites observed a seven-day week and a yearly calendar composed of seven periods of fifty days followed by feast days. Their temples were probably of similar construction and their modes of sacrifice similar. Undoubtedly, Israel drew upon Canaanite lore in developing its own sagas and traditions. While the Canaanites worshipped the gods of the natural, agricultural order, however, Israel followed the transcendent God who acts in history and who shapes human destiny.

Despite the predominance of the Canaanites, who lived primarily in the fertile plains, the population of the land at the time of the conquest was very mixed. The Bible lists no less than six other ethnic groups: the Hittites, the Hivites, the Perizzites, the Girgashites, the Amorites, and the Jebusites (Joshua 3:10). No archaeological evidence has been found that Hittites did inhabit the land, but there may have been some small settlements. The Hivites were probably Hurrians, but we know virtually nothing about the identity of the Perizzites or the Girgashites or precisely how the Amorites were distinguished from the Canaanites. Probably what were called the Amorites were the "country cousins" of the Canaanites who inhabited the hill country of Judah and areas east of the Jordan. The Jebusites were probably Hurrians who lived in Jebus, i.e., Jerusalem. Despite the many people there was still open country left in Canaan, particularly in the central hill-country; it is here that Israel settled.

The story of the conquest found in Joshua is one of a relatively brief and victorious march through the land. Although this book does contain many accurate historical reminiscences, it is shot full of oversimplifications. In the first place, archaeological investigation has made clear that Jericho and Ai were already in ruins when Israel entered in the thirteenth century. Apparently, the authors took over older conquest stories and fused them with their own or made up accounts to explain, for instance, why Ai was a ruin. Secondly, there is no mention at all of the conquest of the central hill country where the Joseph tribes settled; yet it was at Shechem where the tribes first gathered and the first central shrine was established. Did the invading Israelites find at Shechem relatives who welcomed them home? Had the Joseph tribes, Ephraim and Mannassah, invaded and settled in the land somewhat earlier? Was the exodus experienced by only a few of the tribes while the rest remained in Canaan? At this time no final answers can be given to these questions.

Third, although the story implies that Joshua and his troops routed the Canaanites once and for all, both Joshua and Judges admit implicitly that the victory was by no means total. The Canaanites continued to hold most of the large cities and the fertile plains for a long time. Jerusalem did not fall into Israelite hands until the time of David. Gezer was given to Solomon by an Egyptian Pharaoh as a dowry. Askelon and Gaza never did become integrated into the Israelite nation.

Thus the historical facts concerning the conquest are far more complicated than the authors of Joshua wished to admit. In Joshua we find fused together, embellished, and theologically corrected, accounts of several invasions of Canaan by various people. Nevertheless, we can say that a major invasion did take place in the thirteenth century through which a far less "culturally sophisticated" people overcame the sedentary population in certain areas and began the slow process of building a new civilization on the ashes of the old.

In the Time of the Judges (app. 1200-1050 B.C.)

MANY OF the Tells excavated by present-day archaeologists have contained remnants and reminders of what we believe was the Israelite conquest. In their own way they reveal almost as eloquently as the book of Judges some of the problems which Israel faced in settling and controlling the land. On top of ash levels containing fairly sophisticated Canaanite implements and pottery are to be found the much more "primitive" remains of the invading bedouin tribes. Israel may have triumphed over the Canaanites because of her unity of spirit and her sense of destiny, but she had much to learn technologically and agriculturally from those with whom she settled. As Americans have learned who have tried to export Western technology to under-developed countries, it is difficult to separate the skills and methodology of a particular culture from the world-view which gave them birth. Israel had to learn agricultural methods from the Canaanites in order to survive, but in doing so there was a strong temptation to adopt as well the mythologies and cultic rites which undergirded the whole agricultural life. Hence, despite the protestations of the "faithful," Israel again and again was tempted to accept the world-view of those whom she conquered.

That she did not completely succumb to this temptation is due in large measure to the fact that Israel was called upon repeatedly to renew her vigorous military spirit in order to ward off other peoples who also wished to plunder or settle in the land. At least that is the way the book of Judges tells the story and there is no particular reason to doubt this general thesis. As long as the invaders were bedouin tribesmen as Israel had been, she was generally successful in driving them out.

A few tribes would band together under the leadership of a judge (who was more like a charismatic general than a legal official) and would fight a brief, "citizens" war until the invader was expelled.

One of the great strengths which Israel brought to Canaan was a sense of unity which transcended loyalty to the city-states. All of Israel, ideally at least, was bound together by a common faith. One can overemphasize this unity, however, for, as the book of Judges clearly shows, it seldom happened that all of the tribes united against the invader. Northern and Southern Israel were, as a matter of fact, divided by the band of Canaanite city-states which stretched across the plains of Megiddo. Although the various tribes of Israel were bound together by a common faith, they developed their own, somewhat different cultural patterns and loyalties.

Hence, when met by an aggressive and determined foe such as the Philistines, Israel was unprepared. Without one central government or king each tribe went its own way and all suffered accordingly.

Although we know something "externally" about the Philistines, because no written documents from them have been uncovered, they remain an enigmatic mystery. Virtually nothing is known about their language or their religion, though we do have many evidences of their material culture. Undoubtedly their arrival was a part of the catastrophic interruption of civilization in the eastern mediterranean region caused by a new wave of invasions which took place about 1200 B.C. Not only did the Doric invaders uproot the Myceneaen civilization of Greece, the Sea Peoples even went so far as to attack Egypt. The latter, under Ramesses III, repulsed these people in 1196, but was not as victorious as Ramesses' own stele proclaims. Probably to appease them he allowed these Sea Peoples to settle on what is now the Gaza Strip.

Biblical tradition has it that the Philistines came from Caphtor (Crete) and there is some reason to accept this notion, though they probably were not originally Cretan. The Philistines, at least, produced a kind of painted pottery unknown before in Palestine but quite similar to that found on the Greek islands. They also made a unique sort of ceramic sarcophagus which is a sure sign of Philistine occupation. Somewhere during their travels, they picked up the art of iron working, an art largely unknown in Canaan. Thus with the arrival of the Philistines the Iron Age in Palestine began. For some time, however, they kept their trade secrets to themselves and thus gained a great advantage over their neighbors who continued to make implements of war of bronze.

It was not just the secret of iron which gave the Philistines an advantage. The five city states under their control were bent upon carving a Philistine Empire out of this part of the Near East and their determination and skill at war caused them to prosper. Slowly but surely they gained hegemony over the inland regions until they controlled much of the area. Israel was never totally defeated, but neither was she able to ward off the Philistine advances. The tragi-comic story of Samson reveals the great weakness of the Israelite "judgeship." Samson is able to get in his licks against the haughty Philistines, but his effort is a personal one and in the end he dies pulling the Temple of Dagon upon their heads.

The Book of Judges, a collection of authentic memories, folk legends, and stories designed to teach a moral lesson, is on the one hand an extended glorification of the "good old days" when God alone was king of Israel and when no human potentate told the individual Israelite what to do. But it also offers an equally strong argument for the rise of the kingship in Israel. Dependence upon a charismatic leader who would arise in times of crisis led inevitably to chaos and defeat. Judges, though a literary unit, points forward to the development of the kingship recorded in the books of Samuel and Kings.

The Rise of the Kingship (1050-922 B.C.)

WHEN ONE turns to the books of Samuel and Kings one immediately senses a firmness of historical footing not felt before. Although there is little non-Biblical evidence to support the facts asserted concerning Saul and David, the history is so frankly and plausibly recorded that it is not difficult to believe that most of it is quite accurate. Legendary accretions there are, but they are subordinated to the carefully recorded and sometime embarrassing facts about Israel's first two kings.

The story opens with Samuel, the last of the judges, and his exploits and problems. Against his own better judgment he accepts the people's (and God's) demand for a king and anoints the Benjamite Saul. In many respects Saul was a good choice. He was from a small tribe and thus his selection did not cause great tribal disaffection. He was tall and handsome and looked like a leader. At the beginning he fulfilled

Israel's hopes by winning some minor skirmishes with the Philistines and other enemies, but as time went on the problems of his nation and his own personal idiosyncracies got the better of him.

As a king he certainly faced great difficulties. He had no professional army, no impressive capital, and very little "money." Moreover, Samuel, the man of God, always stood in the background, ready to criticize and, indeed, overthrow. As a consequence, Saul became increasingly moody and paranoic. Instead of accepting the talented David as a comrade-in-arms and wise advisor he soon became jealous of him and turned this trusted friend into an unwilling enemy. Finally, Saul, in a decisive battle against the Philistines, was killed with his son Jonathan on Mount Gilboa in about 1000 B.C. All of Israel was humiliated as the Philistines hung their dead bodies from the walls of Beth-shan.

In the meantime, David bided his time among the Philistines, pretending to fight against Israel, while actually undercutting the power of the Philistine states. When Saul was killed, David returned and was soon crowned king of Judah at Hebron. Saul's son, Ishbaal, inherited the northern kingdom, but he quickly fell before assassins. David, who seems to have truly lamented the assassination, was then chosen to be king of the northern tribes and thus became ruler over all Israel.

David was a man of great leadership ability and an inborn sense of timing which prevented him from making the kind of mistakes which so often are the undoing of lesser men. He could have fought Saul directly. Instead he avoided direct conflict with the legitimate ruler of the realm and thus offended few. When he came to power, he had the nation behind him and was able to expand greatly the power and extent of his kingship. After reducing the holdings of the Philistines to the minimum he turned to the task of solidifying and expanding Israel's holdings elsewhere. During his forty year reign (1000-960 B.C.) he not only conquered many of the remaining Canaanite cities but also gained hegemony over Damascus, Edom, and Moab as well. Thus he carved out an Empire the likes of which the land had never known before. To be sure, he was greatly aided in this by the fact that both Egypt and the Mesopotamian nations were experiencing "dark ages" at that time. Still, a lesser man might well have fumbled the opportunity. With David, Israel's moment of glory seemed to unfold quite naturally.

David, of couse, needed a capital city for his Empire. Significantly, he chose neither Hebron, where he had originally been crowned, nor Shechem, the ancient city of the north-central region. Instead, to avoid all tribal disputes, he chose the Jebusite city of Jerusalem and renamed it "the City of David." Already an impregnable fortress which David himself only conquered by clever strategem, the city served David beautifully as a symbol around which he could build an enduring kingdom. To this day Jerusalem remains a religious, if not a political capital of the Western world. To it Moslems, Christians, and Jews still go to visit the ancient shrines of their religions: the Dome of the Rock, the Church of the Holy Sepulchre, and the Wailing Wall.

Like most men David had one failing which nearly proved to be his undoing. Although fierce in battle and wise in administration, he could not resist the temptation to spoil his children. As a consequence, the last years of his reign were marred by tawdry squabbles among his sons and repeated attempts to usurp the throne. Even on his deathbed David was confronted by an attempted coup by his son Adonijah. In the end, however, David had his way and Solomon, the son of his favorite wife, Bathsheba, ascended the throne in his stead.

Solomon, who ruled from about 960 to 922 B.C. was in many respects a worthy successor to his father. Although not a fighter, he did strengthen Israel's defenses and tried to develop her industrial potential. A great builder, he turned Jerusalem into a truly imperial city with a lavish palace, harem, and temple. During his reign Israel undoubtedly reached literary heights unknown before. It is no wonder that later Israelites looked back upon his reign as a Golden Age and upon him as the wisest of men.

Although Solomon's achievements were great, however, there is another side to the story which must be told. Solomon's building projects were impressive, but they were bought at a price. In order to finance his programs he was forced to levy heavy taxes and to use impressed labor. Beneath the surface of his apparently placid Empire discontent grew. Israelite freedom was being infringed upon, and around the edges the Empire showed signs of decay. It is no wonder, then, that when Solomon was succeeded upon the throne by a lesser man, the Empire fell apart. One wonders what would have happened to Israel and to the world if Solomon had been less of an oriental potentate and had sought to preserve the "democratic" freedoms which characterized the older tribal system of government. Such speculation is, of course, fruitless, for inevitably there is a flaw which spoils the best laid plans of men. Israel knew her moment of glory under David and Solomon, but that glory soon gave way to petty division and then to disaster.

Before that unfortunate development is rehearsed, it is necessary to say something about the development of Israelite religion during this period. Before the development of the kingship Israelite religion seems to have been rather loosely structured and decentralized. There was a central shrine at Shiloh (earlier at Gilgal and then Shechem) where all Israelite males were to worship three times a year, but there were also many other shrines and high-places where sacrifices were offered.

During the judgeship of Samuel the Ark of the Covenant, which had been housed at Shiloh, was captured by the Philistines. David, however, recovered the Ark and brought it to Jerusalem. When Solomon built his Temple, which was originally meant to be a royal chapel, he placed within it this ancient symbol of the faith. The books of Samuel and Kings do not tell the whole story, but it would appear that Solomon conceived of himself not only as secular ruler but as a kind of priest-king and head of the cult. He offered sacrifices at the high place in Gibeon and appointed the high-priest. In doing this he assumed a role which was held by many other potentates in the ancient Near East but which was not appreciated by some Israelites who disliked such centralization of authority. Even the book of I Kings, which generally glorifies Solomon, offers criticism of him for preempting certain cultic responsibilities.

The critics of the king and the development of a royal cult were not without spokesmen within Israel. Along with the development of the kingship there also came the development of a prophetic movement which was to be of supreme importance in the history of Israelite religion. The Near East had known for a long time of ecstatic prophets who would, through inspiration, predict the future and offer counsel to those who sought it. In Greece, the Delphic oracle served such a function. From Egypt and Mesopotamia have also come documents expressing or describing prophetic activity. Doubtless there were ecstatic prophets among the Israelites as well.

The prophets who confront us in the pages of Samuel and Kings and in the books of written prophecies, however, offer far more than cryptic oracles of advice and portent. In Israel the prophets—at least those who are mentioned—appear as spokesmen for God. They are the guardians of the covenant who criticize both the king and the people when they stray from the basic covenantal agreement between themselves and Yahweh. When David commits adultery with Bathsheba, Nathan is there to call him to account. When Solomon oversteps his bounds, Adonijah appears to anoint Jeroboam king over ten of the twelve tribes. When Ahab countenances the worship of the Tyrian Melkart, Elijah and Elisha call down God's wrath upon him. Many of the prophets did predict the future, but they based their predictions upon the political and social realities of their day and upon the terms of the covenant under which Israel lived. The history of Israel from the ninth to the sixth century is the history of the growing tension between the prophets and their followers on the one hand and those who wished to turn the Israelite nations into typical oriental despotic states on the other.

The Divided Kingdoms (922-721 B.C.)

WHEN SOLOMON died in about 922, he was succeeded to the throne by his son Rehoboam. Apparently his succession was unquestioned by the Judahites, but in the north, tribal leaders were more hesitant. Not only did they wish an alleviation of some of the excesses of Solomon; they also wished to express their tribal independence by "electing" their king as they had elected David. When Rehoboam unwisely refused to accede to any of their demands, the northern tribes simply withdrew from the "Empire" and chose as their king Jeroboam I who had recently returned from exile in Egypt. Thus began the division of the kingdom of David which was to last until the destruction of the northern kingdom (now called Israel) in 721 B.C. The southern kingdom (Judah) continued as a semi-independent state until 586 B.C.

Not only was Rehoboam powerless to stop the secession of the north. His own rather small kingdom was reduced severely by the Egyptian Pharaoh Shoshenk I, who went so far as to plunder the temple in Jerusalem. Because of the prestige of the Davidic line, Judah remained politically stable. Only from 842 to 837, when the queen mother, Ataliah, ruled and sought to extirpate the sons of David was the succession of Davidic rulers interrupted. At the same time, Judah was, during most of her history, a politically and commercially insignificant country. Perhaps it was this unimportance which preserved her from total disaster for so long. Most conquerors didn't regard her as worth bothering about.

Israel, on the other hand, sat astride important trade routes and, hence, was economically and politically much more important. Although never a major power, during her best years she was able to prosper commercially and manifested considerable military strength. Since Israel had no long tradition of royal lineage, however, her political situation was always tenuous. One usurper followed another; to the end, Israel was unable to establish a line of succession comparable to that of David. Furthermore, because of her strategic position and wealth, Israel was far more vulnerable to foreign invasion and domination.

The primary threat came first from the Arameans to the north. Once the Davidic yoke had been thrown off, the Aramaic people banded together and formed a considerable, though loosely organized, empire in Syria and the upper Mesopotamian region. Indeed, the influence of this people was so important that Aramaic became a widely accepted official language for trade and international relations. Eventually the Arameans succumbed before the growing strength of Assyria to the east, but not before they had subdued and severely weakened the state of Israel.

Perhaps the most important and successful king of Israel during the ninth century was Omri who ruled from 876-869 B.C. Omri came to the throne through a military coup, but soon established himself as the accepted king. Although the Biblical historians, who regarded Omri as an evil ruler, tell us little about him, non-Biblical sources make clear his importance. Long after his death and the end of his lineage, Assyrians continued to call Israel "the land of Omri."

One of Omri's most important acts was the building of a new capital for the kingdom northwest of the ancient capital of Shechem on a lofty, unoccupied hill. This capital, which he called Samaria, commanded a beautiful view of the valleys around it and must have made an impressive royal seat. Not only at Samaria but all over his kingdom Omri built magnificent buildings whose ruins still reflect the power of his reign.

Unlike Solomon, Omri was not content merely to defend his territories. He was able to expand Israel's borders eastward and to reduce Moab to tributary status. Through the marriage of his son Ahab to the daughter of the king of Tyre he cemented peaceful relations with his neighbor to the north, while his daughter's marriage to the crown prince of Judah improved relations with his sister state immeasurably. When he died, therefore, he left to his son Ahab a relatively prosperous and powerful state over which to rule.

Ahab (869-850), however, did not experience easy sailing as king of Israel. In the first place, his domain was threatened from without by the Arameans, whom he was at first able to push back, and then by the Assyrians against whom the Arameans and Israelites joined in coalition. At the important battle of Qarqar in 853 the allies were able to withstand the advances of Shalmanezer III, but this threat from the east was a premonition of more disastrous events to follow. In the meantime, with Assyria withdrawn, Aram and Israel set to quarreling again and Ahab lost his life in battle against Damascus at Ramoth-Gilead.

Another equally perilous threat to the house of Omri came from within. Ahab's marriage to Jezebel, the princess of Tyre, entailed the introduction of the cult of Melkart into Israel. Although apparently welcomed by the populace, the popularity of this foreign cult met with stern opposition from the prophets Elijah and Elisha. Not content with merely oral polemics against the pagan gods, Elisha fomented revolution by anointing a new king, Jehu, who led an armed rebellion against Ahab's son Joram. In this he was successful, and the blossoming Melkart cult was soon stamped out.

In a way, this prophetic revolution was salutory, for had the "Melkart party" triumphed, Israel would have lost her own unique cultural and religious heritage, and we would not be studying the Bible today. At the same time, Jehu's revolt led to some very unfortunate political and economic consequences. One of Jehu's first moves was to kill off all the members of Omri's family and most of his political advisors. This meant that the nation lost many of its most able administrators and leaders. Furthermore, his revolution destroyed the peaceful and cooperative relations between Israel and Tyre and Judah. Jehu pursued a policy of international isolationism and thus left himself open to attack. When the Assyrians marched westward once more, Jehu was forced to submit meekly and to pay tribute, as the Black Obelisk of Shalmanezer III so clearly depicts. The Assyrians withdrew, but were replaced by the Arameans as the tormentors of Israel. Indeed, it would appear that both Israel and Judah were reduced to tributary status in the Aramean Empire.

The last half of the ninth century, therefore, was one of great weakness and turmoil for both Israel and Judah. Fortunately, however, a turn in world-events allowed Israel to flourish briefly once again. The Assyrians once more pushed toward the sea and in savage warfare defeated Damascus, virtually destroying the Aramaic Empire. Israel and Judah were also forced to pay tribute, but Assyria, threatened by the kingdom of Urartu, was obliged to turn her attention north and eastward and hence withdrew. Moreover, both Israel and Judah were blessed with capable rulers—Jeroboam II and Ahaziah—and soon took advantage of the demise of Damascus.

The first half of the eighth century was, therefore, a time for prosperity and modest expansion. Together Israel and Judah controlled most of the old Solomonic Empire and began once more to prosper economically. This moment of glory was to prove illusory, however. The prophets warned that social inequality, constant warfare among the little states of Syria-Palestine, and religious unfaithfulness could only lead to ultimate disaster. In the north Amos and Hosea prophesied imminent doom. Isaiah and Micah, who prophesied in the south were almost equally pessimistic about the immediate future. Hosea, Isaiah, and Micah all maintained that eventually God would fulfill his promises to Israel, but for the immediate future they agreed with the dire predictions of Amos. Nor were they proven wrong. In 745 B.C. Tiglath-Pileser III came to the throne of Assyria and set about to create a world-wide Assyrian Empire. An exceedingly able and vigorous leader, he subdued Babylon and Urartu and then turned his attention westward. Unlike his predecessors, Tiglath-Pileser aimed, not only to exact tribute, but to conquer. Although he met with some opposition, his armies were too powerful for those of Palestine and he soon was in control of the whole area. In order to prevent revolution, he adopted the policy of simply moving sizeable segments of the population to another part of the Empire and replacing them with foreign peoples. The hand-writing on the wall now became a reality; Israel and Judah became, in effect, part of the Assyrian Empire.

The final end of the northern kingdom did not come until 721, however, during the reign of the Assyrian Emperor Sargon II. Hoping to take advantage of an alliance with Egypt, Hoshea, the Israelite king, withheld tribute. Sargon, however, soon attacked and the Egyptian aid never arrived. Hoshea was taken prisoner, Samaria beseiged and conquered, and a significant proportion of the population exiled. So ended the northern kingdom as a political reality. Judah continued to exist as a vassal state, but she too was required to pay tribute and had little freedom of political action left. Not until the last decades of the seventh century did Judah regain her independence once more.

Judah Stands Alone (721-586 B.C.)

ALTHOUGH THE FRUITS of disobedience were made clear in the destruction of Samaria, Judah could not long remain content with her submissive lot. As long as Sargon remained on the throne in Assyria, King Ahaz and then his son Hezekiah remained relatively submissive, but when Sennacerib replaced him, Hezekiah's thoughts turned to freedom. When the Babylonian revolutionary Merodach-baladan sent emissaries asking for Judah's alliance against the Assyrian hegemony, Hezekiah, much against the advice of the prophet Isaiah, agreed. Unfortunately, Merodach-baladan was defeated and Sennacerib turned upon Judah. According to the Bible, Hezekiah was saved by divine intervention, but this did not much alter the facts of the case. Hezekiah was forced to submit, pay a huge tribute, and watch his daughters be carried away to Nineveh. Jerusalem was not destroyed, but was placed under the surveillance of Philistine overlords.

Under Esarhaddon and Assurbanipal Assyria reached the zenith of her power in the early decades of the seventh century. Even Egypt had to submit to her force and, for a few brief years, Nineveh controlled the world. Mannassah, Hezekiah's son, reflected the power of Assyria in his own reign. Although the Bible severely censures him for his evil ways, in fact there was little else he could have done. His adoption of Assyrian gods and the consequent desecration of the temple were the natural and expected results of his submission to the ruling powers. To have emphasized the worship of Yahweh would have been to have supported Israel's desire for independence, a dangerous desire, given the nature of Assyrian power.

Like most great empires, Assyria no sooner ended her conquest of the world than she began to decay. Under Assurbanipal stresses and strains began to appear as the conquered peoples began to seek freedom and those still outside the empire sought to share in its riches. After his death in 626 the Babylonians gained their independence. Then in 612 the united army of Babylonians, Medes, and Scythians conquered Nineveh. The prophet Nahum expresses the feelings of many peoples of the world in his exultation over the death of that evil "harlot." The giant Assyria was no more!

Happily, during this time Judah was ruled by a wise and industrious king, Josiah. Taking advantage of Assyrian weakness he was able to expand the territory of Judah to include the province of Samaria as well. Using as the basis for reform a newly discovered book of law, which many scholars believe was none other than an early edition of the book of Deuteronomy, he destroyed out-lying shrines and made the Temple of Solomon *the* cultic shrine for all of Israel. He reinstituted the ancient convenantal agreement between God and Israel, celebrated Passover once more, and generally restored, in a dramatically altered way, the ancient worship of Yahweh. Once again, it looked as though the Davidic Empire might be restored.

Unfortunately, these hopes were dashed by the realities of history. Neccho, the Egyptian Pharaoh, sought to come to the aid of the defeated Assyrian Emperor in order to prevent a total Babylonian take-over. Josiah met him at Megiddo and, either through deceit or warfare—the text is not clear—met his death. The Egyptians placed his son Jehoiakim on the throne, and Judah became, for the moment, an Egyptian vassal.

Almost immediately, however, Babylonia replaced Assyria as the foremost power and sought to reassert her hegemony over Syria-Palestine. Johoiakim resisted and Babylonia sent troops. From this point onward, Judah was on the slippery slide to disaster. Jeremiah, the great prophetic witness of this period, called his people to obedience but foresaw little hope for her in the immediate future. Submit to the Babylonians, he counselled, there is no other way. Unfortunately Judah's rulers did not listen. The tide of nationalism ran high and Jeremiah was accused of treason. History, however, was on Jeremiah's side. In 597 the Babylonians came and deported many Judahites, including the young King Jehoiachin. When the nation still would not submit and sought freedom again under Zedekiah, Nebuchadnezzar returned with force, destroyed Jerusalem and depopulated the country. Many persons were left, of course, but the ruling class was deported along with most of the intelligentsia. Judah became the haunt of the lions and the briars, dismembered and forlorn. Jeremiah remained behind, but when a member of the Davidic family assassinated the appointed Governor, Gedaliah, Jeremiah himself was taken away to Egypt by those who sought his safety.

Exile and Restoration (586-400 B.C.)

SINCE THE BOOK of Kings ends with the fall of Jerusalem and the exile of King Jehoiachin, we have no chronological account of the events which took place among the Jews in Judah and in Babylonia during the Exilic period. Most of what we do know comes through a careful reading of the book of Ezekiel who served as a prophet and theological interpreter for the Jews in exile. Apparently, although many of the exiled people wished to return home, their situation was not too gloomy. They were given freedom to pursue their trades, to meet together for religious purposes, and to move about without restraint. In fact, as time went on many of the Jews prospered and made their permanent home in this foreign land. So began the "Diaspora," the spreading out of Jewry all over the world.

Ezekiel, himself, sought to interpret the events which brought the kingdom of Israel to an end and to provide a way of life for those separated from their land and their temple. Although he emphasized hope for the future—a return to the land and glorious rebuilding of the temple—he also stressed personal obedience to God's law as an essential part of the Jewish way of life. What was once primarily civil law, designed to regulate behavior in the Israelite state, became religious law which was to be obeyed because it was from God. With the exile, then, Judaism as a religion began.

In Babylonia, the men of Israel met, not to offer sacrifices, but to rehearse and hence keep alive the traditions of the past and to discuss plans for the future. It is doubtless out of this situation that the institution called the synagogue became a reality. Even after the Temple was rebuilt the synagogue remained a central feature of Jewish religious life.

Like the Assyrian Empire before it, Babylonia reached its zenith of power and then began to decay. This demise was hastened by the leadership of the eccentric and perhaps deranged king Nabonidus (555-539) who succeeded in alienating the powerful priestly class of Babylon and hence in undermining his own power. His defeat came at the hands of Cyrus, the Persian, who subdued Media in 553 and Lydia in 546 and then turned on the Babylonians themselves. In 539 Cyrus entered the gates of Babylon which had been thrown open for him by the Babylonians, who were glad to be rid of Nabonidus.

Unlike the Assyrians and Babylonians, Cyrus believed that the stability of his Empire depended to a large extent upon the good will of the conquered peoples. Hence, he not only did not interfere with the religious and cultural life of his subjects, but allowed older traditions suppressed by the Babylonians to be restored. Thus it was that the Jews asked for, and soon received, permission to return to their homeland and rebuild the Temple which had been left in ruins by the forces of Nebuchadnezzar.

The prophet who anticipated and exulted in these new developments was Deutero-Isaiah, whose oracles are to be found in Isaiah 40-55. (There is much scholarly debate about whether Chapters 56-66 are also by him or by a still later hand.) His message was one of comfort and hope to the captive people, for he foresaw in the immediate future a glorious return of the Jews to their land and a rebuilding of the kingdom. Cyrus, he overtly proclaimed to be a Messiah, destined to be the instrument of God's mercy (Isaiah 45:1).

In a sense, the prophet's hopes were fulfilled, for Cyrus did release the Jews, but in no sense was the return as glorious or as triumphant as he predicted. Many Jews, who were prospering quite well in Babylonia, decided to stay right where they were. Those who did return found the land overrun with brambles and wild animals, the cities, piles of rubble, and the political situation, highly unfavorable. Very soon they came into conflict with the Samaritans who were fearful of the return of Jerusalem to power and who probably were repelled by the "orthodoxy" of the returnees. The Governor of the era had his seat in Samaria, a city and a region populated by foreign peoples brought there by the Assyrians. Many of them had adopted the religion of Israel as the religion of the land, but mixed with it pagan practices. They wished to retain the political power in Samaria and hence were alarmed at the prospect of the rebuilding of Jerusalem. The Jews, on the other hand, looked down upon the Samaritans as religiously impure and heterodox. Since Samaria held the political "trump cards," the rebuilding of the Temple was soon halted and the Jews were forced to accept their political subservience.

Little more is known about the reestablished Jewish community until 520 B.C. when two prophets, Haggai and Zechariah, appeared upon the scene. Probably encouraged by the rash of insurrections which followed the ascension of Darius to the throne of Persia, these prophets called for an immediate rebuilding of the Temple and proclaimed again that

God would soon act to fulfill his promises to his people. Zerubbabel, a prince of the Davidic line, who was then acting as governor of Judah by Persian appointment, was described in glowing Messianic language. Although the day of fulfillment did not come, these prophets did stir the people to action, and the Temple, now of very modest size, was rebuilt and dedicated in 515.

After this time, little is known about the Jewish community in Palestine for about seventy-five years. During the same period, however, Persia reached the zenith of its power under Darius (521-486). Although the Persians lost the famous battle of Marathon in 490 B.C. and hence failed in Darius' long-planned attempt to conquer Greece, Persia was able to expand its borders on all sides until, at the death of Darius, its boundaries extended from the Indus river to the Aegean and from the Jaxartes as far as Libya. Darius' son, Xerxes, however was by no means as competent and was unable to extend Persian rule any farther. Again an invasion of Greece was attempted and repelled; Persia was finally driven from its foothold in Europe. Xerxes, after putting down a number of rebellions, was assassinated and succeeded by a younger son, Artaxerxes, (465-424). His reign was characterized by both internal disorder and external defeats as the Persian Empire began to show signs of weakness and decay.

It is during the reign of Artaxerxes that the curtain of history again rises and we can glimpse what was going on in Jerusalem. Unfortunately, the books of Ezra and Nehemiah, which give us this picture, cannot easily be reconciled in historical details. Although the Bible says that Ezra came to Jerusalem first, most contemporary historians now believe that Nehemiah preceded Ezra. It is clear, at any rate, that Nehemiah, a Jewish cup-bearer to the Emperor, received reports from Jerusalem concerning the desperate conditions there and, as a consequence, requested that he be allowed to journey to his "homeland" to help to improve the situation. As a result he was appointed by Artaxerxes I Governor of Judah and arrived in Jerusalem in about 445. While Periclean Athens flowered and set the cultural style of the ancient world which was yet to be born, Nehemiah strove to restore the Jerusalem which was of old and to purify the city of David which had reached deplorable depths. Although flanked on all sides by enemies such as Sanballat, the Governor of Samaria, and Tobiah of Transjordan, he was able to rebuild the walls of the city and to initiate the rebuilding of Jewish life according to the ideals developed in Babylonian Jewry.

If John Bright's reconstruction is correct, he was aided in the latter years of his region by the great "scribe" Ezra, who probably came to Jerusalem during Nehemiah's second term of office.[1] Ezra, equally appalled by the lack of obedience to the Jewish law, called for national repentance and, to convict the people of their sins, read from the book of law. Exactly what Ezra read we do not know, but undoubtedly by this time the Torah was in its final form. Ezra's reformation of Jewish life had the effect, not only of calling people to obey the law, but of making the Torah the authoritative law for Judaism. Henceforth, the Jews would be the people of the Torah, intent upon obeying the rules and regulations of the Book. The work of Nehemiah and Ezra resulted in the separation of the Jews from both the pagans and those believers in the God of Israel whom they regarded as heterodox and half-pagan. Mixed marriages were deplored; Sabbatarian laws enforced; rites, rituals, and customs fastidiously observed. This reformation, of course, was hardly as thorough-going as the reformers would have liked. Still, one can hardly overestimate the effect of their work upon Judaism from that day until this.

Before passing on to the last phase of Old Testament history, a word must be said about the influence of the Persion religion, Zoroastrianism, upon Judaism. One of the chief difficulties in assessing this influence is that so little is known for sure about the prophet Zarathustra (the Greeks called him Zoroaster) or about the early development of the religion which he fostered. Some scholars maintain that he lived about 1000 B.C.; others, that he did not live until the sixth century. Still others argue that he never lived at all but was a fictional character. Furthermore, the extent of the influence of Zoroastrianism within the Persian Empire is somewhat difficult to ascertain, though it is certain that it was by no means insignificant.

Be that as it may, it would appear that Zoroastrian theology and religion did have an impact upon pre-Christian Judaism which must not be overlooked. The theology of Zoroastrianism, as it is presented in the Gathas, is thoroughly dualistic. That is to say, Zarathustra teaches that the history of the world must be understood as the struggle between the Good God, Ahura Mazda, and the Evil God, Ahriman. On the side of each are various spirits, the angels and the demons respectively, who aid in the fighting. Man is called to side with the Good God, Ahura

[1] Bright, John. *A History of Israel.* Philadelphia: Westminster Press, 1959 pp. 375-386.

Mazda, and thus participate in the final victory of light over darkness which will occur at the end of time. Each man is free to choose which side he will fight for, but if he chooses the evil side he does so to his eternal dishonor. On the last day, there will be a resurrection of the dead. Those who fought for Ahura Mazda will be ranked among the blessed, but those who fought for Ahriman will be confined to the outer darkness.

This vision of the world, which was carried all over the Near East by the Zoroastrian Magis, clearly influenced Jewish thinking. Within Judaism we find the development of angeology and demonology, an emphasis upon the resurrection of the dead and the end of history, and numerous exhortations to live the good life in order to receive one's final reward. In other words, many features of late Judaism (and early Christianity) seem to be far more Zoroastrian than Biblical. It is significant that Matthew includes in the opening chapters of his gospel a description of the visit of Magi to the baby Jesus.

To the End of the Old Testament Period

THE PERIOD following Nehemiah and Ezra is the most poorly documented era in the history of Israel. A few details about life in Judah are to be gleaned from the Elephantine papyri—interesting texts from a Jewish community of rather heterdox bent which existed at Elephantine in southern Egypt—, but on the whole, the historian must admit that one can hardly write a history on the basis of these few meager references. The most that can be said is that the Nehemiah-Ezra reforms of the fifth century were hardly totally successful, for we find indications of corruption and infidelity in Jerusalem itself.

Strangely enough, Biblical sources do not even mention the famous conquest of the Persian Empire by Alexander the Great in the 330s and 20s. Apparently Judah, like many other small peoples, welcomed the great Hellenizer without great resentment and found the new political situation at least as amenable as life in the decaying Persian Empire. With the death of Alexander in 323 his Empire split, as several of his generals snatched pieces of it for themselves. Egypt fell to Ptolemy, while Seleucus took Babylonia and then extended his control over Syria. Although Alexander had no opportunity to develop his plan for Hellenizing the East in detail, his generals continued the work which he began. New "Greek" cities with their theaters, gymnasiums, and temples were created all over the area, and Greek patterns of life, which had already been influential in the Persian Empire before Alexander, became even more popular.

But for a few exceptions, there is little evidence in the Bible that this Hellenization had much impact upon the Jews. Some of the books of the Apocrypha and some non-Biblical sources, however, reveal that Hellenic culture was far more attractive to the Jews than the Bible itself reveals. In Egypt, for instance, most Jews were Greek-speaking and, as a result, a translation was made of the whole Old Testament. This translation, often called the Septuagint, greatly facilitated communication between Jew and Greek and was of great use in the spread of Christianity a few centuries later.

In Judah—as indeed in all of Jewry—Hellenization, however, had a very divisive effect. Some Jews wished to retain their ancient customs and institutions and thus repudiated those many other Jews who wished to live in the "modern world." Other Jews were so embarrassed by their own ancient culture that they became completely Hellenized and forsook the traditions of their people. Thus there developed the "parties" of the "Pious" (the Chasidim), the Hellenistic Jews, and what might be called the apostate Jews. The Jewish rulers, though usually priests, tended to side with the Hellenists, if only because they had to seek political accommodation with those outside the faith. The conservative group, therefore, was critical of the ruling ecclesiocracy and sought to return the well-tried ways of theological orthodoxy and cultural conservatism. Because this group concerned itself primarily with personal piety, however, the division among Jews led more to mutual recrimination and distrust than to political insurrection.

Besides these rather general observations, however, little more can be said about the history of Judaism, *per se,* until we come to the second quarter of the second century B.C. This period is fairly well documented by the books of the Maccabees, by the Jewish Historian Josephus, and, indirectly, by the book of Daniel. The history of this "moment" in Jewish history is too complex to review in detail, but the essential events may be summarized briefly as follows:

In 198 a vigorous Seleucid ruler, Antiochus III, defeated the Egyptian army and wrested Palestine from the control of Ptolemaic Empire. Apparently the Jews welcomed this change, joined Antiochus against Ptolemy V Epiphanes, and in return received kind consideration. Jewish captives were released, forgiveness of taxes for three years was decreed, and certain privileges were guaranteed. Thus life in the Seleucid Empire began well.

This situation did not continue, however, under the rulership of Seleucus IV and Antiochus IV Ephiphanes (175-163). Unfortunately for these rulers and, hence, for the Jews, the Seleucid Empire faced, during their reigns, difficult problems both at home and abroad. Not only did the Ptolemaic Empire wish to regain its lost territory, the Parthians in the east were growing in strength, while to the west Rome appeared as a considerable threat. Already, under Antiochus III, the Empire had experienced great humiliation and defeat at the hands of the Roman legions.

Because of these external threats and the costs of keeping a large standing army, Seleucus and Antiochus IV found themselves strapped for funds. In their search for money they imposed heavy taxes on their subjects and were open to bribery. They also eyed the rich temples of the land as sources of further gain. To promote the cause of unity they began to emphasize more and more their own status as "gods incarnate" (a conception fostered by Alexander himself) and to demand religious uniformity of their subjects.

The whole crisis came to a head in Judah when Jason, a brother of Onias III the high-priest, offered to Antiochus money for the high priestly position. As a consequence, Onias was deposed and Jason installed. Jason, a Hellenistic Jew, immediately began to foster Hellenistic ideals by building a gymnasium where not only athletic games but the Greek cultic rites which went with them were observed. This only widened the split between the conservatives and Hellenists which already existed.

Jason did not last long at his post, however, for he was outbid for the job by one Menelaus who was probably not even of a priestly family. Jason was ousted by Antiochus and Menelaus pursued the very unpopular course of selling off valuable objects from the Temple. When word came that Antiochus had been killed in an Egyptian campaign, Jason returned and overthrew Menelaus. Unhappily for him, however, Antiochus was not dead and when he heard what had happened was less than pleased.

In retaliation Antiochus sacked the Temple, carrying away many of its valuable objects. Then the next year he went even further, requiring that all Jewish subjects cease to practice their religion. A garrison of troops was sent, Sabbath and dietary laws revoked and the cult of the Olympic Zeus installed in the Temple. Needless to say, the Jews were incensed. Many refused to obey and were slaughtered.

Soon a revolt, started by Mattathaias and his sons in the hill country of Judah, spread. Judas, one of the sons, (nicknamed the "Hammer" or Makkabios) took over leadership of the movement and began armed resistance. Because most of Antiochus' troops were committed elsewhere, the Maccabean revolt was quite successful in repelling the "foreigners." Jerusalem was taken, the Temple cleansed and rededicated, and the country for a time gained a modicum of freedom. Although the Maccabean rulers experienced some set-backs, the country remained semi-autonomous until the coming of Pompey and the Roman legions in 63 B.C.

Just before the revolt began a tract appeared, counselling faithfulness and courage in the face of persecution. This anonymous work, which claimed to be about the sixth century but which held out hope for the intervention of God in the second, was none other than the book of Daniel. Using bizarre and veiled imagery, it was written to assure the people that the day of God was at hand and that in the face of persecution what was required was the steadfast devotion of the great Daniel. This was doubtless the last of the works contained in the Hebrew canon to be written.

The history of Israel during the Old Testament period, then, ends with a note of momentary triumph. The Maccabees hardly fulfilled the author of Daniel's expectations and, eventually manifested some undesirable characteristics themselves. Nevertheless, for a few brief years Judah was once more free and independent. After the coming of the Romans in 63 B.C., Israel was never again to experience such independence until 1948 A.D.

CHAPTER V

The Torah: An Introduction

The Argument
The Composition of the Torah

HE FIRST and most venerable part of the *Tanak* is called in Hebrew *Torah*, a word which has been traditionally translated "Law". In recent years, however, it has been frequently pointed out that this translation is both inaccurate and misleading, for the Torah contains much more than simply legal prescriptions and proscriptions. For many modern readers, indeed, the narrative sections of these five books seem far more interesting and significant than the various codes of law which are collected in a rather haphazard fashion in the last four books. Genesis captivates us; Leviticus puts the average reader to sleep. Furthermore, the word *Torah* etymologically seems to have much broader implications than our word law. Hence, many scholars have proposed that Torah ought to be translated "The Tradition" or "The Teaching."

Although there is much truth in this argument, certainly we ought not to let our own preconceptions and interests blind us to the fact that for many ancient Israelites the narrative portions of Torah may have appeared as primarily a preamble to the important matter, i.e., to the laws laid down by God for the regulation of human conduct. We may not be deeply interested in dietary regulations or other rules of conduct, but clearly the early Rabbis of Israel were. If we approach the *Torah* as a work of art articulated in five stylistically different movements or acts, we cannot fail to recognize that primary emphasis is placed upon the giving of the law by God.

Having said this, however, the modern commentator must also acknowledge that today the greatest interest for the general reader is engendered by the narrative portions of the Torah. Hence, in this analysis much more space will be devoted to the explication of selected narrative passages than to an interpretation of Israel's legal traditions.

Before we can turn directly to the text itself, it is important to ask some preliminary questions concerning the Torah as a whole: What is the overarching argument of the work? When and how was it composed?

The Argument

THE FIVE books of the Torah (Genesis, Exodus, Leviticus, Numbers, and Deuteronomy) contain an account of the history of the people of Israel from the days of the Patriarchs to the eve of Israel's triumphant entrance into the promised land. This narrative is prefaced by an eleven-chapter history of mankind before the time of Abraham and is concluded by the last words of Moses to the people of Israel. In between, the story is interrupted with increasing regularity by various codes of law which purport to have been delivered by God to Moses.

Needless to say, the Torah hardly contains positivistic historiography. Although archaeologists have proved beyond a shadow of a doubt that much of the Torah is based upon accurate historical reminiscences, the narrative represents far more than a compilation of proved facts. Rather, the Torah is best understood as a drama in five acts in which the themes of Israel's faith are set forth and articulated. The first eleven chapters establish the basic problem with which the drama is to concern itself: the problem of man's alienation from the source of his existence and his consequent alienation from himself. The story of Noah also offers an archetypal pattern according to which God is to overcome that estrangement. In Noah, God chooses one man for the salvation of mankind as a whole. The disruptive effects of man's sin are not cancelled out, for when man does evil disaster inevitably follows; yet in the midst of disaster God chooses one to begin new life on earth.

This is the central theme of the whole drama which follows. When human life is again disrupted by sin, God chooses Abram and promises him not only that from him shall come a great nation but that through him all mankind shall be blessed. (Genesis 12:1-3) In a sense, the rest of Scripture is simply a description of how these promises were partially fulfilled in the life of Israel and an expression of conviction that in the future they will find their full realization.

At the same time, the Torah is also a book for the present, for its other great theme concerns God's will for Israel as she lives out her life "between the times." Thus the other pole which supports the Tabernacle of the Torah is the law. Although the bases for several customs and laws are mentioned in Genesis, the giving of the law *per se* is reserved until the time of Moses. According to the book of Exodus, it was at Mount Sinai that God offered to Israel the conditions of his covenant in the form of the Ten Commandments. To Moses he then gave many ordinances according to which Israel should govern her life.

In a sense, the covenant of promise to Abraham and the covenant of commandment to Moses and the people complement each other, for one speaks of the future; the other, for the present. Nevertheless, a tension exists between them, for while the former is a gift from God with no apparent strings attached, the latter calls Israel to strict obedience.

This tension also leads to the curious combination of dramatic denoument and yet incompleteness of the Torah. In one sense, God's revelation of his will to Israel at Sinai marks the fulfillment of the dramatic action. After Israel's acceptance of the Ten Commandments as the basis for her covenantal agreement with God, the rest of the Torah is primarily a matter of amplification and explanation. Still the Torah ends inconclusively, for the promises are yet to be fulfilled. Israel has neither entered the promised land to become a great nation nor has she become the source of blessing for the Gentiles. Thus Joshua follows Deuteronomy inevitably.

Many modern scholars believe this tension to be the result of the fact that the Torah is a synthesis of different, and somewhat incompatible, theological traditions. Although there are, to be sure, different points of view represented in the Torah, one wonders whether such a simplistic solution is adequate, for surely this paradoxical relation of completed and incompleted action lies at the very heart of Israel's view of reality. One can hardly understand the faith of Israel without comprehending that for the Bible life is a paradox in which obedience is demanded and yet grace is given despite disobedience.

In brief, then, the Torah contains an account of the situation in which man finds himself, of how God chose for himself a people, and how God revealed his will as commandment and law at Sinai and how he finally led Israel to the plain of Moab, ready to enter the Promised Land. Although this drama manifests an overarching unity which cannot be denied, however, there are many indications that the narrative is by no means a seamless robe. On the contrary, sudden changes in style, inconsistencies in detail, and strange repetitions indicate that many hands were at work in the making of this drama. Like the great Gothic cathedrals of Medieval Europe, the Torah reflects the changing tastes and ideas of a variety of people. Such an observation leads us to the next important question: When and how was the Torah composed.

The Composition of the Torah

THE FIRST, and perhaps most salient point to make is that the Torah, itself, does not explicitly answer this question. There is mention of the fact that Moses wrote down the words of the covenantal agreement (Exodus 24:4), but no indication of who wrote the Torah as a whole. At a fairly early date, however, Israelites began ascribing the whole of the Torah to Moses. By the time of Jesus this ascription was already taken to be accepted fact, though it must also be noted that ancient people, in general, were not really much interested in human authorship. For them, as for many generations of Jews and Christians who followed, the important "fact" was that the Torah is the revelation of God's will. Therefore, although there were some who raised their voices to question this theory, most scholars did not concern themselves with the problem. For them, it was more important to attend to what God said than to question who wrote down his words.

The Renaissance of the sixteenth century, however, produced considerable interest in critical scholarship and in the question of human authorship. Although few scholars really addressed themselves to the question of who wrote the Torah, the tools of literary criticism, which were later to be applied to sacred Scripture, were sharpened. The literalism of both Protestants and Roman Catholics generally discouraged scholars from turning directly to the Bible, however. Only in the seventeenth century did a few heterodox men such as Thomas Hobbes and Baruch de Spinoza begin to question the theory of Mosaic authorship. Because of the intense religious fervor of that age, they were condemned roundly for their disbelief.

It was inevitable, however, that eventually this theory would be questioned by both heretics and believers, for there are just too many indications in the Torah itself that no one man would have composed it. Even a school boy can see that the five books contain many different types of literary style. One moves quickly from an archaic bit of poetry to a smoothly flowing narrative to the most tedious genealogy or law code. Vocabularic changes are obvious; different names are even used in different passages to refer to the deity; anachronisms abound throughout. Isaac is said to have dealt with the Philistines when, in fact, the Philistines had not yet invaded the land. Laws are given to Moses in the wilderness which could only have been meaningful within a settled agricultural context. Allusions to the kingship (which didn't begin until the eleventh century), references in Genesis to camels (which weren't domesticated until the thirteenth century), and above all, an account of Moses' death, all point to the fact that much of the text must have been composed after the death of Israel's great leader. Then, too, there are obvious contradictions in the narrative and strangely repetitious passages which make any one–author theory untenable. It was only a matter of time, therefore, before students of the Bible began to formulate other theories about the composition of the Pentateuch.

It is easy to see what is wrong with the Mosaic authorship theory, but it is quite another to develop a cogent alternative. Much of the nineteenth century was spent by the more liberal Biblical scholars considering various possibilities. Some proposed that originally there had been one consistent narrative but that editors had added considerable material to the text without due regard to its inconsistency. Others proposed that the Torah is a vast patchwork of fragments "sewn" together by a variety of editors. Still others took a middle course, maintaining that the Torah, as it stands, is composed of several different "documents" coming from quite different times which were welded together by a series of redactors.

It was the last theory which, momentarily at least, won the day among Biblical scholars. Although many had a hand in its formulation, the name of Julius Wellhausen, the great German Hebraist, stands out as its most important spokesman. According to the Documentary theory worked out by him, the Torah is made up of four different documents. The first, often called the J document, is characterized by the use of the name Jahveh (Yahweh) throughout. This, according to the theory, is the most primitive of the four. It begins with the story of Adam in the garden of Eden (Genesis 2-3) and can be found intermittently through Genesis, Exodus, and Numbers. Closely associated with the J document is the E or Elohist source which refrains from using the name Yahweh until it is revealed at the time of the Exodus. In Genesis, the word *Elohim* is used to refer to the Deity in this document. The third document, D, is found primarily in the book of Deuteronomy, but editorial touches by the "author" of last book of the Torah are found occasionally elsewhere. This book is identified by Documentary critics as the scroll of law found in the Temple in Jerusalem at the time of King Josiah (622 B.C.). The final strand of the Torah contains primarily legal and genealogical material, though some beautiful passages, such as the first chapter of Genesis are ascribed to this source. Since the over-all interest of this document is cultic it is called the Priestly source or P. Critics dated this document during or after the Babylonian exile. According to the standard theory, these documents, which contained varying views of Israel's past, were collated by a series of redactors. Although in the editing parts of each document were lost, the redactors often allowed the contradictions among the four documents to stand. According to the original theory, at least, all of the documents were composed long after the fact and hence reveal more about Israel during and after the period of the kingship than they do about the days of the Patriarchs and Moses.

Although a few conservative theologians refused to accept this theory, the majority of scholars during the first half of the twentieth century found it the most plausible way to account for the many inconsistencies, anachronisms, and changes in literary style found in the text. It is not too much to say, in fact, that the theory of J,E,P, and P became almost a new dogma. The theology of each of these documents was discussed in detail; the "personalities" of the authors were even described.

Today, however, new debate has erupted concerning the whole question. This is not to say that the work of the documentary critics has been wholly laid aside, but there are many signs that it can no longer be accepted without considerable revision. Some of the most ardent supporters of the general theory have, in fact, helped to bring about its demise, for in analyzing the four "documents" they have found that these sources are not in themselves self-consistent. Hence, various scholars have posited a considerable number of subsources: J^1, J^2, E^1, E^2, etc. What the student is left with are a great number of fragments rather than four self-contained documents.

Furthermore, archaelogical evidence has made clear that all of the documents contain some very ancient remembrances which, though sometimes dramatically altered, still point to a very early origin for the text. Genesis, for instance, contains allusions to customs and rituals which were in use at the time of the Patriarchs but which passed out of use long before the Documents are said to have been written. Thus, if there ever were an author of the J document, he worked with much older materials which already were well-known within his tradition. Hence, the Yahwist (the writer of J) can no longer be thought of simply as an author. He too was editor and reviser of older materials. If this is the case, however, it is extraordinarily difficult to separate the sources on the basis of literary style, for the styles of various passages may well have been inherited from the past.

This has led at least some scholars to throw out the Documentary Hypothesis entirely and to speak instead simply of oral tradition. Particularly among Scandinavian scholars it has become fashionable to describe the development of the Torah not in terms of the redaction of documents by editors but in terms of a slowly growing tradition which was passed on by word-of-mouth for centuries before it was finally set down in writing at a fairly late date. They argue that we should think of the Torah not as a set of books to be read but as a story recounted orally by a narrator.

Although many scholars still speak of J,E,P, and D, the idea of oral tradition has gained wide acceptance. The argument now is not whether the Torah began as oral tradition but whether or not various strands of oral tradition were written down and then fused together by editors or fused together in one vast oral tradition and then written down. Whichever option is chosen one implication is clear: The Torah, unlike a modern book, cannot be dated. Although its final form may be late, it is made up of a host of traditions, each with its own history, which can no more be dated exactly than can the story of Jack and the Beanstalk.

Essentially, then, what it would seem we have in the Torah is the memory of at least certain segments of Israel as it finally congealed during and after the Babylonian captivity. Sometimes it is possible to trace the origin of a particular passage back to its source. Often, however, the original version of the story is lost in antiquity. When one reads the Torah, what one is reading is an account of how the spokesman for Jewish orthodoxy remembered and thought about Israel's past. Sometimes external evidence and internal hints can tell us how accurate their memory really was. It is important to remember, however, that it is not what "really" happened which affected Judaism and Western culture, but what these people thought happened. The modern archaelogist may (indeed must) take issue with some of the stories told in the Torah, but the student of Scripture must remember that whether or not Israel truly crossed the Red Sea, the myth of the Exodus had a profound effect upon Israel. In order to understand the faith of these people we must not only reconstruct the facts; we must also come to grips with the meaning of the myth.

CHAPTER VI

Genesis: Introduction and Analysis

The Origin of the World and of Man and His Families
The Sagas of Abraham and Isaac
The Jacob Sagas
The Saga of Joseph

ENESIS (Hebrew: *Bereshith,* "In the Beginning") contains primarily the sagas of the four great Patriarchs, Abraham, Isaac, Jacob, and Joseph. To their stories is prefixed an eleven-chapter introduction which traces the history of mankind from the time of creation to that of Abraham and which sets forth Israel's essential myths. Because Genesis expresses most of the important themes which are later to be expanded and developed in Scripture, we will spend what may seem an inordinate amount of time discussing this work. Discussion of the other books will assume an acquaintance of these basic motifs set forth here.

The first and perhaps most salient fact concerning Genesis with which the modern interpreter must deal is that archaeologists have demonstrated beyond a shadow of a doubt that this first book of Scripture is far more accurate historically than earlier generations of critical scholars dreamed possible. While various schools of literary critics debated about precisely which passages belonged to each of the major documents

(J.E.D. and P.), the excavators were uncovering information which was to put the study of Genesis in a new context. Not only did they unearth documents which show that Genesis reflects with great accuracy the customs, religious beliefs, and demographic situation during the Middle Bronze era in Palestine; many of them came to see Genesis as perhaps the best available "Guidebook" to that era.

Having said that, however, we must immediately go on to acknowledge that this does *not* mean that archaeology has proved Genesis correct in all respects. Indeed, there is no proof, for instance, that any of the Patriarchs even existed. All that archaeology has done is to show that Genesis is based upon some very ancient memories which have been preserved through the ages. It is equally true, however, that these memories have experienced many stages in development during which they have been embellished, recorded, and reinterpreted.

Unfortunately, it seems virtually impossible today to determine just how and when these stages took place. If we knew what state the tradition was in at the time of Moses or of David we might be able to unravel the very looped and knotted ball of yarn which is Genesis. What we have, however, is the tradition in its final, post-exilic (post 539 B.C.) form. We can see that different traditions have been woven together, that attempts have been made to bring the narrative up-to-date by introducing new names to replace archaic ones, that the whole narrative has been made more theologically respectable by repressing the most egregious examples of "paganism." In the face of the tremendously complicated issues which Genesis raises, however, a theory which attempts to explain all this by the postulation of four sources seems almost as simplistic as the traditional view that Moses was the author.

Let me give one example. The genealogical material in Genesis is normally ascribed by the critics to the P source which is customarily dated in post-exilic times. Aside from the fact that, since priests were doubtless involved in the formulation and transmission of all the strata of tradition, calling one source "Priestly" is highly inaccurate, there is something very odd about attributing genealogical lists in particular to a late source. Traditional societies all over the world place great stock in genealogies. In bedouin and African tribal communities the genealogy of each individual is carefully preserved so that he can trace his ancestery back for many generations. What for us are tedious lists are, in such societies, highly important means for self-identification. Doubtless, genealogies functioned in much the same manner in Israelite society. To think that some priest in post-exilic times could have made up a genealogy for Israel is quite ridiculous. At most he could only have passed on a tradition which was very well-established and known to many members of the community. In fact, it would be more reasonable to assume that the genealogical tradition came very early and that the sagas of the Patriarchs were woven into it.

My point, however, is not to develop a "new" theory, but merely to illustrate how unsatisfactory the standard one is. As we proceed in our examination of the Torah, more examples will present themselves. At this point it hardly seems appropriate to come to any final conclusions about just when or how Genesis took shape. Doubtless it began as oral tradition which gradually was refined, embellished, and supplemented as time went on. Those who wish to learn more about the standard documentary theory can read with profit Cuthbert Simpson's article on the composition of the Hexateuch in Volume 1 of the *Interpreter's Bible.* The reader should be warned however, that Biblical scholarship is clearly moving beyond that theory. The regnal years of J., E., D., and P. seem to be about at an end.

The Origin of the World and of Man and His Families

A. Genesis 1:1-2:4 God Creates!

THE BOOK OF GENESIS opens with the beautiful liturgy of creation, used originally, perhaps, on New Year's Day. This chapter should be read, not as a quasi-scientific account of the origin of the world, but as an antiphonal hymn to be sung in praise of *Elohim* (the "Powers" or God) who is the source of all that is.

A number of the motifs and ideas found in this chapter are paralleled in non-Israelite literature. For instance, the idea of a God creating through speech is to be found in the Mesopotamian *Enuma Elish* in which Marduk creates by speaking and in the Memphite theology of Egypt in which Ptah does the same. The order of creation found here is similar to that of the *Enuma Elish*, though in the latter the world is not created by one God. The notion of creation as the ordering of chaos and the idea of the firmament, the bowl-shaped "sky" which has holes in it to let in the rain, are also quite common in Near Eastern mythologies.

The basic "tone" of Genesis 1, however, is quite unique. Gone are the numerous warring gods of the other ancient mythologies; chaos is no longer a deity (like Tiamat of the *Enuma Elish*) to be defeated, but simply some *thing* which is shaped by God's Word. According to classical Christian theology chaos was created by God, but this cannot be fully substantiated by this text, for it can be legitimately translated, "When God began to create the heavens and the earth, the earth was without form and void." Still, it is clear that *Elohim* is totally in charge of creation; chaos does not rebel against his forming word.

Moreover, unlike so many other ancient theogonies, the emphasis here is placed upon the creation and glory of man who is made in the image and likeness (the reflection and shadow?) of God. God is praised for having made man the apex of his creation. Many interpretations have been given to the phrase "image and likeness." It has been variously interpreted to mean that man is rational, personal, immortal, and psychically triune. None of these ideas, however, seems to be supported very well by the text. The interpretation which makes most sense to this reader is that man reflects God in his actions. That is to say, in the relation between male and female and in man's domination of creation, the love and providence of God are reflected. In Verse 26 *Elohim* (a singular noun which is plural in form) says, "Let *us* make man in our image . . ." Is this a remnant of polytheism? Does he speak to the angels of his heavenly court? Does he use the "royal" we? Or does this phrase imply that the male-female duality of man somehow reflects a duality in God himself? No final answer can, at this time, be given, but it may be that the last alternative is the most plausible.

Throughout this chapter primary emphasis is placed upon the goodness of creation. Nowhere is there any hint of the existence of the devil or demons, nor is the created order regarded as merely *maya* (illusion). The world and its creatures are given to man to dominate and he obeys God in so doing. There are no sacred cows or holy plants which man must venerate. Sexuality, which in so many other religions is regarded as an evil, is conceived as good. Man obeys, and perhaps reflects the creative power of God, in procreation.

The liturgy ends with the joyous assertion that after the creation of man, God rested on the seventh day and hallowed it. The notion of a seven-day week did not originate among the Israelites but was observed by both the Mesopotamians and the Canaanites. Among these peoples the *shabbatu* was regarded as a day of evil portent and hence as a day when all usual activity should cease. In Israel the seventh day was regarded as a day of rejoicing. Why? Because after God created man, he rested. That is, he ceased and desisted; he did not go on creating super and super-super men. The seventh day is holy, because it is a reminder that man is meant to be the dominator of the created world. He is God's vice-regent and is responsible only to him.

B. Genesis 2:4-3-24—The Myth of Adam

THE GREAT LITURGY of Genesis 1 is followed by another, probably somewhat older account of the creation of the world and man. This second version presents a far more anthropomorphic and personal picture of God and hence has been described by some scholars as "naive and primitive." The folk-like quality of the tale should not, however, blind the reader to the highly sophisticated and penetrating meaning which it conveys. Nor should the "factual" inconsistencies with Genesis 1 (in the second account man is created first, then the animals) obscure the more profound agreement. Certainly the knowledge that man came into existence long before 4004 B.C. should not be used in refutation of its mythological import. The very fact that the editors chose to place Chapters 1 and 2 side-by-side shows that they were not so much interested in conveying scientific information about the origins of the earth as they were in painting a mythological portrait of man and his relation to God and the world. Further evidence that the author(s) of this account consciously wrote mythologically is to be found in Verses 10-14. Quite clearly Israelites were aware that the Pishon (the Indus?), the Gihon (the Nile?), the Tigris, and the Euphrates rivers did not flow from a single source. Undoubtedly the passage is meant to suggest that out of the mythical Garden of Eden came the great civilizations of man which grew up around these rivers.

This story, then, is a portrait of man (*adam*) as he was meant to exist and as he exists in the world. Adam is Everyman and every man is adam. What is man like? He is a farmer; he tills the garden and keeps it and is psychically related to his counterpart, the land (*adamah*). He shapes for himself his own personal environment by naming the animals. Adam is "bisexual;" he is male (*ish*) and female (*ishshah*) taken together. In marriage these "fragments" are united to form one flesh, *adam*. Human sexuality is exalted as one of the glories of creation. "The man and the woman were both naked, and were not ashamed." (Genesis 2:25)

The creator of this myth of man knew that man ought to be at one with the land, with woman, and with God, but he also knew that something has gone wrong. Man, who was created to be a farmer, dislikes the sweat and labor of his work. The female, whose great and mysterious glory is the ability to bear children, hates the pain and subordination involved. Male and female are suspicious and envious of each other. And both feel shame and fear before the Power of the universe and dread the death which is the natural end of each living thing.

What has disrupted the goodness of creation and made man discontented with his lot? According to the story, this disruption has occurred because man has eaten of the fruit of the tree of the knowledge of good and evil. Many interpretations have been given to this explanation. Some have argued that the description of the fruit is purely arbitrary; the important fact is that man disobeyed God. Others have claimed the knowledge of good and evil implies a knowledge of all things, from the best to the worst. The temptation, then, was to want to know all that God knows. Perhaps. The interpretation which appeals most to this reader, however, runs as follows: Since God created the world good, there was, originally, no evil at all. Man's temptation was (and is) to judge some aspects of God's good creation evil, to make value judgments about what God has given to man. The serpent is not the devil, but only the subtlest of the creatures which God created. Still, the serpent, which in the ancient world was both a symbol for wisdom and immortality and a source for emotional uneasiness, elicited the question, "Is this creature really good?"

If this interpretation is correct, Genesis is saying that man's alienation from, and trouble in, the world stems from the fact that man is unwilling to accept the world as it is, but inevitably rejects certain aspects of it as evil. That is, through his power of self-transcendance man is tempted to stand in judgment over the world and hence over God. The punishment fits the crime. Although man was made to till the garden, he now judges his labor a great evil. The woman despises her subordinate position and the pain of child-bearing. Both are ashamed of their genitals and hide from God as though their sexuality were evil. Death, a most natural conclusion to all life, looms before them as a curse. No explanation is given as to *why* God allows man the opportunity to so alienate himself, though the myth may imply that for man to dominate creation he must be able to transcend himself. Explicitly, however, the myth only points to the fact that man's judgment of the world and his consequent alienation from it are a reality.

C. Genesis 4:1-5:32—Cain and Abel; the Book of Generations

THE STRIFE which pervades Chapter 4 contrasts sharply with the idyllic harmony of Chapter 2 and bears further witness to the fruit of Adam's action in Chapter 3. In this story of Cain and Abel various forms of human rivalry and hate—between sibling brothers, between farmer and shepherd, between Canaanite (Cain comes from the same root) and Israelite—are united with mythical concreteness. Significantly, the locus of the conflict is religion. In Eden there were no altars or sacrifices, for man was at one with God. Now that man is alienated from his Creator he begins the practices of religion to overcome this estrangement, but this only leads him into conflict with his fellows. Cain becomes jealous of his brother, whose offering is accepted by God, and slays him. As a consequence, Cain is condemned as a wanderer; he is cut off even more decisively from the land. Yet God's judgment is tempered by his mercy. Cain receives a special mark (the tattoos of the gypsies?) and thus is protected from the blood avenger. Strangely enough, it is *his* descendants who develop the arts of animal husbandry, music, and metal working, the essential rudiments of human culture. Still, the hope of mankind comes through the youngest brother, Seth, through whom the "lineage" of mankind is traced. (Cf. the many stories of three brothers found particularly in Semitic literature.) After the birth of Seth, men begin to call upon God by his "true" name, Yahweh.

Chapter 5 contains a typically Biblical genealogy which serves as a link between the Cain and Abel story and the myth of Noah. Those interested in the literary form of Genesis should note how the story is articulated through the use of these genealogical "dividers." As in the Sumerian and Babylonian king lists, the ages of the men are greatly exaggerated to indicate great antiquity. Of these ancient men only Enoch is described as particularly righteous—"he walked with God." The whole genealogy points forward to the birth of Noah to whom

Lamech looks as "he who shall bring us relief from our work and from the toil of our hands." Here is, in brief, a basic Biblical motif—the hope for a son who will somehow save mankind. Noah does so, but not as Lamech expects, for Lamech's hope is conditioned by his alienation from the land and labor. This again is typical—hopes are fulfilled, but never quite as the hoper anticipates.

D. Genesis 6:1-10:32—Noah and his Sons

THE MYTH of the great Flood is one of the most common myths known to man. Not only is it mentioned in Mesopotamian and Egyptian literature; flood stories have been found among the Chinese, the Incas of Peru, and in many other civilizations. No geological evidence has been found for a world-wide flood in "human" times, though there have been many extensive floods which have, at various times, wiped out sizable human settlements.

The closest parallel to the Biblical Flood story is to be found in the ancient Mesopotamian Epic of Gilgamesh in which the hero visits the immortal Utnapishtim who survived the great flood in much the same way as Noah did and thus achieved immortality. The Biblical writer(s) doubtless knew some form of this ancient myth, but completely revised it in order to convey ideas more consistent with their own world view and perhaps to attack the pagan mythology itself.

A number of motifs found in the Biblical story distinguish it from the Mesopotamian version. First, unlike the latter version of the myth which ascribes the flood to the rather fickle action of the Gods, the Biblical flood comes as a punishment for human sin. The Bible accepts the wide-spread notion that in antedeluvian days the earth was populated, at least in part, by demi-gods and great heroes. These semi-divine beings (like Gilgamesh and Heracles) are regarded, however, as particularly evil. This was no "Golden Age," but a time of violence and sin. The source for this sin is not found in the fact that man is fleshly but in his "evil imagination." God, in his wrath, therefore, sends a Flood to wipe out this perverse race.

But not quite, for God chooses one man, Noah, to be a source for the salvation of many. The idea of God's choosing one to save the many is found throughout the Bible. Noah receives his call, not so much as a reward for his righteousness, but because God has mercy upon mankind. Noah, the prototype of all "chosen ones," obeys God and in so doing saves mankind and the animals which man is called upon to dominate. The Biblical account is composite, for it is clear that different, sometimes inconsistent, passages have been joined together. (Compare 6:19 and 7:2) Nevertheless, the whole story forms a unity held together by the over-arching theme of God's judgment and choosing mercy.

After many days in the ark (the text is somewhat inconsistent about the time span) Noah discovers through the use of a raven (commonly used by ancient mariners in navigation) and a dove that the flood waters have subsided. On the first day of the first month the earth is dry. The dating is significant, for it reflects the liturgical use to which this myth was put. Doubtless it was used to celebrate the ending of the winter rains and the coming of spring and hence was repeated each year. The more important repetition, however, is the repetition of God's choosing mercy within history—an event which must be expected but cannot be dated.

Noah and his family descend from the ark and give thanks to God by offering sacrifices from all the ritually clean animals. When one considers the number of clean animals, this must have been quite a holocaust. Is God pleased when he smells the "pleasing odor"? Not really. The sacrifices merely remind him that the imagination of man's heart is evil from his youth (8:21), but he takes pity upon man accordingly and promises that no such disaster as the flood will occur again. Here we find a prototype of the many covenants (*berith*) found in the Bible. God takes the initiative by making his promise first. Then he gives to man certain commandments to be obeyed. Man must be fruitful and multiply. He is given not only plants but animals for food, but he must not drink their blood nor may he shed the blood of another man, for man is made in God's image. The sign of the covenant is the rainbow. Clouds will appear repeatedly as a sign of God's primordial wrath, but with the clouds and rain will appear the rainbow, the sign of God's affirmation of mercy to man and to all flesh. Thus, symbolically, the "No" and the "Yes" of God are bound together.

The story of Noah's drunkenness (9:20-28) is enigmatic, yet evocative. Noah, the "new humanity," makes wine, gets drunk, and lies down naked in his tent. His son Ham (or is it Canaan?) sees him naked, but Shem and Japheth cover him without looking at him. As a result, Ham is cursed and his brothers blessed. Probably, this refers to the Canaanite propensity to engage in cultic orgies and their failure to observe sexual proprieties accepted by the Israelites. It is interesting, however, that it is Ham and not Noah who is judged guilty. Unlike Utnapishtim, who received the gift of immortality, however, Noah remains a mortal man and dies at a ripe old age.

Chapter 10 includes a genealogy which most modern readers will gloss over. It is significant, however, for it is really an essay concerning the Biblical view of "race." Noah's three sons become the fathers of the three different types of people known to the Biblical writers. Ham fathers the peoples who inhabit the fertile river valleys and plains of Egypt, Canaan, and Mesopotamia. Japheth is the progeniture of the coastland peoples, the mariners and traders; Shem, the father of the people of the hill country, desert, and plain. Thus the Bible does not really speak of race at all but of cultural types. It is the city dweller who inhabits the rich valleys and not the Negro whom the Bible regards as accursed.

E. Genesis 11:1-32: The Tower of Babel and the Family of Shem

THE FIRST NINE VERSES of this chapter are a mythological description of the building and destruction of man's first great urban civilization in Shinar (Sumer). Although hardly factual, it contains a number of historical reminiscences which have been validated by archaeologists. Sumer was, indeed, the first great center for urban civilization. Sumerians did build their buildings out of kiln-dried, rather than sun-dried bricks (which the Israelites used). The Sumerian city, particularly of the Third dynasty of Ur at the end of the third millenium, was dominated by the ziggurat, a public building and temple which "reached into the heavens." Akkadian did serve as a sort of "lingua franca," not only within Mesopotamia, but all over the Near East.

By 1950 B.C. the Third Dynasty of Ur was brought to an end by invading Elamites from the East and the subsequent centuries brought more invaders and more chaos. Amorites (literally "Westerners") poured into the fertile crescent and established control in many regions. The Hurrians established hegemony in northwestern Mesopotamia and the Hittites, who moved into Anatolia, began pushing southward. Akkadian did not completely lose its status as lingua franca, but there surely was a confusion of tongues and cultures unknown during the period of Sumerian and Akkadian ascendance.

In typically Biblical style, this cultural dislocation is understood as the judgment of God against human pretensions (See the Sumerian "Curse of Agade" for a similar interpretation of history), but it also sets the stage for the next revelation of God's choosing mercy—the call of Abram. These two stories are connected by another genealogy which traces the lineage from Shem to Abram. Left behind are Ham and Japheth; the story now concentrates upon this particular son of Shem and his family. The funnel of history once more narrows as God again chooses one for the sake of all.

The Sagas of Abraham and Isaac

Most scholars recognize that between Chapters 11 and 12 there is an abrupt shift in the narrative and, in a sense, they are quite right. In Chapter 11 we still are in the primordial time of myth. With the story of Abraham we move to the quasi-historical times of the saga. Still, it is probably best to understand Abraham in the light of the disruption of civilization which took place near the end of the second millenium in Mesopotamia and which Chapter 11 mythologically describes. That is, it may have been the collapse of Ur which prompted Abram's father, Terah, to leave that ancient city and move northwestward along the fertile crescent to Haran.

Genesis 11:27-32, which gives Abram's genealogy, indicates that the family lived in Ur, but it also reveals that the homeland was actually to the north. Archaeological discoveries have confirmed that some of the names of Abram's relatives (Nahor and Haran) were in fact names of towns in northwestern Mesopotamia inhabited by Western Semites. Clearly, either the mention of Ur was for some reason later introduced into the text *or* Abram's family, though connected with Haran, had moved to Ur at an earlier time. In 14:13 Abram is called a "Hebrew." Although the meaning of this word is uncertain, it probably was a cultural term to designate those people who did not quite "belong" to any one society but who lived as donkey caravaners and traders. If this is correct, Abram's family was probably in Ur for commercial reasons. When the strength of Ur was shaken, his father decided to set out for the open spaces in the west, hoping to find new territory for himself and his family. On the way they stopped, quite naturally, at Haran, the land of their origin, and settled down for a while. While in Haran, Terah died.

The "call" which comes to Abram in 12:1 is not, then, unanticipated. Yahweh calls Abram to carry out the original plan and go to Canaan. His promise and blessing to him are, however, extraordinary. Not only does he vow to make of Abram's house a great nation and protect him from his enemies, he promises that by him "all the families of the earth shall bless themselves" (12:3). Is this promise to Abram an authentic memory from Patriarchal times or a later addition to the text? There is no easy way to answer this question. Certainly, Israel later remembered the "fathers" as having been the recipients of many such promises and regarded them as revelations of the ultimate purpose and destiny of Israel. For Abram, at any rate, the God who spoke was doubtless not conceived of in the same manner as later Israelites thought of him. We still move very much within a quasi-pagan culture. Probably if the memory is authentic it originally simply signified that Abram received a very propitious omen through some act of divination.

As a result of Yahweh's command, Abram and his family, together with Lot, his nephew, travel to Canaan. When they arrive, Abram immediately goes to Shechem where, at a Canaanite divination tree (the oak of Moreh), he seeks further advice, probably concerning where he should settle. Instead of giving him definite advice, however, the oracle of divination reveals that he is to be given the whole land! (12:7) His first place of residence is near Bethel, in the central hill country (12:8) (which was to house later an important Israelite shrine), but he soon moves on to the Negeb.

Because of famine he then goes to Egypt, a common act among inhabitants of the region during times of disaster. The Tomb of Beni Hasan in Egypt contains an interesting picture of Semites coming to Egypt during this general period. The story, however, is most peculiar. The Pharaoh desires Sarai, Abram's wife, and Abram, to protect his own life, says that she is his sister and allows her to be taken into the harem. God, however, afflicts the Pharaoh and his house with great plagues and, when it is discovered why, the Pharaoh throws Abram and his family out of Egypt. A similar story is told also in Gen. 20:1-7 and in 26:6-11.

A possible clue to understanding this narrative is to be found in documents discovered at the Hurrian site of Nuzi. From them we learn that in this region, from which Abram came, a wife who was also adopted as a sister had a special and higher status in society. Hence, in the original story, Abram, when saying Sarai was his sister, actually claimed that she had special rights and was protected by law. The Pharaoh, not understanding the custom, however, took her any way. Apparently, later transmitters of the tradition didn't understand either and hence turned Abram into a liar in order to make some sense out of the story.

Chapter 13 tells about Abram's return to the Bethel area. He and his nephew, Lot, decide to split up, with Abram staying in the hill country and Lot moving into the Jordan valley and settling near Sodom. Sodom and Gomorrah have never been certainly located, though many scholars would place them near the southern end of the Dead Sea on land which is now covered with water. Again Abram receives a message from Yahweh and as a result he moves to Hebron near what probably were the divining oaks of Mamre.

Chapter 14 contains a very strange account of a war between the kings of Sodom, Gomorrah, Admah, Zeboim, and Bela and Chedorlaomer of Elam (a land east of the Tigris.) It seems unlikely that the Mesopotamian powers would have extended their hegemony so far during this period, but archaeological discoveries may eventually clarify what this war (if there were such) was about. In any event, Lot is taken captive and Abram, who is now pictured as a rich and mighty man, chases after the forces of Chedorlaomer and rescues both Lot and the plunder. Then follows (14:17-24) a very peculiar story of the blessing of Abram by Melchizedek, the priest-king of Jerusalem, who offers to him bread and wine. Abram gives him a tenth of all he has captured. This story may reflect some early incident, but it is most likely an attempt by a later writer to relate Abram, the prototype of the faithful man, to Jerusalem and its shrine. Abram, according to the syncretistic habits of the day, simply equates Yahweh and *El Elyon* (God Most High), the deity of the pagan Jerusalem cult.

Chapter 15 introduces a familiar Biblical theme. Abram is childless, though he apparently has adopted an heir in the person of Eliezer of

Damascus (15:2), one of his slaves. Yahweh promises him that he will have a son and that his descendants will be as multitudinous as the stars in the heavens. Ch. 15:7-21 contains an account of a covenantal sacrifice offered by Abram which, though highly unorthodox according to later Israelite standards, conforms very well with what we know about Akkadian customs during the period. Again Abram receives a favorable response: his descendants will be given the whole land.

In Chapter 16 Sarai, who still has not borne any children, gives to Abram her own maid, Hagar, according to another custom mentioned in the Nuzi tablets. Hagar conceives and Sarai then becomes anxious for her own position. Hagar is treated harshly and flees but subsequently receives a hopeful sign from an angel and returns. Her son, Ishmael, turns out to be the father of the Ishmaelites, a desert tribe. This is one of several stories describing the origin of Israel's neighbors found in Genesis.

In Chapter 17 Yahweh appears to Abram once more. This time God is called by the name *El Shaddai* (God Almighty), which probably signifies his power over procreation. The promise of offspring is repeated and Abram is renamed Abraham, "the father of a multitude". He is also required to undergo the rite of circumcision as a sign of the covenant and to circumcise his household. This is not strange, for circumcision was practiced by the Canaanites and Egyptians, though not by the people of Abraham's homeland. In using this sign, he adopts one of the customs of Canaan, though in the story it is given a new meaning. The rules concerning the rite (16:11-17) may be by a later hand, but the covenantal name for God which is used (*El Shaddai*) is probably authentic.

In Chapters 18 and 19 Abraham entertains three men who prophesy the birth of a son to him even though Sarah (who has also been renamed by God) is now ninety years old! Yahweh then reveals to Abraham that he is going to destroy Sodom and Gomorrah but, after Abraham pleads with him, promises that if ten righteous men are to be found in Sodom he will relent. In Chapter 19 the three men, who seem to be spies for an invading army, now turn out to be two angels (the change in number seems inexplicable) (malak: angel or messenger)! Lot entertains them and tries to protect them from the wicked men of the city. They, in turn, warn Lot of the impending danger and, in fact, have to shove him out the door to save him. As Lot and his family flee, Lot's wife looks back and she becomes one of those several oddly-shaped pillars of salt found in the region. Lot's daughters, sensing that their father has no male heir, take their mother's place after getting their father drunk. Each conceives and from them are born Moab and Ammon, two traditional enemies of Israel who inhabited the eastern bank of the Dead Sea. Clearly this is both an aetiological myth and a bit of comic relief designed to poke fun at Israel's antagonists. Chapter 20 retells the story of Gen. 12:10-20. This time the man who takes Sarah (who by the way is supposedly at least ninety years old) is Abimelech, the king of Gerar.

In Chapter 21 the promised son, Isaac (laughter), is born, and Hagar and Ishmael are thrown out of the household because of Sarah's jealousy, an act forbidden by Nuzi law. God protects the outcasts and Ishmael grows up in the desert. In 21:22-33 Abraham gets into a controversy over some wells with Abimelech. Finally, they resolve the problem and make a typical covenant together. The place of the wells is named Beersheba. The mention of the Philistine is an obvious embellishment of the text, for the Philistines didn't arrive until much later.

Chapter 22 contains perhaps the strangest story in the whole Abraham saga. Abraham is commanded by God to sacrifice his only son, Isaac, in the land of Moriah. Although Mount Moriah came to be associated with Mount Zion in Jerusalem, we have no idea where it was originally located. Abraham takes his son with him and sets off to do this most hideous act. Just as he is about to plunge in the knife, however, an angel of Yahweh tells him not to do so and shows him a ram to substitute in his place. Abraham is praised for his faith and receives once more God's blessing.

The question is: what does this all mean? It would appear that the editorial explanation that God was testing Abraham is an attempt to make the story sound a little more orthodox. Probably in the original story Abraham, who as we have seen made no very sharp distinction between his religion and that of the people of the land, really believed that he should follow the custom sometimes followed in Canaan of sacrificing the first-born son to the deity. (Child sacrifice is mentioned even among the Israelites as late as the seventh century.) Abraham, however, does not go through with the act and substitutes an animal instead, thus founding the practice of the redemption of the first-born as it was later practiced in Israel.

As it now stands, at any rate, the story also conveys one of the archetypal patterns of Israel's mythology. Isaac is the chosen one whose birth is wholly dependent upon the grace of God and whose life is perennially in danger. In a sense, this is a myth of resurrection. Isaac is to die, but is miraculously saved "out of death" to become the son of the promise once more. It is noteworthy that both Jacob and Joseph also undergo such an historicized rite of initiation.

Chapter 23 tells of the death of Sarah and the purchase of a burial ground. Although there is no archaeological evidence that Hittites ever inhabited this territory, the story as a whole bears marks of great antiquity. Abraham wishes to buy a burial ground, but Ephron, a Hittite, offers to give it to him. Despite the fact that he eventually has to pay a ridiculously high price, Abraham insists on buying it. Why? Because the purchase of the property means that Abraham is no longer a mere sojourner on the land; he becomes a property owner. Reference is made to the trees on the property, a typically Hittite way of doing business. (23:17) According to ancient tradition, this burial cave is now located under the great Mosque in Hebron.

Because generations overlap, it is not surprising that sagas of Abraham and Isaac overlap as well. Chapter 24 tells the moving story of how a wife is found for Isaac among the peoples of Haran, apparently to keep the blood-line pure. Rebecca, in fact, turns out to be Isaac's cousin. Although Bethuel's name is mentioned, the fact that Laban, Rebecca's brother, does the bargaining shows that Bethuel may have been dead. If so, the marriage contracted was a sister-wife marriage similar to that between Abraham and Sarah. The whole account of the marriage contract bears marks of great antiquity.

Chapter 25:1-18 provides a genealogical interlude between the Abraham-Isaac and the Isaac-Jacob sagas. In 25:1-6 Abraham is described as the father of several other tribes, including the Midianites who are to figure prominently in the Moses story. Ch. 25:7-10 recounts the death and burial of Abraham, while 25:12-18 lists the tribes of the Ishmaelites and their area of occupation.

The Jacob Sagas

With 25:19 we move immediately to the beginning of the saga of Jacob. Ch. 26 contains more mention of Isaac, but clearly he is only a transitional figure who, in this narrative, has no particular importance in himself. It may well be that originally the Isaac sagas were of much greater significance but for one reason or another have been suppressed.

Rebecca, after a period of barrenness conceives twins, Esau and Jacob. Jacob, whose name is later changed to Israel, is the younger, but it is clear from the beginning that he is the hero of the story. Esau, the father of Edom, is pictured as a rather stupid fellow who is continually being tricked by his younger brother. Right away he exhibits his foolishness by selling his birth-right for a mess of pottage. In so doing he gives away his rights as the eldest son and Jacob becomes the son of the promise.

Chapter 26 gives some "information" about Isaac, but curiously virtually everything said about him has already been said about Abraham. He appears as but a shadow of his father.

The story of Jacob can be outlined rather briefly. In Ch. 27 Jacob dupes his father and wins from him the blessing (*berukah*) which was meant for Esau. As a consequence he is forced to flee to Haran (Ch. 28) where he lives with his uncle Laban. Laban, acting true to form, deceives Jacob into marrying his eldest daughter Leah, but eventually Jacob marries his beloved Rachel as well (Ch. 29). Jacob, who knows some tricks of his own, cons Laban into giving him the best from his flocks. (Ch. 30) Subsequently, Jacob flees to Canaan Laban chases after and catches him, but they arrive at an uneasy "peace." (Ch. 31) Esau, though still angry with him, (Ch. 32-33) does not kill him and Jacob settles near Shechem and then near Bethel. (34-35) The rest of the story of Jacob is tied directly to that of his son Joseph.

The saga of Jacob is so well-told that it is best for the reader to enjoy it for himself. There are a number of comments, however, which ought to be made about several episodes in the story. Clearly, the whole narrative reflects the tensions which existed between Israel and Edom (Esau) and Israel and the Aramaeans (Laban). This has led many scholars to conclude that the Jacob saga is more legendary than historical. The saga can, in fact, be read as a portrait of the people of Israel as a whole. Still, there are a number of authentic touches which reflect the saga's great antiquity.

The emphasis upon the importance and unretractable nature of the father's blessing is very ancient. The *berukah* was believed to contain power, and once the father had spoken his words, he could not withdraw them. Later Israelites may have believed similarly, but this idea fits well into a Middle Bronze Age context. The account of Jacob's dream at Bethel also bears marks of great antiquity. This dream of angels ascending and descending a stairway (not a ladder) (28:12) is reminiscent of the ziggurats of Mesopotamia with their stairways leading to the place of sacrifice (where the deity dwelt) on top. When Jacob sets up a pillar and anoints it (28:18), he acts as a typical man of his time. Canaanite *masseboth* (stone pillars) have been found all over Palestine. Sleeping on such a stone in a sacred place (28:11) also was undoubtedly a typical act of divination.

Rachel's theft of Laban's teraphim (30:31) has been clarified by archaeological discoveries too. In Haran the household idol was not simply a deity to be worshipped; it was also a symbol of the family inheritance. Laban wanted to pass this symbol on to his own heir, but Jacob's wife stole it, hence producing a very difficult situation for Laban. It was no wonder he chased after Jacob in anger. The covenant made between Laban and Jacob at Mizpah also is performed with due regard to very ancient practice.

Chapter 32 contains some very difficult problems of interpretation and must be commented upon. After Jacob leaves Laban he soon meets some "angels." Thereupon he immediately sends messengers of his own to Esau. They return with news that Esau is coming with some four hundred men! In a panic, Jacob sends Esau huge droves of cattle, apparently to try to placate him. He then sends his wives and children across the River Jabbok and remains by himself. There, it is said, he wrestles with a man until the breaking of day and from him wins a blessing. Through this wrestling his name is changed to Israel, that is, "he who strives with God" (32:28; cf. 35:10). The next morning, when Esau arrives, the expected battle does not take place. Instead, Esau, though accompanied by his armed men, welcomes Jacob with an outward show of forgiveness. Why? Why would a man who obviously has started with an armed force for a purpose be so suddenly placated?

Let us go back first to the original messengers (*malakim*: messengers or angels) whom Jacob meets. They are described as angels of God, but it is clear they bring a message of warning from Esau. Why else would Jacob immediately send messengers of his own to his brother? Apparently Esau has heard of Jacob's coming, perhaps from his crafty uncle Laban. It would appear that Jacob's consequent show of strength convinces Esau that instead of all-out war there should be a trial-by-combat instead. This seems to be what takes place between Jacob and the man at night. Because Jacob wins and wrings a blessing from Esau's champion, Esau does not press the matter the next day. His tactic is to bide his time and gain his revenge later on. Jacob, however, is too wily for that. He convinces Esau that he should travel by himself, but then, instead of heading to Esau's home makes for the north-central region.

Chapter 34, which tells of the rape of Dinah and the consequent slaughter of the Shechemites by Simeon and Levi, obviously contains more than meets the eye. Probably this reflects a struggle between the original Shechemites and the people of Israel which was more than a fight conducted by the two men! The fact that when Israel later invades the land under Joshua she finds apparently friendly people in Shechem may indicate that this story is a telescoped account of an early conquest of this city.

Chapter 35 is really a kind of summary of the whole Jacob story. Jacob returns to Bethel where he receives once more God's promises. His name is confirmed by God to be Israel, and the deity identifies himself as *El Shaddai.* Chapter 35:16-21 tells of the birth of the twelfth son, Benjamin, and of the death of Rachel. The reference to Reuben's sin in 35:22 seems to allude to the fact that although the eldest son, Reuben, soon passed out of existence as an historical tribe and never played much of a role in the history of Israel. Ch. 35:23-26 then lists Jacob's twelve sons (cf. 29:31-30-13) who are to become, according to tradition, the fathers of the twelve tribes of Israel. The saga of Jacob comes to a rather strange close with an account of Jacob journeying to Hebron where his father, Isaac, is dying. Subsequently Esau and Jacob bury him. The story is strange, because Isaac appeared ready for death when Jacob started out for Haran many years before. Perhaps this account comes from a different source. More likely, however, it was added to picture Jacob as a dutiful son. Although Jacob is seldom, if ever idealized in the story, it may well have been unthinkable to the authors that Jacob would not be present when his father died.

The story of Jacob, taken as a whole, is an odd combination of historical accuracy, legendary aetiology, and mythological honesty. Although many of the details of the story seem reliable enough, one can hardly believe the rather simplistic accounts of the origin of the various peoples and tribes who are to play such an important part in the Biblical story. At the same time, as a portrait of Israel the whole account glows with candidness. Jacob, who is Israel, is hardly glorified. He is a clever man who makes it through life by the skin of his teeth, the son of the promise who nevertheless must use every weapon at his disposal to stay alive in a hostile world. If one wishes to know how the people of Israel thought of themselves, one can hardly do better than to read this sometimes comic, sometimes tragic story.

The Saga of Joseph

After a listing of the genealogy of Esau (Ch. 36) which serves as a punctuating interlude in the narrative, we move to the story of Joseph. The saga may be summarized briefly as follows: Joseph, Jacob's eldest son by Rachel, is pictured as a rather overly confident young man who is hated by his brothers. As a consequence, they throw him into a pit and then sell him to the Ishmaelites (or is it the Midianites?) (37:27-28) who take him to Egypt. There, after a number of escapades, he rises to power through, in part, his ability to interpret dreams. Eventually he becomes the Pharaoh's viceroy and as such wields great power.

During a famine his brothers come to Egypt in search of grain for food. He talks with them but does not reveal his identity. After making them feel very uncomfortable, he finally reveals his identity during their second trip to Egypt and arranges to have them settled in the "land of Goshen." There Israel lives until the time of the Exodus.

The whole saga is such a "success story" that it is rather difficult to take it as historically reliable. As has already been pointed out in Chapter 3, however, there are many authentic touches which make the tale appear more plausible than was once thought possible. Whoever told the story knew, at least, a great deal about Egypt during the Middle Bronze Age.

There seems to be no reason to review the tale in more detail in this analysis, for the narrative itself is both clearly and beautifully composed. A word might be said about the two interjections into the text. Chapter 38 disrupts the Joseph story by introducing an account of Judah's dealing with his daughter-in-law Tamar. It is interesting, first of all, because it introduces the custom of a levirate marriage (cf. Deut. 25:5-10). According to this ancient custom, when a husband died his brother was expected to marry his wife so that she could perpetuate the dead husband's name by bearing legitimate offspring. When after two sons have married her and died, Judah refuses to give Tamar a third son in marriage, she tricks Judah himself into sleeping with her and hence conceives for her dead husband the twins, Perez and Zerah by her father-in-law. Doubtless this story was introduced, not only to provide an interlude in the Joseph narrative but to add a word about the lineage of David. Had Tamar not pretended to be a harlot, David, (and Jesus) would not have been born!

The other passage which demands special mention is to be found in Chapter 49 which contains the final blessing offered by Jacob to his twelve sons. Although certainly not historically authentic, for it presupposes the settlement of the tribes in the land, it bears many marks of great antiquity and may well reflect an early view of the strengths and weaknesses of the twelve tribes coming from the time of the judges. Actually the identification of this as the "blessing" of Jacob is somewhat inaccurate, for, in fact, he has some very critical words to say about several of the tribes. Reuben, Simeon, and Levi, in particular, are singled out for censure. This seems certainly to indicate a date of origin prior to the time that the Levites became the priestly tribe. Benjamin, who otherwise is pictured in Genesis as one of Jacob's favorites, is here described in rather unflattering terms. (49:37). Clearly by the time of writing Judah and Joseph are the strongest of the tribes and are hence described at the greatest length. Ch. 49:10 seems to presuppose a post-Davidic date, but this verse may have been added to the original text.

As one moves through Genesis one senses subtle changes in the nature of the narrative. The first eleven chapters, though sometimes based upon historical reminiscences clearly move in the primordial time of myth. The Abrahamic saga contains more authentic memories but still is episodic and highly confusing. Jacob appears as much more of a real personality, but aetiological passages still abound. In the

Joseph story, however, we find a smoothly flowing narrative which, though sometimes historically suspect, still gives the impression of an historical realism not found earlier. Thus the reader is led very artfully from the time of myth to the times of this age. The stage is now set for the great moment of Israel's history. We are now in Egypt, awaiting the Exodus which is at hand.

Although the Joseph cycle is more historical than mythological, it still makes a mythological point. At the beginning of Genesis man's alienation from God is seen as stemming from his propensity to want to know good and evil. The book ends with a series of stories to illustrate that what to man may appear evil may be meant by God for good. Joseph's brothers mean to do him evil by selling him into slavery, but had they not done so his dreams of grandeur would never have been fulfilled; he never would have become viceroy of Egypt. This moment of success, on the other hand, though seemingly good is what eventually leads to Israel's Egyptian bondage. Still, had Israel not become enslaved in Egypt the exodus and the consequent covenant with God would not have taken place. Man continually wants to judge some circumstances good and others evil. The story of Joseph illustrates how impossible it is to make such judgments. One of the themes of Biblical historiography is that out of the worst situation God can make good to come, while out of the best situation evil can arise. The Biblical vision of life, therefore, is neither comic nor tragic. No one lives "happily ever after"; neither is life's stage just strewn with heaps of corpses. Even the worst historical disaster may contain the seeds of future hope.

CHAPTER VII

Exodus: Introduction and Analysis

The Composition of Exodus
The Date of the Exodus
Analysis

HE BOOK OF EXODUS takes its English title from the Vulgate and Septuagint translations. The Hebrew title, *Shemoth* (Names), is, as usual, derived from the first sentence in the book. In this instance, the Septuagint title seems more descriptive, though the revelation of names does play an important part in the story. In any event, this book occupies an incomparably important place among the books of the *Tanak*, for in it Israel's remembrance of undoubtedly the most central event of her history is recorded. Whenever later Israelites expressed their faith (cf. Deut. 26:5-11; Joshua 24:2-13; and Nehemiah 9:6-37) the event of the Exodus received primary emphasis. The Exodus is to the Jew what the event of Jesus Christ is to the Christian. In this book are expressed the most important memories and myths which have guided Israel throughout her long history.

The Composition of Exodus

LIKE GENESIS, Exodus is a composite work made up of passages coming from a variety of eras and traditions. Even the reader of an English translation can observe variations in style as well as inconsistencies and breaks in the text. Not only have the Documentary critics analyzed these phenomena in Exodus with great care. They have also found in Exodus important clues for unravelling the literary composition of the Torah as a whole.

One of the proof-texts of the Documentary hypothesis is found in Exodus 6:2-3.

> And God said to Moses, "I am the LORD (Yahweh). I appeared to Abraham, to Isaac, and to Jacob, as God Almighty (El Shaddai), but by name the LORD (Yahweh) I did not make myself known to them.

Documentary critics have argued that this text shows that its author believed that the name "Yahweh" was not known to Israel before the exodus and therefore used the word *Elohim* to refer to God before that time. Hence they designate the author of this passage "E" and attribute to him many (though not all) of the passages in Genesis which use *Elohim* rather than Yahweh to refer to the deity. Passages in Genesis which use Yahweh are generally ascribed to the J (Yahwist) source. The Yahwist, according to the theory, knew nothing of the revelation of a new name at Sinai and hence used Yahweh throughout his narrative.

Although this reasoning, on the surface of things, seems cogent enough, it needs to be scrutinized carefully. The whole argument hinges upon what the words "did not make himself known" mean. Clearly the word *yada*ᶜ (to know) which is used here ought not to be understood as meaning "to be acquainted with." In a Biblical sense, for instance, a man may be acquainted with many women without "knowing" them, for knowing in this context means engaging in sexual intercourse. In all contexts it implies a thorough involvement with the whole self. For instance, when the prophet Jeremiah says,

> Therefore, behold, I will make them know, this once I will make them know my power and might, and they shall know that my name is the LORD (Yahweh). (Jer. 16:21)

he does not mean to imply that the people of Judah of his time are unacquainted with the fact that their God's name is Yahweh. Rather, he means that they have no idea what the name means because they have not entered into relation with God with their whole being. Only an historical catyclysm like the fall of Jerusalem will bring them to this total knowledge.

What the author of Exodus 6:3 seems to be saying, then, is not that Israel until now has been unacquainted with Yahweh's name, but that she has not known the name fully. Before this time Israel's basic covenant, the covenant of circumcision, has been performed in the name of *El Shaddai* (God Almighty). Now the exodus is going to culminate in a new covenant which will be made in the name of Yahweh. The exodus event itself will reveal what that name means.

To separate sources, then, on the basis of which name is used in the text seems highly arbitrary. The author of 6:3 may well have used the name Yahweh in his account of the Patriarchs, but he never made it a covenantal name. To be fair to the Documentary critics, it must be admitted that the use of Yahweh or Elohim is only one of several criteria used to distinguish sources. Still, if this particular criterion is eliminated completely the task of separating sources becomes far more difficult. Furthermore, some of the other criteria used are equally suspect.

For instance, Documentary critics find another indicator of sources in the alternation of certain other names, such as those used to refer to the mountain of Moses' theophany. One source, they claim, calls it Sinai while another names it Horeb. An explanation for this usage can be found, however, without the postulation of separate sources. Before Moses is first confronted by God in the burning bush (*seneh*) the mountain is called Horeb. After Moses' call (Ch. 3) it is called Sinai, the only exception in Exodus being in 33:6. Although it is possible that the mountain simply had two names from the beginning, it is more likely that because of the theophany of the *seneh*, the mountain was renamed Sinai, a word which may well be derived etymologically from *seneh*. This would fit well with the typical Biblical practice or renaming someone or something after a theophany has occurred.

We have already seen that both Abram and Jacob received new "theophanous" names as a result of divine revelation. Places are also renamed in Genesis for the same reason. Jacob's place of wrestling is renamed "Peniel" (32:30); the place of his revelatory dream is renamed "Bethel." (28:19) So, it would appear that Horeb is renamed Sinai. This does not mean that the old name was completely dropped. Just as Israel is still often called Jacob after Genesis 32 so Horeb remains the geographical name of the mountain. When the theophany is emphasized, however, it is the name Sinai which is used.

These arguments, of course, certainly ought not to be used to argue that Exodus was written by one person. The composite nature of Exodus is quite obvious throughout. What they do militate against is a too simplistic solution of the problem of composition. Doubtless, long before Exodus was put "on paper" the essential story was chanted and retold orally by countless generations. From an early nucleus of tradition it grew into the narrative which we now have, as many hands worked to revise and embellish the story.

It also must be remembered that this story was used primarily within the cult and may well have been thoroughly shaped by this context. Certainly, the book ought to be analyzed, not as a novel or play, but as a series of readings to be used in cultic worship. Many of the breaks in the narrative may, in fact, exist because there was a concomitant break in the reading. Unfortunately, however, we know little about the cultic use of the Torah in pre-exilic days and therefore can only guess about the effects of cultic use upon the book. It may be taken as axiomatic, however, that if we knew more about the cult we would also know much more about the composition of Exodus. At this juncture, the Biblical scholar must be content with the recognition that the work before him is a highly complex "coagulation" of long-standing traditions which finally became authoritative for the people of Israel in post-exilic times.

The Date of the Exodus

Since the event of the exodus is so significant for the history of Israel it is important to date it as exactly as possible so that it can be placed in its proper historical context. Unfortunately, this is very difficult to do. First of all, there are no references to the exodus in non-Biblical literature and because of the nature of the event it is highly unlikely that any will ever be found. The most that archaeology has yielded are some clues concerning the exodus which may be helpful when correlated with the Biblical material but which constitute no absolute proof concerning any specific date.

Second, the archaeological evidence which is available does not fit very well with all the assertions of the Bible itself. If one were to accept the authority of the Bible at face value, it would appear that the exodus took place in the fifteenth Century B.C. I Kings 6:1, for instance, says that the Temple was begun in the fourth year of the reign of Solomon (about 955 B.C.), 480 years after the exodus. This would place the exodus in 1435. Judges 11:26 suggests a similar date, for it says that the conquest took place about 300 years before the time of Jephthah. If Jephthah can be dated about 1100 B.C., this would place the conquest at about 1400 B.C.

The archaeological evidence we have, however, indicates that this date is too early. Excavations in Palestine have revealed that such cities as Hazor, Debir, and Lachish fell before invaders in the thirteenth, rather than the fifteenth century. The first mention of Israel in Canaan in extra-Biblical sources is to be found in the Mernephthah Stele (ca 1220 B.C.). In earlier documents mentioning the people of that area Israel is not listed. Furthermore, Exodus 1:11 speaks about the Pharaoh building the "store-cities" of Pithom and Raamses somewhere in the northeastern region of Egypt. We know that the Pharaohs of the nineteenth dynasty (13th C.) did initiate building projects in this area, while the Pharaohs of the eighteenth dynasty did not. In fact, the old Hyksos capital of Avaris was rebuilt under Seti I and Raamses II (1290-1224) and was eventually named after the latter ruler. This would seem to be a strong indication that Seti I was the Pharaoh from whom Moses fled and that Raamses II was the ruler of Egypt at the time of the exodus.

If Israel really was in Egypt for 430 years before the exodus (12:40), this would mean that if the exodus took place in the thirteenth Century Joseph would have come to Egypt during the age of the Hyksos. This would explain why a Semite, rather than a native Egyptian, was chosen for the high office of viceroy. Joseph's rise to power makes good sense if it occurred while the Hyksos were in power; it would be more difficult to explain if it took place earlier. This also helps to explain what is meant in Exodus 1:8 when it is said that a new king arose who did not know Joseph. After the Egyptians drove the Hyksos out in the sixteenth Century, it is likely that all collaborators with the Hyksos would have been regarded with suspicion. It must be admitted, however, that the reference to 430 years in Egypt may be just as inaccurate as later statements about the time of the exodus. In fact, Exodus 6:16-20 indicates that there were only four generations from Levi to Moses: Levi, Kohath, Amram, and Moses. This would suggest a much shorter interval of time spent in Egypt.

In any event, the best historical scholarship available now suggest a thirteenth Century date for the exodus. The references in Judges and Kings mentioned above are discarded by most historians as inaccurate, for they are based upon the assumption that a generation should be calculated as forty years in length. According to the now prevalent theory Israel left Egypt not long after the beginning of the reign of Raamses II in 1290, spent some time in the wilderness, and then attacked Canaan around 1250 B.C.

One should not conclude from this tentative hypothesis, however, that the exodus took place as the Bible says. We have no external evidence at all about the exodus and must rely almost exclusively on the Bible for our information. Although the basic outlines of the Biblical story seem believable, it is difficult to separate historical fact and legendary embellishment. In particular, the question of whether all the tribes participated in the event is a much debated point. It may be that the story of the exodus functioned in Israel much as the story of the first Thanksgiving functions in modern America. Although Americans tend to speak of the Puritans as forefathers, it is obvious that they are such only in a quasi-mythological way, for the ancestors of most Americans came to the New World long after the Puritans arrived. In the same way, Israelites may have taken this event experienced by a few of the tribes and made it a central myth for all.

Hence, it may be somewhat misleading to speak of *The* exodus or *The* conquest. Quite conceivably different tribes may have come out of Egypt at different times. Others may never have lived in Egypt at all. The conquest may also have taken place at various times and in various ways. What we have in Exodus may well be an historical nucleus transformed into a unifying myth for quite diverse groups of people. What is important about the story, then, is not precisely when the event took place but that the event later came to be regarded as the central myth for all the tribes.

Analysis

A. Moses' Early Life

CHAPTER 1, in a few brief sentences, summarizes the long period which Israel spent in Egypt. After a new king takes over who does not know Joseph the people are gradually enslaved and set to work building store-cities for the Pharaoh. To reduce the number of Hebrews, the Pharaoh decrees that all male infants of the Hebrews shall be killed. The Hebrew midwives outwit the Pharaoh, but eventually he demands that all the sons be thrown into the river.

Chapter 2 tells of the birth of Moses (whose Hebrew name is not given) to a Levite couple. Like many heroes of antiquity (for instance,

Sargon I) he is put into a little basket and floated down the river but is miraculously saved from death by one of the Pharaoh's daughters (he doubtless had many) who then gives him back to his mother to nurse. Moses therefore never totally loses his self-consciousness as a Hebrew even though he is brought up in the Pharaoh's household.

This self-identification as a Hebrew is exemplified by Moses' concern for his people and his consequent murder of an Egyptian taskmaster (2:11-12). When Moses realizes that his act has been discovered he flees from Egypt to the land of Midian. Just where that land was is debatable, for the Midianites were a nomadic people who did not occupy just one area permanently. Probably, their land at the time was either in the Sinai peninsula or northern Arabia. In any event, he marries Zipporah, a daughter of the Midianite priest Jethro, and settles down there as a shepherd of his father-in-law's flocks.

Just how long he served in this capacity is unclear. The Bible simply says that after many days the Pharaoh died and under the new ruler Israel's plight was even worse. This change in leadership meant, however, that Moses' life was no longer in danger in Egypt and may have prompted him to consider returning home. Hence, his "call" found Chapters 3 and 4 is already prepared for.

One day Moses leads his flocks to "the mountain of the God", a designation which seems to imply that it already had sacred significance for the Midianites. Perhaps Moses goes to this mountain in order to seek advice from the deity about what he should do. There he sees the burning bush. Again the use of the definite article seems to indicate that this was a known phenomenon among the Midianites. Moses may conceivably have gone to Horeb to perform an act of divination in order to determine whether or not he should return to his homeland.

The answer which is given, however, seems far more than he bargained for, for God tells him to return to Egypt to bring forth the people of Israel and to lead them to a new land. Like many of the other leaders of Israel Moses is reluctant to accept God's commission and raises as many objections as possible to it. Finally, however, God breaks down his resistance and he returns to Egypt.

Among the objections raised, is one which has particular significance for the whole narrative. In 3:13 Moses asks God what his name is so that he can answer this possible question if raised by the people of Israel. Clearly he is asking not for a new name, but for one which the people will recognize. God's response is three-fold. He gives his name as "I am that I am" (or "I will be what I will be"), "I am," and "Yahweh." Why these three names are given is something of a mystery. This passage suggests, at any rate, that the name, Yahweh, was already known and used among Israelites and hence was not newly revealed at this time. The passage also suggests that this name is to replace earlier designations such as *El Shaddai* as the most important way of addressing God.

Perhaps it is appropriate, at this point, to say a few words about the various names of God used in the text. *Elohim,* which is translated "God" in most versions, is not really a name at all. It means literally "The Powers" and is used with a plural verb to refer to the pagan divinities. For instance, the first commandment (Ex. 20:3) reads "You shall have no other *Elohim* before me. When used with a singular verb *Elohim* refers to the God of Israel and implies that this God encompasses all the powers of the universe which pagans worship singly as gods.

In the book of Genesis a number of names, such as *El Shaddai* (God Almighty) and *El Elyon* are used to address God. Even in the first book of the Torah, however, the name of Yahweh is preeminent. There is much debate about the meaning of this name, but it probably means "He causes to pass what comes to pass." With the exodus this became the convenantal name according to which Israel could speak to God. As time went on, however, the name came to be regarded as more and more sacred until during the post-exilic period Jews believed it to be too holy to pronounce. Hence, when it occurred in the text, they read not Yahweh but *Adonai* (Lord). When vowels were added to the text, the consonants of Yahweh were preserved but the vowels written were those of *Adonai*. Christian scholars, unaware of this development, transliterated what they found as "Jehovah," an impossible Hebrew word. Only in this century has it been widely recognized that Jehovah is an artificial construction based upon the consonants of one word and the vowels of another. In any event, scholars are generally agreed that the original name was Yahweh. The Revised Standard Version, however, still retains the Jewish euphemism, the Lord. When this word, written in capital letters, is found, it should read as Yahweh.

Another interesting feature of the story is the magical tricks with which Moses is equipped. Ch. 7:9-12 indicates that the trick of turning a snake into a rod (perhaps by pressing a nerve to make it rigid) was also known and used by Egyptian magicians as well. Undoubtedly Moses first learned this as a young man brought up in the Pharaoh's house.

Such a use of magic by Egyptians is attested to in much Egyptian literature.

Apparently Moses had some speech impediment or at least was not a very good public speaker. When he raises this as an objection, Yahweh reminds him of his brother Aaron who later becomes Moses' "mouthpiece." Just what the original relation between these two men was is a matter of some debate. It may be that we have two quite separate stories of different leaders which have been woven together. In the Bible, at any rate, Aaron plays an important, if sometimes infamous, role in the narrative. He becomes the first "high priest" and founder of the priestly house of Aaron which is to figure so largely in later Israelite history.

Chapter 4:18-26 doubtless contains some very ancient, though now inexplicable, recollections. After Moses has received Jethro's approval for his plans, he sets out for Egypt. On the way Yahweh seeks to kill him! As a result Zipporah circumcizes their son (or it is Moses?) and touches Moses' feet with the foreskin. Moses is cured. No one is sure what this passage is about, but it probably reflects some cultic rite which is now lost to us. Certainly this *looks* very much like a primitive initiation rite in which the person initiated is threatened by death at the hands of the deity but is saved through the rite of circumcision, an initiatory ritual-torture used in many traditional societies. Through this event Moses personally experiences the passage from death to life which Israel is to know in the exodus.

Immediately thereafter Moses meets Aaron on the way, a sign perhaps that there was some communication between Moses and his people during his exile. Moses tells Aaron what to say and he speaks to the elders of the people and convinces them that Yahweh is indeed about to act.

B. The struggle with the Pharaoh (5:1-12:36)

AFTER HAVING won the support of the people, Moses and Aaron go to the Pharaoh, proclaiming that Yahweh has commanded his people to celebrate a feast in the wilderness. The Pharaoh, who was conceived by Egyptians to be all the gods incarnate, does not even recognize the reality of Yahweh and hence not only denies their request but makes the workload of the Israelites heavier. The Israelite foremen, as a consequence, become annoyed with Moses who has only made their situation worse, and Moses appeals to Yahweh for help. In response

Yahweh not only reaffirms his promises to Israel to give them their freedom and a new land in which to dwell, he promises that he will make a covenant with the people so that they will "know" his name. Now Yahweh warns Moses that the Pharaoh will not listen to him, so that eventually, after he has demonstrated his power, Egyptians will know his name, too.

After a genealogy in 6:14-27, which contains reminiscences of great antiquity, the story continues. Ten times Moses demands that Pharaoh let Israel go; ten times he denies the request. After each denial a plague falls upon Egypt. Significantly, these plagues are not called miracles, but signs (*'ot*) of Yahweh's power. None, except the last, can be described as, strictly speaking, miraculous. Given the flooding of the Nile, which often turns the water dark red, several of the other signs follow quite naturally. Frogs jump out of the polluted water and die (8:1-15). This might well lead to a plague of gnats (8:16-19) and a plague of flies (8:20-24). The flies in turn certainly could bring a disease to the cattle (9:1-7) and perhaps boils and sores to the people (9:8-10). Hail and lightning storms are unusual in Egypt, but have occurred (9:13-26). So too have there been occasional plagues of locusts (10:1-15). The three days of darkness do seem unusual, but may signify a great dust storm (10:21-29).

This does not prove, of course, that these signs actually took place. They could very well be an imaginative expansion of the original story to make the account more impressive. At the same time, there is nothing particularly supernatural about them. All of them *could* have occurred. Since Goshen was not right on the Nile itself, it could very well be that the plagues did not extend that far and so Israel remained unaffected.

Only the last of the plagues appears unbelievable from a scientific point of view. According to the account, Yahweh sends a plague which kills all of the first-born of the Egyptians but does not touch the Israelites. Clearly, this is a plague of a different order, not only because it appears so scientifically improbable but because it is so obviously symbolic. In 4:22 Israel is described as the first-born son of Yahweh. Now Yahweh slays the first-born of the Egyptians so that his son can go free. The many are sacrificed for the sake of the one. This, then, is a plague which symbolically captures the meaning of the rest. After it the Pharaoh momentarily relents and commands Israel to be gone (12:29-32) and the Egyptians, to hasten them on their way, give them jewelry and clothing. (12:35).

Chapter 12:1-28 contains an account of how this event, in which the people of Israel were spared, is to be celebrated and remembered. Passover (*Pesach*) is to mark the beginning of the year. At that time, blood of the lamb is to be smeared upon the door-posts, and the passover meal of lamb and unleavened bread is to be eaten standing with staff in hand. Israel, thus, is to reenact the last moments before the departure for freedom. The New Year is to begin not only with a remembrance of things past but with an eager expectation for the exodus which is coming. It is to be a moment of rebirth, when Israel leaves the death of captivity and is born into a new life of freedom.

C. From Egypt to Sinai (12:37-18:27)

ACCORDING TO 12:37 about 600,000 men with their wives and children, together with a "mixed multitude" left Egypt with Moses. Obviously the numbers have been greatly inflated, for this would mean that about two million people were involved. Not only could such a horde not have survived in the desert. It is unlikely that the Egyptians would have been able to muster a large enough army to deal with such a sizeable group.

Exodus 12:43-13:16 contains another set of laws concerning Passover which emphasizes the exclusion of foreigners from the feast. This section seems to be placed where it is because of the mention of the mixed multitude in 12:38. It also contains laws about the consecration of the first-born to Yahweh to commemorate this event. Undoubtedly this practice was of much older origin but has here been historicized. All first-born males of the cattle are to be sacrificed, with the exception of the ass. This animal was commonly sacrificed by non-Israelites, but, for some reason—perhaps its relation to the pagan cult—was denied sacrificial status in Israel. First-born sons are also to be consecrated, but are to be redeemed rather than actually sacrificed. (Cf. Genesis 22.)

There is great debate about the next section (12:17-15:21) which traces the route of Israel out of Egypt. Unfortunately, most of the places mentioned (Migdol, Baal, Zephon, Pihahiroth, Succoth) have not been certainly located and hence the route can only be guessed at. It is clear, at any rate, that the *yam suf*, which Israel is said to have crossed, was not the "Red Sea" but rather the "Sea of Reeds." Probably this was a marshy area located somewhere in the north-eastern corner of Egypt. It is likely that originally Israel escaped from the pursuing Egyptian armies (the

Pharaoh had changed his mind about letting Israel go) by crossing a marshy area in which the Egyptian chariots became mired.

This last escape was taken by Israel to be the crowning sign that Yahweh was indeed leading Israel, that Israel was saved by his mighty hand and outstretched arm. Doubtless beneath the highly embellished story which stands before us is a kernel of historical truth. It must also be recognized, however, that the parting of waters symbolizes in many cultures the moment of birth. Mythologically, the whole account connotes the birth of Israel out of Death. This is the same symbolism (*mutatis mutandis*) used in the Christian rite of baptism.

Although much of Chapter 15 is a poetic gloss of a later date glorifying this moment of freedom, the first two lines of Miriam's song of exultation (cf. 15:21) are probably very ancient and may, in fact, come from an eye-witness.

Exodus 15:22-17:7 includes accounts of three "miracles" experienced by Israel in the wilderness. First, Moses makes the water of Marah sweet by throwing a tree in the water. This event evokes a promise from Yahweh that if Israel keeps his commandments Yahweh will keep them from the diseases with which he smote the Egyptians.

Second, 16:1-36 tells of Israel's hunger in the desert and the giving of the quail and manna. Although the text describes these events miraculously, there is no need to consider them supernatural. We know that migrating quail do sometimes fall on the desert exhausted and can be picked up easily. Manna, a sweet substance secreted by insects in the desert, can still be purchased at the market-places in Cairo. The fact that manna does not appear on the seventh day reminds Moses that Israel ought to observe the ancient Semitic custom of refraining from work one day a week. The text indicates that Moses did not begin the celebration of the Sabbath, but merely reinstituted an old practice and filled it with new significance.

Third, 17:1-7 tells of the thirst of Israel and of how Moses strikes a rock to get water. Again no supernatural explanation is required, for the limestone rocks of the Sinai often contain pockets of water and can be "tapped" today by someone familiar with the desert. 17:8-16 describes Israel's first battle against the bedouin people of Amalek. This section is important because, although historically suspect, it points to the long-standing feud between Israel and the Amalekites. (cf. I Samuel 15).

Throughout her journey through the wilderness Israel is said to be led by a pillar of cloud and a pillar of fire (Exodus 13:21-22). Whether there is some naturalistic explanation of these pillars is uncertain. As mythological images, however, they clearly convey the conviction that Yahweh is directly concerned about his people. Israel does not wander aimlessly, for God leads her onward to the mountain of the covenant and then to the Promised Land.

Finally, Israel arrives at "the mountain of God" (18:5). There Moses is met by Jethro, his father-in-law, who brings with him Moses' wife and children (when did they return to Midian?). Jethro expresses his faith in Yahweh and, as priest of Midian, offers a sacrifice and eats holy bread with Moses and Aaron and the elders. Like most fathers-in-law Jethro has a word of advice to Moses. Moses has been trying to adjudicate all disputes among the Israelites and is over-worked. Jethro proposes a more workable system and Moses agrees. Then Jethro returns home. This story, among others, has led some scholars to believe that Yahweh was originally a mountain god of the Midianites whom Moses adopted. There seems little reason to accept this thesis as anything more than unproved speculation. Surely the text gives no cogent indication that this was the case.

D. The Covenant

AFTER THREE MONTHS of travel Israel arrives at Mount Sinai. The location of the site is undetermined, but traditionally the mountain has been located in the south-central part of the Sinai peninsula. After arriving, Moses immediately goes up the mountain to receive Yahweh's commands. God responds with a brief but highly significant message (19:3-6) in which he reminds Israel of how he has protected her and calls her to obedience. If Israel will really hear his voice, Yahweh promises that she will be his *segullah*, his treasure among the nations, a kingdom of priests and a holy nation.

The people vow to obey, and God promises that he will come and speak to them. The people then consecrate themselves by washing their clothes and refraining from sexual intercourse. On the third day after the third new moon after leaving Egypt, (a most propitious time), the theophany occurs. A thunderstorm breaks out on the mountain while, at the same time, there are earth tremors. Through this strange coincidence Yahweh addresses Israel with his voice of thunder. What he says becomes the basis for Israel's covenantal agreement with him. Chapter

20, then, contains a human translation of Yahweh's voice of thunder, a voice which provides an interpretation of the whole exodus event.

It is important to recognize that these "Ten Commandments" are not given as a set of "natural laws" meant for all men. On the contrary, they are specifically designed for Israel and express, in terms of command, the significance of the exodus. These commands have often been criticized for their negativity, but such criticism clearly misses the point. The covenant rests upon one very positive fact: that Yahweh has led Israel out of bondage to freedom. The commandments, far from being a negative burden, simply express the meaning and the limits of the freedom into which Israel has been led. Covenanting with Yahweh means that Israel is freed from any obligation to the "Powers" (gods) of this world. Idol worship, which so consumed the attention of the pagans, is abolished. Israel must love and honor Yahweh alone. Because Yahweh is above all the gods he is incomprehensible and hence ought not to be pictured in any way. Israel is called to hold his name in honor and to respect his image which is man. This implies resting one day a week to symbolize man's freedom from slavery. Such freedom also implies that Israelites ought to regard the dignity of all other men. Hence murder, adultery, theft, false witnessing, and coveting are forbidden, for each of these is an attack upon the dignity of the neighbor. Far from being a set of legal burdens, then, the ten commandments is a charter for freedom.

Instead of rejoicing in their freedom, however, the people of Israel respond to Yahweh's voice of thunder with fear. As a consequence, Moses is forced to provide more specific rules in order to quell Israel's rising sense of anxiety. The prohibition of idols is retained, but the people are allowed to build an altar as a means of communication with the incomprehensible deity (20:21-26). Then follows what is often called "The Covenant Code" in 21:1-23:19. This very ancient law code does not deny any of the Ten Commandments, but makes the meaning of them much more specific. The Decalogue is apodictic. That is to say, the commandments are given without regard to circumstances. The Covenant Code, on the whole, is casuistic, specifying what one should do in a particular situation. In this, the Covenant Code is much closer to various other Near Eastern law codes (the Hammurabic Code, etc.) than are the Ten Commandments. While the Ten Commandments are absolute requirements and hence can never be obeyed completely, the Covenant Code can be followed and fulfilled by the individual who takes it seriously.

The Covenant Code may be outlined in the following way:

Laws concernings slaves: 21:1-11
Laws concerning murder: 21:12-17
Laws concerning non-capital offenses: 21:18-32
Laws concerning property rights: 21:33-22:17
Miscellaneous laws and duties: 22:18-31
Laws concerning the perversion of justice: 23:1-9
Cultic laws: 23:10-19

Finally, the people's terror is placated by the promise that Yahweh will send an angel to lead them into the promised land rather than terrorizing them with his own presence. They are to obey that angel (who is identified in later Jewish lore as the Archangel Michael) and are to avoid making covenants with the Canaanites or engaging in their religious practices.

Chapter 24 is highly significant, for it contains an account of the covenant-making ceremony. After Moses, Aaron and his sons, and the elders of the people have set themselves apart from the people, Moses recites before Israel the "words", i.e., of the commandments of Yahweh, and all the ordinances (the Covenant Code) and the people agree to accept them. After writing down the Decalogue before the people, Moses then builds an altar and sets up twelve *massebot* (pillars). Strangely enough he subsequently calls upon teen-age boys to offer the burnt and peace offerings. Again Moses reads from the book of the covenant and again the people agree to it. Half of the blood from the sacrifices is thrown on the altar while half is thrown on the people, thus symbolizing that Israel and Yahweh are united in blood. Finally, Moses, Aaron and his sons, and the elders go apart to consume the sacrificial meal. While doing so they see "visions of God" (24:10-11). Doubtless this whole passage served as the basis for the covenant-renewal ceremony held in Israel at specified intervals.

E. Israel's Apostasy

ALMOST IMMEDIATELY Moses leaves the people and, with Joshua, ascends the mountain to receive the law on tablets of stone. While on Sinai he receives not only the tablets but instructions regarding the cultic paraphernalia, etc. (25:1-31:18) Some scholars have argued that this whole section is very late (post-exilic) and reads back into Mosaic times much later practices. In fact, it is argued that what is really being described here is the Solomonic Temple and not the early Tabernacle at all. Certainly, it seems clear that much of this is post-Mosaic, because, for instance, it appears highly unlikely that priests in the desert would have worn the elaborate garments described in 28:1-43 or that Israel in the wilderness would have been able to make a table overlaid with gold (25:23-24). Still there is no particular reason to see this as only the result of some later scribes' idle imagination. Although there are many embellishments, the description may well be of the cultic shrine used by Israel during the period of the Judges.

It is also important to see the role this section plays in the over-all drama of Exodus. While Moses is up on the mountain dreaming of the fine robes which his brother is to wear, Aaron is down below consenting to, if not fostering, idolatry. Chapter 32 tells of how Israel became tired waiting for Moses and urged Aaron to make gods for them. As a consequence, he makes a golden calf and proclaims a feast day. Although there may be a kernel of historical truth here, it seems apparent that the writer has in mind the calf used in the northern kingdom of Israel during and after the reign of Jeroboam I. In all fairness to Jeroboam (and perhaps to Aaron), it is probable that the calf (bull) was not regarded as an image of the deity himself but the steed upon which he rode. Still, for the orthodox Judean the use of this symbol rather than the ark of the covenant (cf. 25:10-22) constituted idolatry. As Exodus stands, at any rate, the story expresses a very ambivalent view of the priesthood. On the one hand, the priest's role is seen as both necessary and even glorious; yet it is also admitted that Aaron and his sons often were responsible for Israel's idolatry. This ambivalent attitude toward the cult pervades both the Torah and the Prophets.

When Moses comes down the mountain he is angered by Aaron's actions. He destroys the calf and breaks the tablets which he has brought with him. He calls for men to stand with him, and his own tribe, Levi, does. The sons of Levi go through the camp and slaughter some 3,000 men. As a consequence of this "righteous" act, the Levites are set apart for service to Yahweh. (32:25-29) Just how accurate historically this story is is debatable although it seems highly unlikely that the Levites themselves would have made up this account of their bloody ordination. Perhaps this is a story used to link together two diverse traditions found in the Torah which, on the one hand, describe the Levites as warlike and, on the other, accord them cultic responsibilities.

Twice (32:11-14; 30:55) Moses intercedes on behalf of Israel before Yahweh and finally the deity is placated. Again he promises to send an angel before Israel, but this time the people take this as an evil omen (33:1-6). The rest of the chapter describes Moses' relation to God. Curiously, Moses is pictured as both seeing God face to face (33:11) and yet not being able to do so (33:20). This apparent discrepancy may be due to the use of different sources, but more likely it points to the paradoxical relation in which Moses stood to Yahweh. On the one hand, his relation was intensely direct; yet Moses was unable to know what Yahweh would do next. He could only see his back (33:23) as he went before him.

Chapter 34 describes the renewal of God's promises to Israel (34:10) and his regiving of the law. One would expect a reiteration of the ten commandments, but such is not the case. Instead of the original Decalogue of Exodus 20 Moses is given laws which pertain almost exclusively to the cult. Although it is difficult to count ten laws in this passage (34:11-26), it is this set of regulations which is officially called the ten commandments. (34:28).

We see now the "tragedy" of Exodus now unfolding. Israel, through the Exodus, is given her freedom, not only from Egyptian bondage but from human "religion." Because of her fear before God and her apostasy, however, this freedom is gradually curtailed as not only civil but cultic laws are given to her.

Chapters 35-39, strangely enough, contain an almost exact repetition of God's commandments concerning the cult found in 25-31. Now, however, it is affirmed that Israel followed these original commandments and constructed the Tabernacle and the rest of the paraphenalia as commanded. One wonders why the compilers felt it necessary to repeat this section in such detail. Perhaps they did so, not merely to extend the book unduly, but to emphasize that concerning the cult, at least, Israel was obedient. The people were tempted again and again to disobey the words of the covenant and seemingly could not avoid sin, but they could build a Tabernacle as the Lord prescribed! Thus Exodus concludes with a rather plaintive note. Israel's freedom is now qualified because of her sin; yet there is a splendidness to be found in human religion which cannot be overlooked. Aaron may have led the people astray, but his robes are, at least, glorious.

The book concludes with an account of the dedication of the Tabernacle, that portable shrine, in which Israel can meet God, and with a description of Yahweh's glory filling the Tabernacle as it was later to fill the Temple. Israel has sinned almost from the very beginning, but Yahweh remains with her to lead her onward toward the Promised Land.

CHAPTER VIII

Leviticus: Introduction and Analysis

The Date of Composition
Laws for the Cult
The Holiness Code

HE THIRD book of the Torah, Leviticus, derives its name from the title prefixed to it in the Septuagint and Vulgate versions. The Hebrew title, according to Semitic custom, is *Wayyiqra*, "and he called," the first word of the text. Doubtless the title Leviticus was used because the translators believed the book to contain laws for and by the Levites. Clearly, however, this is a misnomer, for the Levites are scarcely mentioned in Leviticus at all. Throughout, it is Aaron and his sons who are emphasized. Though Exodus knows of the "ordination" of the Levites for special service to Yahweh (Exodus 32:25-29) and Numbers specifies their duties (Numbers 3:5-10), Leviticus has virtually nothing to say about them. When they are mentioned in 25:32-33 it is only in connection with their rights regarding Levitical cities. If one were to read Leviticus alone one would not even guess that these Levites are accorded in some sections of the Torah cultic responsibilities. In this Leviticus differs sharply with Numbers, in particular, which mentions the Levites quite frequently.

In a sense, Leviticus continues the story of Israel in the wilderness of Sinai set forth in the last half of Exodus. Those narrative passages which are contained in the book (particularly in Chapters 8-10) do, in fact, seem to come from the same source as Exodus 25-40. Not only does chapter 8 record the ordination of Aaron and his sons, the one act commanded by God in Mt. Sinai (Exodus 25-31) which was not fulfilled in Exodus 35-40. The story of Nadab's and Abihu's unholy (but now obscure) act in Leviticus 10 corresponds with the view of Aaron found in Exodus 32.

The more one examines Leviticus with care, however, the more evident it becomes that this book contains traditions which differ considerably from those found in the other books of the Torah. Not only are narrative sections few and far between; the legal sections of Leviticus differ in emphasis and style from those found in Exodus, Numbers, and Deuteronomy.

In Exodus and Deuteronomy, in particular, the site of Yahweh's revelation of the law is seen to be Mount Sinai. Leviticus, on the other hand, contains Yahweh's commands to Moses in the Tent of Meeting. At the same time, Leviticus has precious little to say about the Tabernacle so glorified in Exodus. It is mentioned only three times: in 8:10, 15:31 and 17:4. Each of these instances can be demonstrated to be an editorial gloss rather than a part of the "original" book. In Numbers references to the Tabernacle again appear frequently, thus indicating a return to the tradition of Exodus 25-40.

A number of other differences also bear mentioning. With the exception of Deuteronomy 32:51, Leviticus contains the only references to the holiness of Yahweh himself to be found in the Torah. In Exodus, Numbers, and most of Deuteronomy only the people of Israel, places and things are described as *kadosh,* i.e., set apart or holy. Numbers, as a matter of fact, seems to deny the quality of holiness to Israel as well. In Leviticus, on the other hand, great emphasis is placed upon the holiness of both Yahweh and Israel.

Although both versions of the Ten Commandments (Exodus 20, Deuteronomy 5) call upon Israel to love God, Leviticus mentions neither the love of man for God nor the love of God for man. It does, however, contain the famous commandment, "You shall love your neighbor as yourself" (19:18) which is missing in the other codes of law.

Finally, as has already been mentioned, Leviticus alone places almost total emphasis upon the house of Aaron, excluding any mention of the cultic responsibilities of the Levites. Exodus and Numbers recognize cultic roles for both the Aaronites and the Levites; Deuteronomy stresses the Levitical priests and says almost nothing about Aaron's sons.

This is not to say, of course, that Leviticus is wholly at variance with the books which surround it. Certainly, it is much closer in thought-form and style to Exodus 25-40 and many sections of Numbers than it is to Deuteronomy. Deuteronomy's emphasis upon remembering what God has done for Israel in the past and upon man's love for God are totally absent in Leviticus. Leviticus, on the other hand, stresses the preeminence of the house of Aaron, the importance of atonement, and the specifics of the sacrifices while Deuteronomy does not. Still, Leviticus differs enough from both Exodus and Numbers to regard it as containing separate traditions which were fused with the rest by some editor. In truth, one can skip over Leviticus without sensing any break in the narrative at all.

Thus far we have been speaking about Leviticus as a whole, but it is clear that Leviticus itself is not of one piece. Most scholars, at the very least, distinguish between Chapters 1-16 and Chapters 17-26 as separate law codes, and many try to make further divisions of the text in a variety of ways. Although there is no unanimity of belief about the many sources which critical scholars severally identify, it does seem clear that 17-26 can be seen as a separate unit. Usually this section is called "The Holiness Code," but this title seems to be a misnomer, for the second half of Leviticus hardly emphasizes holiness any more than the first. What is quite distinctive about 17-26 is the frequent refrain, "I am the Lord." Although used only once (11:45) in Chapters 1-16, it is repeated often in the last half of the book as a statement of justification and warning for the preceding ordinances. In a sense, all of the laws and ordinances are seen as flowing naturally from the Reality to which the name Yahweh points. If one knows Yahweh, proclaims the Code, one will naturally obey these laws which reflect the meaning and implications of his holy name.

The Date of Composition

DOCUMENTARY CRITICS, recognizing the preponderant interest in cultic matters in Leviticus, have assigned virtually the whole of the book to the P source and thus have dated it in the exilic or post-exilic period. If one means by this that the book took final shape at this time, such dating can be accepted. Certainly Chapter 26 bears evidence of post-exilic authorship, for it alludes to the captivity of the people and the desolation of the land. (26:27ff) It must also be recognized, however, that like the other books of the Torah which also were put in final form at a fairly late date, Leviticus is based upon much older material which may have been edited during or after the exile but which surely was in use long before the fall of Jerusalem. Leviticus must be seen, not as the creation of a particular age, but as the final form of a tradition which developed over the centuries. Within its pages we can find not only hints of post-exilic times but very ancient descriptions of rites and customs.

Many scholars, noting the similarity between the Holiness Code and the Code of Ezekiel (Ezekiel 40-48), believe that one can be much more precise about dating 17-26. This code, they say, like the Code of Ezekiel, comes from exilic times. Although some similarities do exist, it seems to this writer that they have been greatly over emphasized. It is true that Ezekiel like Leviticus is concerned about the distinction between the clean and the unclean, about the ritual purity of the priests, and about some of the specifics of sacrificing. Some of their ethical emphases are also similar. The following differences, however, should also be noted:

1. Although Ezekiel uses the phrase "I am the LORD" many times in his book, he never uses it to justify any of the laws and ordinances which he gives. The phrase is not to be found at all in Ezekiel 40-48.
2. Leviticus emphasizes throughout the idea of atonement. Neither this word, nor the Day of Atonement is mentioned in Ezekiel.
3. Leviticus emphasizes the sons of Aaron and says almost nothing about the Levites. Ezekiel criticizes the Levites but recognizes their existence and their cultic responsibilities. He does not mention the sons of Aaron but only the sons of Zadok.
4. Ezekiel, like Exodus 25-40, is much concerned about the structure of Israel's place of worship, an interest almost totally lacking in Leviticus.
5. Ezekiel (46:1,6) speaks of the festivals of the new moon which are not so much as mentioned in Leviticus.

6. Ezekiel places emphasis upon the cultic responsibilities of the prince, while Leviticus has little to say about human sovereignty.
7. Ezekiel, at least one time, offers a law in specific contradiction to the law of Leviticus. While Leviticus allows all priests but the high priest to marry widows, Ezekiel specifically denies this possibility (cf. Lev. 21:7, 13-14; Ezekiel 44:22).

On the whole, a comparison of these two Codes would seem to show not that they came from the same time but that Ezekiel was dependent upon Leviticus, as he also was upon Deuteronomy, for many of his ideas. If anything, then, the similarities between Ezekiel and Leviticus indicate that Leviticus 17-26, at least, was pre-exilic in origin and may well have been used in Judah before the fall of Jerusalem. Just how long before the fall of Jerusalem this book came into existence, however, is a matter of great debate.

It is unfortunate that Leviticus cannot be dated with any great precision, for such dating would greatly enhance our knowledge of the history of the religion of Israel. The origin and history of the Levites and the sons of Aaron is very obscure and a firm date for Leviticus would help us to write a history of this development. Perhaps archaeologists, in the future, will discover evidence which will help in the tracing out the development of Israel's cult. At this point, however, we must be satisfied with the frustrating recognition that the Bible itself, unless taken uncritically at face value, gives us only clues as to how precisely the cult of Israel changed over the centuries. These clues, though tantalizing, are not sufficient to establish any one theory concerning the matter.

Analysis

Laws for the Cult

A. Laws regarding various types of offering (*Korban* 1:1-7:38)

THIS FIRST SECTION describes the way in which Israelites are to offer various types of offering to Yahweh. Emphasis is placed upon how the cultic rite should be performed rather than upon the circumstances which prompt the offering. Only in regard to sin and guilt offerings are the circumstances discussed.

Leviticus 1:1-6:7 is addressed to the people and gives instruction regarding burnt offerings (Ch. 1), cereal offerings (Ch. 2), peace offerings (Ch. 3), sin and guilt offerings (Chs. 4-6:7). Chs. 6:8-7:36 then gives instructions to Aaron and his sons concerning their part in making the same offerings. Ch. 7:22 concerns portions of animals which are proscribed for eating, while 7:28-36 concerns the portion of the offerings to be given to Aaron and his sons. Chs. 7:37-38 is a concluding paragraph which seems to indicate that Chapters 1-7 once constituted a separate Code of Law.

B. Priestly regulations (8:1-10:20)

CHAPTER 8 describes the ordination of Aaron and his sons. The ritual is performed according to the commands of God set forth in Exodus 29. Doubtless this is meant to be a prototype for all ordination services.

Chapter 9 describes the first offerings offered by Aaron and his sons themselves, while Chapter 10 tells of Nadab and Abihu (Aaron's oldest sons) offering "unholy fire" and hence being killed by God. The nature of their act is obscure, but the story underlines a) the importance attached to absolutely correct procedures and b) the potential sinfulness of the Aaronic priesthood. Ch. 10:8-10 forbids the drinking of wine to those priests who are going to serve into the Tent of Meeting and sets forth the basic responsibilities of the priests. They are to teach the people to distinguish between the holy and the common and between the clean and the unclean and are to instruct them in the statutes of Yahweh. The chapter concludes with a brief narrative dealing with the eating of holy things.

C. Laws of Cleanness and Purification (11:1-15:33)

Chapter 11 contains Judaism's basic dietary laws. Another version found in Deuteronomy 14:3-21, generally repeats what is said here in a somewhat abbreviated way. Scholars have proposed many reasons for the prohibition of the eating of certain animals. The old theory that pork was prohibited because of the danger of trichinosis seems untenable, for many of the other meats forbidden harbor no such danger. Others have proposed that those animals prohibited were the sacrificial animals of the Canaanites and other neighboring peoples. It is true that some of the favorite sacrificial animals of the pagans are on the list, but this theory by no means accounts for all of the animals mentioned. Probably the laws are based upon very ancient taboos rather than upon any logical reasoning. Just why the basic criterion for cleanness should involve cleaving the hoof and chewing the cud is unknown.

In Chapter 12 are contained laws regarding the purification of a woman after childbirth. The conception of a new mother as unclean is a very ancient notion which is found the world over. Chapters 13 and 14 concern the diagnosis and treatment of leprosy while Chapter 15 deals with various forms of unclean secretions. As in many cultures, priests in Israel served not only a cultic but a medical role as well. Holiness and health are seen as directly related, for sickness is regarded as a result of sin. There is no implication, however, that faith is the only cure for diseases, as some modern sects maintain. The appropriate offerings are prescribed when the disease has been cured, but the book also shows an elementary knowledge of contagion and the value of cleanliness.

D. The Day of Atonement (16:1-34)

THE FIRST HALF of the book ends with a description of Yom Kippur, the Day of Atonement. Although this holy day is also described in Numbers 29:7-11, Leviticus gives quite a different description of the rites which are to take place on the tenth day of the seventh month. For instance, Numbers mentions not only the sacrifice of a bull and a goat but of one ram and seven male lambs along with cereal offerings. Leviticus stresses particularly the use of a scapegoat to carry away the sins of Israel which are laid upon its head by the priest. This goat is designated for Azazel, but whether this is a place or a demon is a much debated question. The Book of Enoch, which is full of speculative suggestions, identifies Azazel as a demon, but since the author of Enoch specifically sought to explain the otherwise puzzling verses of Scripture, this reference to Azazel must have been regarded as enigmatic by his time (the first century B.C.). It is clear that we have here a very old tradition which may have passed out of usage long before the exile.

The Holiness Code

A. Laws for Killing and Eating Animals

Chapter 17 begins the Holiness Code by specifying that all animals killed must be brought to the Tent of Meeting. This is done, it is said, to prevent sacrifices to satyrs (or perhaps male goats). The punishment for violation of this law is death! Leviticus 17:10-16 then prohibits the eating of blood or the flesh of any animal which has died naturally or has been "torn by beasts". These laws have had profound effect upon the dietary customs of Jewry.

B. Laws Concerning Sexual Relations

Chapter 18 then continues with the prohibition of incest and a careful statement about which relations should be regarded as incestuous. Ch. 18:19 warns against intercourse with a woman during her menstrual period, while 18:22-23 prohibits homosexuality and bestiality. 18:21, which appears to have been interjected into the text, prohibits child sacrifice to the god Molech. Ch. 18:24-30 concludes the chapter with a word of warning against the breaking of these laws.

C. Miscellaneous Laws Which Israel Must Obey to be Holy

This section contains a variety of laws which reveal both high ethical standards and the most primitive taboos. In 19:18, for instance, is to be found the famous imperative, "You shall love your neighbor as yourself." The very next verse, however, prohibits the sowing of a field with two kinds of seed and the wearing of a garment made of two kinds of stuff. On the whole, however, the ethical nature of these laws is very impressive. There seems to be little or no topical order in this chapter.

D. Punishments

Chapter 20 prescribes the appropriate punishments for the following "sins": child sacrifice (death), consultation with mediums and wizards (ostracism), cursing of father or mother (death), adultery (death), various degrees of incest (ostracism, childlessness, etc.) The chapter concludes with an exhortation to be holy as Yahweh is holy and with a misplaced description of the penalty for being a medium or wizard (death).

E. Rules for the Priesthood

CHAPTERS 21-22 contain a variety of rules for priests, describing how they should avoid pollution, whom they may not marry, how they should dress, etc. Chapter 22:1-9 emphasizes that priests must be free of physical blemishes while 22:10-15 explains who may and may not eat the food which has been offered to Yahweh. Ch. 22:17-31 distinguishes between acceptable and unacceptable offerings.

F. Laws Concerning Festivals

CHAPTER 23 sets forth the basic laws concerning the various holy days: The Sabbath (23:1-3), Passover (4-8), The Feast of first fruits (9-14), Pentecost (15-22), The feast of trumpets, i.e., New Year's (23-25), the Day of Atonement (26-32), and Tabernacles (33-43).

G. Miscellaneous Laws

CHAPTER 24:1-4 specifies the use of olive oil for the lamp in the tent of meeting which is to be kept burning constantly. Ch. 24:5-9 describes the twelve cakes which are to be offered each Sabbath Day to Yahweh. Ch. 24:10-16 specifies death as the punishment for blasphemy, while 24:17-23 invokes the law of "an eye for an eye and a tooth for a tooth."

Chapter 25:1-23 contains the law of the Jubilee year which is to be celebrated every fifty years. On that year each family will receive back any inheritance of land lost during the interval and the whole land will be allowed to rest. Some regard this legislation as an ideal which could never be enforced, but there are some indications that at least in post-exilic times, it was observed.

Chapter 25:25-34, which contains the only references to the Levites in the book, concerns the redemption of property. Ch. 25:35-38 prohibits the taking of usury from a poor brother, while 25:39-55 continues this theme by discussing how a poor fellow citizen (brother) who sells himself as a slave should be treated.

H. Conclusion

THE HOLINESS CODE concludes with a description of the blessings to be derived through obedience to Yahweh and of the punishments which will follow disobedience. Particularly in 26:27ff there are strong hints that the writer was familiar with the exile. This does not mean that the whole code need be dated as post-exilic. Furthermore, it is conceivable that even before the exile Israelites regarded historical disaster as a punishment for sin. Surely many of the prophets foresaw coming destruction before it actually occurred. Probably, however, this section was written after the fall of Jerusalem as a way of emphasizing the importance of obedience to Yahweh.

Chapter 26:46 indicates that the original Code came to an end at this point. Chapter 27, which deals with the making of vows and how they should be kept, then, is a later addition to the text. This does not mean that its origin was late, but only that it was tacked onto the book as an after-thought, perhaps to preserve a bit of tradition for which the editor could find no other place.

CHAPTER IX

Numbers: Introduction and Analysis

Israel at Sinai
From Sinai to Moab
Israel in Moab

HE fourth book of the Torah derives its English title from the Vulgate title, *Numeri*, which is in turn based upon the Septuagint name, *Arithmoi*. Doubtless this title was originally given because the book begins with the numbering of Israel, but it hardly accurately expresses the contents of the work as a whole. Much more preferable is the Hebrew title, *Bemidbar* ("In the wilderness"), which describes the locale in which the stories described in Numbers take place.

Numbers, at least in its narrative portions, contains episodes from the history of Israel during its long forty-year stay in the wilderness though, because long stretches of time are completely skipped over, it can hardly be called a history of the period. It begins where Exodus left off, at the foot of Mount Sinai. After some ten chapters describing the preparations for the march, it sketchily traces Israel's movements until the people arrive at last in the area east of the Jordan, ready to enter the Promised land. Just as one can move from Exodus to Numbers without feeling any decisive break in the story, so one can also turn from

Numbers to Joshua just as easily. Only Deuteronomy 34 seems to be an integral part of the narrative story, though Deut. 33 also contains ancient material which was also probably part of the pre-Deuteronomic narrative.

Although Numbers provides many memorable episodes, it is highly confusing to read, for it contains, intertwined with the wilderness saga, various collections of legal material which have been interjected without much regard to context. Hence one moves swiftly from an historical remembrance to a set of ordinances which seems to have no connection with what precedes it. Just why this is so is unclear, but surely Numbers is the most clumsily edited book in Torah.

Numbers has constituted perhaps the greatest problem for source critics. Although most of them have cut through the Gordian knot by assigning the legal sections, by and large, to P and the narrative portions to JE, attempts to unravel J and E in the book have proved highly unsuccessful. Furthermore, though it may be comforting to evoke the name P every time a set of laws is introduced, it has become increasingly clear that this really solves no problems, for P itself comprises the most diverse materials coming from many different periods in Israel's history. In many respects the legal sections of Numbers reveal many affinities with Leviticus. Unlike Deuteronomy, Numbers emphasizes the idea of atonement and contains the only other mention to the Day of Atonement. Many of its laws find parallels in Leviticus. At the same time, Numbers, unlike Leviticus, speaks frequently of the Levites and mentions the tabernacle by name on many occasions.

The precise dating of the various legal and narrative sections of Numbers offers a bewildering variety of problems. Perhaps all that needs to be said at this juncture is that though some legal and narrative sections reveal the hand of post-exilic editing, many portions of the book bear the marks of great antiquity. The task of separating the early and the late strata is still incomplete and perhaps will, by necessity, remain so until such time as we have more information about the legal and cultic history of Israel.

Analysis

Israel at Sinai

CHAPTER 1 contains the results of a census purportedly taken by Moses while Israel was encamped at Sinai. It is about as stimulating for the beginner as reading the Telephone Book. If one stops to consider the account carefully, however, it soon appears that there is something wrong, for one can hardly imagine this many people living in the Sinai desert. Some scholars have suggested that these figures are from the census taken by David several centuries later. Others maintain that the word *aleph* which is translated 1,000 ought to be read "tents." Both theories help to explain the inflation of numbers, but neither is very convincing, for it is difficult to see either why David's census records should have found a place here or why the word *aleph* ought to be rendered as "tents."

Chapter Two describes the marching and camping order of Israel. In the middle go the Levites with the ark and Tent of Meeting. Before them are the tribes to camp on the east: Judah, Issachar, and Zebulun, and on the south: Reuben, Simeon, and Gad. Behind them come those camping on the west side: Ephraim, Manasseh, and Benjamin, and on the north: Dan, Asher, and Naphtali.

Chapter 3 concerns the position and duties of the Levites. Here the distinction between the sons of Aaron, the priests, and the Levites, the custodians of the cultic paraphenalia, is made clear. Apparently, all first-born Israelites originally had cultic responsibilities, but the Levites now take their place.

In Chapter 4, a census of the Levites, previously forbidden in Ch. 1:47-54, is taken and the duties of the three Levite families, the sons of Kohath, Gershon, Merari, are spelled out. Then in Chapters 5 and 6 is found a series of miscellaneous laws. Ch. 5:1-4 deals with Israelites who contract leprosy, while 5:5-10 contains laws pertaining to restitution for sins committed. Ch. 5:11-31 gives the law to be used in cases of jealousy. That is, when a man suspects his wife of infidelity the woman is required to drink of a certain potion (the water of bitterness) which will reveal her guilt or innocence. As in many ancient laws, the burden of proof is totally on the woman. Ch. 6:1-21 contains laws pertaining to Nazirites. The origin and purpose of the vow of the Nazirite is somewhat obscure, but apparently the Nazirites constituted a special order of men and women who "separated themselves to Yahweh" and who consequently neither drank wine nor cut their hair. This was not a lifetime vow as 6:13-20 shows. Chapter 6 concludes with the famous Aaronic blessing which is still used today in many churches.

Chapter 7 lists the offerings brought to Moses and the Levites by the leaders of each tribe after the tabernacle had been dedicated. Just how or why Israelites would have had so many gold and silver dishes and plates in the wilderness is an interesting question! Doubtless the whole passage reflects the practice of a post-Mosaic period, but the possibility of dating the section exactly seems remote.

Chapter 8 speaks of the lamps and lampstand of the sanctuary (8:1-4) and then describes the rite through which the Levites are to be purified and ordained. Ch. 8:23-26 establishes the time of service of the Levite as between the ages of 25 and 50. In Chapter 9 the keeping of the second Passover is briefly described and the question of what happens to a person who is ritually unclean at the time of Passover is settled. Those who are in such a state shall celebrate it on the first day of the second month. Ch. 9:15-23 describes the miraculous cloud which covered the Tabernacle and which led the people through the wilderness. Finally, in 10:1-10, the making of silver trumpets to be used for camp signals is commanded. These trumpets, which also are to be used cultically (10:10), should be distinguished from the *shopharim* which are made out of ram's horns and are to be blown on New Year's Day.

From Sinai to Moab

AT LAST ISRAEL begins her march, led by the cloud of the Lord. Just before they leave Moses asks Hobab, his father-in-law, to go with them as a guide. Why the name used here is Hobab is somewhat obscure. So also is it unclear whether Moses actually convinces him to accompany them. Why Moses felt the need of a guide when the cloud of the Lord was operative is also not explained.

Until this point things have seemingly gone quite well for Moses and the people. Chapter 11, which describes Israel's complaints about misfortunes and food, marks a turning point in the story, for from this point in the narrative until Chapter 25 the text is filled with stories of Israel's various rebellions against Yahweh and Moses. While Yahweh appears as an avenging God who is quick to destroy the offending Israelites, Moses is normally pictured as a mediator who, though also offended by Israel's unfaithfulness, still pleads with Yahweh for mercy. In 11:4-9 the people complain about the lack of meat. Moses prays to the Lord for help (11:5-15), and Yahweh responds with a promise that meat will be given. He also sends his Spirit upon the seventy elders so that they prophesy. Finally the quail arrive just as they did in Exodus 16:13, but when the people eat them they immediately fall ill from the plague. Thus Yahweh punishes them for their excessive craving.

In Chapter 12 Miriam and Aaron, Moses' sister and brother, speak against his Cushite wife and hence, in effect, attack Moses' position of leadership. As a result Miriam is struck with leprosy; she is cured after seven days of "excommunication."

In Chapter 13 twelve spies are chosen to be sent out to reconnoiter the land of Canaan. They find the land rich and bring back a bunch of grapes to demonstrate its fertility, but they also are disheartened by the impressive fortifications and the strength of the inhabitants. Despite the encouragement of Caleb and Joshua who believe a successful invasion is possible, most of the spies are negative. Chapter 14 describes the fearful reaction of the people, the anger of Yahweh in response to their lack of faith, and Moses' intercession for the people. Yahweh responds by saying that only Caleb and Joshua will finally enter the Promised Land. Because of their infidelity the rest will die in the wilderness. Only after 40 years will their children enter the land of hope. When the people take matters into their own hands and attack they are defeated by the Amalekites and Canaanites.

In Chapter 15 we turn suddenly from narrative to ordinances. Ch. 15:1-16 contains regulations concerning cereal offerings while 15:17-21 pertains to course meal offerings. Ch. 15:22-31 concerns the making of atonement for sins unwittingly committed. Atonement, both in Numbers and in Leviticus, is available only for unpremeditated sins. Only guilt which results from ignorance or error can be "covered over." The man who consciously acts against the commandments of Yahweh is liable to punishment. The chapter ends with a story which sets the precedent of death by stoning as punishment for the breaking of Sabbath law (15:32-36) and with an ordinance commanding that Israelites wear tassels on their garments as a reminder of God's commands.

Chapter 16 contains an account of still another rebellion against Moses and Aaron, this time by Korah, a Levite, and Dathan, Abiram, and On of the tribe of Reuben. Their complaint seems to be based upon a belief in "the priesthood of all believers." They argue both that Moses has gone too far in setting apart the priesthood when all Israel is holy and that he has become far too pretentious in claiming the role of "prince" for himself. The sympathy of the reader may well be with the rebels, but the sympathy of Yahweh is not. He causes the ground to open and the rebels are simply swallowed up and taken alive into Sheol, that shadowy pit where departed spirits go. When the people murmur against this seemingly inhumane act, Yahweh sends a plague and 14,000 of them are destroyed. Chapter 17 gives further evidence of Aaron's preeminence when Aaron's rod not only buds but bears ripe almonds.

Clearly, this whole section, which seems so very barbaric today, is meant to communicate a message to the reader. The sons of Aaron may sometimes be sinful, but their office has been ordained by God and ought not to be questioned. Those who wish to rebel against the religious authorities ought to remember the fate of Korah, Dathan, and Abiram. Happily this is not the only attitude toward the priesthood represented in Scripture, for many of the prophets, in particular, were highly critical of the priests, if not of the priestly office.

With Chapters 18 and 19 we return to a code of laws once more. Chapter 18 describes the proper relation between the sons of Aaron and the Levites and prescribes, in particular, the duties of the latter. Chapter 19 contains, first of all, a curious passage describing the sacrifice of a red heifer whose ashes are to be used in the preparation of "the water for impurity (19:1-10). Ch. 19:11-20 then describes how this water is to be used in the purification of uncleanness.

In Chapter 20 we return to the narrative once more. Israel is now encamped at Kadesh, where apparently she stayed for a long time. There Miriam dies (20:1) and Moses again strikes a rock and brings forth water. For some reason, Moses and Aaron are accused of sin in connection with the latter incident, though what they did wrong is really not made clear. In any event, because of it they are to be excluded from entrance into the Promised Land (20:10-13).

Although the text certainly gives no indication that forty years have elapsed since the return of the spies in Chapters 13-14, Moses now prepares to enter the land from the east rather than from the south, by asking for passage through Edom along the King's Highway. When Edom refuses, Israel is forced to take a more circuitous route through the desert. Near Mount Hor, on the border of Edom, Aaron dies and is succeeded as high priest by his son Eleazar (21:22-29).

Chapter 21:1-3 contains an account of Israel's defeat of the king of Arad. This story seems to be misplaced, for Arad was hardly on the route around Edom which Israel is said to have been taking. As a matter of fact, the site now identified by archaeologists as Arad was not even inhabited at this time. Ch. 21:4-9 contains an equally puzzling story of Yahweh's sending of seraphim serpents (RSV: fiery serpents) to punish the people for their griping. Moses makes a bronze serpent and sets it upon a pole and this cures the people. Perhaps this story is told to explain the presence of the bronze serpent (seraph) in the Temple (Cf. II Kings 18:4), though it may be based upon some ancient tradition. In any event, the legend traces the introduction of Canaanite serpent veneration into Israel's cult back to Moses himself!

Chapter 21:10-20 reviews briefly the course Israel took through the wilderness and includes very ancient poems taken from "the Book of the Wars of Yahweh." Ch. 21:21-30 tells of Israel's victory over Sihon, the king of the Amorites, while 21:31-35 describes their defeat of Og of Bashan. With these battles conquest of the Promised Land, in effect, begins. The conquest of the major area west of the Jordan, however, is not described until the book of Joshua.

Israel in Moab

CHAPTERS 22-24 tell the very interesting story of Balaam, a diviner who is brought by Balak of Moab to curse Israel. Although embellished by legendary accretions, the story is very ancient, for it reflects quite accurately how an eastern diviner did his work during this era. Balaam, at first, refuses to perform the divination required, but then goes, warning that he cannot guarantee what God will do. The result is that, though Balaam performs his rite meticulously, Israel is blessed and not cursed. Four times the rite is performed and four times the result is blessing and not cursing. Even the pagan diviner must obey the will of Yahweh!

This assertion makes Chapter 25 even more ironic. While the pagan diviner does Yahweh's will, the Israelites engage in fertility rites with the women of Moab and "yoke themselves" with the pagan deity, Baal of Peor. As a result, Moses has all the chiefs of the tribes hanged. Even so, a plague strikes Israel and kills 24,000 people before Phineas, the son of the high priest, kills an Israelite cohabiting with a Midianite woman and by this act of "virtue" ends the affliction.

The rest of Numbers takes place on the plains of Moab. Chapter 26 contains an account of the second census taken by Moses. As in the first census, the numbers seem greatly inflated. Chapter 27 begins with a precedent case which settles the question of inheritance when a man has only female offspring. 27:12-22 describes Moses' choice of Joshua as successor and the rite by which he is invested with his office.

Chapter 28 then provides the laws of the various offerings: the daily burnt offering (28:1-8), the Sabbath offering (9-10), the new moon offering (11-15), the offering for the Feast of Unleavened Bread (16-25), and the first fruits offering (26-31). Chapter 29 continues the discussion with a description of the Feast of Trumpets (29:1-6), the offering for the Day of Atonement (7-11), and the Offerings for the Feast of Tabernacles (12-40).

Chapter 30 includes various laws concerning vows while Chapter 31 describes the supposed extermination of the Midianites. This story is told in order to introduce various laws regarding the laws of *herem* (a war in which the enemy is to be exterminated). Ch. 31:25-54 describes the division of the booty and the offering of various articles to make atonement with Yahweh.

Chapter 32 describes the settlement of the tribes of Reuben, Gad, and half the tribe of Manasseh east of the Jordan, while Chapter 33 recounts briefly the route of Israel from Egypt to the Promised Land. Unfortunately, most of the places mentioned in this list cannot be identified. In 33:50-56 Yahweh commands Israel to attack and drive out the Cannaanites, while 34:1-15 describes what the external boundaries of Israel are to be. In 34:16-29 men who are to be responsible for the division of the land among the tribes of Israel are appointed. Chapter 35 then describes the allotment of certain cities to the Levites and the commandment to set up cities of refuge for those who have committed murder unintentionally. The book ends on a very inconclusive note with some laws regarding the marriage of heiresses. This chapter is directly related to the story of Zelophehad's daughters in 27:1-11.

Conclusion

WHAT is to be made out of this bewildering mass of material? If one separates out the legal material and examines it, one finds a preeminent interest in the cult. In particular, the place of the Levites and their relation to the Aaronic priests is especially emphasized (Chs. 3, 4, 8, 18, and 35:1-8). So too are the various rites and rituals of the cult (Chs. 9, 15, 19, 28, 29), though only occasionally is anything said specifically about the cultic paraphenalia (8:1-4). On the whole, very little is said about what might be called criminal or moral law. In fact, from Numbers alone it would seem impossible to reconstruct the ten commandments or even to determine the basic ethical impulses underlying Israel's faith. In this Numbers stands in marked contrast to the Covenant Code of Exodus 21-23, Deuteronomy, or even to Leviticus. In Numbers there is no emphasis upon Israel's responsibility to love God and only one reference to Yahweh's love for Israel (14:18-19).

In both the legal and the narrative passages Yahweh appears not as much as a loving father or husband as a dreadful power whose wrath is overwhelming. Yahweh leads Israel, but upon the slightest provocation he can turn upon his people and destroy them. Only the rebels argue that Israel is holy to Yahweh. For the authors, the cultic paraphenalia and the priests and Nazirites are holy; Israel is pictured, particularly in Chs. 11-25 as thoroughly sinful. Although in Chapter 25 Israel's sin is described in terms of idolatry, in most passages Israel's chief sin is her unwillingness to trust in and obey God and his servant Moses. In Numbers there seems to be no hint that faith in Yahweh might lead to rebellion against the human authorities.

Although many scholars describe Numbers as, on the whole, quite late, it is difficult to imagine such a work's being produced after the prophets of Israel had done their work. Neither their emphasis upon human justice nor their attack upon primarily cultic religion is to be found here. Not only does the story of Baalam reflect the authentic practices of an early pagan diviner. The picture of Yahweh presented here also seems highly primitive and non-ethical. He is sheer power whose will is to be obeyed. It is Moses and not Yahweh who throughout shows some sympathy for his fellow Israelites and who seeks mercy for them. For these reasons, it would appear that Numbers, though edited in post-exilic times, reflects an early stage in Israel's development.

CHAPTER X

Deuteronomy: Introduction and Analysis

The Contents of Deuteronomy
The Uniqueness of Deuteronomy
Conclusion

HE NAME DEUTERONOMY is derived from the Septuagint and means, literally, "The Second Law." Although, because the book purports to contain the words of a second covenant which Moses made with Israel (29:1), there is some justification for this title, this is surely not the second or even the third corpus of legal materials to be found in the Torah. The Hebrew title *Eleh Ha'devarim*, "These are the words (of Moses)" is far more descriptive for it points to the book's most distinctive feature, i.e., the fact that the words of this book are directed from Moses to the people rather than from Yahweh to Moses and the people. It is, in effect, a long "Farewell Speech."

The Contents of Deuteronomy

The Contents of the book can be summarized briefly as follows:

I. The first speech of Moses (1:1-4:43)

THIS FIRST SPEECH, which shows obvious acquaintance with the historical traditions contained in the book of Numbers, calls upon Israel to remember what has happened to her in the "recent" past. Israel is now on the plains of Moab, ready to enter the Promised Land. She is reminded of how Moses organized the people (cf. Ex. 18), how Israel was disobedient at Kadesh-barnea, and how, after being commanded not to attack either the Edomites or the Ammonites, she finally won victories over Sihon and Og, the Amorite kings. After the distribution of the land east of the Jordan to the Reubenites and the Gadites, Moses is forbidden to enter the Promised Land himself. It is significant that in Deuteronomy it is because of Israel's sin and not his own that Moses is refused entry (4:21-22). In a sense, Moses is conceived as vicarious sufferer who bears upon his own shoulders the sins of the people. In 4:1-4 Israel's sin of idolatry at Baal-Peor is seen as paradigmatic. Israel is thoroughly warned not to worship foreign gods again. Then Moses reminds Israel of her special relation to Yahweh (4:32-40). In this extraordinary passage, the author expresses belief in the gods worshipped by other peoples as real powers subservient to Yahweh. What makes Israel distinct as a people is the fact that she alone is directly related to Yahweh himself. The section ends with Moses setting apart three cities east of the Jordan as cities of refuge.

II. The second speech of Moses (4:44-11:32)

AFTER a brief introduction in 4:44-49 Moses proceeds to set forth the basic commandments (The Decalogue) and undergirding attitudes which ought to dominate Israel's covenantal relation with Yahweh. In a highly hortatory style he calls upon Israel to remember Yahweh's many acts of *chesed* (steadfast love) and to respond to his covenant with total love (*ahavah*). Above all things, Israel is commanded to avoid idolatry and to fight against idolaters. Her own past sins are reviewed and she is exhorted in the future to remain faithful and to teach Yahweh's commandments to the succeeding generation.

III. The statutes and ordinances of the covenant (12:1-26:19)

THIS SECTION contains a rather disorganized collection of laws of various kinds. Perhaps the most important ordinance, from the point of view of the author, is placed first. In Ch. 12 Israel is commanded to sacrifice at only one central shrine where Yahweh will cause his name to dwell. This commandment was to have profound effects in Judah in the seventh century. Chapter 13 contains warnings and laws about false prophets and idolaters, while Chapter 14 gives basic rules about clean and unclean animals and about the tithe of seed.

Chapter 15 gives laws regarding slaves and the sacrifice of firstling male animals. Ch. 16:1-17 sets forth the basic rules regarding festivals. Ch. 16:18-20 deals with the structure of civil government, including the kingship, while 18:1-22 concerns Levites and prophets. Chapter 19 sets forth basic criminal laws and Chapter 20, laws of war. Ch. 21:1-25:19 contains a whole host of ordinances loosely put together without much topical structure. This section ends with a description of the ceremony of the offering of the first fruits. Particularly interesting is 26:5-10 which contains a brief, historical confession of faith. Ch. 26:16-19 gives Moses' exhortation to Israel to obey the commandments with all her heart and soul and is, in effect, a sealing of the covenantal bond.

IV. *The Covenantal Renewal Ceremony (27:1-30:20)*

IN THIS SECTION Moses commands Israel to build an altar at Mount Ebal (near Shechem) and to celebrate the rite of blessing and cursing which is then given in the text. (At least the 12 curses to be uttered by the Levites on Mount Ebal are included (27:15-26), though no parallel blessings are offered.) Chapter 28 gives, in prose form, the blessings of obedience and the curses of disobedience. Chapter 29 contains an exhortation to keep the covenant and prescribes the punishment which will follow upon infidelity. In Chapter 30 Israel is promised forgiveness if she repents after her punishment. Ch. 30:11-20 includes Moses' final exhortation and word of warning. Israel is called to choose between life and death and is reminded that what is demanded of her is not impossible. She can do it if only she will!

V. *The last days of Moses (31:1-34:12)*

MOSES prepares for death by first of all appointing Joshua as his successor (31:1-6). In 31:9-13 Moses writes the words of the Law (presumably the code contained in this book) and commands the Levites to gather the people every seven years for a covenant renewal ceremony. In 31:14-23 Yahweh speaks to Moses and Joshua, but the speech has become garbled by an editor who wished to introduce the Song of Moses at this point. Somehow it is never quite clear whether Moses is writing the Law or the Song which is to follow. In 32:1-42 the Song of Moses is given to Israel to be remembered and sung. Then, after Yahweh announces to Moses that his death is at hand Moses again breaks into poetry, this time offering blessings to each of the tribes (33:1-29). Finally in Chapter 39 Moses goes to the top of Mount Nebo (or is it Pisgah?), views the land which his people are about to enter, and dies. After 30 days of mourning for the greatest prophet of all, Israel is united under the banner of Joshua son of Nun. The conquest of the land is at hand.

The Uniqueness of Deuteronomy

Any thoughtful reader who is at all acquainted with the other books of the Pentateuch soon recognizes that in Deuteronomy we have a work which differs both in style and in thought-form from the rest of the Torah. In the first place, since it purports to contain Moses' last words to the people of Israel, it is written in the first, rather than the third person. Just why the first person used is sometimes singular and sometimes plural is an unresolved question. In any event, a hortatory tone is in evidence throughout much of the work as Moses calls Israel to hear, remember, love, and obey.

Second, there are a number of characteristic phrases (such as "the place Yahweh will choose," "to cause his name to dwell there," "the commands of God which I command you," "With your whole heart and your whole soul," "A land flowing with milk and honey," etc.) which mark the Deuteronomic style as distinctive. Only the most insensitive reader could imagine this work to be by the same author as Leviticus or Numbers.

Third, Deuteronomy is dominated by a distinctive theology which, through not wholly out of accord with the rest of the Torah, surely entails some new emphases. Throughout the work Moses explicitly calls Israel to remember what God has done in the past and to respond to that remembrance with grateful thanksgiving. Such remembrance is seen to provide the undergirding *raison d'etre* for obedience. More than any other part of the Torah, Deuteronomy also stresses Israel's obligation to love God. Righteousness is seen, not simply as conformity to certain legal norms, but as the love of God with the whole self. Yahweh's attitude toward Israel is also understood as characterized primarily by steadfast love (*chesed*). Nothing, however, is said about man's obligation to love his neighbor, though the love of God does imply justice and sympathy for one's fellow men.

Among the most distinctive features of Deuteronomy's message is the demand (found especially in Chapter 12) that Israel offer sacrifices only in the one place where Yahweh will make his name to dwell. Although other parts of the Torah emphasize the Tabernacle and/or the Tent of Meeting there seems to be no clear requirement elsewhere that all sacrifices must be made at one central shrine. In fact, Exodus 20:24 would seem to imply quite the reverse. Deuteronomy, on the other hand, explicitly calls for the destruction of all outlying shrines and reshapes the sacrificial law so that only one shrine need be used.

It is this emphasis, in particular, which has led scholars to identify Deuteronomy as the scroll of law found in the Temple during the reign of King Josiah in the seventh century. According to II Kings 22-23 this scroll led Josiah to initiate a reform of the religion of Judah which, in particular, involved the destruction of all places of sacrifice except the Tmple in Jerusalem. Since only Deuteronomy, of all the books of the Torah, calls for such a reform and since it is inconceivable that such an important book of the law would have been lost after Josiah's time, it is likely that the identification of Deuteronomy as the discovered scroll is correct. The fact that Deuteronomy often reflects both the language and the thought of the eighth century prophets helps to confirm this identification.

This does not mean, however, that when one has said that Deuteronomy was found in the seventh century all problems of composition and dating have been solved. On the contrary, it means that the work of the critical scholar has just begun. In the first place, it seems reasonably clear that the law book found in the Temple may well have been supplemented and edited after the time of Josiah. Deuteronomy, for instance, really has two "introductions" and most scholars agree that 1:1-4:43 may well have been added after Josiah's time. The Song of Moses (Ch. 32), although written in a somewhat archaic style, reveals many similarities to the literature of the exile and probably was added by a later editor. Chapter 31, which, in part, introduces the Song is quite confusing and shows signs of clumsy editing. The Blessings of Moses (Ch. 33) appear to be much older and, though probably not as ancient as the last words of Jacob (Gen. 49), may well have been first composed during the period of the judges. Like "The Song of Moses," this set of blessings was probably added to Deuteronomy by an editor who wished to find a place for this ancient poem in the text of the Torah.

One can conclude, then, that Josiah's scroll of law was somewhat shorter than the present book of Deuteronomy and may well be generally equated with Deuteronomy 4:44-30:20. Doubtless later additions are to be found within this corpus too, but the basic shape of the scroll is still intact. Chs. 4:44-11:32 constitute an extensive prologue to the legal corpus itself. In this prologue Moses reiterates, in slightly different words, the Decalogue of Exodus 20 and then proceeds to interpret the essential meaning of God's covenant with Israel. It is here that special emphasis is placed upon God's love for Israel and Israel's love for God. Idolatry is severely attacked and Israel is called upon to remember God's mercies in the past and to forsake her own penchant for sin. The whole section is highly hortatory in nature and may well be based upon Levitical preaching and teaching in the eighth and/or seventh centuries.

Chapters 12:1-26:19 contain the central corpus of Deuteronomic law which is extensive and wide-ranging. Although many of the ordinances found in this section find no parallel elsewhere in the Torah, it is striking how much the Deuteronomist draws upon other Law Codes. Scholars have noted in particular the many parallels between Deuteronomy and the Covenant Code of Exodus 20-23. In fact, about one half of the ordinances of the Covenant Code are found in some variant form in Deuteronomy. The nature of the variation is, however, significant. The author of Deuteronomy clearly attempts throughout to bring the Covenant Code up-to-date and to reinterpret its provisions according to present circumstances, as a comparison of, for instance, Ex. 23:10f and Deut. 15:1ff shows.

Deuteronomy also reveals many legal affinities with Leviticus. Not only does it include a parallel version of Leviticus' laws concerning clean and unclean animals (Cf. Deut. 14:3-20; Leviticus 11:2-45); many other similarities are to be found as well. Although it may be that Leviticus is the later Code, Deuteronomy 24:8 seems to indicate the prior existence of laws concerning leprosy similar to those found in Leviticus 13-14. An analysis of the various parallels between Deuteronomy and Leviticus indicates that Leviticus (and this includes 17-26 as well as most of the rest of the book) is probably the earlier law.

Numbers is also alluded to many times in Deuteronomy. Certainly 1:1-4:43 reveals good knowledge of the narrative portions of Numbers and, in fact, appears to be an attempt to clear up certain historical difficulties engendered by the fourth book of the Torah. The legal sections of Numbers are less frequently called to mind though Deuteronomy sometimes presupposes the responsibilities of the Levites set forth in Numbers. On the whole, however, it is difficult to determine whether the Deuteronomic Code or the legal material in Numbers is earlier. The opinion of this writer is that Numbers largely precedes Deuteronomy, though any assertion concerning this matter is highly speculative.

At any rate, Deuteronomy seems to be an attempt to draw together and modernize the legal traditions of Israel for the author's own time. Not that the author meant that this Code should totally replace earlier legal *corpi*. On the contrary, in many places the existence and general authority of older codes is presupposed. The author, however, did see the necessity to revise certain ancient laws and to introduce other ones to meet the exigencies of his own day. Of particular importance, as has already been said, is Deuteronomy's emphasis upon one central sacrificial shrine for all of Israel. The elimination of all the other sacrificial altars, of course, meant, in fact, a rather radical revision of the whole cult. Leviticus' requirement that all killed animals must be offered in sacrifice (Lev. 17:1-7) could no longer be enforced and hence is abolished (Deut. 12:15). The number of yearly festivals had to be reduced, for Israelites could not be expected to travel to the central shrine so many times a year. Hence Deuteronomy reverts to the three Mosaic feasts established in the Covenant Code (Ex. 23:14-17), thus eliminating the festivals of the new moon, the feast of trumpets, and the Day of Atonement mentioned in Numbers 28:11-29:40. In accordance with the attack of the prophets upon Israel's solemn assemblies, Deuteronomy emphasizes the joy and gladness of the three feasts (Deut. 16:1-16). The destruction of the outlying shrines also, of course, put many Levites out of work. Deuteronomy reflects this situation by urging that Israelites be generous to the Levites "who sojourn among you" and by allowing the Levites the right to minister whenever they like in the central shrine (18:6-8).

Throughout Deuteronomy the Levites and the Levitical priests are spoken of many times, but the sons of Aaron are not mentioned at all. Eleazar's succession to Aaron is described (10:6), but no special emphasis is placed upon it. Some scholars have argued that when the Deuteronomist speaks of the Levitical priests (in contrast to the Levites), he really means the sons of Aaron, but there is no clear evidence that this is the case. In any event, it is strange that a Code of Law which places such emphasis upon one shrine says nothing much about the priests who are actually to do the sacrificing there. Furthermore, neither the tabernacle nor the tent of meeting plays an important part in Deuteronomy. The book has really nothing to say about how the cultic shrine ought to be constructed nor about the paraphernalia of it. Neither the lamps, nor the lampstands, nor the laver of bronze, nor the table, nor the Bread of Presence is mentioned. The ark is spoken of in Chapters 10 and 31, but only to indicate that the contents of the ark are to be the law.

It is usually assumed that when Deuteronomy speaks of "the place where Yahweh will cause his name to dwell" it refers to the Temple in Jerusalem. Certainly Josiah must have taken it this way. The only reference to an exact location, however, is found in Chapter 27 where Yahweh specifically commands the people to build an altar on Mount Ebal. The inclusion of this whole passage concerning the blessings and cursing on Mount Gerizim and Mount Ebal seeems very strange, coming from the Deuteronomist's mouth. Why would an author who wanted to emphasize the centrality of Jerusalem have included this tradition from the north? Perhaps the truth is that Deuteronomy did not originate in Judah at all but was an attempt by eighth century Northerners to reform religion by denying the preeminence of both Jerusalem and Bethel in favor of the ancient shrine of Shechem. By the eighth century Shechem was in ruins and, because of its political impotence, could have been proposed as the correct center for cultic worship. If this was the author's intention, the suggestion was not followed. The scroll found its way to Jerusalem and there was used to bolster the preeminence of Solomon's Temple.

Deuteronomy also expresses a number of other distinctive concerns and ideas which must be mentioned. First of all, Deuteronomy is concerned about the false prophets who lead the people astray. His criteria for judging between true and false prophets are two: a) Any prophet who urges Israel to worship other gods is, by definition, false and should be executed (13:1-5), and b) a true prophet is one whose words come true (18:22). The criteria aren't very helpful, but the mention of prophets seems to preclude a premonarchic date for the book. In the eighteenth chapter Moses also predicts that a new prophet will come whose authority will be like his own. Of whom does the author speak? Of some eighth or seventh century prophet? Of the Deuteronomist himself? or some Law-giver of the future? Ch. 18:18-19 is very reminiscent of the call of Jeremiah (Jer. 1:4-10), but it is more likely that Jeremiah's call was based upon this passage rather than vice versa. In any event, this passage is unique in that is portrays "He who comes" as a prophet and lawgiver rather than as a Son of David.

A second emphasis of Deuteronomy concerns the ordering of civil government and the administration of justice. In 16:18-20 a system of judges and officials is proposed for every town, and the importance of true justice is particularly underlined. Ch. 17:8-13 concerns the setting up of a court of appeals which is to be in the hands of the Levitical priests and a judge. Ch. 17:14-20 continues the discussion of civil government by, for the first and only time in the Torah, mentioning explicitly the kingship. The Kingship, says Deuteronomy, is legitimate, but the king must be an Israelite and ought to act righteously in accordance with the Law. Of particular interest is the fact that the sins of the king which are criticized are precisely those attributed to Solomon in I Kings 10:26-11:7. Again, this may be a clue that the author speaks from a Northern point of view, for it was Solomon's excesses which forced Israel, the northern kingdom, into rebellion.

Not only is Deuteronomy concerned about the structure of civil government. The book also provides a number of "decisions" concerning criminal and civil law. Chapter 19, for instance, includes provisions concerning accidental murder, intentional murder, and the removing of landmarks as well as basic ordinances regarding the importance and examination of witnesses. Ch. 22:13-30 gives a number of ordinances concerning sexual relationships. Ch. 24:1-4 contains the only legislation regarding divorce to be found in the Torah.

Another rather surprising emphasis is to be found in 20:1-20, 23:9-14, and 24:5, 17-19. All these passages give various rules and admonitions concerning warfare. These are complemented by the martial pronouncements found in 7:16-26, 9:1-6, and 31:3-8. This emphasis upon war and how it should be conducted seems strange if the Deuteronomic Code came into existence during the era just preceding Josiah, for at that time Judah was, for all intents and purposes, part of the Assyrian Empire and had little military power of her own. To be sure, during the reign of Josiah Judah did regain some military strength, but that development came after, not before Josiah's reforms. It would seem, then, that either these passages were added to the book of law after Josiah had begun to prosper militarily or they were written during the eighth century when Israel and Judah were still independent political entities. In either case, these "War" passages hearken back to Israel's ancient military heritage and may, in fact, preserve old traditions almost completely lost in the other books of law.

Conclusion

WHAT then can we conclude from all this? It would appear that like all the other books of the Torah, Deuteronomy had a long history of its own, for within its pages are to be found some very ancient recollections and ordinances as well as some comparatively late ones. By the time of Josiah these various traditions had been molded into a document whose shape was that of a covenantal renewal ceremony. Chs. 4:44-30:20 are clearly patterned after other, much older covenant agreements which characteristically begin with an historical prelude and exhortation, continue with a set of ordinances, and conclude with a series of blessings and cursings. Into this mold has been poured hortatory sermonic material from eighth century Levites, ordinances from various earlier codes of Law, and some ordinances designed especially for the eighth-seventh centuries.

The process of development did not cease with the discovery of the scroll. Various ordinances were added to the main Code of laws, poetic insertions were made, and the whole book was reedited so that it would fit within the over-all framework of the Torah. During the post-exilic period the final editing was done, and Deuteronomy assumed the form in which we have it today.

Of the importance of Deuteronomy one can hardly say too much, for without this book the Torah and the Judeo-Christian tradition would be much poorer. Throughout her post-exilic history Israel has used the great *Shemah* of Deuteronomy 6:4-5 as the most profound expression of her essential faith. The book's emphasis upon love and remembrance has also been one of the central themes of Jewish life.

The Gospels illustrate over and over again that Jesus not only knew but was greatly influenced by this last book of the Torah, for he repeatedly refers to it as a source of authority. Hence, though modern quibblers may think that the author of the book was a forger who put words in the mouth of Moses, history has proved that this forgery has withstood the test of time. Moses may not have spoken these words attributed to him, but the book as a whole surely expresses very beautifully what many regard as the essence of Judaism.

CHAPTER XI

The Prophets: A General Introduction

HE BOOKS of the prophets (the *Nevi'im*) constitute the second major section of the canon of Israel. There is no clear historical record concerning when these scrolls were accepted by the Israelite community as canonical, but internal evidence points to a date somewhere around 200 B.C. This does not mean, of course, that none of these books was used before this time. On the contrary, canonization implies that the books had already found such wide acceptance that they could be considered authoritative by the community. Until that time, however, the various books were open to revision and we find some passages which were probably added as late as the third century. After 200 B.C. the books were considered "closed" and only very minor modifications in the texts were made.

The books of the prophets are divided into two major sections: the former prophets and the latter prophets. This division is not based particularly upon chronological considerations. In fact, it might be better to label these two sections: the prophetic histories and the prophetic oracles. The first section, which includes the books of Joshua, Judges, I and II Samuel and I and II Kings, contains a more or less continuous history of the people of Israel from the time when they entered the promised land to their defeat at the hands of the Babylonians in 587/6 B.C. Thus it is a continuation of the historical narrative set forth in the books of the Torah. One might entitle the work as a whole "The Rise and Fall of the Israelite nation."

Since these books are historical, one might wonder why they are labelled "prophetic" at all. A number of complementary reasons may be given for including them in this second section of the Tanak. First, these books recount the historical background of the prophetic movement and hence set the stage for the prophetic oracles. Since the prophets themselves consistently "heard" in historical events the word of God and addressed themselves to the crucial events of their own time, this historical background is essential for understanding them. Second, these historical books contain many accounts of various prophets (such as Nathan, Ahijah, Elijah, and Elisha) who were of great importance for the history of the prophetic movement but who left no written oracles for posterity. Without these books we would have no knowledge of the predecessors of Amos, the first of the "written" prophets. Finally, and perhaps most important, these historical books are termed prophetic because they contain a prophetic interpretation of history. In no sense were the authors of the Former Prophets positivistic historians who merely wished to record "the facts." They recount the history of Israel in order to proclaim their prophetic judgment upon the people of Israel. Their intent is to show how God fulfilled his promises to Israel but how Israel, in turn, failed to live according to the covenant and hence was punished. Joshua proclaims triumphantly that God gave Israel victory over the Canaanites and hence kept his promise that Israel should inhabit the land flowing with milk and honey. Judges, however, depicts how Israel repeatedly strayed from faith in Yahweh and only through God's grace was saved from sheer disaster. Samuel recounts the story of the origin of the kingship and traces David's triumphant victory over his enemies. Kings goes on to show that this triumph was only momentary and that one king after another refused obedience to God and hence led the people down the road to final and complete destruction. Although the form is different, the message is the same as that of the latter prophets. Israel has sinned; therefore she has been punished by God.

Although there are many disputed questions concerning the authorship of these books, it is clear that they depend, in part, upon rather ancient traditions. Both archaeological discoveries and internal evidence show that many features are quite authentic. It is equally clear, however, that all of these works received their final editing by "Deuteronomic" editors during the exilic period. This is not to say, however, that these last editors composed all the books. Although Kings was certainly written during this time, it is likely that Joshua, Judges, and much of Samuel were already in existence before the exile. The exilic editors added some comments of their own to these books and brought them together to form one coherent history, but were certainly not responsible for their basic shape. Both Joshua and Judges reveal that they came from the northern kingdom and hence must have come into existence some time before 721 B.C. Samuel is somewhat later, but also must have been extant long before the fall of the northern kingdom. The precise dating of these books, however, is a complicated issue which need not concern the nonspecialist unduly.

The oracles of the prophets are contained in four scrolls: Isaiah, Jeremiah, Ezekiel, and the Twelve Minor Prophets. Each prophetic book (with the exception of Jonah) is based upon the oracles of a particular man who addressed his message to his own particular age. One should not think of the prophets, however, as authors who wrote books. On the contrary, few, if any of these men wrote down their messages. Some of them may well have been illiterate. Rather these were preachers who delivered fairly short oracles or what might be called "protest songs" for specific occasions. These oracles were in poetry and were committed to memory by some of their hearers. In some cases, such as Jeremiah, a scribe was employed to write down the messages as delivered. In other cases, the oracles must have existed for some time only in oral form before they were committed to writing. Hence the composition of the books of the latter prophets parallels to a certain extent the composition of the Torah. The oracles of a prophet were preserved by a "school of prophets" who remembered, repeated, and sometimes added significantly to them. Thus, although each book bears a particular prophet's name, the final product is the result of perhaps several generations of prophetic followers.

Sometimes it is relatively easy to distinguish between the original oracles and later additions. A sudden shift from poetry (the usual vehicle for prophetic messages) to prose is often a sign that a follower has added a comment or elaboration. Sometimes the message changes so dramatically or events referred to are so long after the original prophetic message that it is obvious that a new voice is speaking. This is particularly the case in the book of Isaiah which is by at least two different prophets who were separated in time by almost two centuries. In any event, although an individual invariably initiated a particular prophetic tradition, it is clear that the books of the prophets are the products of prophetic schools which themselves had a long and important existence.

Therefore, it is difficult to order the prophetic books chronologically. Isaiah of Jerusalem certainly preceded Jeremiah, but there are many passages in his book which were not composed until long after Jeremiah's death. Occasionally, also, a later prophetic book may incorporate a section from an earlier period. Still, it is fruitful to try to date at least the original prophets around whom later traditions clustered. Four prophets can certainly be dated in the eighth century B.C.: Amos, Hosea, Micah, and Isaiah of Jerusalem. The seventh century saw four more: Habakkuk, Zephaniah, Nahum, and Jeremiah. Obadiah, Ezekiel, and probably Joel, can all be dated in the sixth century during the exile, while Haggai, Zechariah, Malachi, and probably Jonah are from the post-exilic period. In this volume these books are treated in their canonical order. The reader, however, may wish to study them chronologically and hence ought to begin, not with Isaiah but with Amos.

The writings of the prophets differ decisively in both form and content; yet nearly all of them contain, in one way or another, the same essential arguments. In fact, the message of most of the prophets can be reduced to two basic syllogisms. First, the negative one: God has warned that he will punish Israel when she is unfaithful. Israel has been unfaithful. Hence God will punish Israel. This is the argument which dominates the prophets of the eighth and seventh centuries, but it is seldom unaccompanied by the positive syllogism: God has promised that Israel will be blessed; God keeps his promises. Hence Israel can hope for the future; she will be blessed. In these two arguments, one finds the heart of the prophetic paradox. Israel will meet disaster; yet there is still hope. God may abandon his people, but the alienation is not forever. Nearly all of the prophets seek to keep both of these truths in focus. There are, of course, some exceptions to this rule. Amos has little to say about Israel's hope, though later followers sought to balance his message by adding a final chapter depicting in brighter terms Israel's future. Nahum says little about either argument, for his oracle is simply an exultation over the fall of Assyria. Jonah breaks with the prophetic mold completely for the book is not a prophetic oracle at all but a short story which makes a prophetic point. Still, for most of the prophets this basic format applies. What is particularly interesting is not that each prophet speaks of both doom and hope, but how each describes the details of Israel's future.

As one proceeds from the eighth century prophets toward the final destruction of the kingdom of Judah in 586 one senses a rising mood of pessimism concerning the possibility for repentance and renewal on the part of the people. At the same time, there is a striking development and elaboration of Israel's hope for the future. Israel's day of glory and fulfillment is pushed further into the future, but it is also magnified until it is conceived of as a thoroughly eschatological breaking in of God's power to a thoroughly corrupt world.

CHAPTER XII

Joshua: Introduction and Analysis

The Entering of the Promised Land
The Conquest of the Land
The Division of the land and the affirmation of the Covenant

HE BOOK of Joshua, which records Israel's victorious conquest of the promised land, completes, in a sense, the narrative of the Torah, for it provides the denouement toward which the preceding books point. For this reason, some scholars speak of the Hexateuch rather than of the Pentateuch and try to show that the various sources for the books of Moses are also in evidence in this work. There is no need to engage in an elaborate literary analysis at this juncture to prove or disprove the point. To be sure, Joshua does continue and, in a sense, complete the early history of Israel, but it also serves equally well as an introduction to the new stage in life during which Israel settles and eventually gains control over the promised land. It is the first chapter in a long narrative which leads from conquest to kingship to eventual decline and fall.

Of the several scrolls which relate this story (Joshua, Judges, I and II Samuel, I and II Kings), Joshua is undoubtedly the most optimistic and nationalistic. The invasion and conquest of the land under Moses' successor and shadow, Joshua, is described as lightning fast and thoroughly successful. For the moment, Yahweh sides with his people and brings about an almost miraculous victory against great odds. The great odds, however, are only great from a human point of view. From the vantage point of faith in Yahweh, the Canaanites and other inhabitants never had a chance. In those days, God was the king who led Israel into battle and his armies were invincible.

As it has already been indicated in Chapter Three, the author of Joshua has greatly over-simplified and embellished the history of this period. Archaeological excavations at Lachish, Debir, and Hazor have proved that someone, in all probability the Israelites, did attack and destroy these cities. On top of the burned-over levels of fairly sophisticated Canaanite remains from the thirteenth century, we find the much more primitive artifacts of invading tribes. At the same time, it is equally clear that the description of the conquest of Jericho and Ai are, if not entirely fictitious, at least highly embellished and misplaced historically. We shall return to these stories when the book is analyzed by chapter. All that needs to be asserted here is that though the book of Joshua does contain some accurate historical reminiscences, it also is a radically simplified and telescoped account which serves the "mythological" purposes of the author.

Joshua is, in a sense, a retelling of the creation myth in historical terms. Through the power of his Word God puts down the power of chaos and orders the world according to his will. Like Marduk of the Babylonian *Enuma Elish* who destroys Tiamat, Yahweh now vanquishes the powers of darkness, the Canaanites. The cosmos is then ordered as each tribe receives its parcel of land. The saga comes to an end with a call to Israel to remember God's actions in the past and to live a life worthy of this new creation. The covenant is reaffirmed and all go to inhabit their inheritances. The old generation dies and a new age of hope is born.

The book of Joshua may be very distorted history—surely archaeology has proved it to be such—but it is a very accurate expression of one aspect of Israelite mythology. This is the basic archetypal pattern according to which Israel shapes her hope. This is the way it was at the beginning and this is the way it will be at the end. It is a revelation of primordial time, the time normally hidden from sinful men. In this sense, Joshua is thoroughly prophetic.

There are many who are angered or upset by the Yahweh of Joshua who turns out to be a rather blood-thirsty and highly biased God. Who could worship a God like this? Surely such questioning is justified if the book is read on a purely historical plane. The story, however, is not just history, but is the retelling of a myth and as such functions in much the same capacity as those many movies in which the good cowboys get the bad Indians. In the world we live in, things don't happen quite that way, for there is too much evil in the best of us and too much good in the worst of us to make any human battle a war between good and evil. Still, we watch the late-late show, not because we believe the story is factually accurate, but because we believe, very deeply believe, that this is the way things ought to be. Not now, but perhaps on the last day, the honest cowboy will root the varmints out.

The danger of this myth is, of course, that the believer may fail to distinguish between primordial time and the time in which we live. When this happens, the believer becomes a fanatic who imagines himself as a man with a white hat on horseback who fights only for the good. Certainly Israelites fell prey to this temptation over and over again. Still, without the hope that eventually the good will win the final battle, human life appears as meaningless. If good does not finally win, is there any real distinction between good and evil at all?

Analysis

The Entering of the Promised Land

THE SAGA begins immediately after the death of Moses with Joshua's exhortation to the people to enter the promised land. This introduction is doubtless from the pen of a much later editor, for he refers to "the book of the Law" (1:8) which probably was not extant until long after Joshua. Preparations are made, the tribes who will eventually inhabit the territory east of the Jordan agree to cross over and fight (1:12-18), and spies are sent out.

The spies go to Jericho and meet a certain harlot named Rahab who hides them and keeps them safe. They, in turn, agree that she and her family are to be protected. This story may have been told to explain why one section of the wall of the ruin of Jericho (Rahab's apartment) remained standing while the rest had fallen. Her name may also conceivably have mythological connotations. In the Masoretic text the name is spelled with a hard "h" and means literally "broad." Possibly, however, her name was spelled originally with a soft "h." If so this is the name of the monster against which Yahweh fought in Hebraic mythology (cf. Isaiah 51:9). In Joshua the "monster" (notice that she is a harlot—the very symbol of the Canaanite fertility cult) collaborates with Yahweh, and Israel wins an easy victory. It is her word of acquiescence and that alone which gives the spies great hopes for taking the city.

The spies return and, despite the floods, the Israelites cross the river, which parts before them miraculously. One can explain this event naturalistically, for occasionally land-slides occur which do dam up the Jordan for a short time, but that is to miss the mythological meaning of the story. This is the Red Sea crossing all over again. Joshua is Moses *revivus.* And both events are symbols of birth out of death. This time it is the ark of the covenant which is endowed with miraculous powers. Everyone but the priests must stand back as the ark does its mighty work. Just as on the day of creation, once the dragon of chaos is quelled, the waters are divided so that the creation of earthly life can begin. Twelve stones are taken from the river as a memorial to this mighty act and to the fact that all twelve tribes have been saved. Then the waters close together once more. Word of the miracle reaches the kings of the land and melts their courage to fear.

The Conquest of the Land

THE NEW BIRTH has taken place, so Israel must once more be treated as a new born babe. Israel goes to Gilgal and there is circumcised. In the wilderness, circumcision had not been practiced. Now all the men submit to that ancient rite and wait several days until they are healed. Again this sounds more like myth than history. Why didn't Jericho, which lay but a few miles south, attack while they were in such a vulnerable position? Why would an invading tribe, well aware of the perils of battle ahead, spend the first days of the invasion enduring the rite of circumcision and then celebrating Passover? Surely the whole event is being told to evoke certain mythological patterns.

After the ceremonies of birth are over, Joshua sees a vision of an angel of the Lord which is plainly reminiscent of Moses' call at Horeb (Joshua 5:13-15) and the invasion *per se* begins, as Joshua and his army attack Jericho. Clearly this story, though in an historical setting, is highly mythological. From archaeological excavations at Jericho it is evident that Jericho had been in ruins for at least two hundred years when Israel attacked in the thirteenth century. Even if this is a reminiscence of an earlier invasion by the *'apiru* tribes which attacked the land during the reign of Aknaton (cf. The Tell El Amarna Letters), the story is told for its mythological import rather than its historicity. The attack is hardly a military attack at all but is rather a miraculous creation story. For seven days the armies of Israel march around the walls of Jericho blowing their ram's horns. On the seventh day all the people shout and the walls simply fall flat. Since the ram's horn (the *shophar*) was (and is) connected with the celebration of the New Year and since the motif of the seven days is also clearly related to God's creative act, this is, again, an historicized myth of creation. It may, in fact, be a dramatization of a cultic festival in which the evil powers were attacked ritually through the use of circumambulation, the blowing of ram's horns, and a final shouting to drive them away. If this is so, the myth of the defeat of Jericho may be much older than the historical Joshua and may, in fact, be an attempt to legitimize a myth and rite of pagan origin.

If Chapters 1-6 are an historical retelling of the myth of creation, Chapter 7 is an historical account of the fall into sin. Achan (whose name probably means "troubling") tries to keep for himself some of the plunder from Jericho, and Israel therefore suffers defeat at the hands of the city of Ai. The sin, however, is revealed by lot and is rooted out. The purity of creation is thus, momentarily, preserved.

Having made his "mythological" point the author can now turn to a slightly more historical account of the conquest. The story of the defeat of Ai, however, is certainly not historically reliable. The name, Ai (or better Ha'Ai), means "the ruin." Archaeologists have confirmed that this city, like Jericho, was already in ruins by the thirteenth century. Probably, in this case, this story originally came from pre-Israelite days and is an account of an earlier conquest which was later incorporated into the tradition. The emphasis upon the smoke rising from the city (8:20) could conceivably symbolize the sacrifice performed after the beginning of the New Year, but that may be pressing the mythological interpretation too far.

After the conquest of Ai through the typical ploy of drawing the forces of the city into an ambush (cf. Judges 20:29-48), there is a very strange passage describing the building of an altar on Mount Ebal and the performing of a rite of blessing and cursing before Mount Ebal and Mount Gerizim. It is strange because there is no preceding account of the conquest of the ancient city of Shechem which lay between these mountains. Many scholars argue that this indicates that the conquest did not take place all at once and that some Israelites (or sympathetic tribes) were already living in and around Shechem when Joshua arrived. This may be the case. It could also be, however, that this mythological introduction properly concludes with the traditional rite of blessing and cursing on these mountains and that the author therefore mentions it without regard to the historical difficulties it entails. Just as the passover event ended at Mount Sinai, so the new passover ends at the holy mountains of the northern kingdom. It is even possible, though by no means proved, that in the Northern Kingdom the New Year began with the celebration of Passover at Gilgal and then with liturgical rites at the ruins of Jericho and Ai. The whole pilgrimage might have been concluded with the ceremony of blessing and cursing at Gerizim and Ebal. Since, among other things, it is clearly indicated that the offender, Achan, was from Judah, a southern tribe, (7:1), there seems to be a good reason to think this first section of Joshua came from a northern author.

The conquest of southern Palestine takes place, not by design, but in response to the attack of the southern Amorite kings. Chapter 9 tells of how the people of Gibeon cleverly tricked Joshua into protecting rather than annihilating them. They are made "hewers of wood and drawers of water" (9:21), but when the southern kings attack them, Joshua is compelled to go to their aid. As a consequence he defeats the kings of Jerusalem, Hebron, Jarmuth, Lachish, and Eglon and subdues the land before him.

Chapter 11 then recounts Joshua's victory over the city-states of the north (including Hazor), while Chapter 12 lists all of the kings, both east and west of the Jordan who were defeated by him. The list claims, in effect, that Joshua conquered the land once and for all, and that it was therefore available to be divided among the tribes. As the Book of Judges clearly indicates, however, such was not the case. In fact, most of the major cities remained unconquered; Israel settled primarily in the hill country, not in the plains.

The Division of the land and the affirmation of the Covenant

THE HISTORICAL "myth of creation" found in Joshua now continues in Chapters 13-21 with the final ordering of the world, i.e., with the division of the land among the tribes. There is no need to review this account in any detail, for nearly any Biblical Atlas will give a map of the land as apportioned to each tribe. It might be noted that the tribe lists are somewhat older than the city lists found in these chapters. With the apportionment of the land, Israel is finally reconciled with the land and one of the basic promises of God to Abraham is fulfilled.

The whole book concludes with the farewell addresses of Joshua and with a covenant renewal ceremony. Joshua speaks first to the two and a half tribes who are to inhabit the eastern side of the Jordan. They are sent home, but later rebuked because they set up a cultic center of their own at which to offer sacrifices. The unity of Israel, it is emphasized, is to be found in the common worship of God at one central shrine. Although Shiloh is mentioned here (22:12) it is apparent from 24:1 that the cultic center is really still at Shechem, for it is to this place that Joshua summons all the tribes for a covenant-renewal ceremony. Joshua reviews the holy history of the people (24:2-12) and then calls the people to put away all foreign gods. As at Sinai they are given a choice of serving Yahweh or the other gods. They choose Yahweh, and Joshua warns them that such a choice involves important responsibility (24:19-20). Again the people reiterate their faith and enter into covenant with Yahweh and Joshua. Like Moses, Joshua then makes statutes and ordinances and writes these words in the book of the law of God. (24:26) A *massebah* (a memorial stone) is set up and the rite is concluded. With this event the new age is finally begun. It is appropriate, therefore, that the bones of those from the old age are laid to rest. Joshua dies and is buried at Timnathserah; Joseph's bones are interred at Shechem; and Eleazar, the high-priest, is buried at Gibeah. All of these sites are said to be in the north-central region, another sign that this is a book from Ephraim, not Judah.

Conclusion

THROUGHOUT this discussion, the mythological rather than the historical aspects of the book of Joshua have been emphasized. It should not be inferred from this that the historical aspects are worthless or unimportant. Doubtless, the book does contain many accurate historical reminiscences and traditions. Clearly, however, the author uses the historical facts for his own purposes. If we knew more about the rites, rituals, and myths of the people in vogue at the time of writing, it is almost certain that the mythological aspects of the story and their connection with the cult would stand out much more clearly. Until such time as this information is uncovered, we must remain content with suggestions and hypotheses.

CHAPTER XIII

Judges: Introduction and Analysis

F THE BOOK of Joshua can be considered an historicized version of the myth of creation, Judges can be seen almost equally well as a similar description of the myth of man's fall into sin. When we begin the book of Judges we move abruptly from primordial time when God rules and man responds with faith, to human time with its cycle of guilt, punishment, and salvation. In Judges God still continues to fight for the righteous, but Israel repeatedly fails to serve God with faithfulness. As a result, Israel is subject to defeat at the hands of various enemies and only survives because of God's enduring mercy.

Joshua ends with Israel totally in control of the land and totally committed to Yahweh. Judges immediately belies this ideal situation, for the book opens with the admission that Israel still had to fight against the Canaanites and other dwellers in the land. It also soon indicates that not all of the tribes were very active or very successful in doing this. Furthermore, Chapter 2 underlines the fact that Israel quickly was tempted to forsake the God of the covenant and worshipped instead the Baals and Ashtaroth of the people of the land. Thus begins the cycle of guilt, punishment, and salvation which dominates the major portion of the book.

After apostasy and a period of military defeat, salvation is invariably provided by Yahweh who sends a judge to lead Israel to victory once more. The title "Judges" (*Shophetim*) seems quite strange and inappropriate, for these judges are hardly described as legal interpreters or arbiters at all. Rather, they are charismatic leaders who sense suddenly the call to serve Yahweh by leading the people against their enemy. Many reasons have been given for the use of this term, but the one which seems most natural is this: later Israelites who looked back upon this period before the monarchy knew that Israel's political system, before David, depended upon judges who dispensed judicial verdicts. The reminiscences which they had of the period, however, were of military leaders who raised up Israel to defeat the enemy. Hence, these leaders came to be called judges even though they scarcely served in this capacity. Phrases such as "And he judged Israel twenty-three years" (10:2) are simply used to gloss over this basic inconsistency. The Judges are more accurately called "Champions" or "Heroes" of Israel.

In all there are twelve judges mentioned in the book. One might expect there would be one for each of the twelve tribes of Israel, but such is not the case. Othniel and Ibzan (both minor figures) are from Judah; Jair and Gideon, from Manasseh (the first from the east bank, the second from the west); Deborah and Abdon are Ephraimites; Ehud, from Benjamin; Shamgar, probably from Naphtali; Jephthah, from Gad; Tola, from Issachar; Elon, from Zebulun; and Samson, from Dan. Thus, the tribes of Simeon, Reuben, Asher, and Levi are unrepresented.

Clearly, though the book claims that these leaders judged all of Israel, each was a fairly local figure who led, at best, a few tribes into battle. In no case does all of Israel fight as a unit. In fact, the ancient Song of Deborah (chap. 5) criticizes the tribes of Reuben, Gilead, Dan, and Asher for failing to engage the Canaanites in battle under Deborah and Barak. In most of the other battles even fewer tribes participate. Thus the judges can hardly be considered national leaders at all.

The author and/or editors of the book have arranged the stories of these judges according to a rather artificial chronological system devised to relate these traditions of the judges one to another. There is no evidence, however, that the compilers of these stories ordered them in the proper chronological order or that some of the judges were not contemporaries. What we have in this book are a number of more-or-less authentic traditions about the heroes of pre-royal Israel put together to fill out the period between the Conquest and the kingship and to meet the didactic and mythological purposes of the author.

Clearly one of the main points of the author is that almost from the beginning Israel fell into sin and therefore was subjected to historical punishment by Yahweh at the hands of her enemies. Only when Yahweh raised up a new hero to lead the people was Israel revived once more. As the story proceeds, however, the cycle becomes more and more disastrous for Israel, and the heroes become less and less competent to deal with the situation. The last of the judges, Samson, is simply a great buffoon who kills a few Philistines but who does not lead Israel in battle at all. The story moves, then, from a glorification of the heroes to a call for a new and better way of organizing Israel politically and militarily. That is to say, Judges points forward to the books of Samuel and the rise of the kingship. The book ends with two rather gruesome stories (17:1-18:31 and 19:1-21:25) which illustrate graphically the corrupt condition of religion and justice under the judges. The whole account concludes with the sardonic words.

> "In those days there was no king in Israel; every man did what was right in his own eyes." (Judges 21:25)

Analysis

I. Introduction (1:1-2:5)

THE STORY opens with the events closely following the death of Joshua. Judah wins a major battle at Bezek and then defeats Jerusalem. Subsequently, Judah under Othniel takes Debir while the Kenites settle near Arad at the northern edge of the Negeb. The whole account is filled with apparent contradictions. Judah is said to have conquered Gaza, Askelon, and Ekron, but it is admitted that they could not drive out the inhabitants of the plain (1:19). Judah is said to have conquered Jerusalem, but the Benjaminites did not. Hence the Jebusites continued to reside in that city (1:21). The last half of the chapter explains that many of the tribes (particularly the northern ones) did not drive out the Canaanites but lived among them (1:22-36). Chapter 2:1-5 further explains that the inhabitants of the land were not fully defeated because Israel broke the covenant with Yahweh by making covenants with the Canaanites.

II. A Second Introduction (2:6-3:6)

This appears to be a separate introduction to the book, 1:1-2:5 having been added by a later, Judean hand. It includes an account of the death of Joshua, a description of the apostasy of Israel (2:11-15), and a brief summary of the way Yahweh repeatedly saved her by sending judges (2:16-21). Ch. 3:1-5 lists the nations of inhabitants who were left by God in the land to test Israel. This section spells out the basic "theology" of the book as a whole and therefore is especially significant.

III. The First Four Judges (3:7-5:31)

1. The first oppressor of Israel is named as Cushanrishathaim of Mesopotamia, but historians have been unable to identify this person further. The whole story is suspicious, for it is doubtful that any "oppressor" came from Mesopotamia during this period. Othniel, the brother of Caleb, finally throws off his yoke (3:7-11).
2. Eglon of Moab is the next oppressor. Ehud, a left-handed Benjamite, assassinates him and leads the army of Ephraim to victory against the Moabites. This brief story is deftly and amusingly told (7:12-30).
3. Shamgar is said to have killed six hundred Philistines with an oxgoad, but nothing more appears to have been known about him (7:31).
4. The first major judge who is described at any length is Deborah who, with Barak, wins a major victory over the Canaanites near Megiddo. Particularly important and impressive is the ancient "Song of Deborah" found in Chapter 5. This is doubtless a poem of great antiquity, probably coming into existence shortly after the victory. It is very important, therefore, as a source for understanding the thought and religion of the time.

IV. Gideon and Abimelech (6:1-9:57)

THIS TIME, it is Midian with its camel cavalry which attacks and decimates Israel.. Gideon (Jerubbaal)—notice the pagan name—is called by God and despite local resistance to his destruction of an altar of Baal, leads a hand-picked army to victory over the enemy. The whole account, with its miraculous angel (6:11-24), its use of special signs (6:36-40; 7:9-14), and its extravagant heroism (7:1-8), has all the marks of a folk legend; yet there are also good indications that it is based upon historical events. Chapter 8:1-17 reveals how disunited Israel really was, while 8:22-28 shows to what extent Canaanite religion had penetrated the spirit of Israel. Gideon is offered the kingship, but refuses, arguing that Yahweh alone ought to be regarded as king. Then, however, he makes a typically Canaanite ephod out of gold, and this image becomes very popular among the Israelites.

After the death of Gideon, his son Abimelech talks the Shechemites into making him king of that city. Subsequently he kills all of the other sons of Jerubbaal (Gideon) except Jotham, who from Mount Gerizim employs a "tree fable" in order to criticize and curse his ruthless brother (9:7-21). Abimelech eventually loses the loyalty of the Shechemites and, though he puts down the rebellion of Gaal and destroys Shechem itself with fire, is killed in an attack upon neighboring Thebez. Thus the curse of Jotham is effective.

With Abimelech we find an Israelite assuming the role and the attitudes of a typical Canaanite king. He rules over a relatively small city-state, seems to have no concern for the unity of Israel as a whole, and is destroyed in a typical intra-city-state skirmish. It is interesting that excavations at Shechem have confirmed a few details of the story. In 9:46 it is said that the people of the Tower of Shechem entered the stronghold of the house of El Berith. That temple has now been excavated and has revealed walls of amazing thickness (hence the term "stronghold") as well as an impressive *massebah* outside it. There is also some evidence of the destruction of the city at about this time. This destruction may have led to the moving of the central shrine from Shechem to Shiloh.

V. *Tola, Jair, Jephthah, Ibzan, Elon*

WITH the exception of Jephthah all of these judges are mentioned only briefly in the text and seem to have been of only minor importance.

A. Tola of Issachar is remembered simply as a man who judged Israel in Ephraim for twenty-three years (10:1-2).

B. Jair is noted only for his thirty sons who rode thirty asses and had thirty cities in the area south of the Sea of Galilee (Chinnereth) on the east side of the Jordan (10:3-5).

C. Jephthah's story, however, is told at some length. This time it is the Ammonites who attack the tribes east of the Jordan. Jephthah is the bastard son of Gilead who is thrown out of his father's house by the legitimate sons and who, thereupon, becomes a kind of brigand. Despite his rather disreputable past, the tribes of Gilead call him to lead the army. Jephthah does so, but with the provision that if he defeats the enemy he will become their head.

Jepthah attempts to deal with the Ammonite king peaceably by sending him a letter. In it he outlines Israel's claims to the land and appeals to the verdict of past history. The letter is of particular interest, for Jephthah seems to admit the reality and power of the Ammonite god, Chemosh (11:24). The king of the Ammonites refuses to listen to him, however, so Jephthah, vowing that he will sacrifice to Yahweh the first thing that meets him when he returns victorious, attacks and defeats the Ammonites.

When he returns home, he is met by his only child, a virgin daughter. He is distraught, but will not take back his vow. His daughter is allowed two months to go into the hills with some companion to bewail her virginity, but is finally sacrificed. The story is interesting, for it clearly reflects the adoption of certain pagan customs by Israel. Many Near Eastern peoples celebrated rites during which women bewailed the death of a god of fertility. This story seems to be an historization of this archetypal pagan myth and an attempt to explain why Israel engaged in much the same practice (11:39-40).

The story of Jephthah ends with an account (12:1-7) of his quarrel with the Ephraimites who were annoyed that he did not call them to help him (and to share in the plunder). Through the use of the famous password Shibboleth he is able to distinguish the Ephraimites from the Gileadites and hence, slays 42,000 Ephraimites at the fords. The numbers are undoubtedly greatly exaggerated, but the story clearly reveals something of the linguistic differences among the tribes. Then follow three more minor judges.

D. Ibzan of Bethlehem seems to have been rather wealthy. No exploits of him are mentioned (12:8-10).
E. Elon from Zebulun is even more briefly described (12:11-12).
F. Abdon's only claim to fame is that he had forty sons and thirty grandsons who rode on seventy asses (12:13-15).

VI. Samson

THE STORY of Samson begins quite auspiciously with an account of Samson's birth. Samson's mother, it seems, is barren, but one day is greeted by an angel who tells her that she will now conceive and bear a son who will grow up to be a Nazirite (cf. Numbers 6:1-21). Manoah, his father, prays that the angel will return to tell them more specifically how to raise the boy. The angel returns but says little more than before. The mother is to drink no wine nor eat anything unclean, that's all. Manoah offers the angel food, but the angel suggests a sacrifice. When it is offered, the angel ascends in the flame and disappears. The child is then born, named Samson, and the Spirit of the Lord begins to stir within him.

So far so good. This sounds very much like the story of the birth of Samuel (I Samuel: 1-2) and of Jesus (Luke 1:26-38), and one expects that Samson will grow up to be the greatest and most pious of the judges. Nothing, however, could be further from the case. Instead of doing great and holy acts the young Samson goes down to Timnah and falls in love with a young Philistine wench. His father and mother are a bit upset but acquiesce and arrange for a wedding. On his way to Timnah, Samson kills a lion and then, later, discovers honey in the carcass. At a pre-marital wedding feast, Samson propounds his famous riddle to his thirty Philistine companions. When he is tricked by his wife-to-be, who then reveals the answer to the riddle to his guests, he pays off his bet by killing thirty men of Ashkelon and giving their festal garments to his guests.

Samson returns to his wife, but her father won't let her see him, so he burns the fields of the Philistines who, in turn, burn his wife and her father. The Philistines then try to capture him, but he is seemingly all-powerful and defeats them again and again single-handed. Finally they discover his weak-spot, women, and through Delilah bind him, cut off his hair (the source of his strength), and gouge out his eyes. In the final episode Samson, his hair regrown, pulls down the Temple of Dagon and kills both many Philistines and himself. So dies the last of the great heroes.

Certainly this story contains more than meets the eye. One of the clues to its original meaning is that the saga takes place not far from Beth Shemesh, i.e., from the house of Shamash. Shamash was, of course, a widely worshipped Sun god, and in many respects Samson mirrors his image. In fact, the name *Samson* means *sun*. Just as the sun's strength is contained in the rays that emanate from it like hairs on the head, so Samson's strength lies in his hair. Like Shamash, Samson is all-powerful as long as his locks remain unshorn and uses fire against his enemies (15:4-5, 14, 16:9). He is the symbol of male virility and strength whose weakness (like the weakness of many of the pagan gods) is women. When his locks are shorn and darkness comes (symbolized by blindness), he is momentarily weakened, but the rays return and the power of light vanquishes its enemies.

The story, then, undoubtedly originated as a pagan myth, but was historicized by the Israelites and used against the Philistines. At the same time, the story of Samson clearly reveals the historical weakness of the institution of the judgeship. The tragic-comic figure of Samson argues for a better political and social structure for the nation, i.e., for the kingship.

VII. Micah, the Ephraimite, and His Priest (17:1-18:31)

THE LAST two episodes of the book (17:1-21:25) are often termed appendices, because they do not relate stories of judges. Clearly, however, these are no mere appendages or after-thoughts, for they are the final illustrations to prove the argument of the book. That is, these stories are included to illustrate that Israel during the period of the judges was both religiously and politically corrupt and that the rise of the kingship was absolutely necessary.

The first story (17:1-18:31) is a rather complicated narrative which makes some less-than-subtle points. The story begins in Ephraim with a man named Micah who first of all steals 1100 pieces of silver from his mother and then returns them to her. She, to express her gratitude, dedicates the silver to God and has a molten and graven image made. At first, Micah has one of his own sons serve as priest in the idol's shrine, but later is able to convince a Levite to be the priest of his household.

At just this time the tribe of Dan is being forced out of its territory by the Philistines and moves north to find safer territory. While on the way the tribe stops at Micah's, steals the image and his priest and takes them along. Micah tries in vain to get them back. The clincher of the story is that not only does this pagan idol, forbidden to Israel by the ten commandments, come to be the central idol in the shrine of Dan, one of the two major shrines of the northern kingdom, but that the priest who goes with the Danites and who founds the priesthood of the shrine is none other than the grandson of Moses himself! Such were the depths to which Israel's religion had sunk.

VIII. The Levite, His Concubine, and the Men of Benjamin

THE BOOK of Judges closes with another, equally shocking story of a Levite whose concubine, because of his abuse, leaves him. He goes to her home to persuade her to return. Her father agrees and after many false starts they leave for home rather late in the day. As a consequence, they decide to spend the night at a Benjamite town, Gibeah. Only one man (an Ephraimite) shows them any hospitality and when they are making merry in his house, some base fellows demand that the Levite come out. The Levite refuses, but gives them his concubine whom they rape and then let go. She is found dead on the door-step the next morning. So much for the great hospitality and sense of kinship found among Israelites! So much also for the great esteem in which the priesthood was held!

The Levite then cuts his concubine into twelve pieces and sends a piece to each of the tribes. Soon the whole of Israel has assembled against Benjamin. At first, the Benjamites defend themselves successfully, but eventually are caught in ambush and well-nigh annihilated. The question then is: what will happen to this tribe? They need more wives to reproduce quickly to regain strength, but the other tribes have vowed not to give wives to the Benjamites in marriage. Two solutions are found. First, they remember that the people of Jabesh-gilead did not engage in the battle. The Israelites smite that city, but save the virgins for the living Benjamites. Second, they remember that once a year there is a feast at Shiloh at which the women dance. The Benjamites are allowed to attack the dancers and carry away the virgins they desire. Thus is Benjamin restrengthened! Clearly this last solution reflects certain rites practiced the world over during which women are carried off as a part of the fertility ritual. Again Israel has historicized a myth and given some justification for the Israelite adoption of an essentially pagan practice. Thus, curiously enough, although Judges consistently inveighs against Israel's adoption of pagan customs and declares that this was the source of her woe, the book at the same time, cryptically baptizes several pagan myths and practices into the faith and reveals, in so doing, how powerful a force pagan religion really was in Israel.

One more hidden point ought to be mentioned before passing on to the books of Samuel. The town which showed such poor hospitality to the Levite is Gibeah, the home-town of the future king, Saul. When Saul dies and is hung on the walls of Beth Shan, it is the people of Jabesh-gilead who come to take down and bury the corpse! Hence, although Judges offers a powerful argument for the kingship, the final story clearly is a less-than-complimentary comment about the ancestry of the first king, Saul.

CHAPTER XIV

I and II Samuel: Introduction and Analysis

I. The birth and judgeship of Samuel
II. The reigns of Saul and David

HE TWO BOOKS of Samuel, originally a single work which was divided when translated into Greek, form the third major chapter in the history of Israel stretching from conquest to captivity. Although this narrative is named for the first major figure to appear in its pages, the hero of the whole saga is David, whose trials and triumphs are recorded in some detail. Virtually nothing is known of David from extra-Biblical sources, but through Samuel we learn more about this great king than about almost any other figure in the Bible.

Just when and how Samuel was composed is a matter of great debate among scholars; a full elaboration of the various theories of authorship clearly lies beyond the scope of this work. Certainly, however, the several inconsistencies in the story, together with changes in style, indicate the use of several sources. Whoever wrote the book used a number of divergent traditions which he wove together to create the narrative which now stands. Precisely how this was done and which passage belongs to which source is the subject of the basic scholarly argument. Some argue that the sources of Samuel continue J. and E. of the Torah; others believe it to be a patchwork of relatively short fragments. It seems clear, at any rate, that the basic work was written long before the exilic period. During that time an editor or school of editors under the influence of the book of Deuteronomy edited Samuel along with Joshua, Judges, and Kings, to produce one extensive "Deuteronomic" history. In so doing they introduced a few comments of their own. In Samuel these editorial additions are quite minimal and we can say that basically we have before us the work as it was compiled during the period of the divided monarchy.

Just as Joshua and Judges can be seen as historical versions of the Israelite myths of creation and fall, so the books of Samuel can be understood as an historicization of the myth of election first set forth in the story of Noah. Israel, imperilled by the Philistines, appears to be near extinction as a nation. David, God's elect man, makes order out of the historical chaos, saves Israel from disaster, and for a moment leads Israel to a moment of brilliance. David is Noah and Abraham all over again, for he is the elect one and the recipient of God's promises. So too is he preeminently the prototype of the hope of Israel which is to come. After David's and Solomon's time chaos again began its reign, but Israel believed it would last only for a season. In God's good time, a son of David would arise and once more usher in a golden age. David's story is rehearsed in such detail because, though a sinful man, he is still a type of him who comes.

Although Samuel has mythological import, however, one feels oneself to be on rather firm historical ground in the book. Legends and inconsistencies there are, but the whole story is so honestly told that its main outlines seem undebatable. Probably the compilers of the books relied to a large extent upon well-substantiated traditions and eye-witness accounts. It may well be, in fact, that most of the sources for these books were already in existence during the reign of Solomon. At this point in the history of Israel, the historian can therefore begin to speak of names and dates with some assurance.

Not only are the books of Samuel historically fairly reliable. Stylistically they represent some of the finest historical writing from the ancient world. Indeed, one searches in vain through the writings of Mesopotamia and Egypt for anything like the psychological insight, vivid characterization, and candid honesty of these books. Even Herodotus and Thucydides scarcely measure up to the literary brilliance of this work. From a purely humanistic point of view, these scrolls are worth all the genealogies and law codes and archaisms which one must plow through to get to them.

Analysis

THE BOOKS of Samuel are relatively long and dramatically very involved. In this volume, therefore, only the highlights can be summarized and analyzed. Perhaps this is as it should be, for nothing will replace reading the books for themselves.

I. The birth and judgeship of Samuel

CHAPTER ONE contains an account of the birth of the last of the judges, Samuel, which is very reminiscent of the birth stories of Samson and Jesus. Hannah, his mother, prays for a child and vows to dedicate him to God, probably as a Nazirite. The petition is granted and their son, Samuel, is taken to the cultic shrine at Shiloh and placed under the tutelage of Eli, the priest.

Chapter Two contains Hannah's song of praise to God which is very similar to the Magnificat of Mary in Luke 1:46-56. Unlike Samson, Samuel turns out to be a particularly righteous boy, even though the sons of Eli are very corrupt (2:12-17, 22-25). Ch. 2:27-36 is particularly interesting for it marks the first introduction of a prophet into the story. A man of God comes to call down the judgment of God upon the house of Eli. Shortly thereafter Samuel has a message from God with a similar content. Eli accepts the message with stoic trust (3:18) and Samuel becomes himself a prophet (3:20). As such he is not so much a seer who tells fortunes as one who, through the inspiration of God, sees the historical implications of the actions of sinful men. In Chapter 4 the scene shifts to the conflict between Israel and the Philistines. Israel gets the worse of a battle and decides rather belatedly to seek Yahweh's help. The ark of the covenant is brought into the fray, but instead of helping Israel win, it encourages the Philistines to fight harder. Israel is defeated, the sons of Eli killed, and the ark itself captured by the enemy. Thus begins a long period of wandering for the ark which finds a final home only when the Temple of Solomon is built.

When Eli hears that the ark is lost, he falls backward off his seat and breaks his neck. His grandson is born soon thereafter and is named

Ichabod—the glory has departed (4:12-22). The Philistines are soon to learn, however, that the captured ark is no boon to them. Not only does the image of their god Dagon fall over when the ark is placed in its house; the Philistines themselves are afflicted with tumors (5:6-12). As a consequence, the ark is sent away, pulled by the two milk cows. The cows finally stop at Beth-Shemesh and the Israelites recover their sacred portable shrine. Eventually, the ark ends up in Kiriath-jearim where it remains for twenty years. Although this whole story has a rather legendary character, it reflects quite accurately the superstitious attitudes of the Philistines and other pagan peoples and may well be reliable in so far as it represents what the people at the time believed happened.

In the last episode of this section, Samuel calls Israel to repentance (7:3-4), and the tribes gather at Mizpah to cleanse themselves. The Philistines attack them there, but are frightened by a thunderstorm and Israel wins the day. The story concludes with a significant description of Samuel's work. Apparently, he was much more of a judge than the previous heroes, though his area of operation was quite circumscribed. His circuit included Bethel, Gilgal, and Mizpah (7:16), a rather small area for a judge of all of Israel!

II. The reigns of Saul and David

CHAPTERS 1-7 have been by way of introduction. With Chapter 8 the main theme of the story is set forth as the people of Israel ask Samuel, who is now old and without a worthy successor, for a king. Samuel eloquently warns the people of the dangers of the kingship (8:10-18), but the people demand one nonetheless. Samuel is hesitant, but, when Yahweh commands him to "make them a king," he acquiesces.

Chapter 9 now introduces Saul, a young and handsome Benjamite, who is looking for his father's lost asses. Thinking Samuel to be a clairvoyant, he goes to seek his aid. Instead of just learning about his father's animals, however, he is anointed king over all Israel. The story is amusing and sets the stage for the tragi-comic reign of King Saul; yet one must also see that there were some good reasons for the selection of Saul as king. In the first place, he was from Benjamin, a small and relatively unimportant tribe. Hence, his selection did not cause the tribal antagonisms which might have been produced by the choice of someone from Judah or Ephraim. Second, he was tall and handsome and looked, at least, like a leader. Third, he had no great yen for power. He came looking for some donkeys, not for the kingship, and that fact in itself was a point in his favor.

Chapter 10 describes the anointing of Saul, first in private (10:1-8) and then before all Israel (10:17-25). Verses 9-13 are interesting for they describe some ecstatic prophets whom Saul momentarily joins and hence give a brief picture of pre-classical prophecy in Israel.

The reign of Saul begins auspiciously with a victory over the Ammonites through which he wins the favor of the people of Jabesh-gilead who proclaim him king at Gilgal. Apparently the eastern tribes did not fully recognize him until this point. Samuel then makes a "Farewell Speech," calling the people to follow their king, to repent of their sins, and to obey the commandments of Yahweh. In a sense, Samuel, in this speech, steps down as leader, but unfortunately for Saul he stays around to be the king's chief critic and antagonist.

Such criticism is not long in coming. When Saul, hard pressed by the Philistines, takes matters into his own hands and offers a sacrifice to Yahweh, Samuel roundly condemns him for having overstepped his bounds. Saul may be king, but Samuel is still in charge of the sacrifices. The king may be the political leader, but he must not meddle in the affairs of the cult. Samuel, the judge, now plays the part of the prophet, i.e., the spokesman for God and the covenant.

Verses 16-23 describe briefly Saul's rag-tag little army and its tenuous situation. The Philistines, who alone know the secrets of iron-working, seem to hold all the military trump cards.

Chapter 14 introduces Saul's son, Jonathan, and describes some of his exploits. It ends with a brief description of some of Saul's battles and a list of the members of Saul's family.

Chapter 15 marks the turning point in Saul's career. Saul fights with the Amalekites and, according to the *herem* tradition is expected to destroy totally all of the goods and captives taken in battle. When he does not do so, Samuel calls down God's judgment upon him. Saul repents, but it is too late. Samuel regrets that he has anointed him king and, in Chapter 16, more-or-less secretly anoints David in his stead. Saul, who is troubled by an evil spirit, requests some one to play music for him and David gets the job.

Chapter 17, which contains the famous story of David and Goliath, is obviously from a different source, for in it Saul does not recognize

David, even though supposedly the young man has frequently played the harp before him (17:55-58). Doubtless this is one of many legendary tales which was told about the great hero, David.

In Chapter 18 David wins the friendship of Jonathan and is successful as a warrior, but soon attracts Saul's jealousy and hatred. Saul grudgingly gives to David one of his daughters, Michal, as his wife, but covertly both fears and hates him.

In Chapter 19 Jonathan informs David of Saul's plot to kill him, and David, with Michal's help, escapes. The chapter ends with another account of Saul prophesying with the ecstatic prophets.

Chapter 20 tells the touching story of the continued friendship of Jonathan and David and of how Jonathan helps his friend despite the hatred of his father. David is forced to flee permanently from the court of Saul. Chapters 21-26 record David's various exploits while in exile in the desert and in Philistia. David gathers about him a group of social outcasts and welds them into an effective fighting force. Saul tries to catch David, but never succeeds. On two occasions, David actually holds Saul's life in his hands, but refuses to kill him because he is the anointed king (chs. 24, 26). Still, David recognizes that his situation is perilous and that eventually Saul may capture and kill him.

In Chapter 27 David decides to go to Philistia. He convinces the Philistines that he is anti-Israelite and they allow him to operate out of their territory. Instead of attacking Israel, however, he actually fights Israel's age-old enemy, the Amalekites.

Chapters 28-30 depict the last days of Saul and his final death. Saul is seen as a pitiable man who even goes so far as to consult a medium (an action condemned by the law) in order to get advice from the now-deceased Samuel. The ghost of Samuel has only criticism and a word of woe to offer the king. Tomorrow, he says, you and your son will be killed (28:19).

The Philistines gather at Aphek for the great battle, but refuse to let David and his men join them because they are suspicious of his former connection with Israel. David returns to Ziklag to find that the Amalekites have raided his camp. He sets out after them and, with the aid of an Egyptian informer, finds and defeats them. In the meantime, Israel loses her battle against Philistia. Saul is wounded badly, but is actually killed, at his own request, by his armor-bearer. His sons are slain by the Philistines and they, with Saul, are decapitated. Their bodies are hung from the walls of Bethshan but are buried by the men of Jabesh gilead (31:1-13). So the first book of Samuel comes to a bloody end.

II Samuel continues the story with the account of David's hearing of Saul's death, his anger against the armor bearer for having killed Yahweh's anointed, and a beautiful lament for Saul and Jonathan (Chapter 1).

In Chapter 2 David is made king over Hebron while Saul's son, Ishbosheth, is anointed king over the rest of Israel. For seven years and six months (2:11) both kings rule and there is intermittant civil war between them. Chapter 2 explains how a blood feud between Joab, the right hand man of David, and Abner, the commander of Saul's army, began. Abner, who is the power behind the throne in the north, seeks peace with David, and David agrees, with the proviso that Michal be returned to him. Joab, however, assassinates Abner while he is in Hebron, and though David laments his death, the deed has been done.

In Chapter 4, Ishbosheth, whose power has been shaken by the assassination of his staunchest supporter, is himself cut down by cut-throats who then present themselves to David, expecting some reward. Instead, he has them executed for their pains. David may have lamented the deaths of Abner and Ishbosheth, but their deaths surely facilitated his rise to preeminence over the whole of Israel, his conquest of Jerusalem which he makes his capital city, and his victories over the Philistines. The chapter is brief, but the deeds recorded are monumental. Not only does David rather quickly drive the hated enemy out of his territory. He turns a formerly Jebusite city into a capital which has ever since had a special place in world history. Jerusalem may still be small in size, but it remains today a preeminent religious center for much of the Western world.

David almost immediately acts to make Jerusalem more than just another city of his domain. With thirty thousand men (undoubtedly an exaggeration) he goes to get the ark of the covenant. After a false start (6:6-11) and the subsequent sojourn of the ark at the house of Obed-edom, he finally brings it to Jerusalem with great jubilation. Thus the religious center for Israel is moved permanently from the north-central region to Judah. Michal wins David's eternal disfavor by criticizing him for dancing unclad before the ark as it is led into the city (6:20-23).

The David of Samuel, unlike the David of Chronicles, is hardly a man who spends most of his time worrying about cultic affairs. He is a vigorous general, a virile and sometimes lustful hero, and a keen politician. At the same time, the David of Samuel is a fervently pious man who does more than simply manipulate religion for the benefit of the state. His dancing before the ark in an "uncovered" state is just one example of his enthusiasm for Yahweh and his cult.

Chapter 7 tells of David's desire to build a temple in Jerusalem. At first the prophet Nathan, who is to play an important part in the history of David from now on, gives his approval, but God, in a nocturnal vision, informs Nathan that it is not up to David to give him a house. On the contrary, God will give David a house and will establish his lineage upon the throne of Israel forever (8:11-16). This promise, which is in many respects comparable to God's blessing of Abraham, became an important factor in Israel's Messianic expectation. Almost from the beginning, it would seem, Israel (at least the southern tribes) recognized David and his house as especially blessed and placed her hope for the future in a new "Son of David."

In any event, David offers a prayer of humble acquiescence and thanksgiving in 7:18-29 and ceases his plans to construct a Temple in his capital city. This building project is left for his son and successor, Solomon.

Chapter 8 returns to David, the successful general, and describes his various victories over the Philistines, the Moabites, the Syrians, and the Edomites. Through these victories David's little kingdom becomes an Empire stretching from the Euphrates to the brook of Egypt, from the mountains of Lebanon to the Arabian desert. Chapter 9 describes David's kind treatment of Jonathan's son Mephibosheth, while Chapter 10 tells of his victory over the Ammonites and Syrians.

Throughout the books of Samuel David is portrayed as *the* great king of Israel who established the nation's one hour of greatness. Unlike so many hero stories, however, Samuel refuses to gloss over David's equally notable faults and sins. What makes the whole account so plausible is that David is depicted as a real man, not as a one-dimensional hero-type. Chapter 11, in accordance with this penchant of the author, describes David's act of adultery with Bathsheba and the consequent murder of her husband. The story is surprising for two reasons. First, one would not expect an author so favorably disposed to a ruler to have included the story. Second, when the prophet Nathan calls David into account for his sins, David, unlike most oriental potentates, repents. Chapter 12 contains Nathan's famous rebuke of his king, David's confession of guilt, and the pathetic story of the death of the child born from the union. Like most evil acts recorded in Scripture, David's adultery has some good, as well as some evil consequences. Ch. 12:24-25 cryptically adds that another son is born to Bathsheba and his name is Solomon! The chapter concludes with a brief account of another victory over the Ammonites.

David is pictured throughout Samuel as a magnanimous ruler, an heroic general, and a clever politician. Chapters 13-19 reveal one great weakness on his part—his indulgence toward his spoiled children. Chapter 13 is a beautifully graphic account of the rape of Tamar by her half-brother Amnon, one of David's sons, the consequent murder of Amnon by Absalom, and of Absalom's flight to exile. Chapter 14, then, explains how Joab, through a ruse, convinces David to allow Absalom to return. Absalom is brought back, but is not allowed in the king's presence. Instead of accepting this situation humbly, however, Absalom foments a rebellion and, for a time, takes over the kingdom. Chapters 15-17 describe the political intrigues which took place during this period. While Ahithophel advises Absalom, Husai, a friend of David, offers counter-advice.

Because Hushai is listened to, David is allowed to escape across the Jordan and the eventual battle is fought on his ground. The outcome, given the situation, is almost a foregone conclusion. David's forces are triumphant and Absalom, against the wishes of his father, is killed. Joab is exuberant, but David only laments the death of his son. The picture of the victorious David weeping for his son is one of the most moving scenes in the whole Bible.

Finally, in Chapter 19, Joab makes the king come to his senses. David returns to Jerusalem, generally forgives those who submit to him, and reestablishes his reign. In II Samuel 19:41-43 is given the first hint of the disaffection of the northern tribes which was to explode after the death of Solomon.

Chapter 20 records the details of another rebellion, this time by Sheba, a Benjamite. Joab, acting in David's behalf, quickly quells the revolt. In Chapter 21, David, apparently using a famine as an excuse, extirpates the blood-guilt of Saul by killing seven of his sons. Doubtless, this was a way to prevent further revolts, for the sons of Saul were obvious rallying points for revolutions. The chapter ends with another victory over the Philistines. In the battle, David grows tired and he is urged not to engage in actual combat again. Curiously, in the next battle with the Philistines one Elhanan slays a giant named Goliath. The relation between this brief reference and the earlier story of David and Goliath is unclear.

In Chapter 22 the narrative is interrupted by a psalm of David, which is similar in most respects to Psalm 18. Then, in Chapter 23, follow the last words of David and a listing of David's mighty men. Chapter 24 is obviously a later addition to the text, for instead of describing David's death, it tells of a census which David takes, a census which is regarded as sinful by Yahweh and hence the cause of a pestilence. Finally, David is advised by the prophet Gad to buy a threshing floor and upon it to build an altar. David does so and the pestilence ceases. On this rather inconclusive note, II Samuel comes to an end.

CHAPTER XV

I and II Kings: Introduction and Analysis

From Solomon until the Fall of Jerusalem

HE TWO BOOKS of Kings, which complete the long history of Israel which began with Joshua, were, like the books of Samuel, originally one. They were divided first in the Septuagint translation of the *Tanak*, for the Greek, having written vowels, made the work too long to be placed on a single scroll.

Since the book concludes with the fall of Jerusalem, it could not have been put in final shape before the exilic period. There are some indications, however, that an earlier version without the final chapters may have existed during the reign of King Josiah. The traditional Talmudic attribution of the book to Jeremiah is certainly incorrect, for clearly Jeremiah's style differs from that of Kings. Still, the final version is quite possibly by one of Jeremiah's contemporaries.

Whoever the authors were, it is obvious that they used several documents from earlier times in order to write their history. I Kings 11:41 refers to "The book of the acts of Solomon" which doubtless contained the annals of this illustrious king's reign. Although it included some very reliable material, there were also in it some legendary and historically suspect sections as well. Even the legends are of great value, however, for they show how Solomon was remembered by those of a generation or two after him.

"The Book of the Chronicles of the Kings of Israel" is also referred to seventeen times and seems to have been a court chronicle containing basic information about the exploits and character of the various northern kings from Jeroboam to at least Pekah. The authors of Kings consistently refer the reader to this book and to "The Book of the Chronicles of the Kings of Judah" for further information about those many kings whom he treats only briefly. Needless to say, these works ought not to be confused with the books of Chronicles found among the Writings in the Old Testament.

Beside these mentioned sources, the authors doubtless had before them court memoirs from the reign of David, upon which they based their description of the last hours of King David; materials concerning Elijah, Elisha, and other prophets derived from the traditions of various prophetic schools; and some extra material concerning the reign of King Ahab. These sources the authors excerpted and rearranged according to their own purposes. Sometimes they would adhere rather slavishly to their contents and therefore include comments which seem out of place in their own era. At the same time, the choice and the arrangement of materials reflects very much their own theological position and world view, which appears to have been thoroughly shaped by the book of Deuteronomy. For this reason Kings is often designated a "Deuteronomic history." The same term is sometimes applied to the other books of the former prophets as well, for they too contain Deuteronomic touches, but it is in Kings that the Deuteronomic theology is most in evidence.

Essentially Kings is composed of several large blocks of material concerning David and Solomon, Ahab, Elijah, Elisha, Hezekiah, and Josiah. These materials, excerpted from the sources mentioned above, are connected by much shorter notices concerning the other rulers of Israel and Judah. Nearly all of these brief accounts follow the same general format as that found in 15:1-8 where the reign of Abijam is described. The account normally begins with the dating of the reign in terms of the reign of the contemporary king from the other Israelite kingdom, for example,

> Now in the eighteenth year of King Jeroboam the son of Nebat, Abijam began to reign over Judah. He reigned for three years in Jerusalem. (15:1)

Although fairly accurate, this synchronous dating system is sometimes unreliable, as a comparison with contemporary Assyrian and Babylonian king lists shows. For instance, according to the synchronistic dating there were 170 years between the revolution of Jehu and the fall of Jerusalem. There were 165 years if computed according to the Judean regnal years; 143 years and seven months according to the Israel regnal years, and 120 years according to the Assyrian king lists. Hence there is much debate about the actual dating of most of these kings.

Then follows a more or less brief account of the king's exploits and an evaluation of his reign. This evaluation is based upon one criterion: did the king emphasize worship in the Jerusalem Temple and destroy the various high places of Israel and Judah? When this yardstick is applied, all of the northern kings fall under censure, for the northern kingdom had its own separate shrines. Of the southern kings only Hezekiah and Josiah receive the authors' full approval. Favorable decisions in regard to Asa, Jehoshaphat, Jehoash, Azariah, and Jotham are qualified by the recognition that during their reigns "the high places were not taken away" (I Kings 15:14).

This criterion reflects the influence of Deuteronomy, for of all the books of the law only Deuteronomy emphasizes the importance of one central shrine for all Israel. One might also give a pragmatic justification for this seemingly rather peculiar standard of judgment. The existence of several places of sacrifice symbolized, in effect, the political and religious disunity of Israel and Judah. This lack of unity was one of the primary factors which led to the downfall of both. Although the authors show some sympathy for Israel's initial revolt against Rehoboam (I Kings 12:1-24), they place full responsibility for the continuation of the schism upon the northern kings. This book, unlike Joshua and Judges, is written, then, from a Judaen point of view. The authors attempt to explain the reasons for the decline and fall of the Davidic-Solomonic Empire and find them in the twin sins of disunity and idolatry.

The typical description of a king ends with words to this effect:

> The rest of the acts of Abijam, and all that he did, are they not written in the Book of the Chronicles of the Kings of Judah? And there was war between Abijam and Jeroboam. And Abijam slept with his fathers; and they buried him in the city of David. And Asa his son reigned in his stead. (I Kings 15:7-8)

Although Kings rises at times to great literary heights, this format has a rather dampening effect upon the style of the book as a whole. The average reader usually finds the review of the various kings rather dull and unproductive. Still, it must be recognized that the author was dealing with highly complex material which did not lend itself well to simple treatment. The very fact that he had to jump back and forth between the northern and the southern kingdom was itself a great difficulty. Literary excellence may not at all times be in evidence, but at least Kings provides us with a great deal of highly important information within a few pages. Were it not for this work and for the book of Chronicles, which is in large measure based upon Kings, we would know virtually nothing about the history of Israel from Davidic to exilic times. Archaeologists may find data to correct and to expand upon Kings, but they, barring some great literary find, can never replace it as the primary source for the history of this period.

Analysis

From Solomon until the Fall of Jerusalem

THE STORY begins with David drawing near to death. His strength and virility are gone, and he must be cared for by a nurse (1:1-1:4). With his weakening, his eldest son, Adonijah, moves to secure the throne for himself. In so doing, he is not just presumptuous, for as the eldest living heir, the throne would most naturally fall to him. Both Abiathar and Joab back him and it looks as though his succession to the kingship is a foregone conclusion.

Unfortunately for him a number of David's close advisors think otherwise. Nathan, the prophet, Zadok, the priest, and Benaiah, a leader of the military, oppose Adonijah and favor Solomon. Bathsheba, Solomon's mother, tells David of Adonijah's actions and calls upon him to fulfill his vow to make Solomon king. This he does and Solomon is anointed by Nathan and Zadok.

Chapter 2 includes the last words of David. He urges Solomon to be pious and strong and to deal swiftly with two men who have displeased him: Joab and Shimei. Chapter 2:10-12 records briefly David's death. Then the blood-bath begins. Adonijah acts presumptuously and is struck down by Benaiah, Solomon's hatchet man (2:13-25). Abiathar is banished to Anathoth (2:26-27), while Joab is slain (2:28-35). Shimei breaks an agreement with Solomon to stay in Jerusalem and also knows the fatal blade of Benaiah's sword. So Solomon establishes himself with strength.

I. *The reign of Solomon (3:1-11:43)*

One of Solomon's first acts is to make alliance with the Pharaoh of Egypt by marrying one of his daughters. This essentially political relationship shows how powerful Solomon appeared in the eyes of the Egyptians, for normally Egypt would have entered into such an entente only with a major power. According to I Kings 9:16, the Pharaoh conquered Gezer from the Canaanites and gave it to Solomon as a dowry. This is a significant bit of information, for it shows that even during David's day part of the land was under non-Israelite control.

Chapter 3:3-15 tells of Solomon's customary sacrifices at the high-place in Gibeon and of a dream he has there. In the dream God asks Solomon what he would like from him. Solomon replies, "Give me an understanding mind" (3:9). God is pleased with this request and grants both it and riches and honor as well. Chapter 3:16-28 then exemplifies Solomon's wisdom by telling of his judgment concerning two women who both claim the same child as her own.

Chapter 4 lists Solomon's various court officials and the provisions required for his household. His strength is underlined by a description of his stables of horses. The chapter ends with a lyric account of Solomon's wisdom, his proverbs, and his songs.

In Chapter 5 Solomon's preparations for the building of the Temple, including his agreement with Hiram king of Tyre, are described. Then, in Chapter 6 a lengthy description of the Temple is included. It is said (6:1) that the Temple was begun 480 years after Israel came out of Egypt, but this figure, like so many other round numbers in the Bible, seems quite inflated. If it is correct, the exodus took place in the sixteenth, rather than the thirteenth century. The assertion that it took seven years to build the Temple (6:38) could be accurate, but it may reflect the mythological motif of creation "in seven" rather than historical fact.

Chapter 7 describes the building of Solomon's palace and the making of various fixtures (bronze pillars, a molten 'sea', ten brass lavers, etc.) for the Temple, while Chapter 9 describes the service of dedication. The ark is brought into the Temple and Solomon offers a dedicatory speech and prayer. Finally he blesses Yahweh and Israel and then offers sacrifice before the LORD. The small part the priests play in this service is significant. Quite clearly Solomon has taken over the role played by so many other ancient Near Eastern monarchs. Not only is he political leader, he is really head of the cult as well. Gone is the "separation of church and state" so emphasized by Samuel. What Saul was criticized for doing (I Sam. 13:8-15), Solomon does quite openly and naturally.

Chapter 9 records Yahweh's conditional covenant with Solomon in which he promises to establish Solomon's throne forever—if he and his successors will be faithful to him. The passage bears the certain marks of the Deuteronomist who has lived through the fall of Jerusalem and the destruction of the Temple and who here attempts to explain these events. Had Solomon's successors kept the covenant Jerusalem would never have fallen, he says . . . but they did not.

The chapter concludes with an account of Solomon's disagreement with Hiram, his use of forced labor, and his developing of a fleet of ships which operated out of Ezion-geber on the Red Sea. Chapter 10 tells of the visit of the Queen of Sheba, Solomon's great wisdom, and the fabulous material splendor of his kingdom.

Throughout this description of Solomon's reign there have been some slight hints of criticism, but in general the praises for him have been glowing and, in fact, exaggerated. Chapter 11, however, is highly critical of Solomon's foreign wives and even more of his turning toward other gods and his building of high places for them. God not only warns Solomon; he raises up adversaries in the persons of Hadad of Edom, Rezon of Syria, and Jeroboam who is later to become king of the northern kingdom of Israel. Although the text is not entirely explicit, it implies that both Edom and Syria regained enough strength to gain their freedom from the Solomonic Empire at this time. The section ends with a typical Deuteronomic conclusion (11:41-43).

II. Rehoboam and the divided kingdom (12:1-16:20)

CHAPTER 12 tells the tragic story of the division of the kingdom after Solomon's death. Rehoboam, his son, ascends to the throne with the firm backing of Judah, but the northern tribes, wishing to ameliorate some of the excesses of Solomon, call for reforms. Rehoboam consults with advisors and, taking the advice of the princelings rather than the older men, refuses to promise any changes.

As a consequence, the northern tribes simply walk out and form their own kingdom in the north with Jeroboam, a critic of the reign of Solomon who had been exiled in Egypt, as their king. Rehoboam is powerless to stop the schism, and, as a matter of fact, is forbidden by a prophet of God from starting war against the schismatic state (12:21-24). Jeroboam, to lessen the influence of Jerusalem, builds calves of gold and establishes them at Dan and Bethel. These two shrines are to figure prominently in the religious life of the north from then on. Jeroboam is also said to have built other high places and to have made priests men who were not even Levites.

Chapter 13 then tells the story of a prophet who not only criticizes Jeroboam for his idolatrous actions but foretells that King Josiah will tear down the shrine at Bethel some two hundred years later! The story is obviously told by someone from a later time, for it states that the prophecy was fulfilled (13:5). The prophet then disobeys God's command and is killed by a lion.

Chapter 14 continues the denunciation of Jeroboam—this time through the words of the prophet Ahijah who anointed Jeroboam in the first place. Little else is said of the first king of Israel (as the northern kingdom now is called), for, to the author, all that needed to be said has been said. Jeroboam was an evil king because he promoted idolatry. Beside this fact his good qualities and his victories did not seem important to mention.

With 14:21 we return to Rehoboam, the idolatries taking place in Judah, the victory of Pharaoh Shishak over Judah, and the death of Rehoboam. Then, in the 15th chapter the author begins a brief summary of the reigns of several kings. In 15:1-24 he describes the deeds of Abijam and Asa, kings of Judah. Then he turns in quick succession to Nadab, Baasha, Elah, and Zimri from the north (15:25-30). Clearly the northern kingdom was politically unstable for all but Baasha came to power through a coup d'etat.

III. The House of Omri and Elijah (16:21-II Kings 2:12)

THE STORY of the most powerful house to rule Israel begins inauspiciously in Kings with a brief account of Omri's coup d'etat which brings Zimri's seven day career to an abrupt end and with just a short synopsis of Omri's reign. Kings simply condemns Omri as one more evil king, but we know from external sources that he was by no means just another ruler. He was quite successful in strengthening Israel and in expanding her borders on all sides. He also began building programs, the remains of which are still in evidence in the Holy Land. Even the major powers regarded him with respect and referred to Israel as "the land of Omri" long after his death. The author of Kings, of course, was not impressed by such achievements. For him the house of Omri spelled idolatry and that was all that really mattered.

Ahab, Omri's son, is dealt with at much greater length, not because he was a righteous king, but because of his connection with the prophet Elijah. Chapter 17 begins the famous saga of Elijah the Tishbite and his prophetic "war" against the house of Omri. His stories, surrounded with the miraculous as they are, represent a type of "saint" story popular in prophetic circles. Elijah is a strange figure who appears suddenly to offer a word of woe and then to disappear. He is a prophet par excellence who, with the freedom of the desert in his veins, represents Yahweh and the faithful against the encroaching power of the sovereign king and his evil queen.

The account of the struggle between Ahab and Elijah is introduced in 16:29-34 with a brief synopsis of Ahab's evil ways. According to the judgment of the Deuteronomist, "Ahab did more to provoke the LORD, the God of Israel, to anger than all the Kings of Israel who were before him" (16:33). Suddenly Elijah the Tishbite (the meaning of Tishbite is uncertain) arrives to announce a drought. Elijah then leaves for the eastern desert where he is fed by the ravens (a word which might also conceivably be rendered "Arabs"). Then he goes to Sidon, the homeland of Jezebel, Ahab's queen, and performs miracles at the home of a widow.

In the 18th chapter, Yahweh tells Elijah that the drought will end and that he should seek out Ahab. He meets first Obadiah, one of Ahab's officials who is faithful to Yahweh, and tells him that he will meet with Ahab. He does so and calls the prophets of Baal and Asherah to a show-down at Mount Carmel, a high promontory which juts out into the Mediterranean. Then follows one of the most memorable scenes in the Elijah cycle. Each side builds an altar and calls upon its god to light the sacrifice. The prophets of Baal cry out and cut themselves (an act of sympathetic magic) but to no avail. Elijah, however, prays simply to Yahweh and fire falls from heaven on his water-drenched sacrifice. Elijah in his moment of victory has all of the prophets of Baal cut down. Elijah then seems to perform a bit of sympathetic magic himself, crouching (like a cloud?) on the top of Carmel. After seven (!) trips by his servant to look over the water a cloud finally appears and Elijah tells Ahab to hurry home because the rains are coming. Ahab drives his chariot, but Elijah runs before him to the entrance of Jezreel. The drought is ended.

Chapter 19 contains the almost equally famous story of Elijah's flight to Mount Horeb. Jezebel is angry because of the slaughter of the prophets of Baal and vows to have Elijah killed. Elijah flees to the southern desert and there is miraculously fed (19:4-8). Finally he arrives at Mount Horeb and waits for a word from God. At last it comes, not in the wind or earthquake or fire, but in a still small voice. Many who have spoken of God's still small voice have failed to see what it commands Elijah to do. He is called to anoint Hazael (who turns out to be a vicious enemy of Israel) king of Syria, to anoint Jehu king of Israel and hence start a revolution, and to anoint Elisha as his prophetic successor. Elijah performs the last act, but for some unexplained reason, leaves the anointing of Hazael and Jehu to his successor. In any event, we see here the political and revolutionary role of the prophet who could, like Samuel, step in when the political situation got out-of-hand and simply anoint another man king.

While Elijah is preparing for revolution, Ahab is working for victory. In Chapter 20, Ben-hadad, the king of Syria, challenges and then attacks Samaria, but Ahab, with the assurance of a prophet that he will win (!), attacks while Ben-hadad's guard is down and defeats him. Ben-hadad attacks again the next spring as the prophet warns, but Ahab once more attacks and wins. Ben-hadad, in fact, is captured, but Ahab spares his life. For this act of clemency, Ahab is severely censured by the prophets.

Chapter 21 returns to the Elijah cycle of stories. Ahab wants a vineyard owned by a free citizen, Naboth, but the owner refuses to sell it. Ahab simply sulks, but Jezebel, without any regard for property rights in Israel, arranges to have Naboth falsely accused and put to death. For this act, Elijah condemns Ahab and prophesies that both Ahab and his wife will die violent deaths. Ahab repents and gains a momentary respite from disaster, but the staying of judgment lasts only briefly.

In Chapter 22 we turn from the "Elijah" to the "Ahab" source again. Ahab and the Judean king Jehoshaphat (whom Chronicles depicts in the most glowing terms) make an agreement to attack Syria which has taken the border fortress of Ramoth-gilead. Several prophets predict victory, but Micaiah, though he at first does the same, finally tells the truth—Ahab will be defeated. Micaiah is imprisoned until Ahab is proved right, but the word of the prophet comes true. Ahab is struck by an arrow in the chest and dies. Chapter 22:39 speaks of the ivory house which Ahab built, an interesting comment since many ivories have been uncovered by archaeologists both in Samaria and in Nineveh where they were later transported.

The first book ends with a very brief synopsis of the reign of Jehoshaphat (22:41-50), who is described in much greater detail in II Chronicles 17-20, and Ahaziah, Ahab's son and successor (22:51-53). The story of Ahaziah, however, is concluded in II Kings:1 which tells of the king's illness and his attempt to find out from Baalzebub, the god of Ekron, whether or not he will recover. For this Elijah severely censures him and as a result is himself sought after. He is protected, however, by fire from heaven which kills the men sent after him (1:9-16). The story of Ahaziah is concluded in the typical Deuteronomistic way.

One sentence in this story is of particular interest. In 1:1 is said that after the death of Ahab, Moab rebelled against Israel. In 1868 the famous Moabite stone which tells the story from the Moabite point-of-view was discovered. In this stele, Mesha (Cf. II Kings 3:4) tells of his land's subordination to Israel during the days of Omri and of Mesha's final victory over the Israelites. The stone is important, not only because it confirms this sentence in Kings, but because it shows that the Moabites also regarded their god, Chemosh, as a deity who acted in history, punishing Moab by allowing Omri to dominate them and then eventually leading Moab to victory. Clearly the Biblical motion that God is a God of history was not peculiar to Israel but was shared by other peoples of the time as well.

Chapter 2 includes an account of the last day of Elijah during which he is taken up into heaven in a chariot of fire (2:11). Elisha, before he leaves, asks for and receives a double portion of his spirit, and then becomes his prophetic successor. On his return home he strikes the water of the Jordan with Elijah's mantle and performs a water-parting miracle, thus identifying himself with the Mosaic-Joshuaic tradition.

IV. *Elisha and Jehu's Revolution*

ELISHA'S MINISTRY begins with even more miracles than those ascribed to Elijah. Not only does he part the waters of the Jordan (2:12-14). He also sweetens the water of the spring at Jericho (2:19-22) and has some forty-two small boys killed by she-bears for jeering him (2:23-25). In Chapter 3 he is called by Jehoshaphat and Jehoram, the new king of Israel, to help them and, through the playing of a minstrel, brings water to them in the desert during their march on Moab. As a consequence, the Moabites are defeated. The list of miracles continues in Chapter 4. He makes a jar of oil continually full of oil (Cf: I Kings 17:14-16), prophesies the birth of a son (4:8-17), and then later raises the child from the dead (4:18-37). He makes poisonous pottage harmless (4:38-41), miraculously feeds one hundred men (4:42-44), and cures Naaman, the Syrian, of leprosy (Chapter 5). This last miracle story also contains an attack upon those who cure for money. Gehazi, Elisha's servant, accepts money in payment and hence is struck with leprosy himself. Elisha's miracles come from God; to him and not to the prophet belongs the glory and the pay.

In Chapter 6 Elisha makes an axe head float on the water (6:1-7) and then helps Israel in her fight against Syria by striking the Syrian armies blind (6:8-23). Again the Syrians attack, but Yahweh frightens them away as Elisha predicts (6:24-7:20). Chapter 8 contains a rather strange story about the widow whom Elisha had helped earlier (Ch.4), who at the word of Elisha flees to Philistia and then returns.

Suddenly, the miracles end and we return to political realities. After helping Israel Elisha now goes to Syria and anoints Hazael king there and thus sets on the throne of the enemy a vicious and energetic ruler (8:7-15). The Deuteronomist then interjects a brief summary of the reigns of Jehoram and Ahaziah, kings of Judah, which prepares us for the next great moment, the revolution of Jehu in Israel.

In Chapter 9 Elisha finally fulfills God's command to Elijah to anoint Jehu king of Israel. He sends a messenger (one of the members of his prophetic school) who announces God's will for him. The revolution begins. Jehu, a commander of the army, drives furiously with his troops to Samaria. The kings of Israel and Judah, stationed as they are on the heights of Samaria see him coming. When their messengers do not return, they set out themselves and discover what is happening too late. With poetic justice Joram, the son of Ahab, is killed and buried in the plot of Naboth which his father had confiscated. Ahaziah, the king of Judah, is also killed in flight and his body is taken back to Jerusalem.

Then begins the bloodbath. In a very dramatic moment, Jezebel is thrown out the window by the command of Jehu and is trampled by the horses (9:30-37). Jehu beheads Ahab's seventy sons (10:1-11), and slays the forty-two princes of Judah and the other relations of Ahab (10:15-17). Then, in a ruse, he slaughters all those who worship the Baals (10:18-27). Thus he establishes the worship of Yahweh alone in Israel. In one sense, Jehu's bloody methods were salutory, for he rid Israel of idolatry. Still, his massive slaughter left Israel administratively weak and without allies. The Black Obelisk of Shalemenezer shows the result of all this. On it Jehu is depicted as supinely offering obeisence before the king of Assyria!

Kings says little about Assyria during this period, but we know from other sources that that great giant of the east was growing in strength and was eyeing the rich lands of Syria-Palestine. Ahab may have been an evil king, but his various coalitions with the other states of the area kept Assyrian power more or less in check. Jehu, however, broke these bonds of alliance in his Yahwistic fervor and helped to produce the ultimate disaster which was to take place in the next century.

Significantly, the book of Kings has little good to say about Jehu. It is admitted that he rooted out the idolators, but he is also accused of continuing the sanctuaries of Bethel and Dan (10:28). It is also mentioned that Israel lost considerable territory during his reign (10:32-33).

V. *The post-Jehu period until the fall of the Northern Kingdom*

PARADOXICALLY, the Jehu revolution, though against the house of Omri, led to the reign of Ahab's sister, Ataliah, in Judah. With the death of Ahaziah, the queen mother assumed the throne and cut down all of the royal family except Jehoash, an infant, who was hidden by a nurse. Thus, for a brief period the ruler of Judah was non-Davidic. Jehoida, the priest, however, led a coup d'etat after seven years of her rule and brought the boy Jehoash to the throne.

Jehoash is described in Chapter 12 as relatively pious, because of his repairing of the Temple, but it is admitted that he was militarily weak (12:17-18) and not wholly orthodox (12:3).

In Chapter 13 the reigns of Jehoahaz and Jehoash, kings of Israel, are described along with an account of Elisha's last days. Characteristically, even after Elisha's death, his grave becomes a source for miracles (13:20-21). Under Jehoahaz, Israel is severely defeated by Hazael of Damascus, but recovers some of the territory under Jehoash.

Chapter 14 contains brief summaries of the reign of Amaziah in Judah (14:1-22) and Jeroboam II in Israel (14:23-28). We know from other sources that the reign of Jeroboam II was a prosperous and victorious one for Israel, but little of this is mentioned by the authors of Kings. They do mention that Jeroboam did restore some territory according to the word spoken by Jonah the son of Amittai, the prophet. This prophet later was to become the chief character in an imaginative short story found among the twelve minor prophets.

Chapter 15 contains summary statements concerning the reigns of no less than seven kings: Azariah (Judah), Zechariah, Shallum, Menahem, Pekahiah, and Pekah (Israel), and Jotham (Judah). Again, while Judah experienced political stability, Israel was wracked with revolution. During this period there were three coups d'etat as Israel repeatedly felt the sting of Assyria's military strength. In 15:19 we find the first reference to Pul, i.e., Tiglath pileser III, whose imperialistic activities as king of Assyria were to extend the hegemony of that Empire over much of the Near East. Kings says relatively little about him, but he was, in truth, one of the major world-conquerors of the ancient world. Not much is said either about the reigns of Ahaziah and Jotham, but we know from other sources that the reign of the former in particular was quite prosperous and relatively peaceful.

Chapter 16 then describes the reign of Ahaz who is censured for sacrificing his own son and for introducing a pagan altar and other novelties into the Temple. The story of Ahaz' struggle against Israel and Syria is also told in Isaiah 7:1ff., though his alliance with Tiglath pileser is not mentioned.

In Chapter 17 the final defeat of the northern kingdom at the hands of the Assyrians during the reign of Hoshea is described briefly and without pathos. Chapter 17:7-23 provides a summary of the reasons for the destruction of the larger of the two Israelite kingdoms which can be spelled out in one word: idolatry. Israel deserved exactly what she got; therefore, no one ought to bewail her fate. Chapter 17:24-41 describes the resettlement of foreign peoples in the northern kingdom and how they both accepted Yahweh as the god of the region and yet continued their pagan practices. This whole passage is a not so subtle attack upon the Samaritans whom the Jews, recognizing their heterodoxy, despised.

VI. From Hezekiah to the Fall of Jerusalem: Judah stands alone.

IN CHAPTER 18 Kings turns to one of the few righteous kings, Hezekiah. This account, which is paralleled, in part, quite closely in Isaiah 36-39, praises Hezekiah for his reform of the cult and for his generally righteous behavior. When the Assyrian king's envoy, Rabshakeh, comes to Israel with force and taunts Jerusalem, it looks as though Hezekiah's days are numbered, but, as Isaiah predicts (II Kings 19:20-28), the Assyrians leave without total conquest. Sennacherib returns to Nineveh only to be assassinated by two of his sons (19:36-37).

Although there is no non-Biblical confirmation of this Assyrian setback, something, in all probability a plague, forced Sennacherib to retreat without capturing Jerusalem. This event was one of the factors which led to the widespread belief among Judeans that Jerusalem would not fall. Still, this was no major victory for Hezekiah. Quite clearly, much of Judah had been ravaged by Assyria and was but a pawn in her hands. Perhaps the Judaic decimation had been so successful that the Assyrians saw no point in a long seige of the fortress city.

Chapter 20 tells of Hezekiah's sickness and of his temporary reprieve from death (20:1-11). Then follows a brief account of Hezekiah's attempt to join with the revolutionary Merodach-baladan of Babylonia who sought to throw off the Assyrian yoke. Isaiah, who consistently advocated a policy of neutralism and isolationism, condemned this adventurous act in no uncertain terms. He proved to be correct;

Merodach-baladan's revolt was quelled and Assyria, under Esarhaddon, extended her domains to include even Egypt.

Chapter 21 begins with a bitter tirade against Hezekiah's son Manasseh who not only adopted a pro-Assyrian policy but who countenanced many abominable pagan practices. In fact the final fall of Jerusalem is seen as primarily a result of his sins which even the righteousness of Josiah could not wipe away (21:10-14). Amon's two-year reign is then summarized. Like his father he is roundly condemned for his sins (21:19-26).

Chapters 22:1-23:30 then describe the actions of the righteous king Josiah. Of particular importance is his repair of the Temple during which a scroll of Law is found (22:8-10). This scroll is generally identified by most scholars as a version of what is now called the book of Deuteronomy. As a result of this find, Josiah sets about to reform the religion of Judah, tearing down all the out-lying shrines and making the Jerusalem Temple the place of sacrifice for all Israel (23:4-20). He calls all Israelites to renew the covenant (23:1-3) and orders the celebration of Passover which, according to Kings, had not been observed since the days of the Judges! (23:21-23) He also "put away" all mediums and wizards and all the other pagan "abominations" which abounded in Judah.

Still, Yahweh is not placated. Josiah, for all his righteous reforms, comes too late and the judgment can not be diverted. Josiah himself is killed as he goes to meet the Egyptian Pharaoh, Neco, at Megiddo (23:29-30), and Judah plunges once more toward disaster.

Jehoahaz, his son, is placed on the throne, but is soon deposed by the Egyptians who replace him with Jehoiakim, a pro-Egyptian sympathizer. Much more is said of this brutal king in the book of Jeremiah. In any event, the Babylonians, who had taken over much of the Assyrian Empire which crumbled during Josiah's era, reestablish control over the area (24:1). When Jehoiakim rebels, the Babylonians come in force, but Jehoakim does not have to face them. He dies, leaving the disastrous situation for his son Jehoiachin to face. The Babylonian forces under Nebuchadnezzar beseige Jerusalem and Jehoiachin is forced to submit. He, along with many officials and leading men, is taken into exile in Babylonia leaving his uncle, Zedekiah, on the throne.

Chapters 24:18-25:30 tell briefly of the revolt of Zedekiah, the dreadful seige of the city and its final destruction. The Temple is torn down and Judah depopulated. Zedekiah is forced to watch while his own sons are killed and is then blinded and taken into captivity. Gedaliah is appointed governor, but he is also cut down by assassins (25:22-25). Those responsible and many others then flee to exile in Egypt. Probably some people remain behind, but the land is generally depopulated. Jerusalem is in ruins. The end has come.

After this rather terse summary of the major disaster in Israel's history, the author ends with a brief ray of hope. In exile King Jehoiachin is freed from prison and is even given a regular allowance from the king. Considering the magnitude of the disaster, however, this mildly optimistic conclusion is a faint hope indeed. Yet the Davidic line still lives and maybe some day—some day—

CHAPTER XVI

Isaiah: Introduction and Analysis

The Life and Times of Isaiah
Part I: Isaiah 1-39.
Part II: Isaiah 40-66.

HE SCROLL of the prophet Isaiah stands first among the three major prophets, perhaps because it is the oldest, perhaps because it is the longest, of the three. Although the whole work has been traditionally ascribed to one man, one of the firmest conclusions of modern scholarship is that the book is composite, the work of several men living at quite different times. In this respect Isaiah does not differ particularly from the other prophetic books which, for the most part, also reveal editorial glosses and additions. What does make Isaiah unique is that such large segments of the work can be clearly singled out as not by the "original" prophet and dated with some precision. Clearly the last half of the book, Chapters 40-66, is by a later hand or hands who wrote two centuries or more after the Isaiah to whom the opening chapters are ascribed. Therefore, this discussion of Isaiah will be divided into two parts dealing, respectively, with 1-39 and 40-66.

This division does not totally mitigate the over-all unity of the book, however. Rather it points to the fact that Isaiah, like many other prophetic books, was the product of a guild of prophets which doubtless had a long and illustrious history of its own. We have already seen in the book of Kings (II Kings 6: 1-2) that Elisha gathered about him a group of disciples who worked with him and may have continued his labors after his death. Surely it was in this school that the traditions concerning Elijah and Elisha took shape and were transmitted.

The prophet himself was a preacher and poet, not a maker of books. He proclaimed his oracles as messages of God for a particular situation. Most of the prophets probably did not write their messages at all. In so far as they wished to have their words preserved for posterity, they depended upon the memories of their hearers. The disciples, in particular, were responsible for remembering the poetic oracles and passing them on to future generations. Eventually the school of disciples would arrange these oracles in writing and add to them biographical material, editorial glosses, and perhaps new prophecies of their own. Thus a prophetic book came into being.

That Isaiah had such a circle of followers is made clear in 8:14 which reads, "Bind up the testimony, seal the teaching among my disciples." (This section may not be by Isaiah himself, but it witnesses to the existence of a prophetic school all the same.) The fact that the writers of 40-66 adopted many of his key terms and images, if not his poetic style, seems to indicate that they were members of the school who added Isaianic prophecy appropriate for their own day.

The probability that the scroll of Isaiah is really the scroll of a whole prophetic school, however, does not mean that the original Isaiah fades into total obscurity. On the contrary, the personality and poetic genius of Isaiah of Jerusalem dominate the first half of the book (and to some extent the second half as well). By "reading between the lines" we can learn a great deal about the man who initiated the prophetic movement which produced the book.

Before turning to a discussion of his life and times, however, it is appropriate to look first at the types of material we find in Isaiah and the way these passages were arranged.

FIRST, there are relatively short poetic oracles delivered on various occasions to speak to particular situations. Clearly, these were not meant to be read all in one sitting. The person who reads one oracle after another soon becomes numb to their impact and perhaps even bored by their repetitiousness. 1:2-31, for instance, is a complete sermon and should be read by itself. It is preferable to read it aloud, for that is the way it was originally delivered. In so far as it is possible, each oracle should be read with the situation in which it was first preached clearly in mind. Only then will its impact "come clear."

SECOND, there are autobiographical passages, as in Chapter 6. This is not, strictly speaking, an oracle, but a "confession" included, perhaps, to underline the authenticity of the prophet's vocation and to set forth some of the major themes of his message. Often times these passages are the best place to begin in the study of a prophet, for they express in a short compass the various prophetic motifs which are expanded elsewhere.

THIRD, there are biographical passages added by the prophetic school to give the reader some information about the man from whom the oracles issued or to illustrate some aspect of his message. These passages are usually in prose and, though not always historically reliable, usually contain highly authentic memories of the school concerning their "master". Chapters 36-39 include materials of this sort.

FOURTH, there are scribal glosses, also often in prose, which expand upon an idea set forth by the prophet himself. A typical example of such a gloss is to be found in 3:18-23. Sometimes, as has already been said, there are also prophetic additions to the words of the prophet which are new oracles written for a later day. 13:1-14:21 is a good example of this type.

One of the problems in reading any of the prophetic books is that they are, for the most part, arranged topically rather than chronologically. There is no guarantee, therefore, that the first oracles presented are the earliest ones. Chapter 1, for instance, may well have been placed where it is because it is a good example of Isaiah's basic message. Just when in his career it was delivered is a matter of some debate, but it probably was delivered in 701 B.C.

The Life and Times of Isaiah

Part I: Isaiah 1-39.

ACCORDING to 1:1 Isaiah prophesied during the reigns of four Judean kings: Uzziah (Ahaziah), Jotham, Ahaz, and Hezekiah. This means that he was active no earlier than 783 and no later than 687 B.C. If Chapter 6 describes his initial call to be a prophet, he began his prophetic ministry in 742. In any event, he may well have been a "working" prophet for more than forty years.

These were some of the most crucial years in the life of the people of Israel. After a relatively prosperous time under Jeroboam II in the north and Ahaziah in the south, Syria-Palestine was plunged into chaos through the machinations of Tiglath-pileser III and his successors to the throne in Assyria. Isaiah, who was a Judean, witnessed from a distance the political turmoil of the northern kingdom and then its eventual collapse in 721. He was also an eye-witness to several invasions of Judah by Assyrian forces, particularly during the reign of Hezekiah. He knew of Egyptian intrigue and revolutionary plots and experienced both the temerity and timidity of the Judean kings.

Unlike his predecessors, Amos and Hosea, Isaiah seems to have been a member of the aristocracy. Perhaps he was also of a priestly family as Jeremiah and Ezekiel were, for he seems to have entered the inner temple, a place reserved for priests alone. His father is identified as Amoz (not to be confused with Amos) but this tells us little about his family background. A more important clue is that he is often as pictured as speaking rather intimately with both king Ahaz and king Hezekiah. Probably only a member of the ruling "Establishment" would have been able to enter into such familiar relationships with royalty.

Isaiah apparently was married to a woman called "the prophetess" —a sign that Isaiah's own "prophethood" was a recognized occupation. In other words, she may well have been called such because her husband occupied an accepted position of prophet within Jerusalem society. They had at least two sons, Shearjashub (A remnant shall return) and Mahershalalhashbaz (The spoil speeds, the prey hastes). Like Hosea (cf. Hosea 1:4-8) Isaiah gave them names which expressed some aspect of his prophetic message. In contrast to Hosea, Isaiah seems to have experienced no marital difficulties.

As counsellor to kings Isaiah promoted a policy of political isolationism. That is to say, he believed that the only way Judah could live through the years of Assyrian aggression was by avoiding as much as possible all foreign alliances. Hence, he was equally critical of Ahaz and his pro-Assyrian policy and Hezekiah, who cooperated with the Babylonian revolutionary Merodach-baladan who, upon the death of Sargon II, tried to throw off the Assyrian yoke.

Although pragmatically defensible, this isolationistic policy of Isaiah was based upon his vision of Yahweh as the "Holy One of Israel." Yahweh is seen as *kadosh,* (holy) that is, as set apart from the world. Israel, says Isaiah, should reflect the holiness of God by being "set apart" herself. Only then will her glory, like the glory of the Lord, radiate throughout the world.

Isaiah, unlike Micah and Jeremiah, seems to have placed great stock in the Temple of God. Not only did he see his great vision there (Chapter 6); he may have regarded the Temple as invulnerable to destruction, at least during his own day. Although this belief may have been defensible when he prophesied, it was to lead to a rather naive optimism in the next century. Judeans came to believe that because the Temple was Yahweh's, he would protect it and its city, Jerusalem, from harm. The failure of Sennacherib to conquer the city during the reign of Hezekiah only strengthened this belief.

Isaiah, however, was certainly not one who believed that Yahweh would side with Judah no matter what. On the contrary, he called upon Judah to fulfill the terms of the covenant and, in particular, to promote social justice. More than almost any other prophet, Isaiah emphasized the plight of the orphan, the widow, and the poor. Furthermore, he saw that failure to live up to the covenant had spelled doom for the northern kingdom and would mean doom for Judah as well. Isaiah saw the whole of history as expressive of God's will. The Assyrians might be ruthless and ungoldly men, but they were also the "rod of God's anger" (10:5). Through them, God brought his judgment to his unfaithful people.

As a Judean, Isaiah seems to have placed great faith in the Davidic kingship as a source of hope. At the same time, he was quite critical of the particular kings who sat on the throne of Judah during his day. His messages say little about Uzziah and Jotham, but concerning Ahaz he is less than laudatory. Hezekiah receives somewhat more favorable treatment, but he too is attacked when he seeks to secure himself through political alliances. On the whole, however, Isaiah spends less time talking about the present kings than about the future king who will restore the glory of Israel. Although he does not use the term Messiah (the anointed one), the prophecies of Chapters 9 and 11 are thoroughly Messianic. There is much disagreement among scholars as to whether these passages are original with him, but to this author there seems to be no compelling reason to think they are not. If they are, Isaiah looked forward to a son of David who would again lead Israel to greatness, not through the power of the sword but through the strength of holiness. There are some indications that Isaiah actually expected the fulfillment of these dreams during his life-time, but such was not to be the case. In fact, after Hezekiah, the evil Manasseh came to the throne and adopted a thoroughly pro-Assyrian policy and many pagan religious practices. Tradition has it that in his old age Isaiah was killed by Manasseh who could not countenance his pronouncements. There is no way to confirm or deny this belief, but it is certainly within the realm of possibility that Isaiah eventually met a martyr's death.

Analysis

A. God's Yes and No to Judah (Chapters 1-5)

AFTER AN OPENING superscription in verse one which gives the father and time of Isaiah, an oracle, proclaimed, perhaps, after the decimation of Judah by Sennacherib in 701 or by Sargon in 711, introduces Isaiah's work as a whole. Isaiah begins by branding Judah a sick society which has lost its "instinct" for God. Animals know their masters, but Judah neither knows nor understands Yahweh (1:1-6). Then he describes the country as ravaged and desolate with only a few survivors (1:7-9), a situation which presupposes one of the Assyrian invasions mentioned above.

In 1:10-17 Isaiah becomes more specific about the faults of the people, pointing to hyprocritical religion as displeasing to God. Yahweh is pictured as thoroughly disgusted with all the sacrifices and special feast days and solemn assemblies. What he wants is not more "religion" but more justice.

> Cease to do evil,
> learn to do good;
> Seek justice,
> correct oppression;
> Defend the fatherless,
> plead for the widow. (1:17)

God calls Judah to reason with him and promises forgiveness in return for faithfulness (1:18-20), but Jerusalem is hardly capable of that, for she is full of rebels, murderers, and money-hungry men.

Therefore, punishment is to come so that the evil may be purged and the righteous remnant saved. Chapter 1 offers a worthy introduction to the thought of Isaiah as a whole, for in it the essential argument which he returns to repeatedly is set forth. Judah is called to know (*yadaʿ*) God, not just through the formalism of the cult but with the whole self. Such knowledge implies not merely a spiritual feeling but acts of justice and mercy. Because Judah does not have such knowledge, she will be punished by historical disaster. But beyond that disaster is hope, at least for a remnant. Zion will be redeemed by justice (1:27).

Chapters 2-4 contain a number of shorter oracles which continue and expand upon these themes. In 2:1-4 the hope of Judah beyond disaster is expressed in the most lyric way. Finally, when the judgments end, the hope of Israel will be fulfilled. All nations and peoples shall flow to Zion and learn the law of God. Then peace shall reign, as swords are beaten into ploughshares and spears into pruning hooks. Whether this passage was actually by Isaiah himself is a matter of some debate. If it is not, it is certainly consistent with the Messianic vision found elsewhere in the book.

Having set forth the glorious hope, the text returns to Isaiah's critique of the present time. Judah, in a word, is full of idolaters and Isaiah foresees only disaster for the immediate future. Here he sets forth a theme which is repeated often throughout his oracles. God will have a day against all that is proud and haughty and men will hide like moles in the ground to try to escape his consuming anger (2:12-22).

In Chapter 3 Isaiah turns specifically to Judah and graphically describes the disaster which will befall all classes and types of men. The elders and princes will be judged with especial harshness for grinding the faces of the poor in the dust (3:13-15). Then he turns on the women, mocking them for their vain and haughty ways and promising them the most shameful condition because of their pride (3:16-4:2). This section ends with a prose passage, obviously by a later follower of Isaiah which again paints a glorious picture of the hope which is to come and which must be held in juxtaposition to the present situation.

Chapter 5 is a beautiful parable-song in which Isaiah compares Judah to a vineyard which bears no fruit and which therefore must be cut down by the vine-dresser. It begins with the most pastoral tone and ends with telling bluntness. This "protest song" may have been sung by Isaiah at a Tabernacle feast at which the vine harvest was traditionally celebrated. In it the symbol of the vine and the vineyard, which is seen so often in Isaiah, is developed.

B. The Holiness of God (Chapters 6-12)

PERHAPS the most important chapter for understanding the message of Isaiah is Chapter 6, in which his famous vision in the Temple is described. Many scholars place this at the very beginning of his ministry, but there seems no absolute reason to do so. Isaiah may have been a prophet for some time before he heard this particular "call." Whether Isaiah actually was in the Temple, serving perhaps as a priest, or whether this vision came in a dream or trance is not certain. In any case, it is a beautiful description of the experience of the Holiness of God. Isaiah sees Yahweh seated upon a high throne with the awful seraphim (not to be confused with the haloed and draped angels of the Hellenistic world) above him. As he gazes, the seraphim chant the now famous Trisagion,

> Holy, holy, holy is the Lord of hosts;
> the whole earth is full of his glory. (6:3)

God is set apart, thrice set apart; yet his influence fills the world. Before this vision of the holiness of God, Isaiah can only confess his sins. A seraph cleanses him with burning fire, however, and when God asks who will speak for him, Isaiah answers affirmatively.

Then follows a most peculiar command. Isaiah is to proclaim God's Word; yet so that no one will perceive or understand. This he is to do until disaster has overtaken his nation and only a stump remains of the tree of Judah. Whether this command was added later as a rationalization for the ineffectiveness of his message or whether Isaiah knew from the beginning that Judah would not listen to him is a much debated point. Significantly, Jesus also saw this as his appointed role (Luke 8:10, Mark 4:12). In any event, Isaiah's vision of holiness was to shape decisively the way in which he spoke about God and conceived of Israel's role in the world.

Chapter 7 contains a biographical narrative set in 734 B.C. in which Isaiah confronts Ahaz while he is examining the defenses around Jerusalem's water supply. Israel and Damascus have formed an alliance against Judah and seek to defeat her and put their own candidate on her throne. Ahaz and the people are very much afraid, but Isaiah advises Ahaz not to worry. God is not with the enemies, he implies. Therefore, they will be defeated and destroyed by Assyria. He offers to give a sign, but Ahaz demurs. Isaiah, however, insists, and in a now famous passage predicts that a young woman (formerly translated virgin) shall bear a son and his name shall be called Immanuel. Before that child is old enough to refuse evil and choose good, both of the attacking nations will be destroyed by Assyria.

Clearly the debate over whether the text should be translated virgin or young woman is beside the point. Isaiah is not speaking of an event several hundred years hence (the birth of Jesus), but of an event which will take place in the immediate future. He is predicting, not the coming of the Messiah, but the fall of Damascus and Samaria.

Chapter 8 continues the story. Isaiah, himself, goes to the prophetess and she conceives and bears a son. Apparently because Ahaz failed to heed his word but instead entered into alliance with Assyria, he names the child not Immanuel (God with us) but Mahershalalhashbaz. (The spoil speeds, the prey hastes). God is with Judah, but because Ahaz has not listened, he is with Judah for judgment! (8:5-15) The chapter ends with a prose passage criticizing the people for listening to mediums and wizards rather than to the Word of Yahweh.

Chapter 9 opens with the famous Messianic passage read so often during the Christmas season: "The people who walked in darkness have seen a great light . . ." The question is, what did this passage mean to Isaiah? He seems to be speaking about an event which was occurring in his day: "For unto us a child is born . . ." (9:6) Is this a poem celebrating the birth of a new prince (Hezekiah) in whom Isaiah placed great hope? If so, the author of the prose introduction in 9:1 attempted to give it a more eschatological meaning by speaking of the hope as coming in "the latter time" (9:1). Isaiah certainly found Hezekiah less than the magnificent figure described and may, himself, have reinterpreted this poem as referring to the far future. As it stands, it expresses profound hope that out of the Davidic lineage will come the expected leader of Israel who will establish justice and righteousness forever.

In 9:8-10:34 Isaiah returns to an oracle of woe, particularly against the northern kingdom. In 10:5-19 he pictures Assyria as the rod of

Yahweh's anger, but also predicts that that ruthless nation will also eventually stand under judgment and be cut down. After a prose passage (10:20-27) which speaks of the survival of a remnant of Israel after the destruction of Assyria, Isaiah returns to a telegraphic portrayal of the approach of the Assyrians and a prediction of their defeat.

In Chapter 11, Isaiah again voices his Messianic expectations, portraying the son of David who is to come to establish justice and peace. Significantly Isaiah's "Messiah" is not so much a warrior as a man of wisdom and understanding. This picture of the peaceful Messiah is mitigated somewhat by 11:10-16 in which Israel and Judah in the Messianic age fight together against their common enemies. Chapter 12 contains a song of thanksgiving which will be sung on that day.

C. The Judgment of the Nations

CHAPTERS 13-23 contain a series of oracles criticizing the various nations. Some may be by Isaiah, but the oracle concerning Babylon in chapter 13:1-22 seems to presuppose a later date. Chapter 14:24-27 concerns the overthrow of Assyria and may well be original. So may the oracle against Philistia in 14:28-32. Chapters 15-16 contain a description of the fall of Moab, while Chapter 17 speaks of the end of Damascus and Samaria. Then follow oracles against Ethiopia (18), Egypt (19-20), Babylon (21:1-10), Edom (21:11-12), Arabia (21:13-17), and Tyre (23). Chapter 22 contains a description of the decimation of Judah (22:1-14) and a prose account of the replacement of a corrupt steward (Shebna) by Eliakim.

D. A Collection of Sermons (Chapters 24-35)

THIS SECTION contains a number of poetic oracles in which many of the characteristic Isaianic ideas and images are expanded and reexpressed. The double-edged symbol of wine, which suggests both joy and drunkenness, is used repeatedly. So too are repeated the symbols of the vine and the vineyard and the stone which is both a foundation and a stone of stumbling. Isaiah's criticism of those who rely upon political alliances is expressed most powerfully in 31:1-3 and 30:1-5. Throughout this section, the present judgment is held in tension with Isaiah's hope for a Messianic age of peace. Chapter 32:1-8 contains a beautiful description of the new age in which the wrongs of the present age are righted and the king will reign in righteousness.

There is considerable agreement among scholars that much of the material in this section is post-eighth century. Chapters 24-27 are often described as "apocalyptic" and are given, accordingly, a very late date. To this writer, there seems to be no absolute reason to deny these passages to Isaiah. Although they do speak of the final judgment and the coming new age, they lack the symbolism, pseudonymity, and bizarre imagery of much later apocalyptic writing, while they do contain several Isaianic phrases and symbols. If these are by a later hand, the author quite consciously sought to use many of the motifs of the prophet of Jerusalem. Chapter 35, on the other hand, is very similar in style and content to the work of the author of Chapters 40-55 and may conceivably be by him.

E. Isaiah and Hezekiah (Chapters 36-39)

This final section of the first part of Isaiah contains a largely prose account of certain events during the reign of Hezekiah which is paralleled rather closely in II Kings 18:13-20:19. Most scholars agree that the compilers of Isaiah borrowed this material from Kings. To this writer, however, it would seem more logical that the material was preserved by Isaiah's school and then used by the authors of Kings.

Isaiah 36:1-37:37 contains the dramatic story of the invasion of Sennacherib in 701. The story of Rabshakeh's jeering challenge to Jerusalem is particularly well told (36). Chapter 38 contains an account of Hezekiah's sickness and Isaiah's prediction of his recovery. Chapter 39 concludes the story of Isaiah, the prophet, with a brief account of Hezekiah's dealings with the envoys of Merodach-baladan and Isaiah's word of warning to him.

In many respects, Isaiah's prophecy is much like that of his predecessors, Amos and Hosea. Like both of them he sees that Israel's sin will lead irrevocably to punishment by God in history. Like Hosea in particular he also foresees beyond the disaster an age of hope and peace. Isaiah's major contributions to the prophetic movement lie not in the realm of new insights but in the further development and beautiful expression of old ones.

In Isaiah we find the development of the description of Israel's hope in terms of a Messianic king who is to come. Isaiah also elaborates much more fully the meaning of Yahweh's holiness to Israel. Isaiah is a poetic genius who knows precisely how to weave the traditional prophetic motifs together to achieve the greatest impact. He is particularly the master of the double-edged symbol which can mean both hope and doom, depending on how it is read. Throughout his oracles he attempts to say both Yes and No to Judah all at once and he does so with great success.

Part II: Isaiah 40-66.

There are many reasons for thinking that this section of Isaiah is by one or more later authors rather than by Isaiah, himself. With Chapter 40 the style of poetry changes, the theological message is developed if not altered, and the historical references concern the sixth century rather than the eighth. Particularly telling is the mention of Cyrus, the Persian Emperor who defeated Babylonia in 539 (44:28, 45:1). Conservative scholars argue, of course, that these are the result of Isaiah's ability to predict the future, but other examples of such precision in the Old Testament are rare. Furthermore, if Isaiah did speak of Cyrus, one wonders what possible meaning this could have had for his hearers. The name is introduced, without explanation, as one apparently quite familiar to his hearers.

Another possibility is to excise these references to Cyrus as later additions to the text, but if one does so one must also explain why the audience addressed is so patently different from the audience of Isaiah of Jerusalem. Chs. 40-55 speak of the judgment which has come rather than of the coming judgment (40:2). The audience clearly lacks political power and responsibility. There is no word of the oppression of the poor by the Judean kings but only of the oppression of the Jews by a foreign nation. When such a foreign nation is named, it is Babylonia, and not Assyria which is mentioned.

Moreover, the author speaks not of the impending exile, but of a glorious return from exile to Jerusalem. The prophet sometimes criticizes Israel for her lack of faith, but his message, as a whole, is a message of hope, not of doom. Zion is now forsaken and forlorn, but soon the people will return to her with great joy.

All of these considerations indicate that Chapters 40-55 are best dated during the exilic period, probably sometime shortly before the conquest of Babylon by Cyrus in 539 B.C. Because of the affinities with Isaiah 1-39, it is reasonable to assume that the author was a member of the Isaianic school of prophecy who sought to "complete" the message of his school's master by adding a prophetic word of hope for his own day. Significantly, his hope is not in a son of David but in Cyrus who is identified as Messiah (45:1). His vision for Israel is one of a new exodus rather than a new David.

In some respects, Second Isaiah's hope was quite accurately fulfilled. Cyrus did defeat the Babylonians and, because of his enlightened policy, did allow many captive peoples, including the Jews, to go home. In fact, according to Ezra 1:1-4, he not only freed them but offered financial assistance! Still, the way back was hardly along a glorious highway built for the benefit of the Jews. Life in the desolate land was hard and the returnees faced many obstacles. Chs. 56-66 reflect more accurately this latter situation and therefore stem in all probability from the early post-exilic period. Still, the exiles were released and Second Isaiah served as the herald of those good tidings. In Isaiah, as in the Old Testament as a whole, salvation and redemption are terms to describe the winning of this-worldly freedom, not the joys of some heavenly paradise after death.

Simply because the author of 40-55 is an unnamed figure who only added to the tradition of his school, one should not think of him as a lesser prophet than Isaiah himself. Indeed, there are few other places in Scripture where prophetic poetry rises to such heights of brilliance. Second or Deutero-Isaiah is a master of the rhetorical question and of majestic, transcendent description. Moreover, in his writings we find the development of a far more explicit theology for Israel. Here we find spelled out the idea of God as creator and as elector of Israel as the traditions of Israel now come into a common theological focus. Above all, we find in 40-55 the expression of a radical monotheism which is sometimes implied, but not often clearly stated in the writings of the other prophets.

One of the most striking and perplexing features of 40-55 is the Servant Songs found in 42:1-4, 49:1-6, 50:4-9, and 52:13-53:12. No other passages of the Old Testament have received such a variety of interpretations. One must ask, first, are these passages by Second Isaiah himself? They intrude into the text rather unexpectedly and hence *may* be later additions. An analysis of poetic form and language, however, is inconclusive and scholars are thoroughly divided about the issue. So also is there great divergence of opinion about the identification of the servant mentioned. Only the most conservative scholars regard these passages as predictions of Jesus, though Jesus may have regarded himself as fulfilling the role outlined in them. Some argue that they refer to Second Isaiah himself (note the use of the first person singular in 49:1-6 and 50:4-9). Chs. 52:13-53:12 would then have been added by his disciples. Others, cognizant of the fact that the prophet himself hardly seems to have fulfilled the role described, argue that the servant is either a) Israel understood corporately, b) Israel understood as an ideal, c) some historical figure such as Moses or Jeremiah, or d) some historical figure of the future.

To this writer, b) seems the best option. Since II Isaiah refers to Israel elsewhere as Yahweh's servant and since he is concerned about the meaning of Israel's suffering in exile, it would appear that this is his description of what the true Israel's role in the world ought to be. Israel is called to suffer for the sins of the world and in so doing to bring God's law and his hope to the nations. Israel died in the exile (53:7-9) but can hope in a corporate resurrection from the grave of historical death (53:10-12, Cf. Ezekiel 37:1-14). Although these passages do appear rather unexpectedly in the text, there seems no sufficient reason to regard them as by a later hand.

Third Isaiah

MOST SCHOLARS distinguish 56-66 from 40-55 as by still a third author or set of authors. The reasons for so doing are not quite as compelling as for separating 1-39 and 40-55, but on balance are fairly cogent. Surely, if Second Isaiah wrote 56-66 his poetic genius had, for the most part, left him. So too had his concern for many of the themes which dominate 40-55. Not only does the author now seem more concerned with observance of the Sabbath, the prohibition of swine's flesh, and other cultic matters; there are indications that he now addresses a people who again are inhabiting Judah and who are disturbed that the glorious return described in 40-55 was not so glorious after all.

It has been suggested that 56-66 is the product of Second Isaiah's old age and is addressed to those Jews who have now returned to Judah as he predicted. This is not at all beyond the realm of possibility. It is more probable, however, that this section is by a number of members of the Isaianic school of prophecy who added their own oracles to the tradition of their school. The various prophecies found in this section, though echoing the vocabulary and style of both First and Second Isaiah, seem less connected than those of their predecessors.

Certainly, however, there are important consistencies throughout this section which must not be overlooked. In contrast to Ezra and Nehemiah, 56-66 is highly universalistic in scope. Foreigners and eunuchs are offered a place in Israel (56:3-5) and Israel's mission is conceived as to and for the Gentiles (66:18-21). Although concerned about observance of the Sabbath, one author at least is highly critical of the rebuilding of the Temple and the offering of sacrifices (66:1-4). The slaughtering of an ox, in fact, is seen as equivalent to murder!

Because of the lack of highly eloquent poetic style, Third Isaiah is often glossed over as of lesser importance than the other parts of the book. Surely, the writing is not quite so memorable. Still, one finds in its pages the most extraordinary development of prophetic thought in which Temple worship is set aside and Israel is called to enter the world empowered by the Spirit of God. It is a happy fact that Isaiah does not end with Chapter 55.

Analysis (40-66)

SECOND ISAIAH opens in Chapter 40 with eloquent words of comfort to Jerusalem. She has now been pardoned and will apparently soon return home on a glorious highway prepared to her. Ch. 40:6-11 contains a highly stylized prophetic call in which the prophet "overhears" a conversation in the heavenly court. The prophet resists because he knows of the mortality of life, but he is reminded that the word of God stands forever (40:8) and that now Yahweh is coming to care for Israel once more.

Chapter 40:12-13 contains a whole series of rhetorical questions which indirectly depict the majesty of God and the foolishness of idols. There are few places in the Bible where radical monotheism is more eloquently set forth. 40:27-31 encourages Israel to have faith that this creator of the universe and Lord of history will grant her strength once more.

Chapter 41 points to the approaching conqueror (Cyrus) who is, in his conquest, serving Yahweh. The pagans may make idols (41:7), but Jacob can look forward to a glorious future. Israel will be redeemed (i.e., bought out of slavery) and made strong. God knows and declares the future; no pagan can do the same (41:21-24).

Chapter 42 begins with a servant song (Vs. 1-4) which describes the servant as a bringer of justice. Vs. 5-9 then depict Israel's role in history as a light to the nations (V. 6.) 42:10-13 is a psalm of joy, while Vs. 14-17 proclaim that Yahweh through his actions will put the idolaters to shame. Then the author turns upon the unfaithful Israelites, criticizing them for their devotion to idols (42:18-25). Despite her sins, Yahweh will now save Israel (43:1-7) and call her once more to be his witnesses (8-13). In fact, Babylon is being defeated for the sake of Israel! (14-21) Yahweh was more than justified in punishing his sinful people (22-28), but now they are to be given another chance through the power of his Spirit. This time Israel will respond favorably (44:1-8).

After a prose passage by a later hand (44:9-20) which restates Second Isaiah's critique of idol worship, the themes already set forth are repeated in 44:21-45:25. In 44:28 and 45:1 Cyrus is identified by name as God's anointed (Messiah) who is the instrument through which Israel's freedom will be obtained. Once more Isaiah attacks idolatry (45:9-13) and promises a great future to Israel (45:14-25).

Chapters 46 and 47 (a taunt song) describe the fall of Babylon while Chapter 48 again declares that all this has taken place for the benefit of Israel. The chapter ends with a call to flee from Babylon with joy and trust that Yahweh will care for Israel as she was cared for during the Exodus (48:20-22).

In Chapter 49 the prophet addresses the coastlands and their peoples, explaining to them that he has been called by Yahweh to bring Israel back to God to be a light to the nations. Whether he speaks in his own right or as the "Suffering Servant" mentioned elsewhere is a debated point. If he speaks of the latter, the suffering servant must have been an historical personality living during his time. If this refers to himself then it tells us much about his own self-understanding. In 49:1 he speaks very much like Jeremiah (1:4), recognizing that from birth he was chosen for his appointed task. The prophet is discouraged, thinking that he has worked in vain, but now he is called to actually lead Israel back and to be a light to the nations (49:6).

Chapter 49:8-13 is apparently a separate oracle, but continues to describe the role of whoever it is who is supposed to be speaking. The speaker is given as a covanent to the people, to establish the land, to apportion the desolate heritages, and to free the prisoners. If this does indeed refer to Second Isaiah, himself, he was then to be one of the leaders of the band of exiles who returned shortly after 539 B.C. Could he possibly have been the Sheshbazzar mentioned in Ezra 1:8? This is only an hypothesis, but it is, as least, a possibility. Ch. 49:14-26 then contains a "dialogue" between desolate Zion and Yahweh who returns to her her children. This is but one of several Zion songs found in Second Isaiah.

Chapter 50 begins by seeking to answer a question raised earlier by the prophet Jeremiah who indicated that with the fall of Jerusalem Yahweh and Israel were divorced (Jeremiah 3:1). Second Isaiah denies such a divorce and points to the fact that no bill of divorce was issued (50:1). Yahweh punished Israel but he can also bring her back. Ch. 50:4-9 is a description of how the prophet himself suffered for his message (V. 6) and yet was strengthened by God. In a sense, he here plays the role of the suffering servant himself. 50:10-11 is a call to trust in God and not in one's own "light."

In Chapter 51 the prophet returns to his familiar themes. He reminds Israel of Yahweh's blessing to Abraham (51:2) and again announces the imminent salvation. Vs. 9-10 refer to a no longer extant myth of creation in which Yahweh slew Rahab, the dragon. Chapter 52 is again addressed to Zion who receives the joyful news of salvation.

Chapters 52:13-53:12 contain perhaps the most important servant songs found in Isaiah. The servant is pictured as despised and rejected by men, as a man of sorrows, acquainted with grief (53:3). His suffering, however, is vicarious, for upon him was laid the sin of all the people. Finally he is executed, but his hope is not dead. "He shall see his offspring and prolong his days and shall receive a portion with the great" (53:10-11). Although this passage may refer to some historical person, it is more probable, as it has already been said, that this is a poetic description of the life and death and resurrection of the true and righteous Israel.

Chapter 54 is again an exultant song of joy which promises peace and protection to Israel. Chapter 55 emphasizes that God's salvation is free for the asking. Israel must only return to Yahweh and allow him to lead her out to the promised land. Second Isaiah ends then as it began, on a note of comfort and joy. The author of 40-55 knew the reality of both sin and suffering and did not hesitate to depict them. His, however, was a moment of exultation and he expresses that moment to the full. To the modern reader he may perhaps repeat himself too often and may, in retrospect, appear far too optimistic. It must be remembered, however, that he addressed a community which had largely lost hope and could hardly believe that any good news was in the offing. Furthermore, though the age to follow was, in many respects, a dreary one for the returnees, the joy which the released prisoner feels can hardly be over-emphasized. For Second Isaiah the winds of freedom blew through the land and he was bound to dance upon the mountain tops.

Third Isaiah

CHAPTER 56 begins with an exhortation to do righteousness and keep the sabbath (1-2). Then assurance is given to the foreign convert and to the eunuch that there is a place in Israel for him (3-8). Chs. 56:9-57:21 contain a scathing denunciation of wicked rulers, prophets and idolatrous Israelites. Chapter 58 contrasts hypocritical fasting (1-7) and the truly righteous life (8-13). In Chapter 59 the author turns to a pressing question: why is Yahweh's redemption not complete? The answer is clear: because of Israel's continued propensity to sin. Doubtless this was included to explain why Israel's return was not as glorious and victorious as Second Isaiah had predicted.

Chapters 60-62 are so like the prophecies of Second Isaiah that they may in fact be by him. The prophet pictures Yahweh as rising like the sun upon Zion while the rest of the world lies in darkness. Clearly this prophecy must have been uttered before the return to Judah, for a later date would have belied such optimism. In the latter days, which are eschatological in nature, Israel will be served by foreign kings. She will no longer need the sun and moon, for she will be lighted by Yahweh himself.

Chapter 61, which was read by Jesus in the synagogue at the beginning of his ministry (Luke 4:18-19), again speaks of the call of the prophet to preach good news to the oppressed and proclaim Yahweh's salvation which is at hand. Chapter 62 expresses the prophet's expectancy that Jerusalem shall soon be redeemed. Chapter 63:1-6 contains a curious dialogue between the watchman and Yahweh who comes covered with blood from his judgments.

Isaiah 63:7-64:12 is a moving communal lament which calls upon Yahweh to remember his steadfast love and save Judah. Clearly this comes out of the post-exilic community whose expectations were heightened by Second Isaiah's glorious message but who were frustrated by the political and social realities which faced them upon their return.

In many respects the tone of this section is similar to that of the book of Lamentations.

Chapter 65 is reminiscent of the pre-exilic prophets, for it paints a vivid picture of idolatry and unrighteousness in Israel. The author predicts that such evil will not go unpunished. God's servants will be rewarded while the unrighteous shall perish (65:13-16). The chapter ends with an eschatological vision of the new heaven and new earth to be created by Yahweh in which the old sins will be wiped away, in which joy and prosperity will prevail, and in which old natural enemies will live in peace (65:17-25).

Isaiah closes with both a word of judgment and a word of hope. The author attacks the rebuilding of the Temple and the offering of sacrifices. To the faithful, however, Yahweh promises joy. The wicked will be punished (66:15-17) but God's servants will prosper. Finally, Yahweh will gather all the nations and reveal to them his glory. The exiled Israelites shall return to Jerusalem, carried by the believing foreigners! In the new heaven and new earth all flesh shall worship the Lord, for the unrighteous will have perished.

So ends the book of Isaiah. As usual, the promised salvation of Israel has come after a fashion; yet still remains in the future as a pillar of fire and a pillar of cloud. The Jews have again a homeland, but their destiny remains incomplete.

CHAPTER XVII

Jeremiah: Introduction and Analysis

The Nature of the Book
Jeremiah's Life and Times
Analysis

LTHOUGH THE BOOK Jeremiah contains many powerful poetic oracles and some interesting vignettes concerning the prophet in prose, its over-all impact upon the reader is likely to be one of confusion. It seems, upon first reading, to be a vast hodgepodge of undated poems and unchronologically arranged prose passages designed to bewilder rather than help the student of Scripture. To be sure, some basic divisions of the book can be discerned, but one can hardly help but wonder why its editors put together the materials as they did.

This is no time to berate the ancient redactors for a job poorly done nor to try to determine just why they did their work as they did. It *is* however, important for the reader to remember that the book of Jeremiah, like the book of Isaiah, is an anthology, not a biography, and must be treated as such. The editors probably had no intention of producing a volume which would be read from cover to cover like a novel or play. Their purpose was not biographical or historical but theological. The emphasis is upon the Word of God which Jeremiah spoke rather than upon Jeremiah himself.

Those of us who wish to learn about the prophet and his times will find plenty of material to work with in this book, for many sections of it are biographical or autobiographical. Still, we must work carefully if we are to piece together a fairly continuous life of the prophet. Even when such scholarly work has been done with the greatest meticulousness, there still will remain many hypotheses unproved and many questions left unanswered.

The Nature of the Book.

The best way to begin this task is to examine the materials which lie before us. The book of Jeremiah, first of all, contains a large number of poems, most of which seem to be by the prophet himself. Although there may be some additions to the text, Jeremiah, unlike Isaiah, is by and/or about one man, not two or three. Among the poems are found several which are autobiographical in nature: Jeremiah's call (1:4-10), and his so-called Confessions (11:18-12:6, 15:10-12 (in prose); 15:15-21; 17:14-18; 18:18-23; 20:7-13; 14-18). These passages not only tell us much about the prophet but allow us to see him "from within," as he expresses himself most candidly to Yahweh. Also among the poems, of course, are a large number of oracles delivered in Judah on a variety of occasions.

Three types of prose are to be found. First of all, there are the many passages which purport to be direct quotations from the prophet. Since most prophets proclaimed their messages in poetry, many scholars suggest that these are by a later hand. Some find in them hints that their author was attempting to modify Jeremiah's own message somewhat. Although there can be no absolute proof in this regard it seems to me that, on the whole, these passages express a message quite similar in content, if not in style, to that of the poetic oracles. It is even conceivable that Jeremiah dictated some of them to his scribe Baruch in prose. The question is certainly by no means a minor one, for if one were to excise all the prose passages as by a later hand, one would be forced to attribute both the famous Temple sermon of Chapter 7 and the vision of the new covenant of 31:27-34 to someone else. One would then have to reassess Jeremiah's original message accordingly. In this chapter, at any rate, we will assume that most of these prose passages do reflect the substance of Jeremiah's message and may be used in describing his prophetic vision.

Second, there are a large number of chapters relating stories about Jeremiah and his work. These are found throughout the text (beginning with Chapter 7), but those in Chapters 21-45 are dated and hence are most useful in studying the life of Jeremiah. Since Jeremiah was accompanied by a scribe, Baruch, who wrote down the prophet's oracles, it is often assumed that he was the author of these biographical sections and that they are therefore quite reliable. Unfortunately all of them relate events which happened in and after 609 B.C. and hence tell us nothing about Jeremiah's early life. Furthermore, they are only vignettes and hardly constitute the basis for a complete biography. Still, because of them we know more about Jeremiah than about any other Old Testament prophet.

Finally, there is the historical account of the fall of Jerusalem found in Chapter 52 which, like Isaiah 36-39, is closely paralleled in II Kings 24:18-25:30. This was undoubtedly a later addition to the text which was copied from Kings, rather than vice versa.

Within Jeremiah, there are several hints that the editors of the book had before them and used earlier Jeremiac anthologies. Ch. 25:13, for instance, sounds like the ending of a collection. We know from Chapter 36 that Jeremiah did dictate a scroll to Baruch which contained his pre-605 B.C. oracles. Baruch proclaimed it in the Temple and eventually it was read before King Jehoiakim. The king, in anger, burned the scroll, but Jeremiah dictated another one with some additions to it (36:32). Many scholars have hypothesized that this collection formed the basis for 1:1-25:13, though no one could regard them as absolutely the same. This section of the book, for instance, contains Jeremiah's confessions, which seem highly inappropriate to have been included in the original work. Some chapters are even dated during the post-605 period. Furthermore, the original scroll was read three times in one day; 1-25, as it stands, seems too long for that.

Chapters 30-31 also seem to constitute a special section. This is often called Jeremiah's "Book of Consolation," for it contains his vision of hope for the future. Another collection of oracles, this time dealing with the foreign nations, is found in chapters 46-51. Like Isaiah 13-23 and Ezekiel 25-32, this anthology presents a prophetic critique of Judah's neighbors and enemies. To what extent 46-51 is by Jeremiah is a matter of some debate.

Jeremiah's Life and Times

WHAT DO ALL these various materials reveal to us about the prophet? Both a great deal and frustratingly little. About some moments in his life we know much; about several long periods there is total silence. According to the superscription (1:1-3) Jeremiah was from a priestly family of Anathoth, a village about three miles north of Jerusalem. Many have speculated that he might have been descended from Abiathar, the high priest who served under David but who was exiled to Anathoth by Solomon. (I Kings 2:26-27) He began to prophesy in 627, the thirteenth year of King Josiah and the year of the death of Asshurbanipal, the last great Emperor of Assyria. Since he was only a boy when he experienced his prophetic call (1:6), he must have been born about the time when Josiah took office. As a youthful prophet, then, he witnessed the crumbling of the Assyrian Empire, the reforms of Josiah (622), the expansion of Judah under Josiah, and the king's tragic death in 609. Unfortunately, however, though some of the oracles found in his book may come from this period, most of them are not easily identifiable. It used to be fashionable to think that 1:11-19 refers to the Scythian invasions which, according to Herodotus, took place during and after the last years of Asshurbanipal, but this theory is now regarded with suspicion by many, for few, if any, evidences of such an invasion have been found by archaeologists. Chapters 2 and 3 may contain oracles from the time of Josiah, but these have certainly been reedited at a later time.

Just what Jeremiah's attitude toward the reform of Josiah initially was cannot be fully determined, but it may well be that he thought it a step in the right direction. The fact that he is later saved by men who supported Josiah (26:24; 36; cf. II Kings 22:12) seems to link him to that reform movement. At the same time, however, he came to see that Josiah's outward reforms did not really change the heart of Judah and were, after all, only pretense (3:6-10). Josiah may have reformed the cult, but Judah's propensity to sin remained.

Much more is known of Jeremiah under the reigns of Jehoiakim and Zedekiah. In both the prose and the poetic passages Jeremiah is shown to have been at logger-heads with Jehoiakim and all that that petty despot stood for. Jehoiakim, in his turn, both despised and feared Jeremiah and would undoubtedly have had him killed had Jeremiah not hidden from him and received help from friends.

Nor was Jehoiakim alone in his animosity toward Jeremiah. Jeremiah regarded the pre-Egyptian policy of his nation as pure folly, for he believed (and rightly so) that Babylonia, under Nebuchadnezzar, would be victorious over any Egyptian-formed or inspired coalition against him. Hence he counselled what seemed to his hearers a pro-Babylonian policy, a stance which involved submission to the yoke of the great eastern empire. The religious leaders, who believed that Yahweh would protect Jerusalem again as he had during the invasion of Sennacherib, were vitriolic in their abuse. So too were some of the political leaders who desired freedom at all costs for Judah. To them Jeremiah was clearly guilty of treason.

Jeremiah, however, was not a man to back down. Although personally he wished that he had never become a prophet and wanted to keep silence, he also could not suppress his prophetic inspiration. His confessions, in particular, reveal his agonizing struggle with the God whose Word he could not help but utter. Hence he stood as one man against society, always biting in his criticism of his nation, always walking the knife edge between safety and disaster.

Things did not improve much with the death of Jehoiakim. The king had already acted upon his pro-Egyptian sentiments and his son, Jehoiachin, had to cope with their results. Jerusalem was besieged and submitted rather quickly. Jehoiachin and many other officials were taken into exile in 597, but Jerusalem was spared total destruction. To Jeremiah, this was but a prelude to further disaster to follow and he wrote to the exiles, telling them not to expect any early return (Chapter 29). Many of his countrymen, however, unmindful of where their hopes were leading them, still desired freedom for Judah and believed that they could find it through an alliance with Egypt.

Zedekiah, a brother of Jehoiakim, was placed upon the throne by Babylonia and may, himself, have doubted the ability of the nationalists to throw off the Babylonian yoke. He was a weak man, however, and was soon sucked into the whirlpool of disaster which was to follow. The nationalists cried for freedom and despite the fact that Egypt had been decisively defeated at the battle of Charchemish in 605, still clung to the hope that an alliance of little nations with Egypt might be successful against Nebuchadnezzar. Perhaps Babylonia's relatively mild treatment of Jerusalem in 597 gave them some encouragement to try again.

In the meantime, Jeremiah strove through oracle and symbolic action to convince the Judahites not to indulge themselves in such foolishness. Chapter 27 tells of how Jeremiah wore a yoke around his neck to symbolize the whole area's subordination to Nebuchadnezzar. For his pains he received prophetic rebuke from Hananiah, who predicted freedom from Babylonia (Ch. 28). On other occasions, he was accused of attempted desertion (Ch. 37), thrown into a well and left for dead (Ch. 38), and imprisoned. Throughout all this time Zedekiah revealed an ambivalent attitude toward Jeremiah. On the one hand, an attempt was made on Jeremiah's life with the permission of the king. On the other, he repeatedly sought advice from Jeremiah and even asked him to pray for the city.

Jeremiah's attitude was never softened by Zedekiah's requests for prophetic advice. He was consistently critical of Zedekiah's policies and when the king asked for a word of encouragement, told him the city would fall before the Babylonians. Only when the end was patently near did Jeremiah offer a gesture of hope. Just at the time when political and social chaos was breaking he bought a field in Anathoth to symbolize his belief that eventually there would be "business as usual" in the land (Ch. 32). The hope, however, was not for Zedekiah, who lived to see his sons executed before he himself was blinded and taken into captivity. In 588, responding to Judah's pro-Egyptian policies, the Babylonians returned to besiege Jerusalem. The Lachish letters, found in a guard room in the Tell of Lachish, give information about the siege of that city which also fell after holding out for some time. In 587/6 B.C., on the 9th of Av, Jerusalem fell. This time the Babylonians were not so kind. The walls of the city were torn down, the Temple destroyed, and the king, as has just been said, was taken into exile along with large segments of the population.

Jeremiah was offered the possibility of going to Babylonia, apparently as a free man, but he elected to stay in Judah under the new Governor, Gedaliah. Gedaliah was soon assassinated by the remnant of nationalists, however, and the land plunged into even greater chaos. Jeremiah's advice was asked and he told the people to stay in the land. The remaining leaders were afraid of the Babylonians though and fled to Egypt, taking Jeremiah and Baruch with them. In Chapters 43-45 we see Jeremiah, now an old man, attacking the exiled Jews in Egypt for their worship of the queen of heaven and their other idolatries and promising once more God's judgment upon them. Apparently the prophet died in exile, an eloquent but unheeded spokesman of God's Word.

Throughout his career as a prophet, Jeremiah was a blunt and stubborn proclaimer of the Word (*davar:* word, event) which Yahweh continued to speak, a Word which shattered all the vain illusions of a people who believed that the Lord was on their side. More than almost any other prophet, Jeremiah was a "loner," knowing the company and friendship of only his faithful scribe, Baruch. Marriage was specifically denied him (16:1), so he experienced neither the comfort of home nor the joys of a family. He was a man "set apart" (1:5) and "walled up" against all enemies (1:18).

Still, he was not just a prophet of vitriolic abuse. His prophecies reveal a great love for his people, even though he could see little hope for them. Like Hosea, who undoubtedly influenced Jeremiah's thought and style enormously, Jeremiah was at once a forbidding "chastizer" and a sensitive person who cried out his laments and complaints from the depth of this inmost being. In Jeremiah, more than in any other prophet, we come to see the individual behind the oracle and sense the tremendously demanding and paradoxical nature of the prophetic office.

Because of Jeremiah's personal complaints, he is often described as a proponent of "individual" religion. Nothing could be further from the case. Throughout his ministry he thought of the demands and promises of Yahweh as meant for all Israel and therefore called all the people to attend to their responsibilities. Sin, for him, was not an individual matter but permeated the whole community. When hope is expressed, it is in terms of a covenant between the whole people and God.

Jeremiah's contribution to the prophetic movement was not in his innovative ideas (though his hope for a new covenant in 31:31 is rather distinctive), but in the fact that Jeremiah served as the prophetic witness to the great catastrophe of 587, a catastrophe which marked a decisive turning-point in the history of Israel. After Jeremiah we enter a new age, the age of Judaism, which continues to the present-day. Prophetic successors to Jeremiah there were, but they presented messages markedly different from those of Amos, Hosea, Micah, and Isaiah. Jeremiah, then, represents the last of the "classical" prophets who spoke to the nations of Israel and Judah. In him we find their "prophetic syllogism" brought to its logical, if devastating conclusion.

Analysis

After the superscription in 1:1-3 which gives essential facts about Jeremiah's lineage and time, 1:4-10 contains his own description of his call to prophethood. This call is exceedingly important, for it expresses Jeremiah's own understanding of his prophetic mission. He sees himself as having been chosen, even before his birth, to be a prophet to the nations (1:5). He himself is reluctant to serve—an attitude which he never entirely suppressed, but God over-rides his objection that he is too young. Yahweh promises to deliver him from his enemies (a foreshadowing of the suffering ahead) and places words in his mouth. Jeremiah's job is to proclaim the Word which both destroys and builds (1:10). In 1:11-13 Yahweh reveals in common-place things (an almond branch and a boiling pot) what he is to do. Here we see a prophetic penchant to see in puns a revelation of God's Word (1:11-12).

Beginning in Chapter 2 we find a whole series of poems in which Yahweh is the primary speaker. Undoubtedly these are oracles delivered at different times for different occasions, but it is very difficult to separate them one from another. This may be because Jeremiah himself wove earlier oracles together to form the book read in the Temple and before Jehoikim (Ch. 36).

In any event, Chapter 2 ff sets forth most of the basic themes which are to be repeated over and over again during the course of the work. When Israel was first married to Yahweh she loved him and was protected by him (2:1-3), but before long Israel forgot the God who had saved her from Egypt and began to chase after other gods. Israel broke the covenant long ago; yet she unshamefacedly claims innocence (2:20-22). The truth is that Israel has become a nymphomaniac, cohabiting with any and every god. Her lust for idols is like that of an animal in heat (2:23-25). Only when she gets into trouble does she think of calling on Yahweh for help (2:27), but, of course, such calls are now of no value. The covenant has been broken; therefore, Israel can expect only punishment.

In 3:1 Jeremiah makes his message explicit. Yahweh has divorced Israel! How then can Israel, the harlot, expect him to return to her. That would not even be right according to Deuteronomic law (Cf. Deut. 24:4). Yahweh is now willing to forgive the northern kingdom which has already suffered judgment, but Judah can expect only punishment from his hand. She did not even heed what happened to the northern kingdom and therefore is worse than her sister (3:6-4:12).

In 4:13ff the prophet speaks for himself, describing the coming of judgment from a human vantage point and expressing his own anguish concerning what is to happen. Chapter 5 makes clear that it is not only in cultic matters that Judah has gone astray. Were there righteous men in Jerusalem the city might be saved, but where can one find a man who does justice and seeks truth (5:1)? The Judeans are like animals, lusting not only after idols but after prostitutes and each others' wives. Therefore, a nation shall come from afar and destroy the kingdom and its people.

Still, Judah refuses to listen. The prophets cry "Peace, Peace," when there is no peace (6:14), when the siege is about to begin which will spell the end. No one hears the trumpet sound. No one senses the disaster which is coming from the north in the form of foreign armies. It is too late now. They will not listen. The destroyer is on the march. Judah will be destroyed.

Chapter 7:1-8:3 is a prose sermon said to have been delivered in the Temple by the prophet. Jeremiah warns the people not to depend upon Yahweh's Temple to save them. He reminds them that Yahweh's name once dwelt at Shiloh, but look at Shiloh today! If you left your hypocrisy and idolatry, that might help, he says, but don't come to the Temple and ask Yahweh for help while you also cling to your pagan idols. Jeremiah holds out a choice between righteousness and unrighteousness, but even the possibility of repentance seems too late to avert the disaster. Jerusalem must be destroyed!

In 8:4-25:13 these themes are repeated over and over again. Particularly interesting in this long and diverse section are the "Confessions" found in 8:18-9:3; 11:18-12:6; 15:10-12, 15-21; 17:14-18; 18:18-23; 20:7-13, 14-18 which reveal Jeremiah's own personal reaction to this message of woe. The first is placed in the mouth of Yahweh, but surely seems more appropriately said by Jeremiah. In these very personal passages we find the prophet crying out in behalf of his people, calling for God's help against his enemies, and shaking his fist at Yahweh who has placed him in this dreadful situation. Ch. 20:14-18, in particular, is very similar to the complaints of Job and may, in fact, have inspired them.

Also of interest in this section in Jeremiah's use of symbolic actions to convey his meaning (13:1-14; 19:1-15). Such symbolic prophecy will be much more fully developed by Ezekiel, particularly during his period of dumbness. Jeremiah's failure to marry (16:1) may also be considered a symbolic prophecy, for through his celibacy he portrays Yahweh's own "single" state. The covenant has been broken; hence Yahweh has no wife. Chapter 21 contains the first explicitly dated passage in the book (except for the call), but it is quite apparent that it is placed where it is without regard to chronological considerations, for it is dated late in the reign of Zedekiah. Indeed, from now on it would seem almost as if after the editors had arranged various stories and oracles on separate sheets; the wind came along and completely upset the original order. The editors piled up the papers again without much regard to chronology and left us with the task of arranging them properly.

Doubtless the editors did have reasons for ordering the book as they did, but it may be helpful to rearrange the sections chronologically for the modern reader. Not all sections can be dated, but those which are might be reshuffled in the following way:

Chapter 25:1-23 In the first year of Jehoiakim, Jeremiah preaches a sermon in the Temple, which he predicts will be destroyed. The priests and prophets want to kill him, but he is protected by some of the princes and people who remember a similar prediction by the prophet Micah (cf. Micah 3:12).

Chapter 19:1-2, 10-11, 14-15, 20:1-6 Jeremiah symbolically breaks a flask to depict the destruction of Judah. Pashur, the overseer of the Temple, has the prophet beaten and put in the stocks.

Chapter 36:1-32 In the fourth year of Jehoiakim Jeremiah dictates the scroll of prophesy and then is forced to go into hiding.

Chapter 45:1-5 This is Baruch's response to the dictation of the scroll.

Chapter 35:1-19 Jeremiah uses the Rechabites as an example of faithfulness to faithless Judah.

Chapter 24:1-10 This prophecy concerns the exiles of 597 (the good figs) and those who remained at home (the bad figs).

Chapters 27:1-22, 28:1-17 Jeremiah wears a yoke to symbolize Judah's eventual servitude under Babylonia. When Hananiah breaks his yoke, he then replaces it with one of iron.

Chapters 29:1-32, 50:59-64 Jeremiah sends a letter to the exiles of 597 advising them not to expect an early return. They will have to wait until Babylonia's 70 years of rule are over (cf. Daniel 9:24ff). The letter receives a heated response on the part of Shemaiah, a leader among those exiled.

Chapters 21:1-10, 34:1-7 Jerusalem is now under siege and Zedekiah sends a delegation to the prophet to get advice from Yahweh. Jeremiah answers that Nebuchadnezzar is going to conquer without pity. He advises, therefore, desertion to the Chaldeans. In 34:1-7 Jeremiah again warns Zedekiah, but promises that he will not die by the sword.

Chapters 34:8-22, 37:1-10 The Egyptian army comes and momentarily raises the siege. Before that time all slaves had been set free; upon lifting the siege the nobles take them back forcibly and Jeremiah strongly attacks their action. In 37:1-10 Zedekiah asks Jeremiah's opinion and the prophet predicts the early resumption of the siege.

Chapters 37:11-21; 38:1-28; 39:15-18 During the lifting of the siege, Jeremiah attempts to leave Jerusalem and is arrested for desertion and thrown into prison. Several men take him from prison and throw him in a well, but he is rescued. He is eventually visited by Zedekiah who asks his advice. Jeremiah advises him to give in to Nebuchadnezzar. In 39:15-18 Jeremiah offers a word of hope to his rescuer, Ebed-melek.

Chapter 32:1-16 Jeremiah remains in prison, but arranges to buy a plot of land for himself in Anathoth as a sign of hope.

Chapters 39:1-14, 40:1-6 The victory of the Babylonians is described, together with the capture of Zedekiah and the release of Jeremiah.

Chapters 40:1-41:8 Gedaliah is made Governor and then assassinated by Ishmael, a Davidite.

Chapter 42:1 Jeremiah advises the people not to flee to Egypt, but they refuse to listen to him and carry him off forcibly with them.

Chapter 44:1-30 These are Jeremiah's words of judgment to the exiles who went to Egypt.

Besides these prose passages there are many oracles to be found in the last chapters of the book. Chs. 46-51 is made up of a collection of oracles against foreign nations. This anthology seems to have been separated from its introduction in 25:15ff. In it are found oracles against Egypt (46), Philistia (47), Moab (48), Ammon (49:1-6); Edom (49:7-22), Damascus (49:23-27), Kedar and Hazor (49:28-33), Elam (49:34-39), and Babylonia (50-51). If the last oracle is by Jeremiah it shows that he was by no means "pro-Babylonian."

Another collection is to be found in Chapters 30 and 31. This is a particularly important section, for it is one of the few places where Jeremiah elaborates upon his belief in some hope for his people. Particularly significant is 31:31-34 in which Jeremiah foresees a new covenant written upon the hearts of Israel and Judah. In those days, everyone will know Yahweh, for the covenant will no longer be imposed "from without," but will be written within. Jeremiah does not deny a belief in a Messiah, but he places little emphasis upon such a hope. For him, Israel needs renewal from within rather than just a great leader. Without such a change in heart, Judah will remain as sinful as ever. Throughout the book Jeremiah has expressed a very pessimistic attitude toward the possibility of Judah's ever achieving true righteousness.

> Can the Ethiopian change his skin
> or the leopard his spots?
> Then also you can do good
> who are accustomed to do evil. (13:23-24)

In his vision in the book of consolation he sees such a change as possible, but only through the grace of God.

Jeremiah ends in Chapter 52 with an account parallel to that found in II Kings 24:18-25:30.

CHAPTER XVIII

Ezekiel: Introduction and Analysis

The Life and Times of Ezekiel
Analysis

F THE BOOKS of the three major prophets, Ezekiel surely follows the most logical and coherent plan. There are neither the sizeable additions to the text by a later hand found in Isaiah nor the chronological dislocations of Jeremiah. The book begins with the call of the prophet in 593/2 and with his specific commission (Chapters 1-3). Then follow in Chapters 4-24 a compilation of the prophet's symbolic and oral prophecies concerning the fall of Jerusalem which was to occur in 587/6. Chapters 25-32 contain Ezekiel's oracles against various foreign nations, while Chapters 33-48 outline Ezekiel's vision and hope for the future.

Despite this over-all coherency, however, scholarly debate has raged about Ezekiel concerning a number of critical issues. First of all, there has been considerable divergence of opinion concerning where and when Ezekiel prophesied. The book itself claims that he was among the exiles who were carried away to Babylonia with King Jehoiachin in 598/7. The fact that all of his early oracles are directed to Jerusalem and its people, however, has caused many to doubt this. Some claim that he prophesied in the sixth century, but in Palestine. Others have concocted more fanciful theories, dating his oracles during the reign of Manassah in the seventh century or, for a variety of reasons, in the fourth century. The most reasonable interpreters (in this writer's opinion) accept the basic assertions of the book itself. There seems to be no real problem involved in thinking Ezekiel to have remained in exile, for his point in attacking Jerusalem may well have been to communicate to his hearers in Babylonia the belief that they should not hope for an immediate return to Jerusalem nor should they place undue faith in Yahweh's Temple there as indestructible. Thus, although he speaks to Jerusalem, his message is for the exiles. The fact that there are many hints of Babylonian origin (the bizarre imagery, the mud-brick walls for houses, etc.) seems to confirm the authenticity of the work's assertions regarding place and date.

Another type of question is raised by the figure of Ezekiel, himself. Surely he is the strangest of all the prophets, for he performs many actions which reveal him close to the brink of abnormality. In fact, one wonders whether anyone in his right mind would have lain on his side for 390 days to symbolize the length of time the northern kingdom would be in exile (4:5). This has led several scholars to regard the whole work as fictional. Far from being historical, then, Ezekiel is regarded by some as a character like Daniel, created by some later writer to make certain points about his own day.

It is true that some of Ezekiel's actions do tax the reader's credulity, but there seems to be no good reason to doubt his essential historicity. Clearly the message of Ezekiel, unlike that of the book of Daniel, seems to be best understood when it is assumed to be addressed to a sixth century audience. Ezekiel may be a strange man, but his very strangeness testifies to the impact which exile and the ultimate destruction of Israel's central shrine might well have had upon a young priest. Even his visions, which may leave the reader initially bewildered, can be understood rationally within a sixth century context.

This is not to say, however, that Ezekiel himself wrote his book or that there are no later additions to the text. It is quite probable that editors put the book together after his death and may have added some non-Ezekelian materials to the traditions about and the oracles from him. Still, the book on the whole reflects the thinking and action of one man, who, though strange, manifested an obvious consistency of vision and thought.

The Life and Times of Ezekiel

ACCORDING to 1:1-2 Ezekiel was a priest (probably of the family of Zadok) who was taken into exile in 598/7 and who lived "among the exiles" at Tell Abib by the Chebar canal, near Nippur. In 593/2 he saw a strange vision (which will be discussed later) and through it was called to be a prophet. As such his responsibility was to be a watchman for the house of Israel, calling the people to decide for righteousness. At the same time, Ezekiel was struck dumb so that he could only speak when Yahweh allowed him to (3:27).

As a consequence, Ezekiel communicated his prophetic judgments in part through symbolic actions, though he also used various parables and more typical prophetic oracles to make his message plain. Until 587/6 his message was: Jerusalem and Judah must be destroyed for their sins. At about the time Jerusalem fell, Ezekiel's wife died. Apparently he loved his wife and had no marital problems as Hosea did, but when she died he used the event to communicate his message symbolically. He did not mourn her at all, thus reflecting Yahweh's attitude toward Jerusalem (24:15-24). As soon as the fall had occurred, Ezekiel's dumbness was removed and he could speak freely. Chapters 33-48 contain Ezekiel's post-destruction oracles and reveal a decided change in emphasis. Ezekiel now speaks of hope, of return, of rebuilding. He describes the rebuilt Temple and the return of the glory of the Lord to it. He establishes laws which will pertain to the priesthood in its service there. In part, Ezekiel's vision is highly sober and realistic, particularly in the legal sections, but he also speaks in the most eschatological way about Yahweh's protection of the restored kingdom and the idyllic conditions which will exist "in the latter day."

Ezekiel's actions were sometimes odd and even incomprehensible, but he was by no means an alienated outcast like Jeremiah. He is often pictured speaking with the leaders of the exiled community and offering advice to them. Apparently he was respected and listened to, at least by some. Surely, he, more than anyone else known to us, shaped the beliefs and hopes of that exiled community in Babylon and, in so doing, fostered the development of what later was to be called Judaism. Ezekiel, then, is a transitional figure. His early oracles reflect the motifs and arguments of classical prophecy, but his later words speak to and reflect a radically new situation. Far more than Jeremiah he was the harbinger of the new world which was dawning, a world in which the people of Judah (the Jews) were scattered abroad throughout the world. He taught them how to live in that world, obeying the legal requirements of the Law and following the vision of an eschatological kingdom which the future promised. Ezekiel, then, can be called, if not the father, at least the grandfather of Judaism.

Since we know neither the birth-date nor the death-date of Ezekiel, it is rather difficult to describe the "times" of Ezekiel with any precision. It is usually assumed that he was a younger contemporary of Jeremiah, but there is no absolute proof of this. He may have been older than Jeremiah and may even have served as a prophet in Palestine before he saw his famous vision by the river Chebar in 593/2. In that case, he may have died not many years after Jerusalem's destruction. If the "thirtieth year" mentioned in 1:1 refers to his age, however, he was born in about 623 B.C., during the reign of Josiah. Probably he died during the exilic period, but it is conceivable that he lived to experience the victory of Cyrus in 539 B.C. He would have been about 84 years old if he lived that long.

Considerable information is available about the Babylonian Empire under Nebuchadnezzar and about the fall of Jerusalem. About the only picture we have of the situation of the exiled Jews during this period, however, comes by reading between the lines in the book of Ezekiel. From what is said in that book, it would appear that the situation in Babylonia was not as bad as was anticipated by the preceding prophets. At least the Jews were able to meet together and apparently were given some freedom in the expression of their religion. Eventually, many of them settled down, started farms and businesses, and began to prosper. It is not surprising, therefore, that when the exile was over many of them decided to stay where they were. In post-exilic times, Babylonian Jewry constituted one of the largest and most powerful communities of Jews in the world. At the time of Ezekiel, however, the exiles were still strongly motivated by a desire to return to their homeland. One of Ezekiel's chief aims seems to have been to deny such a return as an immediate or easy possibility and then to focus the community's attention upon what the situation would be like in Jerusalem after the waiting period was over.

Analysis

After the superscription found in 1:1-3 which gives essential facts about the date and place of the prophet, the book opens with one of the most imaginative and, at first glance, confusing visions found in Scripture. Ezekiel sees in a cloud coming from the north four creatures in the likeness of men who nevertheless have four faces, and four wings, and straight legs with hooves. Then there are the strange wheels with eyes on their rims which accompany the creatures, and a firmament shining like crystal, and a throne with someone in the likeness of man sitting upon it. Given the nature of this vision, it is not surprising that later Rabbis, to prevent theosophical speculation, prohibited the reading of this chapter in the synagogues!

Although many interpretations may be given, the key to this vision seems to be found in 1:28: "Such was the appearance of the likeness of the glory of Yahweh." Until this time, Yahweh's glory has radiated to the world through the Temple in Jerusalem, but now that Temple is to be destroyed and the glory of the LORD roams the earth (cf. Ch. 10). The vision is strange and incomprehensible precisely because that is the nature of Yahweh's glory (*kavod* - influence). Yahweh is now at work, but in strange and uncharted ways, and the prophet is called to stand in awe before him.

Ezekiel, overwhelmed by the magnitude of his vision, falls upon his face, but Yahweh commands him to rise: "Son of man, stand upon your feet" (2:1). The use of the term "Son of Man" to refer to the prophet is typical of Ezekiel as is the emphasis upon the Spirit which enters Ezekiel and sets him on his feet. The Spirit (*ruach*) of Yahweh is mentioned by many of the prophets, but in Ezekiel and Second Isaiah it seems to become almost a separate force, dependent upon, and yet somehow distinguishable from, Yahweh himself.

Ezekiel is called to prophesy to the rebellious people of Israel, not necessarily to convert them all, but so that they will know that there has been a prophet among them (2:5). Yahweh then gives to Ezekiel a scroll to eat and when he does so it tastes sweet (2:8-3:3). Again God warns the prophet that his hearers may not heed him, but that doesn't matter. He is to speak anyway (3:4-11). Then, the Spirit lifts him up, and brings him again among the exiles where he is "overwhelmed" for seven days (3:12-15). In 3:16-21 Ezekiel is called to be a watchman, the warner of the people. If he warns them, their sins are upon their own heads, but if he fails to warn them, he himself is responsible. Yahweh then commands Ezekiel to confine himself to his own house and to be bound with cords. He will be dumb, except for those times when Yahweh allows him to speak his Word.

Chapters 4-24 contain a whole group of prophecies predicting and dramatizing the fall of Jerusalem. Chs. 4 and 5 contain four unusual symbolic prophecies. First (4:1-3), Ezekiel makes a clay model of Jerusalem and then enacts dramatically the siege against it. Second, (4:4-8) Ezekiel lies on his left side 390 days to symbolize the years Israel will be in exile. Then he lies on his right side for 40 days to symbolize the same for Judah. Third, while so lying on his sides. Ezekiel eats unclean (taboo) food only once a day to signify both the fact that Israel will have to eat unclean food in foreign lands and that food in Jerusalem will become scarce during the seige (4:9-17). Finally, Ezekiel shaves his head. The hairs, which symbolize the people, are largely destroyed by fire and sword and scattered by the wind. A few are finally sewed to his robe, and even these are again partially destroyed. This is what will happen to Jerusalem. Only a small remnant shall be saved (5:1-17).

In Chapter 6 Ezekiel prophesies to the mountains, attacking the cultic high-places and promising that only a remnant, but still a remnant, will be preserved. All this is done to show Judah that the Lord of History is Yahweh. Chapter 7 simply repeats once more Ezekiel's prediction of the fall of Jerusalem and the resultant desolation.

Chapters 8-11 are very strange, for in them the Spirit simply lifts Ezekiel up and takes him to Jerusalem. There he is shown the pagan abominations practiced by the people, even in the Temple. He sees elders worshipping idols (8:7-13), a woman weeping for Tammuz (a pagan god of fertility) (8:14-15), and about twenty-five men worshipping the sun (8:16-18). Yahweh's emissaries go through Jerusalem, marking the righteous with their mark and destroying the rest with a sword. Yahweh tells Ezekiel that none of the unrighteous will be spared (9:1-11). In Chapter 10 the prophet sees a vision similar to that in Chapter 1. Now, however, he sees the glory of the Lord departing from the sanctuary. In Chapter 11 he meets and preaches to Jaazaniah ben Azzur and Pelatiah ben Benaiah, men who have led Jerusalem astray. As he preaches the latter man dies (11:13) and Ezekiel cries out to Yahweh lest he kill everyone. Yahweh assures him that the scattered people will eventually be reassembled and given a new heart (11:14-21). In several respects this vision is similar to the vision of the new covenant in Jeremiah 31:31-34.

Whether Chapters 8-11 tell of an actual trip made by Ezekiel to

Jerusalem is an open question. Probably, however, this is not a real journey but a vision during which Ezekiel is taken up in the Spirit to see "things" unseen by his fellow exiles.

Chapter 12 again contains symbolic prophecies. The prophet digs through a wall and crawls out, like someone escaping into exile, and eats his food with quaking to symbolize the fear of the people of Jerusalem. Chapter 13 is an attack upon false prophets while 14 is against the idolatry and hypocrisy of certain elders. Then, in a brief Chapter 15, he likens Judah to the wood of a vine which is useful only for fires.

Chapter 16 is a much longer "parable" in which Jerusalem is compared to an abandoned baby girl who has been left out in the field to die. A man picks her up, takes her home, and raises her, but she is totally unthankful and becomes a prostitute. That is the way Jerusalem has acted and she will be punished accordingly, says Ezekiel. Eventually, however, Yahweh will forgive and remember his covenant, and the fortunes of Israel shall be restored. Chapter 17 contains a peculiar allegory of the great eagles which again teaches of Yahweh's coming judgment.

Chapter 18, on the other hand, addresses the situation in Babylonia. There the old idea of the sins of the fathers being visited upon the sons is nullified (cf. Jeremiah 31:29-30). In the new situation the righteous man will be rewarded and the wicked man punished. In other words, now that the nation has been destroyed, each man will be treated as an individual. This chapter reveals Ezekiel's strong emphasis upon high ethical conduct as essential for the righteous life.

Chapter 19 contains laments for Jehoahaz, Jehoiachin, and Zedekiah, the kings of Judah, while Chapter 20 again reiterates Yahweh's judgment against Judah. Elders come to Ezekiel to inquire of Yahweh, but God tells them he will not be inquired after. He is speaking his Word, and that Word is judgment. This theme is once more repeated in Chapter 21 in the prophecy of the sword. Of some interest is Verse 21 in which methods of divination used by the Babylonian monarch are described. In Chapter 22 Ezekiel again attacks Jerusalem, while in 23 he tells the story of the two harlot sisters Oholah and Oholibah who, in their lustfulness, represent Samaria and Jerusalem. Finally, this section ends with the allegory of the boiling pot which symbolizes the woe facing the bloody city of Jerusalem. The chapter concludes with an account of the death of Ezekiel's wife and his refusal to mourn for her.

Chapters 25-32 contain a typical collection of prophecies against the foreign nations. Chapter 25 speaks of Ammon (1-7), Moab (8-11), Edom (12-14), and Philistia (15-17). Chs. 26:1-28:19 speak of the end of Tyre, while 28:20-23 deals briefly with Sidon. After a brief word of hope to Israel (28:24-26), the prophet turns upon Egypt and predicts that her doom is near (29:1-32:32).

Chapter 33 begins the final major section of the book in which Ezekiel describes in some detail the hope which Israel has for the future. Again, Ezekiel is appointed as a watchman who calls Israel to repentance. Jerusalem has fallen and Yahweh's day of vengeance is at an end. If the people will only repent, Yahweh will now forgive. In Ch. 34 Ezekiel attacks the evil shepherds of Israel who have led her astray. Now Yahweh will become Israel's shepherd himself (a conception much like that in Psalm 23 and some of the parables of Jesus) and lead back his people to their land. Furthermore, he will send one shepherd, a son of David, who will be their earthly guide (34:22:24). Yahweh will make with Israel a covenant of peace and she will dwell securely in her land (34:25-31).

Chapter 35 is a prophecy against Mount Seir (Edom) and therefore seems to be out of the place in the book though it may be included here because of the references to Edom in 36:5. Chapter 36 continues Ezekiel's account of the way it will be in the future. Israel's enemies will be judged and the people will return to their own land. The exile has taken place because of Israel's idolatry and hardness of heart. In the new age, Yahweh himself will not only lead the people but give them hearts of flesh and a spirit of obedience (36:25-27). Then shall the cities be inhabited and the people once more multiply in number.

Chapter 37 contains Ezekiel's famous vision of the dry bones. He sees a valley full of the dry and dead bones of Israel and wonders whether she will ever live again. Ezekiel prophesies to the bones, and Yahweh himself breathes into them his Spirit and Israel is resurrected from the dead. This vision is particularly important for understanding the doctrine of the resurrection found in the New Testament. The chapter concludes with a symbolic prophecy signifying the reunion of Israel and Judah under a son of David (37:15-27).

Chapters 38-39 contain an eschatological passage describing the invasion of Israel by the forces of Gog from the land of Magog. Many scholars believe that this is not by Ezekiel. If it is not, it still attempts to answer a question which his vision of the future raises. Suppose we go home and dwell in the land. How can Israel, a small nation, expect to protect herself? In these chapters the hordes of Gog descend, but Yahweh himself contends against the foreigners and they are summarily defeated. In fact, the number of their slain is so great that whole valleys are filled with the corpses!

In Chapters 40-43 Ezekiel turns to the Temple which has been destroyed and describes in minute detail how it will be rebuilt. Room by room and wall by wall he gives the dimensions of the new Temple. Although this description may seem tedious to the modern reader, for the person in exile it provided a kind of concrete hope to hang on to. Ezekiel gives not a vague and pious hope of what is to be but a very concrete plan. In Chapter 43 he envisions the return of the glory of the Lord to the Temple and then goes on to describe some of the interior appointments.

Chapters 44-46 contain a code of rules which will govern the new Temple. Here Ezekiel, the prophet, becomes Ezekiel, the priest, revealing his intense interest and concern for ritual purity and obedience to the letter of the law. Particularly important is his emphasis upon the sons of Zadok who are to play a preeminent role as priests in the Temple of the future (44:15-31).

Chapter 47 transcends the bounds of human possibility in a way most of the preceding chapters do not. He describes a stream a water issuing from below the threshold of the Temple and forming a river which flows to the Dead Sea. The water from the fountain purifies the Dead Sea of its impurities and turns it into a lovely lake where men can fish and beside which trees will bear fruit each month.

47:13-21 describes the exterior boundaries of the land. Then in Chapter 48 Ezekiel describes briefly the allotment of territory to each tribe, to the priests and Levites, to Jerusalem, and to the ruling prince. Finally, he describes the gates of Jerusalem and says that old Jerusalem shall be renamed *Yahweh Shamah*, "the Lord is there."

So ends the book of Ezekiel. The last sections may seem to the modern reader to be rather dull, but, in truth, they represent an important aspect of the prophecy of Ezekiel. Many prophets prophesied doom and destruction just as eloquently as he did. Others also depicted the future in rosy terms. No prophet other than Ezekiel, however, ever attempted to draw a blue-print for the new age so specifically that one could visualize it in imagination. Ezekiel spoke to a people who were despondent and, who after the fall of Jerusalem, wondered whether they ever could or should return home. Ezekiel, in his specificity, gave them something to hang on to. His plan was a plan to be pored over, meditated upon, and prayed for. Through it he helped to save Israel from the destruction which comes, not from swords, but from purposeless despair.

CHAPTER XIX

The Minor Prophets: Introduction and Analysis

Hosea	*Jonah*	*Zephaniah*
Joel	*Micah*	*Haggai*
Amos	*Nahum*	*Zechariah*
Obadiah	*Habakkuk*	*Malachi*

HE SCROLL of the minor prophets contains twelve collections of prophetic oracles which come from the three major centuries of prophetic activity. They are arranged, in part, chronologically. At least Nahum, Habakkuk and Zephaniah come from the seventh century, while Haggai, Zechariah, and Malachi probably come from the sixth. Just why Joel, Obadiah, and Jonah are grouped with eighth century prophets, Hosea, Amos, and Micah, however, is not wholly clear. Jonah is at least about an eighth century prophet, though the manuscript was written at a much later time. Joel and Obadiah are undated, but are generally believed today to have come from the exilic period. They may have been grouped with the eighth century prophets because the early compilers thought they came from that time, but it is more likely that they were placed where they were because they contain certain phrases which are reminiscent of Amos and Hosea.

In any event, the modern reader may prefer to read these works in what is now believed to be the correct chronological order. The following list is given to facilitate that task:

Amos	
Hosea	EIGHTH CENTURY
Micah	
Zephaniah	
Nahum	SEVENTH CENTURY
Habakkuk	
Obadiah	
Joel	SIXTH CENTURY (Exilic Period)
Haggai	
Zechariah	SIXTH CENTURY (Post-exilic period)
Malachi	
Jonah	LATE SIXTH OR FIFTH CENTURY

Hosea

THE BOOK of Hosea stands first among the so-called minor prophets, probably because it is the longest of these works to come from the eighth century. Although the over-all meaning of the work is quite clear, Hosea raises some very complicated questions of interpretation. In the first place, it is quite apparent that the Hebrew text is very corrupt, for many of its sentences make less than good sense. Reference to the LXX and other early versions sometimes helps, but any translation which purports to represent the original words of Hosea must be regarded as tentative at a number of points. A glance at the footnotes of the RSV will indicate how often the translators felt compelled to abandon the Hebrew text in order to make good sense of it.

Another very serious problem of interpretation is raised in Chapters 1-3. Ch. 1:2 reads, "When the Lord first spoke through Hosea, the Lord said to Hosea, "Go, take to yourself a wife of harlotry and have children of harlotry, for the land commits great harlotry by forsaking the Lord." Because of the rather shocking nature of this command, several different interpretations have been given to it. First, numbers of scholars have read this whole section as a non-historical parable of God's love for Israel. According to this theory, Hosea never really married an unfaithful harlot but only used this image of unfaithful love in order to describe Israel's apostasy. Second, some scholars have claimed that Hosea did marry Gomer, but only later did she become a prostitute. Third, others have accepted the story as told, believing that Hosea consciously married a prostitute, probably one who served the cultic purposes of a pagan temple, in order to symbolize graphically the shocking relation between Yahweh and Israel which actually obtained at his time.

Although there can be no absolute proof concerning this matter, it would seem to this writer that the last alternative is the best. Surely that is what the text strongly implies. If so, this is one of the first and most jolting examples of symbolic prophecy to be found in the Bible. Several other prophets (Isaiah, Jeremiah, Ezekiel, for instance,) act out their prophecies in startling ways but none of them quite approaches the shock that Hosea's action entails. Perhaps only Jesus' act of dying on a cross to symbolize the death of the old Israel surpasses Hosea's most intimate involvement in his own prophetic words.

The whole issue is complicated even more in 3:1 where Hosea is again commanded to love "a woman" who is an adulteress. Some scholars maintain that this is a second woman whom Hosea buys out of slavery and disciplines with love. Others, and I am among them, regard the woman mentioned as the same Gomer who was thrown out of Hosea's house and who later was sold into slavery. Surely the second alternative fits best with the idea of Yahweh buying back his unfaithful wife, Israel, from Assyrian bondage.

What we can say about the life of Hosea depends in large measure upon how literally one takes this first section of his book (1-3), though certain other facts can be gleaned from the superscription and his poetic prophecies. According to 1:1, Hosea prophesied during the reigns of Uzziah, Jotham, Ahaz, and Hezekiah (kings of Judah) and during the reign of Jeroboam II of the northern kingdom. It is usually assumed that the reference to the southern kings was added later by a Judeau hand and should not be taken as historically accurate. Surely there is very little in Hosea's prophecies themselves which would indicate that he prophesied very long after the end of Jeroboam's reign in 746 B.C. 1:4 predicts the end of the house of Jehu which took place with the assassination of Jeroboam's son in that same year and hence must have preceded that date. At the same time, most of Hosea's prophecies seem to presuppose not the prosperity of Jeroboam's reign but the social chaos which prevailed after him. Hence, it can be concluded that Hosea spoke his prophecies during the period after 747 but before 721 when the northern kingdom finally fell.

Because of his primary attack upon the northern kingdom and his specific references to Ephraim, it is usually assumed that he came from the northern kingdom. There is nothing, however, which proves this to be the case. Like Amos he could have come from Judah to deliver his message. Occasionally he has words of judgment for Judah as well, but there is considerable debate about whether most of these were original with him. The assertion of the primacy of the Davidic kingship in 3:5 is generally regarded as by a later hand.

About all we know factually about Hosea, then, is that he prophesied during the last half of the eighth century, that he married a woman who was or became a prostitute, and that she bore him three children whom he gave names which conveyed his message to Israel (1:4-9). Beyond this his prophecies reveal a man of a deeply sensitive nature who could both utter the most damning oracles of judgment and yet express, in a way that Amos did not, the deeply abiding love (*chesed*) of Yahweh for his people. Just as Hosea hates his prostitute-wife and yet loves her still, so Yahweh is pictured as both brutal in his judgments and yet ever yearning for the return of Israel to him.

Analysis

Chapter 1 relates the story of Hosea's marriage to Gomer and of the children who are born to them. Like Isaiah, Hosea gives his children meaning-filled names (Jezreel, Not Pitied, and Not My People) which communicate his word of judgment to Israel. The children become living symbols of the wrath which is born out of sin. Notice that Yahweh not only speaks to, but "through" Hosea (1:2). In Hosea the Word is infleshed and acted out. Ch. 1:10-11 recalls God's promises to the Patriarchs (Gen. 32:12) and on that basis holds out the hope that one day Israel shall be restored.

Chapter 2 is a poetic oracle in which the prophet urges his children to plead with their mother who is to be punished, obscenely punished, for her adulterous loves. This chapter also ends with a word of tender hope (2:14-23) in which Yahweh takes Israel back to the desert and wins her love once more. No longer will she cry to her Baals, for she will know Yahweh as her husband. Here we see set forth most beautifully the "Nevertheless" of divine love (*chesed*). God may punish Israel, but his steadfast love (*chesed*) will endure.

In a brief Chapter 3 the reconciliation of Yahweh of Israel is then dramatized as Hosea buys a woman (is it Gomer?) out of slavery.

Chapters 4-14 contain a collection of poetic oracles which seem, by and large, to be authentic Hosean prophecies. They are arranged in a fairly random way and hence are difficult to outline. Chs. 4:1-9:9 contain primarily Yahweh's judgments against Hosea's contemporaries. Ch. 4:1-10 seems to be a covenant law-suit in which the prophet brings formal charges against Israel for breaking the covenant. He charges the priests and prophets in particular with responsibility for the people's lack of knowledge of Yahweh (4:4-6). In 4:11-19 drunkenness and idolotry are assailed, while in 5:1-7 the prophet attacks both priests and king.

Chapters 5:8-6:6 seems to have been delivered after the Syro-Ephraimite war of 734/3. In the words of repentance in 6:1-2 we find a significant statement of Israel's resurrection faith. This is the one place in the Old Testament where resurrection on the third day is mentioned (cf. Luke 24:46). Ch. 6:6 contains Hosea's view of what Yahweh demands of Israel. Rather than sacrifices and burnt offerings, Yahweh requires steadfast love (*chesed*) and the knowledge of God (*yadaʿ*). The parallelism of this verse shows that in fact, love and knowledge are really the same in the prophet's eyes. That is, he who knows Yahweh with his whole being will manifest abounding and overflowing love in his life. Conversely, the man who so loves his neighbor, knows God.

Hosea 6:7-9:9 contains a series of oracles which reflect the rather chaotic situation which followed the assassination of Zechariah in 746. The kings, who are not legitimate (8:4), are drunken and irate (7:5-7). Banditry abounds in the country (6:9; 7:1) as do various forms of idolatry (7:16, 8:4-5, 8:11-13). Political policy vacillates as first a pro-Egyptian, then a pro-Assyrian attitude is adopted (7:11). All of this means that Israel is on the brink of disaster. Whether the victory be Egyptian or Assyrian does not really matter. Israel must fall. To such a nation the true prophet may appear mad, but in truth it is the nation which is insane. The prophet is a watchman who signals the disaster to come (9:7-8).

In 9:10-13:16 Hosea repeats many of these themes, but in a more historical context. He reminds Israel of her early sin at Baal-peor (9:10; cf. Numbers 25:1-5), her crimes at Gibeah (10:9; cf. Judges 19-20), her apostasy at Gilgal (9:15; 12:11). Throughout his oracles, Hosea shows a good acquaintance with the traditions of Israel, particularly as they are found in the Torah (12:2-6, 12, etc.). These remembrances of things past lead Hosea to indict Israel for her sins, but they also prompt him to go beyond a message of mere judgment. God has loved his people and promised to them great blessings. Therefore, beyond the disaster there is hope. Ch. 11:1-11 expresses beautifully the paradoxicality of Hosea's message. Yahweh is pictured as Ephraim's father, a father who brought up his son with love and tenderness. The son has become rebellious and must be punished; yet Yahweh, like the father of the prodigal son (cf. Luke 15:11-32) yearns for Ephraim to return and hence will not destroy Israel completely. Throughout the Old Testament the image of Yahweh as the father of Israel is used rather sparingly, perhaps because a similar metaphor was used by the Canaanites. Here, however, it is employed with great impact.

For a moment, Hosea reveals the tenderness of Yahweh's love for Israel, but he is no sentimentalist. In Chapters 12 and 13 he returns to his bitter indictment of Israel for her apostasy and her self-centeredness. Ephraim must bear Death and the Grave, and the sting of them is none other than Yahweh himself (13:14) (following the Hebrew).

Chapter 14 is a final call for repentance in which Hosea even offers to Israel the appropriate words to use before God (14:2-3). Yahweh responds with a promise to restore his people to faithfulness and to cause the land to prosper once more (14:4-8). The book concludes with words from the editor to the reader, advising the wise and discerning to take the message of the book to heart (14:9).

If Amos is preeminently the prophet of justice and Isaiah, the prophet of holiness, surely Hosea can be described as the prophet of *chesed*, steadfast love. Hosea's love, however, is neither sweet nor sentimental. His prophecy reveals the brokenness of an abundant love which is not reciprocated. The text is sometimes difficult to read, not simply because of problems of scribal transmission, but because the prophet himself attempts to express both the joys and the fearfulness of such love all at once. The forgiveness of which he speaks is born out of grief and suffering and his words quiver with paradoxicality.

Joel

THE BOOK of Joel, though it contains some superb Hebrew poetry, raises a number of critical issues which are not easily solved. In the first place, the work is undated and gives few clues as to the time of origin. Some have taken the mention of the Greeks in

3:6 as a sign of post-exilic origin, but this reasoning is specious to say the least. Not only were the Greeks known of for centuries before the rise of Alexander the Great, but 2:30-3:8 is in prose and may constitute a later addition to the text anyway. Traditionally, Joel has been dated in the eighth century, perhaps because of its position among the minor prophets, but few arguments can be offered for this dating. More critical scholars have variously assigned it dates during and after the exilic period. The basic reason for so dating it is that it contains an eschatological vision somewhat similar to those found in Ezekiel and other exilic and post-exilic prophets.

The book of Joel opens (1:2-20) with a very accurate and moving description of a locust plague, but whether the prophet meant to use this as a symbol for the invasion of a foreign army or whether he simply describes an historical plague as like an army is unknown. In any event, this plague kindles in the prophet's imagination a vision of Yahweh's day of judgment which is at hand (2:1-11) and prompts him to call his nation to repentance (2:12-17). After repentance the prophet predicts the coming of a new age of joy. Not only will the land prosper agriculturally; in 2:28-29 Joel foresees that God will pour out his Spirit upon all flesh so that there will be dreams and visions and prophecies once more.

In 2:30-31 Joel speaks of the cosmic portents which will accompany the great and terrible day, while in 3:1-16 he pictures Yahweh's judgment against the nations. As in Ezekiel's vision of Gog and Magog (Ezekiel 38-39), the nations descend upon Israel, but are defeated by Yahweh's hosts in a great slaughter. Egypt and Edom will suffer because of the violence they have done Judah (3:19), but Judah shall prosper and Yahweh will be avenged.

Although no final proof can be given, it would appear that Joel spoke at a time when prophecy had ceased, when Judah in particular suffered, and when Israel's hope for the future was conceived in terms of a cosmological disaster followed by an eschatological victory. This would seem to indicate that Joel probably prophesied sometime during the exilic or post-exilic period.

Within the book of Joel there are many hints of the influence of the cult. It may well be that Joel was written for and used in an annual day of repentance held in connection with the celebration of the New Year each fall. In this case, Joel speaks of the deadly reaper, Time, who produces each year a desolate earth which must be renewed and restored through cultic rites. This interpretation depends in large measure upon whether one accepts the hypothesis that Israel, like many other ancient nations, had a cosmic renewal cermony annually. Certainly, if there were such a rite, Joel could have been used cultically at it.

Amos

HIDDEN among the minor prophets is Amos, the oldest and one of the most eloquent books of prophecy found in the Bible. Unlike Joel, Amos is dated quite exactly: "In the days of Uzziah, king of Judah, and in the days of Jeroboam the son of Joash, king of Israel, two years before the earthquake" (1:1). Unfortunately, we do not know when this earthquake occurred, but clearly it was to Israelites a memorable event. The precise dating also seems to indicate that Amos prophesied for only a brief period during this momentarily prosperous era. Most scholars believe that he preached about 750 B.C. in the northern kingdom.

Amos, however, came from the south, from the little Judean village of Tekoa where he worked as a shepherd. Unlike Isaiah and Ezekiel, Amos was neither a priest nor an "official" prophet, but a migrant laborer (7:14). During the summer months, when water was scarce, he led flocks of the ugly but hardy desert sheep out into the wilderness to find pastureland and water where he could. During the fall and winter months, however, the sheep could find enough grass around Tekoa, and Amos was not needed there. By his own testimony, he was also a "dresser of sycamore trees" (7:14). That is to say, while the sheep were grazed around Tekoa, Amos was employed pruning sycamore fig trees, cutting off the excess blossoms and pinching the remaining buds so that the fruit would ripen more rapidly.

Probably, then, Amos could neither read nor write; he was one of the poor people of the land. Still, his prophecies show that illiteracy does not necessarily entail a lack of "culture" or poetic skill. Like many bedouins of today, he was a master of the spoken word who could put his literate contemporaries to shame. From his mouth came the biting voice of the desert, calling an effete and decadent culture to task for its sins. Even today—perhaps especially today—the reader of his words cannot help but be arrested by his consummate poetic gifts and his clear-eyed vision of the way things are.

The age of Amos was one of relative peace and prosperity for both the northern and the southern kingdoms. Jeroboam II and Uzziah were able rulers and under them the two nations flourished and expanded their borders. Both Assyria and Egypt were momentarily under a cloud, more concerned with internal difficulties than outward expansion. For the political leaders and rich merchants of Israel and Judah this was a time for optimistic hopes (5:18) and idle pleasures (6:1-7).

Amos, however, as a spokesman for the poor, saw things quite differently. To him the whole economy was based upon the oppression of the poor and a false sense of security. While the rich got richer and the poor, poorer, the leaders of the country indulged themselves more and more in their little pleasures, unaware that the season of peace would soon be over. Instead of working together for the benefit of all, the little nations of Syria-Palestine squabbled and fought, thus allowing Assyria to arise once more to conquer. Not that the people were not religious; apparently cultic religion was highly popular. For Amos, however, religion and righteousness were hardly to be equated. Yahweh had had enough of feasts, and solemn assemblies, and sacrifices! What he wanted is justice and there was little of that to be found. Therefore, Israel was bound to stumble and fall before the judgment of God.

Like most of the other books of prophecy, Amos was compiled and edited by followers who remembered and eventually recorded his words for posterity. Much of the poetry can be attributed to Amos himself, but most scholars question the attribution of 9:11-15 to him. This passage, which strikes about the only note of hope in the whole book, speaks of the rebuilding of Israel and the days of peace and prosperity which will follow the disaster. Apparently, though Amos saw only doom ahead, the editors felt compelled to add this word of promise to mitigate somewhat the sense of awful terror which Amos evokes and to express not only Yahweh's judgments but his unqualified promises as well.

Analysis

Chapters 1 and 2 contain Amos' prophecy against the nations, which was probably delivered at the cultic shrine at Bethel. The occasion may well have been a celebration of the festival of Tabernacles. Into the merry scene steps Amos with a Word from Yahweh against the enemies of Israel. He begins with Damascus and then moves on to indict Gaza,

Tyre, Edom, Ammon, and Moab. All are censured for their inhuman treatment of fellow human beings and for their petty wars and conquests. Having encircled the people of God with judgments, Amos turns to his own people, Judah, and offers a stinging rebuke (1:4-5). Doubtless his listeners were delighted with his vitriolic attack against their enemies. But Amos doesn't stop. In 1:6-16 he offers his final word of judgment —against Israel—and it is the harshest word of all. Israel has sold the needy for a pair of shoes and has trampled the poor into the dust (2:6). Therefore, she stands condemned and will be punished. The applause has now ceased as his listeners realize that their sins are the burden of his message.

In Chapter 3 Amos offers a new oracle, this time attacking the commonly-held belief that Israel's election means that Yahweh will protect her from harm. Israel has been chosen, says Amos, but that means that she has greater responsibilities. Because she in particular has been chosen, she in particular will be punished for her sins. Yahweh is source of both good and what, to Israel, may seem evil. "Does evil befall a city unless the Lord has done it?"

Verse 12, which speaks of a bit of Samaria being rescued, seems to offer some hope, but it does not. Just as a shepherd whose sheep has been eaten by a lion has to bring back a piece of the ear or some of the cartilege to prove that the sheep was devoured and not surreptitiously sold, so what remains of Samaria will only prove that she indeed has been devoured.

In Verses 13-15 Amos speaks of the destruction of what to him are the idolatrous shrines of the north and of Samaria's palaces. His mention of the "houses of ivory" (15) is of particular interest, for both in Samaria and in Nineveh remains of the beautiful ivories of Samaria have been recovered by archaeologists.

Chapter 4 contains an attack upon the women of Bashan who are in Samaria—those cows who pay more heed to their pleasure than to the needy. The enemy will come and put hooks in their mouths and lead them away. Documents from the time show that this, indeed, was the way Assyrians led their captives. Amos continues by sarcastically calling Israel to continue her apostasy and then by reminding Israel of the many warnings which Yahweh has given to her.

Chapter 5 begins with a brief lament over Israel. 5:4-15 then contains a call to repentance and to justice. Of special importance is Verse 8 in which Yahweh is pictured as the Lord of nature and creator of the constellations. After another lament (5:16-17), Amos calls down woe upon those who desire the day of Yahweh which Amos sees, not as a time of idyllic peace, but as a veritable nightmare (5:18-20). In one of his most memorable passages Amos continues by attacking Israel's hypocritical religion, warning that God's justice will roll down like waters and inundate Israel. 5:25-27 is a prose insertion attacking the pagan practices of Israel and reminding her that in the desert she did not even offer Yahweh sacrifices and offerings!

Chapter 6 returns to an attack upon the idle rich, painting in graphic detail their self-centered pleasures. Because justice and righteousness have been perverted, Israel must inevitably fall.

In Chapter 7 Amos sees three visions (7:1-3; 4-6; 7-9). Each is a vision of judgment, but after the first two God relents. After the third, a vision of the plumbline, however, God promises that the judgment will surely follow and that the house of Jeroboam will perish by the sword. The biographical section which follows is related to that assertion. Amaziah, the priest of Bethel, accuses Amos of treason and then urges the prophet to flee to his own land to "drool" his prophecies there. Amos responds that he has been called by Yahweh and that, because Amaziah has not listened, he and his family will be severely punished (7:16-17).

Chapter 8 records another of Amos' visions—this time of a basket of summer fruit—which communicates to him the coming of judgment (8:1-3). Again Amos returns to attack Israel's hypocritical religion and to predict woe. Those interpreters who believe that predictions of cosmic catastrophe must come from the post-exilic period ought to pay attention to 8:9 in which Amos predicts the same. In 8:11-14 Amos foresees the ultimate judgment, which is not one of fire or sword but of silence. In those days, he says, people will want to hear Yahweh speak, but because they have not listened now, they will know only silence, no matter how hard they try to hear.

Chapter 9 includes another vision, this time of Yahweh himself commanding the destruction of the altar (presumably at Bethel). Then follows another section depicting the inescapable nature of the doom to come. He concludes by reminding Israel that Yahweh not only chose Israel; he also brought the Philistines from Caphtor and the Syrians from Kir (9:7). Israel is doomed and there is no way for her to escape.

As it has already been said, 9:11-15 undoubtedly is a later addition to the text designed to relieve the unmitigated gloom of Amos' message by offering a typical word of hope. For Amos, however, there seems to have been no such relief. Assyria is on the move; Israel is doomed.

Obadiah

THIS BOOK, which is the shortest of the Biblical books of prophecy, contains an attack upon the Edomites primarily for their gloating over, and vicious attack upon Judah during a period of distress. Although the book is undated, the actions criticized and the mention of exiles from Jerusalem (1:20) would seem to indicate that the prophecy was uttered sometime shortly after the fall of Jerusalem in 587/6. Both Jeremiah 49:7-22 and Ezekiel 25:12-14 also condemn Edom for her unbrotherly actions connected with the fall of Jerusalem. In fact, Jeremiah contains some of the same verses found in Obadiah.

Thus although its position in the canon would seem to indicate an eighth century date and some scholars have even argued that it was produced in the ninth century, the book itself offers clear evidence of having come from Palestine during the sixth century.

Like many of the prophets Obadiah predicts that Judah will eventually conquer and that Edom will be destroyed. In Obadiah, however, there seems to be no eschatological hope. His vision of the future is limited to a restoration of the old Davidic Empire and to the defeat of its perennial enemies. Certainly the last verse which is translated, "Saviors shall go up to Mount Zion to rule Mount Esau; and the kingdom shall be the Lord's," ought not to be taken in an eschatological sense. The word for Saviors used here is "Messiahs," i.e., men who are anointed—the kings.

Jonah

THE BOOK of Jonah is unique among the books of the prophets, for it is not a collection of oracles at all. Rather it is a well-wrought, comic novella which, through its broad humor, makes a very decisive prophetic point. It was written with tongue-in-cheek and must be read accordingly if its message is to be properly assessed.

The chief character is one Jonah ben Amittai who is mentioned in II Kings 14:25 as a man who prophesied in the eighth century B.C. In a word, Kings pictures him as a nationalistic prophet who forecast victory to the otherwise criticized Jeroboam II. Clearly the author chose his "hero" carefully. What if, the author suggests, the great nationalist, Jonah, had been commanded by God to preach a word of warning to the hated Assyrians? With that most preposterous assumption the book begins.

We have become accustomed to prophets preaching God's Word without regard to the consequences, but not Jonah. He goes to Joppa and takes the first boat in the opposite direction, probably to Spain. Apparently, he thinks that Yahweh's domain is confined to Israel! But Yahweh won't be denied and creates a great storm. Throughout this crisis the heathen sailors, who are highly devout, are contrasted with Jonah who goes to sleep! The casting of lots reveals that Jonah is guilty, but the sailors do their utmost to save him. Finally and with great reluctance they throw him into the sea. It is the sailors and not Jonah who throughout manifest the greatest faith and sense of humanity.

Jonah is cast into the sea and the storm abruptly ceases. While the sailors are offering sacrifices and vows to Yahweh, Jonah is being swallowed by a great fish. There he stays for three days and three nights. The psalm which he recites while in this state, though declared by some to be a later addition to the text, is clearly part of the comedy. It is a "take-off" on all those pious prayers uttered by the supposedly righteous. Jonah doesn't really repent. He only expresses his desire to see the Temple again and conceives of his relation to Yahweh in a most legalistic way (2:9). In the psalm Yahweh is still conceived of as a thoroughly circumscribed God who seems only to hear prayers in his holy Temple (2:7). Still, when the fish vomits Jonah out (who wouldn't, considering the unpalatable nature of the psalm?), Jonah does obey God and goes to Nineveh.

Clearly, however, he has little concern for the Ninevites whose doom is virtually sealed. He simply proclaims to the capital of Assyria (which is described as laughingly huge) that "Yet forty days, and Nineveh shall be overthrown" (3:4). Much to his surprise, not only the people but the king of Assyria (who historically was not noted for his openness to the words of foreign prophets) repent and declare a fast. Even the animals are covered with sackcloth! This act of righteousness causes God to repent and he does not destroy the city.

Now Jonah becomes indignant and pouts, proclaiming that he knew all along God would be merciful and not do what he said. Jonah asks for death and goes out to sulk. The sun becomes very hot, but God causes a plant to grow up and shade Jonah—who then becomes glad because of the plant. When God causes the plant to die, however, Jonah again becomes spiteful. The story ends with a question from Yahweh,

> "You pity the plant, for which you did not labor, nor did you make it grow, which came into being in a night, and perished in a night. And should not I pity Nineveh, that great city, in which there are more than a hundred and twenty thousand persons who do not know their right hand from their left, and also much cattle? (4:10-11)

The question is: What does the story mean? Perhaps it is best to see first what it does not mean. Though some scholars would disagree, the story does not teach that the pagans would repent if only Israel would proclaim to them God's Word. Any Israelite who knew anything about history knew that the king of Assyria never repented at any time because he heard Yahweh's Word. Therefore the example of Jonah's story proves nothing about the openness of the Gentiles. Neither does the story claim that Yahweh will forgive anyone who repents. No general law can be drawn from a single instance like this.

What the story does "speak to" is man's self-centered egotism which leads him inevitably into either rebellion or a prideful death-wish. Jonah is Judah, so caught up in her conceited piety and pre-conceived notions of God that she can neither appreciate the good qualities of the pagans nor the ridiculous nature of her own egotistical piety. It is a book directed against all those self-righteous people who believe that "we have the answer" and that everyone else is excluded.

The book of Jonah neither commands Israel to go into the world and preach the word nor promises God's love for all men, but it does at least point to possibilities unseen by many men of super-piety. Don't try to tell God what to do, the book says. Watch him work and you may be surprised by his actions!

There is no easy way to date the book of Jonah. This attack upon Jewish self-righteousness seems most appropriately placed during the post-exilic period when Judaism tended to turn inward and cut itself off from the world. Essentially, however, the message is timeless and may have been written any time after Assyria had no longer become a threat to Israel's existence.

Micah

MICAH, the fourth and last of the eighth century prophets, was a younger contemporary of Isaiah of Jerusalem. His home was in Moresheth, one of the villages of Gath, a Philistine city which was for a time incorporated into Judah. According to the superscription he prophesied against both Samaria and Judah during the reigns of Jotham, Ahaz, and Hezekiah (1:1). Although he does condemn Samaria in Chapter 1, however, most of his oracles are directed against his own nation, Judah.

Because of their many similarities (compare in particular Micah 4:1-4 and Isaiah 2:2-4) it has often been asserted that Micah was a disciple of Isaiah. This, indeed, may be a possibility, but it should not blind the reader to Micah's own distinctive style and his differences with Isaiah. The very fact that he was a villager rather than from the capital city in itself gave Micah a different perspective from which to view his nation. On the whole he seems blunter, more concerned about the sins of the Establishment, and less sanguine about the immediate future of Jerusalem.

There has been considerable debate among scholars about how much of the book is actually attributable to Micah himself. As usual, the more radical scholars perform amputative surgery and remove most of the passages of hope (that is, most of 4-7) as later additions. A few conservatives attribute every word to the original Micah. The truth, however, seems to lie somewhere between the two extremes. Certainly there are several passages (for instance, 4:10 which speaks of exile in Babylon) which were probably added later. On the other hand, it hardly seems necessary to deny to Micah most of what is found in the latter half of the book. One can only do so by assuming before hand that an eighth century prophet *must* have said this and not that. The truth is that we know so little about the prophetic movement as a whole that no such hypotheses can be very fully substantiated.

Analysis

Micah begins with a general prediction of the judgment which is soon to fall upon both Israel and Judah for their sins (1:2-16). And what are these sins? Quite simply, Samaria and Jerusalem (1:5). These cities of idolatry are rotten to the core. Ch. 1:9 seems to refer to an invasion of Judah by the Assyrians and may indicate a date in either 715-11 or 701. In 1:10-16 Micah speaks to the towns and villages in the Shephelah region around Moresheth. The city of Lachish is singled out for particular criticism, for apparently it adopted some of the idolatrous practices of the northern kingdom. (1:13)

Chapter 2 contains a much more specific oracle concerning those covetous men, probably the big land-holders, who oppress the common folk (2:1-5). In 2:6-11 Micah attacks all those who wish to silence his prophetic words, sarcastically remarking that the people would much prefer a preacher of wine and strong drink (2:11). 2:12-13 speaks of the return from exile and is doubtless by a later hand.

In Chapter 3 Micah bitterly attacks the political leaders of the country, describing them as cannibals who devour the people (3:1-4). Then he turns upon the prophets who are more interested in being paid properly than in the truth. They shall be put to shame, but Micah is filled with the power of Yahweh's Spirit (3:5-8). Again he returns to the rulers of Israel and Judah, attacking them for their perversion of justice. All the leaders (the kings, the priests, and the prophets) are more concerned about making money than about justice and equity. Therefore Jerusalem shall be destroyed! This is the first time that any prophet known to us predicted the fall of Jerusalem. When Jeremiah does the same more than a century later, he is saved from execution when some of the people remember Micah's words (Jer. 26:18).

With Chapter 4 we suddenly move from words of woe to a message of hope. Ch. 4:1-4 is similar in almost all details to Isaiah 2:2-4 and may have been taken from that slightly earlier prophet of Jerusalem. It is possible that both works are dependent upon an older, common source for this vision of the future glory of Zion. Chs. 4:6-5:1 contain a series of short oracles in which the disaster of the immediate future is held in tension with the future glory of Zion. Now Zion writhes and moans under siege, but in the latter days she shall triumph over her enemies.

Chapter 5:2-4 contains Micah's familiar prophecy that Bethlehem, the home-town of David, will produce yet another ruler who will restore Israel and usher in an age of peace. Ch. 5:5-6 depicts the coming triumph of Israel over Assyria while 5:7-9 depicts Jacob as both triumphant over, and yet a blessing to, the Gentiles. Ch. 5:10-15 contains Yahweh's word of warning to the disobedient nations. Eventually their strength and their idols will be destroyed.

In Chapter 6 Yahweh pleads his case before the witnessing mountains by reminding Israel of the good he has done her in the past (6:1-5). Then, in the most famous words to be found in Micah, Yahweh describes what he demands of his people. He is not interested in sacrifices, not even very grandiose ones. He simply requires that Israel do justice, and love steadfast love (*chesed*), and walk humbly with him (6:8). Ch. 6:9-16 contains Yahweh's indictment against Israel and his promise of coming desolation.

Chapter 7, which concludes the book, begins with the prophet's lament for his people. Instead of lamenting their downfall, however, he emphasizes that what is to be lamented is their wickedness. As the doom approaches, Micah turns to a word of hope. He remembers God's promises to the Patriarchs of old (7:20) and is sure that Yahweh will again show mercy to his people. The people shall return to their desolate land (7:11-13) and the nations which now torment Israel shall fear Yahweh and be ashamed (7:16-17). Whether all the sections of this chapter are by Micah himself is a matter of some debate. Probably there are some later additions. It is certain, however, that the central argument is his. Israel and Judah may face doom, but Yahweh is to be trusted. Tomorrow promises a day of hope.

Nahum

THE LITTLE book of Nahum is undated, but it clearly comes from about 612 B.C., for it speaks of the fall of Nineveh, the capital of Assyria, which took place at that time. Nahum is said to come from Elkosh, but that town has never been certainly located Some identify it with Capernaum (which means "the village of Nahum"), while others place it variously in the territory of Simeon, in Galilee at el-Kauzeh, or even in Assyria itself. Since Nahum itself gives some indications that the author lived in Judah (1:15), a southern location is probably most likely.

Unlike most of the other prophetic works, Nahum offers no word of woe to Israel. Instead, the whole book is simply a shout for joy that Ninevah, the great oppressor, has fallen before the Medes and Babylonians. After an introduction in Chapter 1 which affirms the avenging nature of Yahweh who eventually destroys evil, Nahum depicts with great art the last days of the Assyrian capital. Through a series of explosive images he brings the reader into the heart of the falling city and one experiences the turmoil and anxiety as the gates of the city are opened and the enemy enters. Chapter 3 might be called a taunt oracle. Again, by piling one image upon another, Nahum allows us to glimpse the last bloody moments which are filled with corpses and destruction. Nineveh has fallen because of her sins, and now her shame is exposed to the whole world. Nahum reminds Nineveh of the fall of Thebes which was conquered by Esarhaddon in 669 B.C. That great Egyptian city fell; why should not Nineveh also be destroyed? At the height of her power Assyrians were everywhere; Assyrian merchants traded all over the world; her scribes were like a cloud of locusts (3:17). But now they have all departed. The shepherds of Assyria (probably her gods) are asleep as are her human leaders. Assyria is dead and no one mourns her. Instead everyone who hears the news applauds and makes merry. It is a funeral at which no one cries.

For Nahum this event presented a great opportunity for Judah, for he seems to have forecast an era of peace in which Judah could again keep her feasts and fulfill her vows to Yahweh (1:15). Unfortunately, however, though his people were to experience a few years of independance under Josiah, the Babylonians soon replaced the Assyrians as world oppressors, and Judah once more became a subject nation. For the moment, however, joy reigned and Nahum expressed it beautifully.

Most of the critical problems connected with Nahum concern Chapter 1. This chapter bears evidence of having been originally an acrostic poem, but in its present state that acrostic has clearly been tampered with. Although this may be the result of later editing, it is probable that Nahum himself, took over an older poem and revised it to meet his own deeds. In any event, the first chapter is the least impressive poetically of the three. In the last two chapters Nahum rises to heights seldom equalled in Hebrew poetry and for this reason alone it is fortunate that his book has been preserved.

Habakkuk

HABAKKUK, like Nahum, is undated in the text, but can also be placed around the close of the seventh century, probably between 605 and 598 B.C. While Nahum exults over the fall of Nineveh, Habakkuk speaks with fearful alarm about the consequent rise of Babylonia (referred to as Chaldea in 1:6) and the menace to Judah and the other little nations which Nebuchadnezzar constituted.

According to the apocryphal book, Bel and the Dragon, Habakkuk was the son of Jesus of the tribe of Levi, but this book is so imaginative in its account of this prophet that the identification hardly seems reliable. Hence we know little or nothing about Habakkuk, the man.

His book begins with a highly personal complaint to God of the type later to be found frequently in Jeremiah. In 1:2-4 he cries out to Yahweh, asking him how long the violence and injustice of this world will continue. Verses 5-11 offer Yahweh's reply which is, to say the least, hardly comforting. He tells the prophet that he is arousing the ruthless and arrogant Chaldeans who are going to sweep across the country leaving destruction in their path.

Habakkuk, in his response in 1:12-2:1, affirms both Yahweh's power and his justice; yet he also wonders how God can allow the wicked to swallow up the more righteous (1:13). The prophet mounts his watch tower to see how God will answer his complaint (2:1). Yahweh answers, not with a comforting word of hope for the present, but a vision for the future. Habakkuk is to write the vision large so that the runner may read it (2:2). Yahweh assures Habakkuk that the vision will be fulfilled and that in the meantime the righteous man must live with only faith. This phrase, "the righteous shall live by faith," has played an important role in Western religion. It was quoted by Paul in both Romans 1:17 and Galatians 3:11. Subsequently, it became the watchword of the Lutheran reformation in the sixteenth century.

Certainly, however, Habakkuk did not distinguish between faith and works as later Lutherans were wont to do. On the contrary, the chapter goes on to reveal that his faith is in the triumph of Yahweh's justice over unrighteousness. Ch. 2:5 sums up this vision by depicting the arrogant man and his eventual downfall. The verse, however, begins strangely, "Moreover wine is treacherous . . . " The commentary on Habakkuk found among the Dead Sea Scrolls probably contains a better reading, for in it "wealth" is found in place of "wine."

Chapter 2:6-19 contains a series of "Woes" directed against evil men. These are appropriately understood as aimed at the Babylonian aggressors, but Habakkuk may well been thinking of the wicked men of Judah, such as Jehoiakim, too. In the light of the vision of the ultimate triumph of Yahweh's justice, Habakkuk offers his taunt to the unrighteous for their plundering, avaricious, inhumane, and idolatrous ways. Chapter 2:20 sums up the vision, "Yahweh is in his holy temple; let all the earth keep silence before him."

Chapter 3 contains a psalm of Habakkuk which many authorities ascribe to a later hand. In it is be found a theophanous picture of Yahweh which calls to mind both ancient mythological cosmogonies and the victory of Joshua (and Yahweh) in the conquest of Canaan. Habakkuk calls upon God to renew his work and, in his wrath, to remember mercy (3:2). The prophet expresses his great fear before the calamity to come (3:16), but he also rejoices in Yahweh who is his strength in this time of disaster (3:17-19). Although this last chapter may well have been added later (it is not be found in the Commentary on Habakkuk of the Dead Sea Scrolls), it still expresses quite well the same message which is found in Chapters 1 and 2. Possibly, it signifies that Habakkuk was an official prophet of the temple who wrote psalms for the cult.

Zephaniah

ZEPHANIAH is dated fairly precisely by the superscription to his work as having prophesied during the reign of Josiah (640-609 B.C.). It is usually assumed that, because he attacks the paganism of the Judeans and does not mention the reforms of Josiah which took place in and after 622 B.C., he must have prophesied during the early part of that king's reign. If so Zephaniah was the first to break the prophetic silence which occurred during the long reigns of Manasseh and Amon.

One fact militates against dating Zephaniah too long before 622. In 1:8 he speaks of the king's sons dressing in foreign attire. Since Josiah was a boy of eight when he ascended the throne, he probably would not have produced any offspring until about 630. His sons would probably not have been clothed in such a way as infants, so this pushes us fairly close to 625, at least.

Chapter 1:1 also gives the genealogy of Zephaniah, the longest genealogy of any of the prophets. Probably the lineage given is as long as it is to make known that his great-great grandfather was none other than Hezekiah, the king. In other words, Zephaniah was a son of David. It is significant, therefore, that in his description of Judah's hope he says nothing about a Messianic Son of David.

Zephaniah, like most of his predecessors, is first and foremost a prophet of doom, but unlike them he does not connect the coming disaster to any specific historical threat. On the contrary, he sees that a day of judgment is coming against all the nations, against the whole earth. As in the days of Noah, Yahweh is going to "cut off mankind from the face of the earth" (1:3). This theme is repeated over and over again. The whole world is going to know the anger of the Lord.

Nevertheless, Zephaniah says little specifically about the sins of the Gentiles. In 2:4-15 he forecasts destruction for Philistia, Moab, Ammon, Ethiopia, and Assyria, but is hardly very exact about Yahweh's reasons for such destruction. Concerning Judah, however, he is far more concrete. Particularly in 1:4-9 he criticizes Judah for her pagan and superstitious ways. Like the heathens, Judeans even step over the threshold to avoid bad luck! (1:9) Zephaniah is also critical of those who do not believe that Yahweh will bring either good or evil (1:12). Ch. 3:1-4 depicts the corrupt and vicious nature of Jerusalem and her leaders. One gets the distinct impression that the whole world is to be destroyed for the sins of Judah!

Still, despite the universality of the wrath to come, Zephaniah does hold out hope. He calls upon the humble of the land to seek Yahweh and follow his commandments with the hope that they may be hidden on the day of wrath (2:3). Furthermore, he sees beyond the doom to a new day in which many peoples will call upon the name of Yahweh (3:9-10), when a remnant of Israel made up of the poor and lowly will be renowned and praised (3:20).

Zephaniah does not mention the Torah at all, but there are many hints that he drew his inspiration in part from the story of Noah. The remnant of Israel, like Noah, will survive the flood and again repeople the earth. The corruption of speech which took place at the Tower of Babel (Gen. 11:1-9) will be removed (3:9) so that all may call on Yahweh's name. At the same time, Zephaniah's prophecy against the haughty and proud sounds very much like Isaiah (compare 3:11 and Isaiah 2:12ff), while his description of the day of Yahweh (1:14-16) echoes Amos 5:18-20.

Thus, in many respects Zephaniah offers to the reader very little which is new besides a few imaginative but grisly images of destruction. His emphasis upon Yahweh's destruction of the whole earth, however, is, if not new, at least more radically stated. Doubtless he was one of the formative influences which shaped the apocalyptic movement which was to begin in the next century.

Haggai

WITH THE BOOK of Haggai we move suddenly in the minor prophets, from the seventh to the sixth century. The book is dated with great precision, for Haggai's first oracle is said to have been delivered on the first day of the sixth month of the second year of Darius, the king of Persia (1:1), i.e., in 520 B.C. Haggai's message, which is addressed to the Davidic Governor Zerubbabel and the high-priest Joshua, is, on the whole, simple and straight-forward. His word is: it is time to rebuild the Temple.

The first exiles returned from Babylonia in about 538 and may have made some efforts to begin the reconstruction, but for a variety of reasons did not get very far. Haggai, Zerubbabel's official court prophet, chides the leaders and the people for being more concerned about their own homes and well-being than they are the house of Yahweh. It is true he says, that the going has been hard (1:5-6), but that may, in fact, be because the Temple remains in ruins. As a result of Haggai's message the work of rebuilding is begun.

Haggai's second oracle (2:1-9) is delivered about 50 days later. Apparently the people are discouraged with the rather small size of the building being constructed, but Haggai is not. He assures then that Yahweh's Spirit abides among them and that God, himself, will glorify the house and make it more splendid than the Temple of Solomon. Somehow, though Haggai doesn't explain how, Yahweh will "shake the nations" (2:7) and gold and silver will flow into his house.

The third oracle, delivered in the ninth month of the same year, is somewhat enigmatic. He questions the priests about the "infectious" nature of cleanness and uncleanness and somehow derives from their answers a message from Yahweh. The relationship between the questions and the message is unclear, but Haggai does promise that from now on Yahweh will bless them and cause them to prosper.

On that same day Haggai also has a word for Zerubbabel (2:20-23). Unlike most prophetic words to kings, this is a word of hope. Haggai predicts a political disruption in which the throne of kingdoms is overthrown (2:21-22). As a result, Zerrubbabel will become Yahweh's "signet ring," i.e., his representative on earth. Clearly, this is a prophecy which did not find fulfillment, for Darius, though occasionally beset with political turmoil stayed on his throne. We hear no more of Zerubbabel who conceivably could have been removed from office because of his Messianic pretensions.

In many respects, Haggai is not a very attractive prophet, for his message seems prosaic and highly limited. Gone are the vigorous denunciations of the earlier prophets; gone are their idyllic hopes. When Haggai does speak glowingly of the future he speaks words which obviously were not fulfilled. Still, one must remember that Haggai spoke to a disheartened people who scarcely needed another word of woe. Haggai's very concrete messages at least gave the people something to hang on to as they sought desperately to reestablish themselves in the land of their fathers.

Zechariah

BY ALL ODDS Zechariah is the most obscure book in the Old Testament. Not only is it filled with strange visions; much of the argument of the book seems so disjointed that it is sometimes difficult to determine just what point it is that the authors are trying to make. There are some moments of clarity, but by the time the reader has reached Chapter 14 is he likely to shake his head in bewilderment.

Although many of the obscurities cannot easily be removed, perhaps a few observations will help to locate where the basic problems lie. In the first place, most scholars believe that only Chapters 1-8 are by Zechariah himself. 9-14 contain a series of oracles, probably by the Zecharian school, which differ considerably in idea and expression. Possibly these chapters, together with Malachi, the last of the minor prophets, once formed a miscellaneous appendage to the collection as a whole. Since 12 seems to be a much more pregnant number than 11, however, Malachi was separated from the rest to form the last book. At any rate, the reader ought not to expect to find much consistency between 1-8 and 9-14 or within 9-14. There are some general trends of thought, but that is about all.

The first half of the book (1-8) can at least be ascribed to Zechariah and fairly carefully dated. Zechariah's first oracle is said to have been uttered in the eighth month of the second year of Darius, that is two months after Haggai's first oracle. Like Haggai, Zechariah also urges the rebuilding of the Temple as Ezra 5:1 and 6:14 say. Nehemiah 12:16 also mentions him as a priest who returned with Zerubbabel to Jerusalem. While Zechariah's own book calls him the son of Berechiah, however, both Ezra and Nehemiah name his father as Iddo. There is no major problem in this, for *ben* can mean either son or grandson in Hebrew.

Zechariah's whole prophecy reflects the mood of the returned remnant from Babylonia. Doubtless the exiles came back filled with the visions of grandeur as set forth by II Israiah only to have their hopes seemingly dashed by the disheartening situation which they actually faced. Where was the Messianic age promised by the prophets? When was the age of glory going to begin? Would Yahweh fulfill his promises, or was this to be just another bad joke of which they were the butt? This was no laughing matter. To preserve the sanity of the community some answers had to be found.

Zechariah speaks to this situation, but he does so, not through the straight-forward prophetic oracle, but through descriptions of a series of visions seen personally by him. Throughout these visions Yahweh seems far away. It is an angel who intervenes to question the prophet and to explain to him what he sees. Without the angelic interpreter each vision would be less than intelligible. The only exceptions to this general format are to be found in 1:1-6 and 7:1-8:23. In 1:1-6 Zechariah calls the people to repentance, arguing that they must return to Yahweh before he will return to them (1:3). He reminds them that their fathers failed to listen to the prophets of old and they were punished for their sins. In effect he calls them to return to the faith of the prophets who emphasized both the demands of Yahweh and the hope of Israel.

His second oracle comes just two months after Haggai's last one, in the eleventh month of the second year of Darius. In that last oracle Haggai had prophesied that Yahweh would shake the nations and that Zerubbabel would become his signet ring. No such thing happened, however, for Darius quelled the political uprisings and remained firmly on the throne. Zechariah's vision of the four horsemen who patrol the earth and announce that all is at rest speak to that situation. Yahweh is angry that the nations are at ease and promises that he now will be with Jerusalem. His house will be rebuilt and Jerusalem shall prosper. The next vision of the four horns and four smiths (1:18-20) is to assure Jerusalem that Yahweh will now punish the powers which have scattered Judah.

Chapter 2 contains a vision of a man who is going to measure Jerusalem. The angel tells him not to, for Jerusalem will over-flow with people and, because of Yahweh's protection, will need no walls (2:5). Not only Jews from the Diaspora but many other peoples as well will join themselves to Yahweh (2:11).

Chapter 3 contains a vision of Joshua, the high priest, being accused by Satan. Satan, however, is rebuked by Yahweh who has Joshua's filthy garments removed and who appoints Joshua as ruler over his house. Ch. 3:8-10 seems to see Joshua, himself, as an omen of the imminent coming of the Messiah.

Chapter 4, which contains a vision of a golden lampstand and two olive trees, is rather confusing, in large measure because 4:6-10 seems to have been interjected into the text. The vision seems first of all to be a sign that the golden lampstand has replaced or will replace the now destroyed ark of the covenant in the Temple. The two anointed ones of 4:14 are doubtless the Davidic ruler, Zerubbabel, and the high-priest, Joshua. Ch. 4:6-10 is out of place but important nonetheless, for it not only predicts that Zerubbabel will complete the Temple but that he will triumph, not through might, but through the Spirit (4:6).

In Chapter 5 Zechariah sees a huge flying scroll which is a curse against all who steal and swear falsely. Through the scroll this evil will be rooted out and the world purified. 5:5-11 then continues with his vision of the ephah, a small measuring basket. In this ephah, Zechariah sees a woman who is wickedness herself. She is being carried in the ephah to be buried in Shinar. This story seems to be that of Pandora's box in reverse. Shinar, (Sumer) where man's confusion of languages began (Gen. 11), now becomes the burial ground for wickedness.

The last vision, in Chapter 6, is like the first, for it speaks of the four horsemen who patrol the earth. Its meaning, however, seems highly enigmatic. The chapter ends back on earth. Zechariah is told to take gold and silver from certain recently returned exiles and make crowns and with them crown Joshua and proclaim his name "the Branch." Something seems peculiar about this, however, for one would expect the man crowned to be Zerubbabel. This is particularly true, since the passage also speaks of the good relations which will exist between the crowned ruler and the priest who stands beside him (6:13). Either the name was changed from Zerubbabel to Joshua by a later editor or this is an act against the authority of Zerubbabel or Zerubbabel has now been removed from office by the Persians. The first possibility seems most likely.

In Chapter 7 Zechariah attacks hypocritical fasting and emphasizes the importance of honesty, kindness, and mercy. Chapter 8 concludes Zechariah's words with a hopeful prophecy that Jerusalem shall again be filled with people and shall prosper. The building of the Temple is a sign that this will be so. But Zechariah also warns that Israel must be faithful to Yahweh by speaking truth and rendering true and peaceful judgments (8:16-17). In other words, the fulfillment of the word of the prophets is dependent upon Israel's willingness to obey. If they are faithful, both Jews and Gentiles will come to Jerusalem to seek Yahweh (8:18-23).

As has already been said, the last five chapters are highly enigmatic and difficult to interpret and therefore will be reviewed very briefly. Chs. 9:1-11:3 contain a series of oracles which, though not all written at one time or for one situation, are difficult to separate one from another. Ch. 9:9 is significant for it pictures the Messiah as entering Jerusalem "on an ass, on a colt, the foal of an ass." This was taken to be a prediction of Jesus by Matthew, who pictures him as riding on two animals at once! (21:1-7) Zechariah, himself, probably meant that the Messiah would ride on a pure-bred ass.

Chapter 11:4-17 is highly obscure, for we have no idea to what situation it originally spoke. In it the prophet acts as a shepherd to dramatize his prophecy. Apparently, the time was one of great suffering for Israel, for the text speaks of the sheep which are to be slaughtered and of evil shepherds who do not care for their sheep. The word spoken, however, offers little hope. The shepherd breaks his two staffs, Grace and Union, and thereby symbolizes the destruction of both the covenant and the union of Israel and Judah.

Chapter 12 is also highly enigmatic. First the author pictures Judah being assaulted and then triumphing through God's Spirit over her enemy. Instead of a day of gladness over victory, however, Jerusalem mourns for him whom they have pierced (12:10). Is this to show that on their day of triumph Judah will receive not only victory but a sense of compassion for the Gentiles? Or does this refer to some historic leader who was killed by the Judeans?

Chapter 13:1-6 is a curious attack upon prophets and prophecy, which seems to indicate that the age of true prophecy is over, while 13:7-9 offers prophetic judgment against some unspecified leader of Israel. Chapter 14 is an eschatological account of the final day. Jerusalem will fall and be plundered (14:1-2), but then, suddenly a new day will dawn with strange natural portents (14:3-10). Finally Judah will triumph and the whole world will worship Yahweh in Jerusalem, which will become the most holy of cities.

Zechariah may be strange and obscure in many places, but its importance ought not to be underestimated, particularly in the development of Christianity. The writer of Revelation turned to Zechariah repeatedly for symbolism. The Gospel writers found in particularly the last half of the book many predictions of Jesus. Throughout the history of both Judaism and Christianity Zechariah has served as a source for both theosophical and mystical speculation. One need not become an obscurantist, however, to see the basic points in this book. Perhaps most important is the repeated assertion that though in the end Judah will triumph, the Gentiles will also share in Yahweh's blessing and will enter into the community of the faithful.

Malachi

Almost nothing can be known for sure about the author of this, the last of the minor prophets. Even his name, Malachi, is suspect, for it means simply "my messenger" and may have been derived from the mention of "my messenger" in 3:1. Usually Malachi is dated some time in the late sixth or fifth century, but even that is uncertain. Aside from the book's position in the canon, its concern with cultic matters, and its allusions to the existence of a Temple, there are no absolutely certain signs of its origin. Had it been placed, say, between Joel and Amos one may suspect that it would be dated much earlier by many scholars.

Certainly, however, a date in the fifth century seems appropriate, for the author clearly seems to be speaking to a discouraged and somewhat doubting people. The prophet warns them, not of their idolatry, but of their failure to perform the cultic rites properly. He particularly censures the priests for offering in sacrifice blemished animals (1:66), for giving poor instruction to the people (2:8), for acting faithlessly toward the brides of their youth (2:14-15). Little is said in the Ṭorah and Prophets about divorce. Malachi, however, expresses God's hate of divorce (2:16) and thus seems to set the stage for Jesus' rather radical words concerning the subject (Mark 10:11, Matthew 5:31-32, 19:3-12). Malachi, like Ezra and Nehemiah, also criticizes the taking of foreign wives (2:11), though this may refer to the providing of a foreign goddess as a consort for Yahweh (cf. the Elephantine papyri).

In Chapters 3 and 4 Malachi warns the priests that the day of judgment approaches and that through swift punishment Yahweh will smite the wicked and purify Israel. In 3:6-12 Malachi turns upon the people, castigating them for their disobedience and, in particular, for their negligence in paying their tithes. (3:10) The day of judgment is coming in which the wicked will be destroyed and the righteous saved. Therefore remember and keep the law of Moses! (4:4)

The book ends with a prediction of the return of Elijah before the great and terrible day to reconcile the fathers and sons of Israel. This prediction was to play an important part in the vision of Israel for the future and was particularly remembered by the followers of Jesus. Some of them identified John the Baptist as Elijah returned, while others (cf. John 1:19-23) seem to have seen Jesus as fulfilling this role.

Malachi's use of a didactic "question and answer" style and his emphasis upon cultic correctness are surely unique among the prophets, but essentially his basic argument harkens back to the earlier prophets. Gone is the expectation that II Isaiah's glorious vision is soon to be fulfilled. The Day of Yahweh has again become a day of judgment which men are to remember and fear.

CHAPTER XX

The Writings

NLIKE THE TORAH and the Prophets, the Writings (the Kethuvi'im) were accepted into the canon in the full light of history. As has already been said, at the time of Jesus only the Law and the Prophets were regarded as, strictly speaking, canonical, but there were several other works, such as the Psalms, which had already been accepted as quite authoritative. The official act of canonization, however, did not take place until 90 A.D. At that time a group of distinguished Rabbis met at Jamnia in Palestine to try to make order out of an essentially chaotic situation and to defend Judaism against its enemies. We hear much about many of these Rabbis in the Talmud.

The position of the Jewish people at the time was by no means a happy one. In the first place, because of strong Jewish nationalism coupled with apocalyptic expectations, the Jewish community in Palestine had become involved some twenty years before in a life-and-death struggle against the Roman rule of the Jewish homeland. As a result, the Roman legions had moved in, smashed the insurrection, and literally torn down Jerusalem stone-by-stone. The Temple lay in ruins and the people were despondent. The Rabbis had to work out a "new" basis for Jewish life which had now to exist again without its central shrine and to plot a course for the people which would avoid the extremes of apocalyptic nationalism which had plunged the people into such a catastrophe.

At the same time, Judaism was threatened from within by a new sect, the Nazareans, who claimed that the Messiah had already come in the person of Jesus, who attacked the Law as no longer relevant, and who were winning converts to their cause both in Palestine and abroad. In their decisions concerning the canon the Rabbis were guided by both of these threats. Works which fostered extreme nationalism had to be deemphasized. The writings of the new Christian sect also had to be excluded. At the same time, they sought to include those writings which were of particular use to the new Judaism or which were already accepted as thoroughly authoritative.

Rabbinical arguments for and against certain books were heated but thoughtful. They struggled manfully to avoid further schism by steering a middle course between extremes. To the apocalyptical faction they gave their due (witness the inclusion of Daniel in the canon), but they chose carefully, so that the real extremists would find no solid Scriptural ground for further militant revolt. To the Hellenistic Jews who were interested in philosophical questions they also listened, but they chose writings which, despite their questioning, stood very much within the Jewish theological tradition. They allowed the new Christian heresy no quarter, however, banning from the canon all books about Jesus and his mission.

The canon which was finally agreed upon was, in any event, a very carefully contrived and well-balanced selection of the best Jewish writings. Unlike the other two sections of the canon, the Writings does not manifest an obvious unity of purpose and idea. Indeed, the most varied kinds of literature are included. Still, the twelve books chosen reflect quite admirably the various tendencies of post-exilic Judaism which the Rabbis thought wise to preserve and emphasize. Not that they made this their overt purpose. Indeed, they chose books which were attributed to men who lived before or during the time of Ezra, the great leader of post-exilic Judaism. Hence they excluded on principle many other books which were written at a later time. Still, the result of their efforts was a set of books which shows to the modern reader what Judaism in post-exilic times was like. Through them we are confronted by both the deepest piety and the most anguished questioning which characterized the people during this crucial period.

The first work, Job, reflects the struggle of men of faith to believe in the face of a seemingly amoral and unconcerned universe. The book of Psalms, on the other hand, is a profound outpouring of faith (and sometimes doubt) before God. This work, which is essentially a book of devotional verse, expresses the most various attitudes of prayer and praise. Proverbs, on the other hand, is a collection of sometimes worldly-wise, sometimes devout, sayings. Basically, it is a collection of the best of Israel's tradition of wisdom. Although ascribed to Solomon it contains the thoughts of many men and many generations who sought for practical wisdom by which to live in this world. Like the *Nevi'-im*, the Writings contains a history of Israel, though the history of the Chronicler begins with creation and ends with Ezra and Nehemiah. In many ways, this history is inferior to the books of Samuel and Kings both in style and historical reliability. It is a late work, written from a "priestly" point of view. It is long on genealogies and facts concerning the cult but rather short on human interest and drama. Still, it is not without worth. Not only does it give a somewhat different account of the pre-exilic history of Israel. It also fills in, albeit somewhat sketchily, the post-exilic history of the people. The books of Ezra and Nehemiah are particularly important, for they give us information about the restoration of Judah which would otherwise be completely unavailable to us. Next there are five scrolls, commonly called the Megilloth, which were chosen at least in part because of their association with five of the chief festivals of Judaism. The Song of Songs, a beautiful and erotic love poem, is read at Passover. Ruth, a simple tale of love and devotion, is associated with Pentecost. Lamentations, traditionally ascribed to Jeremiah, is read on the Ninth of Av, when Judaism laments the fall of Jerusalem and the destruction of the Temple. Ecclesiastes, a book of "pessimistic" wisdom which defies easy analysis, is read on the festival of Tabernacles. Esther, a short story with nationalistic implications, is used at Purim. Arguments against the inclusion of Ecclesiastes and Esther were particularly pointed, but their association with festival days and their obvious expression of contemporary Jewish feelings saved them from exclusion. Finally, the Writings contains the book of Daniel, the one true example of apocalyptic writing in the Old Testament. Daniel is included among the prophets in Christian Bibles, but its differences from the classical prophets are clear to anyone who reads it carefully. Although set in the sixth century in Babylonia, it reflects very well, the hopes and fears of pious Jews of the second century B.C.

As has already been said, the Writings, as a whole, do not convey the same unity of message and faith found in the Law and the Prophets. Affirmations of the essential faith of Israel there are, but there are also equally profound expressions of doubt and despair. For this reason, some of the Writings may provide the best "way into the Bible" for many modern men. Many of us find the Law of Israel or the denunciations of the prophets difficult to bear, but all of us can identify with the anguish of Job or perhaps the skepticism of Ecclesiastes. Furthermore, when one begins with the questioning mood of these books the answers given by the Torah come into new focus. In fact, only when one has wrestled with life's problems as these books do will the Biblical faith come alive. They teach us that faith is not so much belief in a set of answers handed down from on high as the acceptance of certain questions which we are bound to answer for ourselves. Whether the Rabbis who chose these books for inclusion in the canon had this approach in mind is unanswerable. At least one can say that their choice of books reveals that faith is born, not from passive acceptance of orthodox dogma, but in the midst of agonizing about the deepest human questions which face us all.

CHAPTER XXI

The Book of Job: Introduction and Analysis

Job and Wisdom
Analysis
Conclusion

LTHOUGH UNIQUE in many respects, the book of Job is usually classified as a piece of wisdom literature. As such it takes its place in a sizeable corpus of literature produced by wise men all over the ancient Near East. Egypt, Edom, Mesopotamia, and of course, Greece all produced works of wisdom which are still extant today. Since Israel was by no means an isolated nation, she too had her wise men who through parables, epigrams, discourses, and dialogues sought to advise men about how to live in this world. The books of Proverbs, Ecclesiastes, and Job represent the fruits of their work. There are also wise sayings and parables to be found in many other books of the Bible.

What precisely is Wisdom Literature? Although an all-inclusive definition is difficult to formulate, one may say that it is a type of writing which begins with man and his problems and seeks to solve them without particular reference to special revelation. This is not to say that the wise man denied the orthodox teachings of the national religion, but he usually sought answers to life's problems without special appeals to them. For instance, the famous epigram of Proverbs, "Consider the ant, thou sluggard, and be wise," knows no particular sect or theology. It is as relevant to an Egyptian or an American as it was to the ancient Israelite. In the observation of the natural world and in the basic forms of human experience the wise man sought for truth. Hence, wisdom is an embryonic form of philosophy. Socrates and Plato, in a way, simply carried wisdom to its logical conclusion.

At the same time, however, the discursive forms of reasoning emphasized by the Greek philosophers are not usually to be found in typically Near Eastern wisdom. Biblical wisdom is basically intuitive, not discursive. The epigram, an expression of intuitive insight, not logical analysis, is a common vehicle of expression. The truths of wisdom are most often homely and practical, not metaphysical. Even the skeptical writer of Ecclesiastes presents us with a series of insights rather than with any logical proof.

Job and Wisdom

In a sense the book of Job fits this general description of wisdom. It employs a typical moral tale coupled with an extensive dialogue. Moreover, the book certainly begins with man rather than with divine revelation. In fact, the whole story is set in a non-covenantal context. Job is from Uz and although this may be simply an imaginary location, chances are it was in Edom. Neither Job nor his comforters are identified as believing Israelites. Nowhere are the promises or the covenant of God mentioned.

Still, though Job begins with the thought-forms and the questions of the wiseman, the book must be said to stand "at the edge of wisdom." It is, in fact, an impassioned assertion of the awareness that the simple moralism of most wise men is hardly enough. Proverbs is full of the kind of "practical" advice which a father might offer to his son who is starting out to seek his fortune in the big wide world. Work hard, act and speak honestly, beware evil women and you will succeed. Job avoids all such clichés. In fact, the more one reads the book the more difficult it becomes to know just what answer is being given. Only the most superficial reader will put down the book fully convinced that he has understood it. Like Plato, who also wrote in dialogue form and who often ended his dialogues inconclusively, the authors of Job involve the reader in an intense debate which ends, not with a final Q.E.D., but with a new set of questions. If there is truth to be found in the book, therefore, it is born in the midst of struggle. Perhaps the truth is the struggle itself.

But this is to move too hastily to our conclusions. Before we can approach the text directly, we must first examine how the book was composed and what conditions prompted the various stages in its development. The first observation to be made is Job 1:1-2:13 and Job 42:7-16 differ in style from the rest of the book. These passages which constitute the Prologue and Epilogue, are written in archaic, folk-tale prose while the long dialogical interval which constitutes the main section of the work is in highly sophisticated poetry. Because of the striking differences in style and vocabulary it is highly unlikely that the prose section came into existence at the same time as the poetic dialogue. Rather, it is probable that the Prologue and Epilogue, along with an intervening section which has been excised, existed for centuries as a simple moral fable. Some scholars believe that it came into being as early as the Patriarchal age, though it was not written down until sometime around the time of David and Solomon. The point of this original story was quite obvious. Job, an exemplary righteous man, was tested for God by the "tester" Satan who, parenthetically, seems to have been on quite good terms with the Almighty. Although Job lost his wealth, family, and health, he remained faithful to God. As a result of his patience he was rewarded double in the end. The "wisdom" of the story is clear: Remain steadfast in adversity and God will reward you. Remember the patience of Job!

During the sixth century, however, events occurred which called this simple-minded moralism into question. Jerusalem was destroyed by the Babylonians and many Jews were carried off into exile. Although one can over-emphasize the direness of the situation of Israel at the time, it is clear that both the righteous and the unrighteous suffered during the years of exile. In fact, to many the punishment seemed all out of proportion to the crime. Not only did they come to ask the ultimate question: is there any moral order in the universe. They also came to question the moralistic advice of the wiseman who said simply, "persevere". Suppose the suffering has become so intense that perseverance and simple trust in God are no longer psychologically possible! Suppose the "testing" so shatters a man that he can only despair! Are exhortations to patience of any value to a man who has suffered a nervous breakdown?

During the sixth century a poet or school of poets came face to face with these issues. Hence they asked of the ancient moral fable a telling question: Suppose Job had lost his patience? Suppose this paragon of virtue had finally broken down? Their long poetic insertion into the simple text is an attempt to explore these issues in depth. This they do by imagining a discussion among Job, the broken hero, and three pious wisemen who continually mouth the traditional wisdom. Probably a later author added still another "comforter," Elihu, who adds his own piece of bombastic advice to the smitten Job.

Because these authors asked questions which went right to the heart of the meaning of the faith of Israel and because they were unwilling to soften the harshness of the problem, they often put into the mouth of Job words which sounded to orthodox ears very much like blasphemy. When later scribes began to copy this work they were sometimes shocked by what was said. Hence they attempted to mitigate the force of Job's complaint at times by inserting words of their own. This means that the text of Job is quite corrupt. Sometimes a carefully wrought passage is suddenly disrupted by a word which does not fit poetically. Sometimes a sentence or phrase seems to be omitted. Fortunately, the work is in poetry and this means that tampering with the text can be quickly seen by a student of Hebrew letters. Occasionally the original reading can be restored with some confidence. In any event, the Hebrew text now available is probably somewhat less shocking theologically than the original. As unfortunate as this may be, such scribal emendations may have been what saved Job from exclusion from the canon.

With these remarks in mind, now let us turn to an analysis of the text itself.

Analysis

The prologue: 1:1-2:13

As has already been said, this section is the first part of what was once a simple moral tale. Job is presented as a paragon of virtue; he is both rich and pious, the prototype of the wise and upright man. In Verse 6 the scene suddenly shifts to heaven where God and Satan are having a conversation. Satan, who is here no principle of evil incarnate but rather the angelic agent who tests men for God, declares that Job would not be so righteous if he had not had such worldly success. So God commands Satan to test Job by "touching" his worldly possessions. In a trice Job loses his great herds of cattle and his children. But Job remains faithful.

Satan is not satisfied, however, for he claims that if he were to afflict Job physically he would succumb to temptation. God again allows Satan to do his worst and Job soon breaks out with loathsome sores. Job's wife is apparently overcome by the sight of her husband's malady and advises him to curse God and die. But again Job remains steadfast. The situation, however, has become grotesque. Job, forsaken by his wife and consumed by the itching, sits among the ashes scraping his sores. To him come three "correct" comforters, Eliphaz (whose name means "God crushes"), Bildad ("the Darling of God") and Zophar ("Twittering Bird" or perhaps "Jumping Goat"). For seven days and nights the four men sit in silence.

Job's first lament and the first round of speeches: 3:1-14:22

SUDDENLY the prose introduction ends and a long poetic dialogue begins. Job opens the conversation, not by continuing to mouth the platitudes of wisdom but by cursing the day of his birth. Gone is the proverbial "patience of Job." The paragon of virtue has become a man of flesh and blood overcome by suffering. Not that he denies his faith in God, but his suffering has destroyed his internal peace. As he says,

> "for the thing that I fear comes upon me,
> and what I dread befalls me.
> I am not at ease, nor am I quiet;
> I have no rest; but trouble comes. (3:25-26)

Therefore, he can only lament that he was ever born and contemplates the possibility of non-existence. It is noteworthy that for Job this, and not the philosophical 'problem of evil', is the central problem. Job previously disposed of the existence of evil by saying "The Lord gives and the Lord takes away." What is different now is that Job no longer has the capacity to accept internally such platitudes. The one benefit which wisdom was to bring has been shattered. Job no longer knows "peace of mind."

Eliphaz, the oldest and most venerable comforter, speaks first. His words are relatively mild, but it is clear that he has not discerned Job's essential problem. Bear up, Job, he says. No man is perfect and hence all are subject to God's judgment. If you will only accept God's affliction with patience, God will, in the end, reward you. This is the perennial answer of wisdom, but it clearly misses the mark.

In the 6th and 7th chapters Job replies by expressing again his broken response to suffering. May God in truth crush me, he says, for I am not made of iron and cannot stand the torture any longer. Job can see no reason for his suffering and pleads innocence, but the only way out for him seems to be death. Only then will he escape his tormentor.

Bildad cannot stand such blasphemy. God is just, he says. Therefore, your punishment *must* be for some crime; even your loss of confidence and trust speaks against you. If you are not guilty, you will be rewarded. Job answers by, in a sense, agreeing. No one, he says, can argue with God for God is Almighty; he is the Creator. Moreover, his justice is not like human justice and hence cannot be comprehended by man. Job accepts God's justice, but sees it as unfathomable. Since God is angry with him, for reasons unknown, all Job can do is to yearn for death.

Zophar reproaches Job, but it is clear he has not understood him, for he merely reiterates the belief that God's wisdom and justice are unfathomable. His interpretation of this fact is the epitome of self-righteous piety. "If you set your heart aright, you will stretch out your hands toward him" (11:13). Trust in God will produce the strength you need to endure the torment. What Zophar fails to understand, however, is that trust in God is the result and not the cause of this strength. Job's inner strength has collapsed; he cannot trust.

Zophar's very smugness seems to produce in Job, however, a subtle, but distinct change in attitude. He responds almost sarcastically, calling his maxims "proverbs of ashes" and twitting him for his claim to wisdom. Job defends his own integrity, but he still sees human life as full of trouble and hopelessness. He cries out for some hope beyond the grave, but sees none. Man's desperate existence ends in death, and where is there any promise in that?

The second round of speeches

WITH CHAPTER 15 the second round of speeches begins. It soon becomes patently clear that none of the three comforters has really listened to Job at all. They rather reiterate in an increasingly tedious way what they have already said. Man must fear God, because he is All-powerful, and trust in his justice. Because God is just, suffering is a result of sin. The righteous man must accept his suffering as deserved and trust in God.

While the comforters remain complacently satisfied with their "orthodox position," Job becomes increasingly vocal in defense of himself. He may have become the laughing-stock of his community, but he is still righteous. For a brief moment he cries out that after death God himself will judge him innocent.

> "For I know that my Redeemer lives,
> and at last he will stand upon the earth;
> and after my skin has been thus destroyed,
> then from my flesh I shall see God,
> whom I shall see on my side,
> and my eyes shall behold, and not another." (19:25-27)

But Job cannot sustain this outburst of faith in the life hereafter. "My heart faints within me" (19:27). Still, in his final speech of the round in answer to Zophar, he spells out his attack upon the position of the comforters: surely in this world the wicked often do prosper and the righteous suffer! Any talk about any clear correspondence between morality and human destiny in this world is just foolishness.

The third round of speeches

ELIPHAZ begins the third round by trying to convince Job that he really has committed sins, but Job will have none of it. Not that he claims to be perfect, but he points out again that many wicked men receive no apparent punishment while righteous people are often severely afflicted. To this Bildad can only respond that all men are sinners and hence all deserve punishment. Job responds by ironically praising his "friends" for their consummate wisdom. He then goes on to describe at length the righteousness of his life, how he has had compassion for others and how he has kept himself from all iniquity.

The introduction of Elihu

THE FORMAT calls for a third speech from Zophar, but none is forthcoming. Perhaps the author sensed the tedium of a too thoroughly ordered dialogue or perhaps later editors have rearranged the text in order to add a new voice. In any event, in Chapters 32-37 we hear from another quarter. Elihu, the Buzite, introduces himself. Elihu is a younger man and hence has kept silence during the preceding discussion. He can, however, contain himself no longer, for he sees that the older men haven't answered Job. The reader expects that now Elihu will say something new, but on the whole he does not. Rather he emphasizes once more the majesty and inscrutability of God and accuses Job of having acted pridefully in questioning his Maker. Only one theme in Elihu's speech is relatively new, i.e., that God sometimes afflicts man so that he may "see the light." In other words, suffering may serve an educative function (33:29-30). Elihu still affirms, however, that God acts with justice in this world and refuses to admit that the just God is hidden from man's eyes. Job's complaint, to him, is just an expression of human conceit.

God's answer to Job

JOB is given no chance to respond to this rather bombastic speech of Elihu's. Instead, quite unexpectedly Yahweh himself enters the discussion. Out of the whirlwind, a symbol, perhaps, of the apparent meaninglessness of cosmological existence, the Lord speaks in answer to Job. His answer, however, is scarcely such in the usual sense of the term, for God piles one question upon another, calling Job to explain if he can the countless mysteries of the universe. Job, overwhelmed by the presence of God, can only cover his mouth in silence, but God continues, pointing to the Behemoth and the Leviathan as his inscrutable masterpieces.

Finally, Job finds his tongue.

> "I know that thou canst do all things,
> and that no purpose of thine can be thwarted,
> Who is this that hides counsel without knowledge?
> Therefore I have uttered what I did not understand,
> things too wonderful for me, which I did not know.
> 'Hear, and I will speak;

I will question you, and you declare to me.'
I had heard of thee by the hearing of the ear,
but now my eye sees thee;
Therefore I despise myself,
and repent in dust and ashes." (42:2-6)

Thereupon the Lord expresses his anger with the comforters and calls upon Job to pray for them. Job does so and they are saved. He, in turn, is given once more wealth and children and finally dies, an old, but respected man, full of days.

Conclusion

THE PERPLEXING QUESTION is, of course, what does the book of Job mean to teach? When the Lord enters he does not answer Job's questions at all. He neither proves that justice reigns in this world, nor does he promise the righting of earthly wrongs in the life hereafter. He seems to agree with the comforters in their condemnation of Job's questioning, yet he also voices his disapproval of them and commends Job in the end. Thus the story seems to raise more questions than it answers.

At the same time, it is clear that the dialogue has not been merely a fruitless whirlwind of words, for in the dialogical process certain "answers" to the problem of evil and human suffering have been discarded as insufficient. In fact, all "intellectual" answers have been shown to be wanting. One cannot solve the problem by developing a neat and tidy theological or philosophical system, for the question which Job raises is not merely an intellectual one. He cries out because, through suffering, he has lost his capacity to trust in life itself. God is hidden to him and therefore he can only shake his fist at a seemingly implacable heaven.

The very fact that God speaks out of the whirlwind, therefore, answers his condition, if not his questions. It does not matter what God says. God may overwhelm Job with impossible questions, but his very presence is an act of love, for it reveals that there is meaning in the universe even though that meaning may be to man inscrutable. The point of the book of Job seems to be that meaning in life is not to be found in human words, words, words, but in confrontation with the Almighty himself. Having made that point the authors could then return to the original ending. Job receives goods and family, but all these are superfluous, for Job has received all that a man needs to live life. He has seen God face-to-face.

CHAPTER XXII

The Psalms: Introduction and Analysis

OF ALL THE BOOKS of the Bible there is perhaps none more difficult to discuss and analyze briefly than the book of Psalms. Not only do the 150 poems in this book express almost every conceivable attitude and belief of the pious Jew. Scholarly opinion concerning the dating and function of the various psalms is so diverse that no one could deal with it within the scope of a few pages. In this summary analysis, therefore, we must be satisfied with some general observations about the book as a whole.

The word "psalm" comes from the Greek *psalmos,* a word denoting the playing of a stringed instrument. It was used by the translators of the Septuagint to render the Hebrew word, *mizmor,* which is employed 57 times in the book to indicate a religious song accompanied by stringed instruments. Psalter, on the other hand, is derived from psaltery, an ancient musical instrument mentioned in the psalms. Since there is no indication in the book that all psalms were meant to be accompanied by a psaltery, this name for the book is somewhat misleading. Today "Psalter" means a collection of Psalms ordered for liturgical purposes. The title of the book in Hebrew, *Tehillim,* means simply "praises." Thus, the Hebrew identifies the book in terms of its function, i.e., the praise of God, while the Greek title, which Western Bibles have inherited, points to the literary form of its contents.

The traditional Rabbinic belief was that the psalms were written by David, the king, but there are few today who would hold to this theory. Not only does the book itself attribute some psalms to other authors (for instance, 72 is ascribed to Solomon, 90, to Moses, and a number, to Asaph and the Sons of Korah), there are clear references in several psalms to events which occurred long after David's reign. (For instance, 137 refers clearly to the Babylonian captivity.) Although a few psalms might conceivably be by David, nearly all are at most "Davidic", i.e., written according to the tradition of David. This may, in fact, be what the original attribution meant.

Just when the psalms were written is a matter of great dispute. Some scholars argue that nearly all of them are post-exilic in origin, while others maintain that many came from the pre-exilic period. Some would even argue for a pre-Davidic date for several of the psalms. Although it is impossible to reach any absolute certainty concerning the matter, it is becoming more and more evident that those who argue for a post-exilic date for the origin of all the psalms are having an increasingly difficult time defending their position. Surely, the Israelites must have had some sort of psalmic tradition even during the time of the judges, for virtually every ancient religion employed hymns of one sort or another to praise the gods or God. Furthermore, discoveries at Ugarit have shown quite conclusively that Israelite and Canaanite hymnody have many literary similarities. This means that the Israelite psalmic tradition must have originated when Canaanite influence was still strong. The mention of kings in various psalms (20:9; 21:1,7; 45:1,11,14,15, for instance) also seems to imply a date when kings still ruled Israel. All of this points to a pre-exilic date for many of the psalms.

The issue, however, is complicated by the fact that many of the psalms have been edited and revised again and again. New verses have been added and older ones deleted. Thus, though the original poem may have been of great antiquity, the psalm as it stands before us may be quite "late". Psalm 104, for instance, is clearly dependent for its inspiration upon an Egyptian hymn to Aton; yet its contents are now thoroughly Yahwistic. In this case, the psalm looks newer than, in a sense, it really is. On the other hand, editors and adapters may well have retained, at times, anachronisms which make the final form of the poem appear older than it is.

All in all, then, it is extraordinarily difficult to date any of the psalms with confidence. Only Psalm 137, which clearly speaks from the vantage point of the Babylonian captivity, gives explicit evidence of its time. Perhaps the most that can be said is that although the final form of the psalms which we have before us is post-exilic, most are based upon or inspired by older poems which may well be pre-exilic and even pre-Davidic.

Not only did many of the individual psalms undergo a long process of historical development; the book of Psalms as a whole exhibits evidence that it went through many "editions" itself. The first book of Psalms may have included only Psalms 2-41 which are, in the main, ascribed to David in the superscriptions. To this collection was then added another collection which is found in Psalms 42-72. Two of the psalms of this second collection (53,70) vary only slightly from psalms in the first edition (14,40:13-17). Just why the editors failed to delete these repetitions is unknown. To these psalms were added the psalms "of Asaph" (50, 73-83) which probably originated in a guild of Temple singers (Ezra 2:41). The same is doubtless true of the psalms of "the sons of Korah" (42-49, 84,85,87,88) and the "Songs of Ascent" (120-134). The Hallel Psalms (111-113, 115-117, 146-150) may also have been part of an originally separate collection. When and how these various editions came into being is unknown. What is reasonably clear is that the final form of the book of Psalms is post-exilic. If Pfeiffer is correct in his assertion that Psalm 2 is an acrostic poem in honor of Janneus Alexander and his wife, then it may be that the book of Psalms as we now have it came into being in 103 B.C.[1] That acrostic interpretation, however, is questioned by many.

As it now stands, the Hebrew Psalter is divided into five books (patterned after the five books of Moses?). Each book concludes with a doxology, while Psalm 150 serves in this capacity for the whole collection. The five books are as follows:

Book I: Psalms 1-41

THIS SECTION begins with an introductory psalm distinguishing the righteous man from the unrighteous which was doubtless added by some post-exilic editor. Then follows a collection of

[1] Pfeiffer, Robert. *Introduction to the Old Testament.* New York: Harper and Brothers, 1948, p. 628.

Davidic psalms which may be the earliest edition of the work. In it the name of Yahweh is used much more frequently than Elohim to refer to God. A number of these psalms are related by superscription to some event in the life of David (3,7,30,34). Other superscriptions (4,5,8,9,12,16,22,32,39) seem to give some indication of how the psalm ought to be performed musically, though many of these directions are now obscure.

Book II: Psalms 42-72

THIS SECOND "Davidic" psalter forms part of what has been called the "Elohistic psalter" (which includes also Psalms 73-82), for in it the name Elohim is used four times as often as the name Yahweh. Just why this should be the case is not clear. Psalms 42-49 are Psalms of the Sons of Korah, while Psalm 50 is "of Asaph." Of the rest all but 66,67,71, and 72 are ascribed in the superscription to David. Apparently Psalm 72 once ended a collection of psalms, for it concludes, "The prayers of David, the son of Jesse, are ended." Nevertheless, in the next sections there are more psalms ascribed to David.

Book III: Psalms 73-89

THIS MUCH BRIEFER book contains ten "Psalms of Asaph" plus four "Psalms of the Sons of Korah," a prayer of David (86), and a psalm (maskil) of Ethan the Ezrahite.

Book IV: Psalms 90-106

THIS RATHER MISCELLANEOUS collection begins with "A Prayer of Moses" (90) and includes two "Davidic" psalms (101,103). Psalm 92 is designated "A Song for the Sabbath"; Psalm 100, "A Psalm for the Thank offering"; Psalm 102, "A Prayer of one afflicted, when he is faint and pours out his complaint before the Lord."

Book V: Psalms 107-150

BESIDES A LARGE NUMBER of psalms characterized by title as "Davidic" this section contains a collection of "Songs of

Ascent", i.e., pilgrim songs probably used on religious journeys to Jerusalem (120-134), and the so-called Hallel Psalms (111-113, 115-117, 146-150). This last group is composed of songs of praise used particularly at the three Mosaic festivals: Passover, Pentecost, and Tabernacles. They are characterized by great joyousness and praise to God.

The book of Psalms has often been called the "Hymnbook of the Second Temple," and surely there is some truth in this designation, for the singing of psalms played an important part in the Temple worship of the Jews. At the same time, it is also clear that not all of the psalms were written for this purpose and may never have been used in the Temple at all. Psalm 45 is in praise of a royal couple on their wedding day. A number of so-called Wisdom or Torah psalms are not particularly suitable for singing. Pfeiffer argues that Psalms 1 and 79 are really in prose.[1] Therefore, it may be better to characterize the book of Psalms as a collection of devotional verse designed for public and private use. Although many of the psalms were originally means to be sung, they certainly came to be used for private meditation and inspiration.

Although there are many ways to categorize the psalms, perhaps the most fruitful method is according to each psalm's probable function within the religious life of the people. Such a means of classification is by no means precise, but at least it will serve to illustrate some of the various moods expressed in the Psalter and some of the different purposes which the psalms served. By analyzing the basic intention expressed in each psalm, they may be grouped together in the following way.

A. Hymns of Praise:
 1. Exhortations to praise Yahweh: 24, 29, 33, 47, 66, 81, 95, 96, 97, 98, 99, 100, 103, 105, 107, 111, 113, 114, 115, 117, 118, 134, 135, 136, 146, 147, 148, 149, 150.
 In these Psalms Israel, the nations, and/or the whole creation are called to praise Yahweh.
 2. Psalms which praise Yahweh directly:
  a. For steadfast love and faithfulness: 36, 89, 92, 108, 138.
  b. For his majesty: 8, 66, 76, 93, 104, 131, 139, 145.

---

[1] Pfeiffer. *Op. cit.*, p. 619.

c. For his justice: 67
d. For his law: 119
e. For deliverance: 65, 124
f. As a God of war: 144

In these psalms Yahweh is addressed directly, usually for some specific benefit or quality.

3. Psalms in praise of Zion, the city of God: 48, 87, 122, 132, 137. It is not always clear whether the psalmist speaks of the earthly Jerusalem or of the heavenly city of God.

B. Affirmations of trust in Yahweh and of his gracious actions in the past: 4, 9, 10, 11, 14, 16, 28, 22, 23, 27, 30, 31, 34, 40, 41, 46, 53, 77, 91, 116, 121.

These are, by and large, testimonial psalms which declare how Yahweh has helped either Israel as a whole or the individual in particular. Some of them might also be grouped with the psalms of supplication, for they implore Yahweh's aid once more in the present.

C. Penitential Psalms: 38, 39, 51, 123, 130.

It is noteworthy that so few of the psalms express regret for the petitioner's sinfulness. Even in several of these psalms the confession of guilt is not very forcefully expressed. In general the psalmists attempt to present themselves to God in the best, rather than the worst, light.

D. Psalms of Supplication:

a. General: 28, 40, 54, 57, 71, 86, 90, 94, 120, 143.
b. Yearning for God's presence: 42-43, 62, 63, 84.
c. For health: 6, 38, 88, 102.
d. For righteousness and strength: 22, 25, 141.
e. For deliverance from and/or defeat of enemies: 3, 5, 13, 17, 35, 55, 56, 58, 59, 64, 69, 70, 109, 129, 140, 142, 143.
f. For justice: 9, 10, 12, 94, 125.
g. For vindication: 7, 26, 42-43.
h. For the nation: 44, 60, 68, 74, 79, 80, 83, 85, 89, 106, 123, 126.

These psalms, which are often called "Laments," are more accurately called prayers of supplication. It is significant how many of the psalms take this form. Even more striking are the numbers which call upon God for aid against the psalmist's "enemies." There has been considerable debate concerning who these enemies were. Were they the enemies of the king and hence of the nation? personal enemies of the individual? magicians who used their wiles against the believer? or demonic forces? No one answer can be given to these questions, for in some one group may be intended while in another, another. In any event, the number of these psalms gives a mood of almost paranoia to the Psalter as a whole. Groups e., f., and g. might well be lumped together, for all three call upon God to judge between the petitioner and the "wicked."

The last group of psalms (h) implores God to help Israel as a whole. The mood of them seems to be post-exilic for they call upon God to restore his relation to Israel which existed "of old."

E. Wisdom or Pedagogical Psalms: 1, 15, 32, 37, 49, 50, 52, 73, 101, 112, 119, 127, 128, 133.

These psalms are instructional in nature and set forth what the good life should be like. That is, they distinguish the way of the righteous from that of the wicked. Many of them employ the techniques and vocabulary of much wisdom literature.

F. Royal Psalms: 2, 20, 21, 45, 61, 72, 110

These psalms directly mention the king in one way or another and may well have been used during the enthronement festival which many scholars believe took place in the fall at the beginning of the New Year. It is conjectured that at that festival the king, in a special ceremony, received his position anew as the political representative of God in Israel. Psalm 45 is not of this type, for it is a psalm for a royal wedding. After the end of the kingship many of these psalms were read as Messianic, i.e., as expressions of hope for the coming of the new son of David.

G. Psalms for Covenant Renewal: 50, 76, 78, 81, 82, 89.

This is an admittedly hypothetical category, but many scholars believe that these, and perhaps other psalms, were used during the ceremony of the renewal of the covenant which supposedly took place each fall.

Needless to say, the Book of Psalms is by no means arranged topically, but rather moves rapidly from one mood to the next. Still there is a movement in the book from Psalms of supplication to Psalms of praise. While the Davidic psalms of the first book tend to be somewhat pleading, if not vindictive in tone, the Hallel psalms which conclude the book are expressions of a type of pure joyousness which is seldom felt in our own age. One can hardly find a better example of the exhiliration which comes from faith in Yahweh than in Psalm 150.

> Praise the Lord!
> praise God in his sanctuary;
> Praise him for his mighty deeds;
> Praise him according to his exceeding greatness!
>
> Praise him with trumpet sound;
> praise him with lute and harp!
> Praise him with timbrel and dance;
> praise him with strings and pipe!
> Praise him with sounding cymbals;
> praise him with loud clashing cymbals!
> Let everything that breathes praise the Lord!
> Praise the Lord!

Before concluding this discussion of the Psalms, a word ought to be said about their literary form and musical performance. Like much Hebrew poetry most of the Psalms are distinguished by the use of parallelism. A typical example of the psalmist's technique is found in Psalm 6:1-2.

> O Lord, rebuke me not in thy anger,
> nor chasten me in thy wrath.
> Be gracious to me, O Lord, for I am languishing;
> O Lord, heal me, for my bones are troubled.

Line 2 simply repeats in different words the meaning of line 1. Line 3 states the idea in positive terms, while Line 4 repeats the petition in different words. Thus, there is employed a rhyming of idea rather than sound. The art of the Psalmist is displayed in the various ways through which this concept-rhyming is done. Sometimes two or three lines are set forth and then paralleled by two or three more. Sometimes the idea of a verse is contrasted rather than repeated in the next. Occasionally, as in Psalm 42:5, 43:5 a stanza is repeated to tie the poem as a whole together.

The poetry of the Psalms is often "dialectic" in nature. That is to say, a psalm may begin with one idea and then shift suddenly to its antithesis. In Psalm 22, for instance, the psalmist begins with the famous complaint, "My God, my God, why hast thou forsaken me?" This theme is developed through Verse 21. Then, quickly, the speaker turns from his questioning and supplication to a triumphant assertion of his praise of God and of his hope for Israel. In this way, the paradoxical nature of the existence of a man of faith is set forth with beautiful power.

Occasionally psalmists make use of alphabetic acrostical patterns for their poems (9-10, 25, 34, 37, 111, 119, 145). In 25 and 34 additions have clearly been made to the text for the acrostic is disrupted. Psalm 119 is the most elaborate, if not the best, example of the acrostic technique. In this psalm the first eight lines begin with the letter Aleph, the next eight with Beth, etc. This makes 119 the longest of all the psalms.

Many of the Psalms have superscriptions which apparently give directions concerning how the psalm was meant to be performed musically. For instance, Psalm 6 is entitled "To the choirmaster; with stringed instruments; according to the Sheminith. A Psalm of David." What "The Sheminith" means we do not know. In fact, by the time the Septuagint was translated, its meaning was already obscure. Probably, however, it refers to a style of playing or traditional melody or mode used by the Temple musicians. Other psalms are entitled "According to the Gittith," "According to Muthlabben," "According to the Hind of the Dawn," etc. Perhaps one day an archaeologist will uncover a musical handbook which will explain these designations. Until that time, readers must be satisfied with wholly speculative theories about them.

Almost equally obscure is the word "Selah" which occurs frequently in the Psalms. Some commentators believe that it functioned as a Da Capo sign and indicated that the stanza should be repeated. Others believe that it indicated that a musical interlude should be played between stanzas. Still others ascribe to it some hidden religious significance. Again, this is a question which at the present time cannot be settled definitely.

Happily, the meaning of the Psalms is not nearly as obscure as their musical directions. In fact, within this book is set forth what many conceive to be the essential faith of Israel. There is no point, therefore, in examining the "theology of the Psalms" in this analysis. It is, in fact, a summary expression of the faith of the whole Old Testament. Here one finds expressed before Yahweh, the Creator and the Lord of history, the needs, aspirations, doubts, fears, and joys of the believing Jew. It is not surprising, therefore, that this book has served generations of both Jews and Christians as a primary medium for inspiration and self-expression. Times have changed since the days of ancient Israel; yet for more believers than not the words of the psalmists still ring true today.

CHAPTER XXIII

The Book of Proverbs: Introduction and Analysis

Some General Considerations
Analysis

HE BOOK OF PROVERBS, like the books of Ecclesiastes and the Song of Songs, has been traditionally ascribed to Solomon, son of David, king of Israel (1:1), but it is clear that this ascription cannot be taken too literally. In fact, the Biblical text itself credits one Agur ben Jakeh with the authorship for Chapter 30 and Lemuel, the king of Massa, with Chapter 31. Furthermore, the word "of" in the phrase "The proverbs of Solomon" is rather ambiguous in Hebrew and might well be translated "in the style of."

Some General Considerations

Since King Solomon was said to have been noted for his wisdom and to have uttered 3,000 proverbs himself (I Kings 4:29-33), it is understandable that later wisemen called this collection of Hebrew wisdom "Solomonic." Solomon could have fostered the school of wise men from which this book eventually issued and may even conceivably be represented in the collection by a proverb or two from his own mouth. On the whole, however, the collection must be considered the work of many generations of wise men who repeated and taught these vehicles for common-sense morality until they became a part of Israel's common heritage.

The term *proverb* means in English a short, popular traditional saying embodying some familiar truth in expressive language. Although such proverbs are to be found in this book, many of the chapters contain discourses which can scarcely be called proverbial in the usual sense. This is because the Hebrew term *mashal,* which is here translated proverb, has a somewhat wider meaning than its English "equivalent." *Mashal* is an utterance of truth or standard of behavior. Hence, within the book of *Meshalim* are included several discourses and poems as well as what we would call proverbs.

All of these various literary types embody *hokmah* (wisdom) and were doubtless the treasure of many wise men of Israel. As it was said in the introduction to Job, the wisdom movement was not only widely represented in the Israelite tradition but had an international character as well. Indeed, wisdom literature flourished in Egypt, Mesopotamia and Phoenecia long before Israel became a nation. Edom, to the south, was especially noted for her wise men. Because wisdom literature emphasizes the kind of understanding gained simply through experience in the world and rarely mentions any specific theological dogmas or national creeds, wise men could easily borrow from those of another nation without denying their national religious heritage. Hence, despite the vast theological and cultic differences among the religions of the ancient Near East, wisdom literature in these various countries is quite similar. A proverb such as

> "A lying tongue is a man's worst enemy,
> And smooth talk leads to downfall." (Proverbs 26:28)

may be Israelite in origin, but it might be repeated and remembered almost anywhere with profit.

It is not surprising, then, that Israelite wisdom is similar to that of other countries in both style and content. Proverbs 22:17-24:22 contains, for instance, a compendium of thirty precepts which are markedly similar to the Egyptian *Instruction of Amen-em-ope.* The precepts are rearranged, some are dropped, and some are added, but it is clear that the Hebrew author had this Egyptian model before him in memory if not on paper. As more examples of non-Biblical wisdom are recovered by the archaeologists it may well be that many more close parallels will be found.

Be that as it may, there still are some distinctive features of Israelite wisdom which distinguish it from that of other countries. Although many of the proverbs and discourses are universally applicable, the basic theme of the book that the fear of Yahweh is the beginning of wisdom (1:7) ties the collection firmly to the Biblical tradition. Gone are the pessimism and pragmatic cynicism which characterize much of the non-Biblical wisdom literature. God is in his heaven and, if all is not right with the world, it is man's foolishness which has produced the evil. Proverbs exemplifies a type of Biblical humanism which may disturb those who found their understanding of the Biblical faith upon the doctrine of original sin but which satisfies those who desire sound and relatively simple moral values by which to conduct their lives. The book runs the risk of expressing a much too simplistic and optimistic view of the human situation, but it at least avoids the magnetic attraction of cynicism which can undercut all human moral endeavor. The moralistic advice of a father to his son as he sets out to seek his fortune in the big wide world may become tedious if repeated too often, but it has its place. The Bible offers it such a place, albeit a rather limited one, in the book of Proverbs.

Analysis

CHAPTER 1:1-7 The book opens with a brief introduction in which the purpose of the book (to teach men wisdom) and the major theme of it (the fear of Yahweh is the beginning of knowledge) are set forth. Doubtless this introduction is later than the other sections, added by the editor as an indication of what the work as a whole is about.

Chapters 1:8-9:18 This first major section of the book contains ten discourses in which a father advises his son about how to live, together with a few poems and proverbs which were originally of separate origin.

The first discourse (1:8-19) admonishes the son to avoid the company of evil men, the thieves and cut-throats who seek to do others harm. This is followed by a poem (1:20-33) in which Wisdom is pictured as a woman selling her wares in the city streets, seeking to convince the foolish that they should listen to her. The second discourse (2:1-22) is a general call to be attentive to wisdom and to live an upright life. The wiles of the loose woman are particularly warned about. In the third discourse (3:1-12) the virtues of loyalty, faithfulness, and trust in the Lord are especially commended. The father predicts filled barns and vats for the righteous, but he also warns that the Lord sometimes reproves those whom he loves. The righteous must be patient in the face of adversity.

Proverbs 3:13-20 contains another poem in praise of the preciousness of wisdom by which the Lord created the world.

The fourth discourse (3:21-35) commends to the son honesty and peaceableness with all men, while the fifth (4:1-9) merely reiterates once more the importance of obtaining wisdom.

The sixth discourse (4:10-19) commends again the way of righteousness and warns about the evil fruits of wickedness. The seventh (4:20-27) calls the son to be attentive to the father's wise words.

The eighth discourse (5:1-23) becomes more concrete as the father again returns to the theme of the wiles of evil women. Then he adds a personal confession — listens to me. I didn't listen to my father and was almost brought to ruin. Drink from your own fountain, love your own wife, and let no one lead you astray. Chapter 6:1-19 contains three expanded proverbs concerning suretyship, idleness, and sowing discord and one numerical proverb in which seven things which are an abomination to Yahweh are enumerated.

The ninth discourse, which warns once more about the dangers of an evil woman, is found in chapter 6:20-35. The tenth (7:1-27) reiterates this theme by painting in vivid detail the seduction of a man by an adulteress. This is followed by a lengthy poem, related thematically to those found in 1:20-33 and 3:13-20, in which Wisdom is again pictured as a woman who calls men to delight in her (18:1-9:6). Particularly significant theologically is the assertion in 8:22-31 that wisdom was the first creation of God. She it was who worked beside him in the creation of the world. It is this wisdom who calls all the simple to her banquet of insight. The first section of the book then concludes with two expanded proverbs concerning the difficulty in teaching the scoffers and fools and about the evil woman who entices men to folly.

Proverbs 10:1-22:16 The second section of Proverbs contains a collection of "Solomonic" proverbs concerning a variety of subjects. Most of them are couplets and were doubtless used in teaching the young. The teacher would recite the first line and the pupils were expected to respond with the appropriate conclusion. Occasionally there is a third line to the proverb which was undoubtedly an alternative answer which might be given. More often than not the second line offers contrast to the first as in 10:1:

> A wise son makes a glad father,
> but a foolish son is a sorrow to his mother.

Occasionally the second line is simply an expansion upon the thought expressed in the first. Although Solomon is said to have studied the plants and animals in search of wisdom there are few references to animals in this section. Most of these proverbs simply contain straightforward moral advice.

Proverbs 22:17-24:22 This section, as it has already been said, contains thirty precepts for moral behavior which are based upon the Egyptian Instructions of Amen-em-opet. Although the similarities between these two works are too close to be dismissed as the result of chance, the Biblical collection of precepts is by no means a carbon copy of the Egyptian version. The differences, however, do not seem to be so much the result of theological or ethical disagreement as of simply only partial recollection. In both, fair and just treatment of the poor and the afflicted, wise circumspection when dealing with rulers and the rich, and the avoidance of dangerous temptations are emphasized.

This passage is then followed in 24:23-34 by another brief collection of the sayings of the wise which emphasizes honesty and industry as essential for the wise life.

Proverbs 25:1-29:27 This section purports to be proverbs of Solomon copied by the men of Hezekiah, the king of Judah (25:1). These wise sayings are ordered rather topically and deal with: a) how one should act before the king (25:2-16), b) how to deal with one's neighbor (25:17-28), c) how to deal with the fool (26:1-12), d) the results of laziness and lying (26:13-28), e) boasting, faithfulness, and prudence (27:1-16), f) how earthly goods are ephemeral and do not satisfy (27:17-27), g) how the wicked and the righteous are distinguished (28:1-28), righteous and wicked authority (29:1-27).

Proverbs 30:1-33 This section purports to contain the words of Agur, son of Jakeh of Massa who is otherwise unknown. Among these sayings are a brief expression of skepticism concerning man's ability to understand the universe (30:1-6) and a number of numerical proverbs and sayings.

Proverbs 31:1-31 Proverbs concludes with the words of Lemuel, king of Massa, which he learned from his mother. In 31:2-9 Lemuel is advised concerning how a king should act. To these admonitions is appended an acrostic poem describing the virtues of a good wife. Watch out, says the poem, for mere beauty and charm. The good wife fears the Lord and because she does so she is industrious, faithful, kind, and ever watchful for the needs of her family.

CHAPTER XXIV

The Megillot

Ruth
The Song of Songs
Ecclesiastes
Lamentations
Esther

s has already been said in the introduction to this part of the Tanak, the Megillot is composed of five festal scrolls (*Megillot*—scrolls) used respectively at five festivals of the Jewish liturgical year. Although of diverse origin and idea, they may be fruitfully considered as a unit, for together they express the many-sided nature of human life. Indeed, one might say that they present a portrait of man as the Bible knows him.

Stylistically, the five scrolls exhibit considerable diversity. Ruth and Esther are both short-stories, but while the former is pastoral in tone, the latter is highly melodramatic. In each the chief character is a woman of considerable devotion and beauty who wins out in spite of adversity. Ruth, however, is a Moabitess while Esther is a Jew of Jews. Both marry outside their "race" and in so doing help to contribute to the life of Israel. Ruth gives birth to the grandfather of David, while Esther uses her position in the Persian court to save the Jews from an anti-Semitic pogrom. In a sense, one story is the obverse of the other. While Ruth emphasizes the debt which Israel owes to the Gentiles, Esther stresses the great threat of their anti-Jewish feelings. Only when both "pictures" are seen simultaneously can Jewish life in a heathen world be comprehended.

Lamentations and the Song of Songs are both in verse, but how different they are in style and outlook! Lamentations is, as its title indicates, a tortured lament over the fall of Jerusalem. The picture painted is grim, for the author describes in vivid detail the horror of war and destruction. He speaks of desolation, of hunger, of dreadful anxiety. The Song of Songs, by way of contrast, is an erotic love poem. Although it would appear that the love remains unrequited, it is intense and beautiful nonetheless. Nowhere in the Bible are the joys of love and sexuality more delightfully expressed. The author speaks of kisses and apples and lovely breasts. Again, the Megillot holds up mirrors of life for our observation and we see it paradoxically as a strange combination of dreadful disaster and wonderful delight.

Of the Megillot Ecclesiastes stands alone. Stylistically it is neither narrative prose nor poetry, for the author employs the epigram and discourse of the wise man to make his point. Nor is his message like that of the other four. Quoheleth, the speaker, is a wise man who has found wisdom wanting and yet the answer. He has looked at man from the perspective of eternity and has found him finite and frail, subject to all the folly and fickleness that flesh is heir to. He has looked at eternity from the perspective of man, and has found God's justice lacking both in this life and beyond. Still he is able to assert, paradoxically, that life is worth living and that wisdom is the key to the good life. He is a man of questioning doubt, but not of cynical despair.

This is the life of man as the Bible sees him. He knows the joys of love and the gloom of disaster; he can be faithful to others or chauvinistically clever. And always beneath the surface there lurks the man of doubt who in his more contemplative moments is bound to ask "Why, Why, Why?"

The Megillot is a man-centered series of books. In none of them (except perhaps in Lamentations) is the thunderous voice of the prophet or law-giver heard. Rather we are faced with man in the world, man without a comfortable set of answers upon which to rely. The writers do not confront us with "Thus says the Lord," but only with "Thus asks man!" Still, throughout these books there whispers the almost inaudible voice of eternity, and the answer is "Yes!"

Ruth

ALTHOUGH PENTECOST (Shevuoth) is not the first festival of the year, its book stands first among the Megillot, perhaps because it is concerned with the earliest period of time. Ruth is set "in the days of the judges" and hence seemingly should precede books ascribed to Solomon and Jeremiah. Although its present form may be post-exilic, Ruth doubtless is based upon stories coming from the time of David, at least.

The story is a relatively simple one. Elimelech, his wife Naomi, and their two sons go to live in Moab. Elimelech dies, but Naomi is able to marry off her sons to two Moabite girls. After ten years the sons die too and Naomi is left alone in a strange land. She decides to return home, but counsels her two daughters-in-law to return to their mothers and marry new husbands. Orpha returns home, but Ruth, with touching devotion, will not leave Naomi.

Naomi and Ruth journey to Bethlehem where Ruth, to get food, gleans grain in the field of a kinsman of Elimelech, Boaz. Boaz, with Ruth's help, falls in love with her, and fulfills his obligation as nearest of kin and marries her. All of this occurs with a good deal of backstage direction by Naomi. Subsequently, a child is born who turns out to be the grandfather of David.

Just what the point of the story is is somewhat debatable. Is it an attempt to quell rumors that David's ancestry was Moabite and that the great king was not truly an Israelite? If so, the story clearly shows that although his great-grandmother was from Moab she was a devoted Yahwist and was properly married by Boaz. Perhaps, however, the point is more subtle. Perhaps, like the book of Jonah, Ruth is a gentle reminder to Israel that foreigners are not all bad and that in fact the great king David was descended from one. If so, it may well have been included in the canon to offset what might be regarded as the excessive exclusiveness of such men as Ezra and Nehemiah who forbade foreign marriages entirely.

In any event, it is a beautifully contrived short story whose folk-like simplicity can still serve as a model for story-tellers today. Probably it was connected with Pentecost because of its mention of the barley harvest.

The Song of Songs

LIKE ECCLESIASTES AND PROVERBS, The Song of Songs is ascribed to Solomon, but this ascription, like the others, is hardly to be taken literally. The use of several Persian and Greek words in the text shows that it was, at least, "touched up" in post-exilic days. On the other hand, its imagery indicates that it may be pre-Solomonic and even non-Israelite in origin. Surely the emphasis upon the beauties of the natural world is unique in the Bible and calls to mind certain Egyptian or perhaps Persian writings. Although many theories have been proposed, there is no definitive answer to the questions of date and place of origin.

In one sense, the Song of Songs is very easy to understand, for it is filled with the images of erotic love. The opening line,

> O that you would kiss me with the kisses of your mouth!
> For your love is better than wine,

speaks for itself. Still, when one reads the text with care, one soon becomes bewildered by the disjointed nature of the text. Is this simply a collection of occasional love poems which have only stylistic relation one to another or is this a kind of drama with a "plot"? Who are the "I" and the "you" of the poems? Why is the figure of Solomon introduced? And why are so many floral metaphors used?

Although the text does appear to be somewhat disjointed, there seems to be no good reason to think that this is merely a collection of love verses composed by various authors. The style and imagery certainly seem to be quite consistent throughout. Furthermore, the more one reads these lyrics, the more one discerns the outline of dramatic plot. The principal characters are three: the comely Shulammite girl, her shepherd lover, and King Solomon. Just why the girl is called a Shulammite (6:13) is unclear. Some think that the word should really be read Shunammite and that the girl should be identified as Abishag the Shunammite, a girl who kept King David warm in his old age (I Kings 1:3-4) and who later became Solomon's. Others believe that Shulammite really means a Solomoness, i.e., the female counterpart of Solomon.

In any event, it would appear that this girl is in love with a shepherd lad but has been taken by Solomon for his harem. Solomon woos the girl, using the most elaborate, almost laughable, poetic images. (Her eyes are compared to doves, her hair to a flock of sheep moving down the slopes of Gilead, her teeth, to a flock of shorn ewes, etc. 4:1-2) She is unimpressed and she remains faithful to her beloved shepherd. She dreams that her lover comes to her bed chamber at night and knocks, but when she goes to let him in he is gone. She chases after him but is caught by the guards and beaten (5:2-8). Solomon continues to woo her, perplexed that she will not respond favorably (6:5) yet still persistant. His lovemaking technique is somewhat limited, however, for he uses the same images of praise over again (6:5-7). He reminds her that she is only one girl among many in his harem (6:8-9) and yet is astounded by her attractive, yet forbidding, glances (6:10).

While Solomon speaks, the girl's mind is elsewhere as she imagines her lover a prince who takes her away in his chariot (6:11-13). Solomon continues his praise (6:1-9), but the girl can only dream of her shepherd lad. Would that you were my brother, she says, for then I could kiss you in public and could go with you to our mother's chamber (8:1-4). In 8:6-14 the Shulammite makes her final speech. She will not give in, for "love is as strong as death "(8:6). No amount of money can buy her love (8:7). Some girls may be physically unattractive and need to be adorned for marriage. She, however, is quite attractive physically but her love for her shepherd is a wall to Solomon (8:8-10). Solomon has many vineyards and has, indeed, rented out some to others. He can have his vineyards, she will keep her own—her virginity. She ends her soliloquy with another plaintive cry to her lover:

"Make haste, my beloved,
and be like a gazelle
or a young stag
upon the mountains of spices." (8:14)

If this interpretation is correct, the whole poem is one of unrequited love, of a lovesick maiden who cannot unite with her true lover. Although it may contain images derived from or inspired by Canaanite fertility-cult literature (the Shulammite sometimes is pictured as like a goddess of the flowers (2:1), it is clear that the principals in the story are human and that the plot is basically non-mythological.

This does not mean, of course, that an allegorical interpretation is wholly misguided. Indeed, this book would probably not have been included in the canon had it not been for the fact that it was interpreted as an allegorical poem depicting Israel's love for God. It is read during Passover, when Israel's escape from Egyptain bondage for marriage to

Yahweh at Sinai is remembered. If one chooses to read it in this manner, however, it is important to apply the allegorical method properly. Attempts to see Solomon as a Christ or Yahweh "type" seem wholly misguided, for Solomon is pictured as an opulent ruler whose love-making technique is almost grotesque. His attempts at love are repulsed by the maiden who hopes against hope that her true love will return.

If the Shulammite is an image for Israel, it is the absent shepherd lad who tends his flocks in the wilderness who is Yahweh. Allegorically, then, this poem ought to be seen as an expression of the absence of God and of eschatological hope. The Shulammite is Israel in Egypt and Solomon is the Pharaoh! The heroine rejects the temptation of mundane love for the hope that her savior will come. In post-exilic times, this allegory could also have been read as an expression of Messianic hope.

I do not mean to imply, of course, that the author of this "dialogue" had any allegorical meaning in mind. His theme was human love and he played upon it well. Still, great art is always open to reinterpretation. Certainly, it must be admitted that this poem would be lost to the modern reader were it not for the fact that it was given a theological interpretation. Like so many other books of the Kethuvi'im it was read as an exhortation to devotion in the midst of separation and adversity and as an expression of hope that Yahweh, the God of the covenant, would again return. It was the post-Christian Rabbis, who wished to minimize Israel's eschatological hopes and refused to admit that Yahweh had ever departed from Israel, who tried to see Solomon as God. Such an allegorical interpretation surely is misguided and ought to be rejected by the modern reader.

Ecclesiastes

LIKE so many other books of the Kethuvi'im the book of Ecclesiastes is very difficult to date historically. Many scholars, recognizing that there are many similarities between some ideas expressed in this book and those of certain Greek philosophers, particularly Heraclitus, date the book during the Hellenistic period, i.e., after 332 B.C. There seems to this author to be no particular reason to date the book so late. In the first place, though the book contains two Persian words and many Aramaisms, there are no Greek words or constructions clearly in evidence. Furthermore Heraclitus died in 470 B.C. and may well have been known in Palestine long before the coming of Alexander. Even if he were not known, his thought could have been based upon older wisdom literature which was available. It is possible, though by no means probable, that Heraclitus and the author of Ecclesiastes were members of the same wisdom school which expressed a pessimism born out of disenchantment with the Persian Empire.

Little more is known about the author himself or the place of writing than about the date. According to Verse 1 he was Solomon himself; Chapter 2 also claims that he was a king in Jerusalem, but there is no reason to take these claims very seriously. The language of the book and much of what it says places it long after the time of Solomon. Doubtless the author was a wise man who knew wisdom literature well, for he quotes proverbs continually to suit his purpose. Still he is no mere collector of sayings, for his work bears a markedly individualistic stamp.

The author is called, in 1:1, Koheleth, a word derived from *qahal* (congregation) and means probably "he who calls a congregation." This was translated by the translators of the Septuagint as "Ecclesiastes," a word derived from *ekklesia,* church. In the R.S.V. he is termed "The Preacher." Surely, however, he was not a preacher in the usual sense, for his message is hardly the kind normally found expressed in church and synagogue. It is, in fact, the words of a wise man who calls into question much religious piety and orthodox dogma.

There has been great debate among scholars concerning precisely how much of the book is by one author. Some have argued that the book has gone through many editions and shows clear traces of editorial changes. Most believe that, at the very least, 12:13-14 was added to make the work more theologically respectable. Be that as it may, it appears to me that the rest of the book may well be by one man. It is true that many statements are contradicted by others in the book, but I shall try to argue that this is by design rather than due to editorial addition. The object of the author is not to present a thoroughly consistent philosophy of life, but to express the inevitably inconsistent conclusions which a man must draw when he faces existence honestly.

Koheleth begins with a statement of the theme which is to dominate the whole work:

> Vanity of vanities, says the Preacher,
> vanity of vanities! All is vanity.

What does man gain by all the toil
at which he toils under the sun?

In a word, man's life of toil (and leisure) is meaningless; it is a grasping after wind. He then attempts to justify his statement with some illustrations. He describes the world as constantly in flux, yet ever the same. Here his ideas are similar to those of Heraclitus. Then he describes his own quest, as a great and rich king, for meaning (2:1-11). He seeks to enjoy himself and gathers about him instruments of pleasure. He builds houses and plants vineyards. He buys slaves and possessions and hires entertainers. But when he looks at what he has done, he finds no meaning in it. Pleasure has become jaded and life a striving after wind.

So he turns to wisdom, but he soon sees that the wise man and the fool must both die . . . and of what advantage is that? There is the problem—death. Death is the final end of life and renders all existence meaningless. Why toil when your riches may well pass to a foolish son? (2:18-19) The Preacher sees that the best thing for man to do is to "eat and drink and find enjoyment in his toil" (2:24), but this is no easy possibility, for man can transcend himself, he can know that his death approaches and that ultimately he and his work will be forgotten. Thus, the ability to enjoy finite existence is a gift from God; it cannot be "willed" (2:24-26).

In Chapter 3 we find a passage which parallels, and yet subtly alters, the meaning of 1:4-11. He again refers to the question of the temporality of existence, but this time he sees it differently. All is flux and yet "For everything there is a season, and a time for every matter under heaven" (3:1). Birth and death, laughing and weeping, killing and healing, etc. all have their times. The implication is that man ought to accept each time in life when it arrives. In this sense, he sounds like a Stoic, but the Preacher also sees that this is precisely man's problem. A beast can accept its times. When it is mating season, it mates; when it is time to die, it dies. God, however, "has put eternty into man's mind, yet so that he cannot find out what God has done from the beginning to the end" (3:11). That is to say, man has the ability to look at himself from the vantage point of eternity. He can transcend the time which is presenting itself to him and hence can be dissatisfied with it. Above all, he can see the possibility, indeed the inevitability of the time of non-existence which puts a question-mark over all the times of existence. Because he cannot know God's ways or the ultimate meaning of these times, he can only cry out "vanity of vanities." Man's transcendent wisdom reveals that he ought to accept life as it comes, but that same widsom makes him dissatisfied with life, for it shows him other options.

The rest of the book is, in a way, an ethical treatise on how to live the good life, but it is totally unGreek, for unlike the Hellenic and Hellenistic philosophers, the Preacher knows that wisdom is bound to lead to both the acceptance and the rejection of every time and every attitude toward life. Hence his message is thoroughly paradoxical. He sees the value in marriage and counsels that two are better than one (4:9-12); yet he also says that he has found wicked women but never a wise one (7:26-29).

He sees the vanity of man's labor (4:4-7), yet he also sees the folly of idleness (4:5). He counsels man to enjoy life and drink wine with a merry heart (9:7); yet he also says that sorrow is better than laughter (7:3). The day of death is better than the day of birth (7:1), yet a living dog is better than a dead lion (9:4). Man ought to fear God and live righteously (8:10-13); yet he also ought not to be overly religious (5:1-7).

All of this seems quite bewildering to the reader. The layman is likely to become angry, while the scholar is prone to posit a variety of sources to explain the contradictions. Koheleth, however, is wiser than those who yearn for neat consistency. He is painting a picture of man and refuses to omit any of his dimensions. Man lives on the knife edge between being and non-being. He sees the absurdity of life and yet loves it nonetheless. Finite man has eternity in his mind and hence must accept and deny his existence at the same time.

To the Epicurean he says, Pleasure is good, but watch out, it is also folly. To the Stoic he says, Wisdom is good, but remember it is also foolishness. To all the philosophers who teach of the good life he says, beware the yen for consistency, for life is not like that.

In the midst of this confusing contradictoriness of life, Koheleth still manages to hold onto a few unambiguous verities. Death is real and hope beyond the grave is an illusion. Man is not God; he neither created the universe nor does he know what time holds in store. Man ought to remember his Creator and his own created condition. Such wisdom may not bring salvation or even peace, but it is better than blind folly which holds up false hopes. The wise man knows, at least, the limitations of his own wisdom, and perhaps is enabled thereby to laugh at and with life a bit.

Ecclesiastes is read at the festival of Tabernacles (*Succoth*) when Israel remembers those years which she spent in tents, wandering in the wilderness. Although Koheleth does not mention this historical period, his "wasteland" philosophy seems aptly suited to it. To this day, Jews build for the festival booths in the midst of a cultural waste and enter them to drink wine with merry hearts.

Lamentations

THE LITTLE BOOK of Lamentations contains five poems [three dirges (Chs. 1, 2, and 4) and two laments (Chs. 3, 5)], expressing grief over the fall of Jerusalem. The first four employ an alphabetic acrostic, while the last, though having 22 lines, does not. The fifth also uses the usual poetic meter with each verse having two halves of four-stress accents. The others use the "qinah" meter which employes verses with a four-three accent arrangement.

Although earliest manuscripts contain no attribution, these poems came to be ascribed to the prophet Jeremiah at a fairly early date, hence the title "The Lamentations of Jeremiah." Although certainly more plausible than the ascription of Ecclesiastes to Solomon, it is unlikely that this identification of authorship is correct. In fact, it is not at all certain that one man wrote all five poems. Quite likely they were composed by different poets who looked back upon the same catastrophic events with anguish. Chapters 2 and 4 most vividly describe Jerusalem immediately after its fall and therefore may be the earliest. Chapter 5, which calls upon God to return after a long absence, may well be the latest. All five may well have been written during the exilic period, but even this is not certain.

Of all the books of the Megillot, Lamentations is certainly most closely related to the writings of the prophets. Ecclesiastes, The Song of Song, and Esther do not even mention Yahweh and are not concerned about his action in history. Ruth employs the name of Yahweh again and again, but then, Ruth is set in the period of the judges. Certainly, there is no strong prophetic tone in Ruth at all. Lamentations looks to Yahweh as the Lord in history, but unlike most of the prophets, after the fact of destruction. The prophets warn of what Yahweh will do. Lamentations can only mourn concerning what he has already done.

In general, Lamentations accepts the destruction of Jerusalem as the just punishment of God for the sins of that city, though in 2:20 there is some indication that the author believes that God has somewhat overreacted and has punished the people too severely. The basic question is not, "Why did God do this?"—the prophetic answer is accepted for that. Rather, the question is, "When, if ever, will God return?" The only real note of hope is struck in the third poem (3:21-27) where the speaker, who in this lamentation speaks about his own personal sufferings, remembers that the steadfast love (*chesed*) of God never ceases. Even this is not the final word, for the lamenter returns to his tears and a confession of his woe. His final affirmation that God will eventually punish his enemies (3:64-66) is said more in desperation than with calm assurance.

The book concludes with a beautiful lament which calls upon God to remember his seemingly forgotten people. Again the desperate condition of the people is depicted, but no rousing statement of faith is offered. Instead, the poem ends with a series of agonizing questions:

> But thou, O LORD, dost reign for ever;
> thy throne endures to all generations.
> Why dost thou forget us for ever,
> why dost thou so long forsake us?
> Restore us to thyself, O LORD, that we may be restored!
> Renew our days as of old!
> Or hast thou utterly rejected us?
> Art thou exceedingly angry with us? (5:19-22)

With these words is expressed one of the driving anxieties of exilic and post-exilic Judaism. The convenantal agreement has been abrogated and Yahweh has departed. Will he ever return? Will he restore the covenant and again show his steadfast love to Israel? To answer these questions the apocalyptic writers painted elaborate visions of the future to convince a doubting people that their final end would indeed be victorious. The Chronicler, on the other hand, sought to mute them by demonstrating that God had never really departed and that Israel still had access, through the cult, to him.

Probably the five poems of Lamentations were collected for the specific purpose of observing the 9th of Av, the great day of national mourning when the fall of Jerusalem was remembered. Certainly it is not surprising that the Rabbis of the first century A.D., who had seen Jerusalem destroyed once more in 70 A.D., found a place for this book in the canon. From their day until the Six-Day War in 1967, Jerusalem was in foreign hands and Jews offered yearly lamentations for its loss. Today, only the Wailing Wall remains of the great sanctuary where God's name was once extolled. Jerusalem may be occupied by Israel, but the bitterness of these lamentations still remains on her lips.

Esther

THE BOOK of Esther, which for centuries has been honored by Jews as *The* Megillah, is best described as an historical nouvella. It is set in the region of Ahasuerus (which one it doesn't say), in Susa, the capital of the Persian Empire. Ahasherus is depicted as a magnificent, but despotic ruler whose whim is command. When his wife, Queen Vashti, refuses the order to appear before Ahasuerus and his guests at a drunken revel to reveal her beauty, she is deposed and all women of the empire are commanded to be subservient to their husbands.

As a result, the king seeks a new wife and through a "Miss Persia" contest finally selects Esther, a beautiful Jewess brought up by her uncle, Mordecai, a descendant of King Saul himself. Esther conceals the fact that she is a Jew, because Mordecai has told her to do so and apparently eats the "unclean food" of the Persian court. She is hardly, then, a pious Jew like Daniel!

While Mordecai is sitting one day at the king's gate, he overhears the guards plotting the king's death. This, he reports to Esther and as a result the king is saved. The incident is recorded, but Mordecai receives no reward. Instead it is Haman, a descendent of Agag the Amalakite (the melodrama becomes almost laughable at this point) who is elevated to high rank. Mordecai refuses to show him deference by bowing before him and the struggle is on. Haman convinces the king that the Jews ought to be destroyed and sends out an edict accordingly. Mordecai appeals to Esther and, though she takes her life in her hands by entering the king's presence unsolicited, approaches him in his throne room. She is well received, but instead of immediately asking his favor, invites Haman and the King to a banquet the next day.

That night the king cannot sleep so as a soporific the court chronicles are read to him. Surprisingly enough he stays awake and finally arrives at the point at which Mordecai's good deed is recorded. While Haman is building the gibbet upon which to hang his arch-enemy, the king vows to reward Mordecai handsomely. The next day the banquet is resumed and Esther asks her favor. When Ahasuerus finds it is Haman who had plotted the pogrom, he stalks out of the room in intense anger. He returns to find Haman on his knees before Esther imploring her mercy. Thinking him to be assaulting the queen, the king becomes even angrier and has Haman condemned to die on the gallows prepared for Mordecai.

Mordecai now takes Haman's place as the king's right-hand man and all would live happily ever after were it not for the fact that this is Persia and in Persia a royal edict cannot be retracted. The Jews, therefore, are still in danger. Mordecai, however, is empowered to send out a new edict allowing the Jews to defend themselves and plunder those enemies who attack them. Because of this, and because the high governmental officials, sensing Mordecai's high position, aid them, the Jews turn the tables on their enemies. What was to have been a slaughter of the Jews turns out to be a bloodbath for the Gentiles. On the 13th and 14th day of Adar the Jews slay some 75,000 of their enemies and then, on the 15th, celebrate a great feast. The book ends with an explanation that this is how the feast of Purim began and with a brief acknowledgement of the great heights of power and might to which Mordecai rose.

Although conservative scholars through the ages have taken this to be a factual account of an historical event, it is clear that this is by no means the case. The story bears too many marks of a highly contrived melodrama to be considered historical. It is true that the author was fairly knowledgeable about the goings-on in a Persian court, but he also makes a good many mistakes. For instance, the Persian Empire never had 127 provinces, as the story claims (1:1). Persian court records do not name either Vashti or Esther as the name of Ahasuerus' queen, nor is there any indication that Purim was ever celebrated in Jewry during the Persian period.

If Esther is not history, one must ask, why was it written? Is it simply the product of an individual's creative imagination or does it have some deeper significance? And if Purim was not founded in this way, how did it come into being? Perhaps the best way to answer these questions is to look at Purim itself. Purim, to say the least, is a most decidedly nationalistic festival. It is a time when Jews make merry and remember the occasion when the Semites beat the anti-Semites at their own game. Esther, however, is more than just a story about anti-Semitism. It is the prototype of all those melodramatic stories in which the good guys, though hard pressed at the X Bar X corral, finally shoot it out and kill all those rather slick fellows in the black hats. It is, in effect, a myth about good (that's us) triumphing over evil (that's them).

There are some indications that the original story upon which Esther is based was far more mythological and far less "historical" than the present one. Clearly Esther is a variant form of Ishtar, the Babylonian goddess of sexuality and fertility. Mordecai may well have been derived from Marduk, the king of the Babylonian pantheon. Perhaps what happened is this. While in captivity (or perhaps even before) the Jews came into contact with a pagan festival of great merriment. It was a mid-winter festival which celebrated the victory of the good gods over the demonic forces. Although the mythological meaning itself was pagan, the festival was nonetheless attractive.

The author of Esther took the essential myth and retold it as an historical narrative. The good gods become Jewish "patriots"; the demons, the Gentile antagonists. The merriment of the pagan festival is preserved, but the festival now becomes thoroughly Jewish and highly nationalistic. Such a transformation should not surprise any one who knows anything about the history of religion. Halloween, for instance, was originally a Celtic festival marking the end of the reign of the God of life and the beginning of the reign of Samhain, the God of death. The Christian Church did not deny the celebration of the day, but by placing All Saints Day on November 1 converted the original pagan festival into All Hallows Eve. The ghosts and goblins remained, but the theological context was changed.

In this connection, one feature of Esther is particularly striking. Although the author removed nearly all obvious remnants of pagan mythology from the story, he did little or nothing to recloth it with the theological orthodoxy of Judaism. The word GOD, to say nothing of the name of God, does not even appear in the text. There are some hints that the triumphs of Esther and Mordecai took place providentially, but this idea is thrust very much into the background. Neither of the heroes offers prayers nor do their fellow Jews. Esther, as it has already been said, breaks the Jewish dietary laws and only reveals her Jewishness under duress.

Why? Why should such an obviously Jewish book avoid so consistently any kind of theological affirmation? Perhaps the author decided that it would be just too much to put a pious Jewish prayer in the mouth of a figure who was originally a pagan goddess. Perhaps he realized that Purim was essentially a secular festival and therefore decided to keep theology out of it. Or perhaps he was one of those who had decided that the orthodox faith of Israel was no longer relevant in his age. In any event, Esther is a thoroughly secular book which sees Jewry alone in the world, without God, depending upon its own resourcefulness for survival. God may act providentially, but the Jews no longer recognize his action as such. Lamentations ends with a question-mark; will God return? Esther affirms that whether he returns or not Jews will fight for themselves against all comers. The Shulammite is locked in the harem of Solomon, and she has decided, despite adversity, to make the best of a bad situation. When she wins a little for herself, she will exult and be glad.

CHAPTER XXV

Daniel

HE AUTHOR of the book of Daniel, whoever he may have been, was certainly a man who meditated upon the Torah and the Prophets "day and night." He poured over the Scriptures of Israel, not out of idle curiosity but because he sought for a clue to the meaning of Israel's existence in his own day. The situation was critical. His people faced a grim threat of annihilation at the hands of the Seleucid ruler Antiochus Epiphanes, who sought to solve the "Jewish problem" once and for all through their forced conversion to paganism. Many of his fellow Jews doubtless thought that indeed the time for extinction had really come.[1]

Perhaps because he had "opened the books" of Israel, our author did not agree. He believed devoutly in the everlastingness of God's kingship and therefore in the ultimate vindication of "the saints of the Most High," i.e., the true and righteous Israel. At the same time, he was well aware that the relation between God and Israel had been decisively altered by the cataclysmic fall of Jerusalem and the resultant exile. Israel (or at least some Israelites) had returned to her land after being released by Cyrus, but no glorious age such as had been promised by the prophets had begun. Instead the Jews were subjected to one foreign ruler after another. Although Jeremiah had declared the old covenant broken, (cf. Jer, 3:1, 31:31-34), no new covenant

[1] For a more complete historical summary of this period see the last section of Chapter 3 of this work.

such as he envisioned was forthcoming, and many Jews sensed with uneasiness that the Lord of the covenant was strangely absent from their midst. Even the author of Daniel was reticent to use the covenantal name of God but instead employed, in most passages, circumlocutions such as "the God of heaven" and "God Most High."

The vigorous persecution by Antiochus raised in a most intense way the question which had been troubling Israel for a long time: How and when would God act to save Israel and restore the covenant? Our author was sure that the hour was at hand. It had to be at hand, for Israel could not long survive under the present conditions! But how could his faith in the nearness of salvation be made convincing to those who lived in a world in which God seemed so completely absent? The writer of Daniel searched the Scriptures for the answer.

It is not surprising that in his search he concentrated particularly upon those passages of "the books" dealing with the times when Israel had previously lived under the shadow of despair. Apparently our author read and absorbed the stories of Joseph in the book of Genesis, for although he does not mention them explicitly, his hero, Daniel, bears many resemblances to that Patriarch. Like Joseph Daniel is able to survive the envy and distrust of his contemporaries because of his uncanny, God-given ability to interpret dreams and visions. Like Joseph he rises to a high rank in a pagan land because of his righteousness and secret wisdom. And like Joseph he remains faithful to his God despite all adversity.

The author of Daniel, of course, had a purpose in making these unspoken comparisons between Daniel and the Patriarch. Had not Joseph lived at the beginning of a dark age for Israel? And had not that dark age ended after four hundred years with sudden and dramatic swiftness when God, through Moses, led the people out of Egypt to make a new covenant with him? The author sought to console the Jewish community, not by overt argumentation, but through the evocation of the basic archetypal pattern of Israel's existence. The reader is subtly led to remember Joseph with the hope that he will, perhaps, draw his own conclusions. And are not conclusions so drawn the most convincing of all?

The author of Daniel also, quite naturally, returned to the prophets who witnessed and interpreted the fall of Jerusalem and the end of the old Davidic kingdom for insight and guidance. Although he refers directly to only Jeremiah, it is Ezekiel with whom he has the greatest affinity. Like Ezekiel he uses strange and bizarre visions to communicate his meaning. In fact, the vision described in 10:5ff employs typically Ezekielian symbols. His use of the title "Son of Man" (7:13, 8:17), his reference to the resurrection (12:2), and, perhaps, most especially his choice of Daniel as his hero all point to the influence of this earlier prophet.

Although no preceding mention of a Daniel is to be found in Scripture, Ezekiel refers to him three times (14:14, 14:20, and 28:03) as a prototype of human wisdom and righteousness. As a result of the excavations at Ugarit we now know that stories about "Dan'el" were very ancient and even non-Israelite in origin. In the ancient Ugaritic "Tale of Aqhat" a King Dan'el is described as a particularly righteous and exemplary man. It seems quite probable that the Israelites took over this legendary figure from this pagan source, reclothed him with typically Israelite righteousness and used stories about him as exemplifications of the highest type of wisdom and virtue. Ezekiel, therefore, was referring to a familiar figure when he wrote,

> Even if these three men, Noah, Daniel, and Job, were in it (the land of Israel), they would deliver but their own lives by their righteousness, says the LORD God. (Ezekiel 14:14)

An interesting thought! Suppose the great Daniel had been in Israel at the time of the Babylonian conquest and had been taken into exile with Ezekiel. How would he have fared? What would such a man, who saw and interpreted visions, have said about his time and ours? I would suggest not only that the author of Daniel knew the stories to which Ezekiel refers but that he took Ezekiel's remark as a clue to how he might communicate his message of hope to his generation. The book of Daniel, then, can be read as a "what if" book which expands upon Ezekiel's brief suggestion. In this respect it bears marked resemblance to both Job and Jonah.

The author of Daniel not only begins with Ezekiel's hypothesis; he also accepts his thesis that Daniel would have been able to deliver only his own life through his righteousness. Throughout the story Daniel is pictured as very much alone. To be sure, his friends Hananiah, Mishael, and Azariah are with him, but his righteousness does not help them and their righteous actions do not particularly help him. It is not until Chapter Nine, when Daniel offers his great and moving prayer in behalf of his people, that one feels him to be intimately related to Israel as a whole. Daniel's main claim to fame is not that he helps his fellow Israelites escape the exile, but that he is able to convert the Gentiles. The primary result of his righteousness and dream interpretation is that the pagan rulers, Nebuchadnezzar, Belshazzar, and Darius, are convinced that Daniel's God is, indeed the king of the universe.[1]

It is noteworthy that for Daniel the kingdom of God is not simply a reality which will come in the future. God is king right now. As Nebuchadnezzar himself proclaims,

> How great are his signs!
> How mighty his wonders!
> His kingdom is an everlasting kingdom,
> and his dominion is from generation to generation (4:3)

The story of Daniel's life, which constitutes the first half of the book, is punctuated and articulated by four poetic affirmations of this faith (2:20-23; 4:3; 4:34b-35; and 6:26-27). Only the first of these confessions of faith is by Daniel himself. The next two are by Nebuchadnezzar who is finally convinced of God's sovereignty by Daniel's "occult" powers; the last is by Darius, the Medic king, who seems to accept Daniel from the very beginning and who now rejoices when Daniel's God saves him from the treachery of his enemies. These four passages set forth the main point which the book is trying to make: God is sovereign over all the nations. He may at times appear to be hidden, but his kingdom is from everlasting to everlasting. Even the Gentile kings inadvertently do his bidding.

The story of Daniel's life which these affirmations punctuate is related in a simple "folk-tale" style. Its construction, however, is by no means simple-minded, for the author weaves the themes of the story together so that it coheres beautifully. The main point is repeated again and again, but the narrative is constructed in a way which neatly avoids repetitiousness.

Movement in the story is to be found not in the development of Daniel's personality or in a new revelation from God, but in the growing awareness of the Gentile kings that Daniel's God is indeed

---

[1] The author of Daniel was obviously either consciously or unconsciously confused about the history of Babylonian and Persian periods. He misspells Nebuchadnezzar's name, claims that Belshazzar succeeded him as King, and says that Darius, the Mede, conquered Babylon before the rise of Cyrus.

sovereign. Nebuchadnezzar is the first to be convinced through Daniel's ability to interpret dreams. When he fails to live according to his own affirmation of God's sovereign power and commands his subjects to worship a golden image (which is, of course, really a symbol of himself), God again intervenes and saves the righteous from the fiery furnace. Nebuchadnezzar then is afflicted with what appears to be a type of insanity because of his pretensions until he once more affirms the lordship of the Most High God. When his successor, Belshazzar, does not carry on this faith in God, his kingdom is overthrown by Darius' army and he is killed. Darius, on the other hand, accepts Daniel into his service gladly and never seems to doubt the reality and power of his God. When he is tricked into denying God and punishing Daniel, he is distraught. Daniel's salvation from the lion's den leads Darius to promulgate to all his subjects a decree lauding the power of the God of Daniel. This decree is the coda which concludes the first half of the book.

It has often been said that the first six chapters were written to console the people of Israel at the time of Antiochus Epiphanes and to give them an example of daring righteousness by which to live. In a sense this is true, for these chapters do proclaim a faith in the ultimate sovereignty of God. At the same time it must also be said that even if one accepts Daniel as an historical figure (which probably was not easy to do even in the second century)[1] he hardly provides a very useful example for the pious man. Daniel survives the persecution which he faces, not simply because he is righteous, but because he is given by God certain powers to interpret dreams. It is his righteousness which gets him into trouble again and again. Since God gives the wisdom of dream interpretation to only a few, most men would find the emulation of Daniel impossible. Thus, the first half of Daniel is far from consoling for those who live under persecution. Daniel would have died ignominiously had it not been for his God-given abilities and for the special angelic forces which protected him.

This is one of the reasons why I cannot assent to the commonly-held opinion that Chapters 7-12 constitute a later addition to the book. Without this latter section the argument of the book is incomplete. Our author

[1] The fact that Daniel opens with an historical error which any careful reader of the book of II Kings would have seen (according to II Kings 24:13 the temple vessels were taken at the time when King Jehoiachim was defeated), implies that the author may have wished to indicate to his readers that he was writing imaginative fiction and not history.

agrees with Ezekiel that Daniel could have saved himself only through his own righteousness, but he also sees possibilities for help and consolation in Daniel's ability to see visions.

Therefore, our author describes a series of visions which his hero had which, in symbolic terms, relate the history of Israel up until the time of Antiochus' persecution of the Jews. Through them he is able to communicate his own conviction that God is in charge of history and that he will soon act decisively to save Israel. In this way, Ezekiel's "what if" becomes for him a rhetorical device through which his faith can be proclaimed.

Like the first half of the book, Chapters 7-12 are divided into a number of different episodes which are held together by some common themes and one common conclusion. Just as part one is punctuated by four assertions of God's kingship, so the second part is punctuated by four predictions of Antiochus' downfall (7:27, 8:23-25, 9:26-27, 11:40-45). As the book proceeds, these assertions become increasingly obvious in meaning and exact in detail. The movement in this section is from a highly symbolic vision in which one feels "taken up into heaven" to a concrete exposition of historical events.

The first and fourth assertions of Antiochus' fall are followed by descriptions of what will happen after this crucial event. When the battle is over, God's reign will be made manifest and his saints will be established forever. Like many of the prophets before him, the author of Deniel foresees a glorious age in which God's rule will prevail over the earth and his faithful people will be vindicated once and for all. Thus, while the first six chapters proclaim God's kingship in the world as it is, the last six point forward to the full revelation of that kingship in the world which shall be.

Chapter Seven is, in many ways, simply an expansion upon the basic idea already set forth in Chapter Two. Although the author now speaks of four beasts rather than one image with four distinct sections, the meaning and some of the imagery are the same. The first beast, the lion, is set upon its feet and given the mind of a man just as Nebuchadnezzar was restored to sanity after having lived as a beast. The bear is told to devour much flesh, a command which seems to allude to the lion's den incident. Just as the legs and part of the feet of the statue are said to be made of iron, the fourth beast is described as having great iron teeth. Just as the statue was destroyed by a stone not made of human hands which became a mountain filling the earth, so the beast is slain through the power of God and the kingdom of the saints established.

In the latter vision, however, the author became more specific. He speaks of the horns of the fourth beast and in particular of the little horn which obviously symbolizes Antiochus. He also speaks more fully, but still symbolically, of the victory of God and his saints over this evil power. Nevertheless, the predictions are certainly no more exact. The most he says is that in his vision "one like a son of man" came to the Ancient of Days and was given dominion over all kingdoms, nations, and languages forever. That is to say, when God's kingdom is revealed in its fullness, the saints of the Most High will be instruments of God's rule.

Having reviewed symbolically the rise and eventual fall of the four great empires, the author, in Chapter 8, backtracks and begins a much more historical analysis of the events leading up to his own day. He describes first the struggle between Persia and Greece and the final victory of the latter. His description is symbolic, but fairly obvious. Just to make sure that everyone gets the point, however, he has the angel Gabriel interpret the dream in clearly historical terms. As in the earlier visions, he ends with a description of Antiochus and a prediction of his fall.

In Chapter 9 the historical record is interrupted when the author turns to a problem which must have disturbed the people of his generation considerably. This he does, in part, to mitigate the tedium of his historical analysis. This passage is, however, much more than an interlude, for in it the central motivating anxiety of the whole book "surfaces." Jeremiah (29:10) had predicted that seventy years would pass before the LORD would bring the people of Israel back to their land, restore their fortune, and reestablish his relation with them. Although Israel returned to her land in less than seventy years and in a way was reestablished, the optimistic promises of Jeremiah were not fulfilled. Instead Judah was dominated by foreign rulers and led a very meager existence as a nation. Hence Israel was anxious about her relation to God. The last petition and question to be found in the book of Lamentations characterized her mood:

> Restore us to thyself, O LORD, that we may be restored
> Renew our days as of old!
> Or hast thou utterly rejected us?
> Art thou exceedingly angry with us?
> (Lamentations 5:21-22)

The author of Daniel himself expresses very beautifully the same sentiment found in Lamentations 5:21-22 in the prayer which he places in Daniel's mouth. The prayer concludes:

> *O Lord,* hear; *O Lord,* forgive; *O Lord,* give heed and act; delay not for thy own sake, O my God, because thy city and thy people are called by thy name.
>
> (Daniel 9:19)

So different in tone is this whole passage from the rest of the book of Daniel that it is not surprising that many scholars have considered this a later interjection into the text. I would argue, however, that such is not the case. On the contrary, I suspect that the author regarded this ninth chapter as the turning-point of the work as a whole. Until this point the author has bravely and triumphantly asserted the faith of the past. God is king and all nations and events are in his hands. Now, suddenly the repressed questioning and yearning of his generation and of himself are released. Save us, O God! Save us now! Save us now!

Throughout the book the author has been satisfied to use circumlocutions to speak of God. Now, in a dramatic, personal, and almost shocking way he names God by his covenantal name. O Yahweh, hear; O Yahweh, forgive. He calls upon the righteous Yahweh whose covenant has been broken to save us once more. Unlike the book of Lamentations, Daniel does not conclude his prayer with but a plaintive question. Nor does Yahweh, himself, speak as he does to Job out of the whirlwind. Instead the angel Gabriel intervenes to answer the question which is in the heart, if not upon the lips of all Jews. The distance between God and man is preserved; yet there is hope. Yes, says Gabriel, Jeremiah did speak of seventy years, but what he meant was seventy weeks of years. Hence the hour of salvation has not yet come but now is not far off. A desolater will come, but in the end a decree will be poured out upon him. Antiochus will be destroyed and Judaism will be saved.

In Chapter 10 our author again returns to Ezekiel for his inspiration. In fact, the imagery used is so similar to that found in the first chapter of Ezekiel that it is quite obvious that he meant to call that overwhelming vision of that prophet to mind. Unlike Ezekiel, however, Daniel does not hear God speak directly. Instead it is an intermediary angel who sets him trembling upon his knees and then upon his feet. Yahweh is still remote and Daniel speaks his name no more, but his angels are present to fight for Israel and to lead her through the perils of life to the denouement of history.

The author now returns to his recounting of the history leading up to his own day. Gone is virtually any attempt to hide his meaning through the use of symbols. This is simply an historical survey without names and dates. The author, however, goes beyond a mere recounting of the past to predict in rather precise and unequivocal terms how Antiochus will meet his end. The fact that his predictions did not come true helps in dating the book rather accurately. The final chapter of Daniel contains a tantalizing and yet enigmatic attempt to describe what will happen after this time of trouble when the victory of Michael and the angelic forces is complete. Like Ezekiel he speaks of a resurrection of the dead, but whether he speaks symbolically of the rebirth of Israel as Ezekiel does in 37:1ff or of a general resurrection at the end of time is not wholly clear. Since Daniel makes reference to the beginning of the Maccabean revolt (11:34-35), it is reasonably certain that it was written after 166 B.C. Antiochus did die in 163, but not as the author predicted. Hence the work must have been written before that time. Whether the author actually knew of the Rededication of the Temple in 164 is an open question. He does allude to it, but his remarks are probably predictive, for he is somewhat confused about when, exactly it occurred.

Since the book of Daniel depends so much upon Ezekiel, it may be that the author means simply to remind his readers of Ezekiel's hope for the resurrection of Israel. Certainly he is not thinking of a general resurrection of all mankind, for he speaks only about the people of Israel in the preceding sentence and says that only "many" of them will be resurrected.

Just as in Chapter 7 our author predicts the everlastingness of the kingdom of the saints (7:23), so now he reiterates that claim. The first part of Daniel concludes with the story of Daniel's "resurrection" from the lion's den. Now the second ends with the proclamation that Israel will be raised from the lion's den of persecution to a new age of triumph.

The chapter concludes with one of the best examples of specific vagueness ever encountered. When Daniel asks how long it will be until all this is accomplished, an angel replies that it will be "for a time, two times, and half a times; and that when the shattering of the power of the holy peace comes to an end all these things will be accomplished" (12:7). Needless to say, Daniel doesn't quite understand. The angel then advises him to go his way, for the vision is sealed until the time of the end, but he also adds that "from the time when the continual burnt offering is taken away, and the abomination of desolation is set up, there shall be a thousand two hundred and ninety days" (12:11). Although the time interval is specific, when one considers what the author did with Jeremiah's seventy years, one can only admit that the vision is indeed sealed. This is particularly true since the specified interval of days soon passed and the end did not come. It is no wonder that Daniel has been a source for speculation and apocalyptic prediction ever since that time.

When the author of Daniel himself attempted to predict the future specifically, he, on the whole, proved to be incorrect. Antiochus did not die as he said nor did his kingdom come to a sudden end. The world still awaits the full manifestation of God's righteous rule upon earth. Still, he was right about one thing. Antiochus did not destroy Israel. On the contrary, the Maccabees (the "little help" mentioned in 11:34) even led the people to a few moments of glory before the Roman armies put an end to their semi-independent nation. Perhaps our author was wrong in attempting to predict so precisely what was to occur, for the course of history is never easily determined in advance, even by a visionary prophet. He knew, however, that what his people needed was not general platitudes but a specific hope to which to cling. This he provided even at the risk of being wrong. Furthermore, his central, motivating thesis is one which faithful men can hardly reject. Essentially the book of Daniel is an affirmation of the faith that the God of Israel has dominion over the world and that in the end he will save his people. Daniel teaches that the faithful man must live expectantly, with the hope that the Kingdom of God is indeed at hand.

CHAPTER XXVI

Ezra and Nehemiah: Introduction and Analysis

The Composition of the Books
Analysis
Ezra
Nehemiah
Conclusion

LTHOUGH EZRA and Nehemiah are distinguished as two separate books in modern Bibles there is clear evidence that in the Hebrew Bible they were connected as one work until 1448. This fact, coupled with the consideration that a discussion of the historical problems raised by these books involves an examination of both at the same time, is the reason why they will be treated together in this chapter.

The Composition of the Books

As is pointed out in the introduction to the book of Chronicles, these two books are so closely related stylistically and theologically to Chronicles that it is clear they are a part of the Chronicler's history and might well be called simply III Chronicles. Only the memoirs of Nehemiah (Neh. 1:1-7:12, 11:1-2, 12:27-43, 13:4-31) contain a distinctively different style. Since Ezra purports to contain the first person memoirs of the great scribe himself, the traditional view was (and is) that it was Ezra himself who wrote Chronicles and his own book. Although many scholars in the past rejected this attribution as preposterous, there are some today who take a much more open view toward this theory. Certainly, if Ezra did not write this lengthy history, someone who lived soon after him or who even knew him may well have.

One would expect, then, that since these books originated in the late fifth or early fourth century B.C. they would contain a rather accurate and consistent account of what happened in the late fifth century B.C. Unfortunately, this does not seem to be entirely the case. A number of factors make it clear that the accounts of Ezra and Nehemiah don't agree in all details. Ezra is said to have arrived in Jerusalem in the seventh year of the Persian Emperor Artaxerxes (which Artaxerxes is not made clear), having been sent by the Persian "king" to reform the religious and civil order of Judah and to teach the inhabitants the law of God. The Jerusalem which he reaches seems to be well-populated, though not strong. Ezra, upon prompting by certain officials, attacks the practice of marrying outside the "race" but does not read the law before the people until some thirteen years later!

All this seems relatively plausible until one reads the memoirs of Nehemiah, which seem to be reasonably authentic. Nehemiah, a Jewish cupbearer to the Emperor, is sent by Artaxerxes, in the 20th year of his reign, to the Governor of Judah; yet no mention is made of Ezra, who was presumably the leading religious and civil figure in Judah, in his memoirs themselves. Furthermore, it is only during the tenure of Nehemiah that Jerusalem is said to have been repopulated (Nehemiah 11). Nehemiah is also said to have attacked mixed marriages—a problem which supposedly had already been dealt with by Ezra. These and other considerations have led many scholars to question the chronology, if not the factuality of these books.

Basically, there are two questions which must be asked: (1) How could the Chronicler, who apparently wrote about 400 B.C. have been so confused about his own history? and (2) how is the work of these two men to be arranged chronologically? The best answer to question one, as far as this writer is concerned, is that the Chronicler was not confused at all. Rather, like the writer of Esdras, a book of the Apocrypha, he ended his history with an account of the work of Ezra but with no mention of Nehemiah! He may have known about Nehemiah, but did not consider it important to include an account of him in his work because he was interested primarily in the cultic, rather than the political aspects of the history of Israel. In a sense, the inclusion of a discussion of Nehemiah would have mitigated his argument, for his main point was that Ezra, the cultic leader and reformer, was the true heir of the Davidic tradition.

Some later editor, however, had in hand the memoirs of Nehemiah and found them too valuable to be forgotten. Hence, he added them to the original text in what he believed the most appropriate places, breaking up, in so doing, the story of Ezra. In the meantime, however, a scribal error had occurred in the transmission of the text of Ezra which confused the issue. It is conceivable, at least, that originally the text said that Ezra arrived in the thirty-seventh year of Artaxerxes rather than in the seventh year. Because of this error, however, the editor thought that Nehemiah, who says that he came in the twentieth year of that Emperor, arrived after Ezra and therefore fit in his memoirs accordingly.

If one accepts this reconstruction, then, Nehemiah came first, in about 445 B.C. He rebuilt the walls of the city against opposition and began much needed reforms. After about 12 years he returned to the Emperor's court. When he came back to Judah several years later he brought with him or had sent a religious "expert," Ezra, who helped him in the needed reformation of the city in and after 428. This of course, is not the only theory accepted by scholars today. Some still hold to the traditional view; others claim that Ezra came in the 7th year of the reign of Artaxerxes II (398). To my mind, however, the foregoing explanation is the most consistent and involves the fewest problems and hypotheses. Until more information concerning the period is uncovered, this is, perhaps, the most that one can say.

Although the Chronicler wrote about an era which was probably not far from his own, he utilized throughout various written documents. Again and again he quotes from court records, official edicts, genealogical lists, etc. On the whole, then, he writes a reasonably well-informed, if selective, history of the times. Nevertheless, it is clear that when he gives population figures, his numbers are often highly exaggerated and inaccurate. Whether this was due to his own propensity to exaggeration, or whether his way of recording numbers is misinterpreted by modern translators is unclear. In any event, the inflation of numbers found in the text has been one of the reasons why many scholars have criticized the authenticity of the whole historical account and why they have dated the work of the Chronicler so long after the events had taken place. On the whole, this skepticism regarding the basic outline of the account seems unjustifiable. Although the Chronicler may have had his own axe to grind and may have distorted certain features of the history accordingly, there is no reason to doubt that in the main he gives us a fairly factual history.

Analysis

Ezra

CHAPTER I begins with the same edict of Cyrus which concludes II Chronicles. Although it may appear strange that Cyrus would be concerned about the rebuilding of a minor sanctuary, it must be remembered that as the new political leader of the Empire he was responsible for the religious institutions of the various peoples of his domain. The Cylinder of Cyrus reveals that he also took similar action in regard to other peoples. When Artaxerxes sent Nehemiah and Ezra to Jerusalem he acted in much the same capacity. 1:5-11 then describes the preparation of the exiles to return to the homeland.

Chapter 2 contains a list of those who first returned from captivity under the leadership of Sheshbazzar. In a sense, this is given to distinguish their offspring from the odious Samaritans and the corrupted people of the land who had not endured exile. A parallel, but somewhat different, list is given in Nehemiah 7. Just why there are such discrepancies has never been cogently explained.

Chapter 3 describes the rebuilding of the altar, so that sacrifices could again be properly offered, and the laying of the foundations of the Temple. Apparently the second Temple was much smaller than the first, for many of the "old-timers" lament when they see its dimensions. For some reason the project is begun, not by Sheshbazzar, who was commissioned to do it, but by Zerubbabel, a Davidite, and Joshua, a priest.

Chapter 4 records the opposition to the work of the returnees on the part of segments of the local population. Part of the opposition stemmed from the religious exclusiveness of the Jews, who, in Babylonia, had developed a particularly rigorous form of Judaism and who looked down upon the Palestinians who seemed to them impure and unrighteous. For the moment, the opposition won by appealing directly to the Persian Emperor. Their argument was that Jerusalem was historically a rebellious city and that its rebuilding could only lead to new political dissidence.

Chapter 5 tells how, during the reign of Darius, Haggai and Zechariah, the prophets, encouraged Zerubbabel to begin work on the Temple once more. The Governor of the province tries to stop them, but they appeal to Cyrus' edict. Darius has the archives searched, discovers the edict, and not only allows but encourages the rebuilding.

Darius' decree together with a description of the completion of the Temple and the celebration of passover are included in Chapter 6. The stage is now set for the entrance of the main character, Ezra.

In Chapter 7 the Chronicler turns to Ezra and his commission from Artaxerxes to go to Jerusalem. Ezra is described as a son of Aaron and as a scribe; doubtless he was a preeminent leader in Babylonian Jewry. Artaxerxes commissions him to take with him those Israelites who wish to go, and convey to Jerusalem the silver and gold promised by the Emperor for the purpose of buying sacrificial offerings and other needed items for the house of God in Jerusalem. Ezra is also commissioned to appoint magistrates and judges for the people and to teach the law to those who do not know it. The chapter concludes with Ezra's words of praise (7:27-28) in response to this commission.

Chapter 8 lists the new returnees and describes the trip to the homeland. Ezra has been too proud to ask for an armed escort and hence the journey is hazardous. Nevertheless, they arrive safely in Jerusalem after a long journey and perform the acts specified in the commission.

Chapter 9 records how certain officials call to Ezra's attention the fact that many of the people (including many Levites and priests) have married pagan wives. Ezra is distraught, because it seems to him that this is simply a sign that Israel is once more reverting to the sins of the past. As a Babylonian Jew he has been convinced that Jewry can only survive by practicing racial and religious exclusiveness. Israel must be "set apart" and Ezra is determined to do this.

In Chapter 10 Ezra calls the people to repentance in a mass meeting in Jerusalem and nearly all agree to give up their foreign wives. The book ends with a listing of all those men who had married foreign women but who, through the urging of Ezra, "put them away."

Nehemiah

CHAPTER 1 begins the memoirs of Nehemiah, a kind of *apologia pro vita sua* in which the great rebuilder of Jerusalem details his actions. The story opens in Susa, the capital of the Persian Empire. Nehemiah, a Jewish cup-bearer to the Emperor (and hence probably a eunuch) is informed by his brother Hanani and certain other men from Judah of the deplorable conditions which exist in the homeland. No mention is made of Ezra or his reforms. Nehemiah in 1:5-11 prays to God about the matter.

In Chapter 2 Nehemiah pleads with Artaxerxes to let him go to Jerusalem to rebuild the city. Artaxerxes agrees and Nehemiah, accompanied by soldiers, returns to Jerusalem. He encourages the people to begin the work, but immediately runs into opposition from Sanballat, the governor in Samaria; Tobiah, the Ammonite; and Geshem, the Arab. At first, however, their opposition is expressed only as derision.

In Chapter 3 it is described how the work is begun and the gates of the city rebuilt.

Chapter 4 tells of renewed opposition on the part of Sanballat and his cohorts who decide to attack Jerusalem. Nehemiah, however, arms his men and remains vigilant and the attack never comes off.

Chapter 5: There is, however, another threat . . . this time from within. Many Jews have become financially burdened and famine threatens the land. Nehemiah attacks the usurers who are lending at interest and wins the people's favor. At the same time, he receives appointment from Artaxerxes to be their Governor, thus solidifying his political control over the area.

In Chapter 6 Sanballat and Tobiah attempt to trick Nehemiah into a secret meeting, but he refuses to go and remains safely within Jerusalem.

Chapter 7 tells of Nehemiah's appointment of his brother to be in charge of Jerusalem and arranges for the city's defense. A genealogy of the returning exiles similar to that of Ezra 2 is then interjected into the text.

With Chapter 8 the account returns to the story of Ezra. Ezra, from a wooden pulpit reads from the law and the Feast of Tabernacles is celebrated. There is much debate concerning what book of Law Ezra read. Was it the full Torah or only some law code now contained within it? From the various rules and regulations found in Nehemiah 10, it can be gathered that Ezra had more than one code before him, for they are based upon various codes of law found in the Torah. It is quite possible, therefore, that Ezra had in his possession the Torah in its final form.

In Chapter 9 the people assemble to renew the covenant. They confess their sins, and Ezra offers in the form of a penitential psalm a summary statement of the faith of Israel. The holy history of Israel is summarized and on this basis the covenant is reaffirmed. Chapter 10 records those who signed the covenant and lists a number of specific obligations which were agreed to. Mixed marriages are forbidden, the sabbath as a day of economic inactivity is emphasized, and the obligations of the people to the Temple and its staff are outlined.

Chapter 11 describes the repopulating of Jerusalem while Chapter 12 lists the genealogies of the Levites and priests and then describes the dedication of the city walls.

The final chapter (13) describes a number of further reforms by Nehemiah and concludes with the following words:

> "Thus I cleansed them from everything foreign, and I established the duties of the priests and Levites, each in his work; and I provided for the wood offering, at appointed times, and for the first fruits. Remember me, O my God, for good." (Nehemiah 13:30-31)

Conclusion

ALTHOUGH the emphasis of Ezra and Nehemiah upon racial exclusiveness and Sabbatarianism may not appeal to many modern men, it is clear that Ezra and Nehemiah were exceedingly important figures in late fifth century Judaism and were remembered by later generations "for good." Together they reformed and reunited a shaken Israel and established a pattern of life which was to carry Palestinian Judaism through many dark days. Of the two, however, it was Ezra who was to kindle the imagination of Jewry. For the Jews he became virtually a second Moses who restored life in a dying people and who founded the Great Synagogue which ruled over the people. To him were attributed apocalypses which claimed to tear the veil of the future and to reveal Israel's great destiny. Ezra, the pious man, became the exemplary ideal for young and old alike.

It is appropriate, therefore, that the Hebrew canon concludes with Chronicles, the most massive work attributed by tradition to the great priest-scribe. More than any other man he, through example and deed, shaped the life and culture of post-exilic Judaism and made it what it is today.

CHAPTER XXVII

Chronicles: I and II: Introduction and Analysis

Date of Authorship
Sources for Chronicles
I Chronicles
II Chronicles

THE BOOKS of Chronicles contain some of the least-read portions of Scripture and are considered by many to be the dullest books of the Bible. Certainly the nine-chapter genealogical introduction to the work does little to dissuade the modern reader from this opinion. Even when the author finally gets to his main theme, the activity of David and his royal house, the narrative lacks the human interest and the literary style which characterize the books of Samuel and Kings. Occasionally an interesting moment occurs in the text, but one must plough through pages and pages of tedious enumeration to get to it.

Still, it is unfortunate that these books have been so neglected by both layman and scholar alike, for they contain important information and a view into an historical era which are not to be found anywhere else. The long post-exilic period from the return from the exile in the sixth century to the rise of the Maccabees in the second is highly undocumented and, if it were not for the Chronicler who wrote these books plus their sequels, Ezra and Nehemiah, we would know virtually nothing about the life of Israel during the Persian period. The Chronicler not only gives us some otherwise unknown facts; his work reflects the changing world-view and theology of this period and hence provides a key for understanding the growth of Judaism during this time.

Date of Authorship

Unfortunately, the books themselves give us no clear indication about precisely when they were written. Still, there are a number of clues which allow us to date the text with relative accuracy. Since it has been demonstrated on stylistic grounds that Chronicles is by the same author as Ezra and Nehemiah it is clear that it could not have been written before the time of Nehemiah who died in about 424 B.C. The fact that there are a number of Persian, but virtually no Greek, words in the text makes it probable that it was written before the conquest of Alexander in the 330s. Furthermore, the genealogy of the Davidic line in I Chr. 3:1-24 ends seven generations after Jehoiaichin. Allowing 25 years per generation, this would mean that the Chronicler ended his list with the generation of the last decade of the fifth century. Therefore, it seems reasonable to date the work about 400 B.C.

Sources for Chronicles

In writing his "history of Israel"—for this, in a way, is what Chronicles is—the Chronicler used a variety of sources. Clearly he knew the Torah, for he mentions its authority several times, and uses its genealogies as a basis for his own genealogical pre-Davidic history. He also had before him the books of Samuel and Kings which he quotes and paraphrases on many occasions. Indeed, he presupposes that his readers are familiar with these works and therefore do not need to be informed by him about all the particulars of, for instance, the rise of David. His work is clearly intended to supplement what was already common knowledge. The book of Lamentations and some psalms are also used by him. Besides these Biblical books, he also refers to a number of official records and genealogical lists plus the records of various prophets and seers which are now lost to us.

Purpose

Although the Chronicler used many sources, it is clear that he selected the information to be used for his own particular purposes. He had no intention of being a positivistic historian. He writes to convey a message which he finds hidden in the various documents he has before him. Although in his genealogical enumerations he traces the history of mankind and Israel from Adam to David, it is clear that this is a mere preamble to his main subject. His concern is for David and his lineage. Nor is it David, the spoiler of children, or David, the adulterer, or David, the crafty politician, with which he is concerned. Rather his interest is in David, the righteous king who founded the cult of Israel and who won his military victories because he consulted the Lord.

The Chronicler knew, of course, that the Temple was built by Solomon and not by David, but he sees Solomon as merely carrying out the plans and directives already well-formulated by his father. It was David who organized the priesthood and the cultus and began the many religious traditions centering in the Temple which are observed "to this day."

In second Chronicles the history of Judah in post-Davidic times is reviewed. The kings of Israel, the northern kingdom, are mentioned only in passing, for the center of attention is the Davidic line. Throughout this review the Chronicler reveals his preeminent interest in piety and the cult. Although he mentions the "evil" kings, whom he condemns for their unfaithfulness and idolatry, he devotes considerably more attention to the relatively righteous kings such as Asa and Jehoshaphat and to the reformers of the cultus, such as Hezekiah and Josiah. Hence he greatly expands our "knowledge" of several kings who are passed over with a few sentences by the Deuteronomic historian. Just how accurate the Chronicler's information was is difficult to determine, but it is quite probable that in many instances he worked with fairly reliable official records.

The Chronicler is also interested throughout in the unity of Israel. Over and over again he speaks of "all of Israel" and makes sure that the support of David by the northern tribes is emphasized. In a way, his main point is that Israel fell because she was unwilling to accept the unity given the tribes by David and his cult. Chronicles is a call to return to that unity in the fourth century.

This appeal to David as a rallying point for the people was, of course, not new. Many Jews looked forward to a new David who would lead Israel to greatness once more. But the David they envisioned was a military leader who, like his father, would defeat the enemies of Israel and establish the glory of the nation. Such a hope the Chronicler knew could only lead to frustration or disaster in his day, for who could fight against the preeminent power of Persia? To be true to David, he teaches, is to be true to the cult which he founded and which his best successors sought to keep pure. It is in the piety of David that Israel must find her unity and her strength. The true successors of David are not the revolutionaries who wish to take up arms but men like Nehemiah and Ezra who cooperate with the Persians and yet who seek to build a cultically pure and pious Israel.

Such an argument does not particularly appeal to most modern men, for our situation is not that of the Chronicler. Hence we find his fervent argument rather dull and tedious. Still, we must admit that this viewpoint was very important for the shaping of Judaism and, in many ways, saved the people from the oblivion of history. When the revolutionaries became vocal in the first and second centuries A.D., they led the people straight to disaster, leaving the followers of the Chronicler to pick up the pieces. It is not surprising that the Rabbis who met at Jamnia in 90 A.D. after the destruction of Jerusalem excluded the much more exciting books of the Maccabees from the canon, but left room for the work of the Chronicler.

Analysis

I Chronicles

CHAPTERS 1-9 A long genealogical introduction which follows, in general the genealogies of the Torah but which abbreviates them at some points and adds further information at others. Census figures from the time of David, the Davidic lineage until the seventh generation after Jehoiachin, and many other bits and pieces of information are included.

Chapters 10-29 The history of David

THE STORY begins in Chapter 10 with the death of Saul, an account which presupposes that the book of Samuel is well-known to the reader. Chapter 11:1-3 recounts the coronation of David, completely glossing over the kingship of Ishbosheth, Saul's son, and the seven years when David was just king in Hebron. David sets about to conquer Jerusalem as his capital city immediately.

Chapter 10:10-40 enumerates the mighty men who fought for David.

Special emphasis is given to the "fact" that David found early support among the non-Judaic tribes. David's next move, described in Chapter 13, is to attempt to bring the ark to Jerusalem. The move is not made properly (that is, by the Levites), however, and David has to be content to leave the ark with the household of Obed-edom.

Chapter 14 recounts David's construction of a palace and his marriage to several new wives. Then, in 14:8-17, it is told how David defeated the Philistines because he heeded God's advice. After the appropriate preparations, David brings the ark, this time properly, to Jerusalem (Chapter 15) and places it in a tent. Chapter 16 tells of how he, himself offered offerings to God and then quotes a "Davidic" psalm, the first of several such poems found in Chronicles. Chapter 17, which parallels II Samuel 7:1-29, tells of David's desire to build a Temple, but how God denied this desire and yet blessed David and the Davidic house. The chapter ends with a Davidic prayer of exemplary piety. Chapters 18-20 describe briefly David's several victories over his enemies. Chapter 21 includes one of the very few instances in which David is described by the Chronicler as having done wrong. Characteristically, however, he blames Satan for having incited David to take a census of the entire people. When David learns of God's displeasure he acts with great humility and piety and the Lord forgives him. Chapters 22-26 discuss David's preparations for the building of the Temple which his son is to undertake, his organization of the Levites, who are especially emphasized by the Chronicler, and the Aaronites; his appointment of musicians and gatekeepers; his arrangements for a Temple treasury; and his appointment of officers and judges. Chapter 27 continues this discussion with an enumeration of those who were appointed to serve as commanders and officers in Israel. The book ends with David's last words to the people, to Solomon, and to God and with a brief description of his death. (Chapters 28-29) No mention is made of the attempted coup d'etat by his son Adonijah. In fact, the Chronicler smooths over the whole affair, having David turn the reins of office over to his son before his death.

II Chronicles

Chapters 1-9 The reign of Solomon

SOLOMON succeeds David to the throne and strengthens the nation both militarily and financially. No mention is made of the blood-bath described in the first chapters of I Kings. In Chapter 2 Solomon immediately turns to preparing for the building of the Temple. Then in Chapters 3-5 the construction and appurtenances of the Temple are described in some detail. This is followed by a lengthy description of its dedication together with Solomon's dedicatory address and prayer and the favorable response of God (5:2-7:22). Chapter 8 describes Solomon's building projects, his marriage to a daughter of the Egyptian Pharoah, and his sacrifices to God. Chapter 9 extols his wisdom by citing a visit from the Queen of Sheba and describes his enormous wealth. Little is said by way of criticism of Solomon.

Chapters 10-36 The Davidic Kings after Solomon

THE CHRONICLER, in Chapters 10-12, describes the reign of Rehoboam. He begins by quoting a parallel passage from I Kings 12:1-20 almost word for word. He then adds some information from probably some other source, but deletes any mention of Israel's apostasy at Bethel or of Judah's idolatry in the high places. Chapter 13 contains a description of the reign of Abijah which is somewhat longer than that in Kings. In particular, he discusses Abijah's defeat of Jeroboam. Asa's reign is also dealt with more fully than in Kings, for Chronicles (14-16) includes a description of Asa's defeat of Zerah, the Ethiopian, his reform movement, and the prophet Hanani's words of judgment to him. While I Kings 22:41-53 describes Jehoshaphat very briefly, Chronicles 17-20 treats his reign in some detail. Quite clearly the Chronicler regards him as a man of great righteousness, for although he allows the prophet Jehu to criticize him (19:2-3), his reign is pictured as one of wealth, strength, and religious purity. Like II Kings, Chronicles (Ch. 21) pictures Jehoram, Jehoshaphat's successor as an evil king, but goes into greater detail about his wickedness (he is described as slaying his own brothers) and his punishment. The reigns of Ahaziah and Athaliah are described in almost the same words as in II Kings, though Ahaziah's death is differently pictured and the person who saved the crown prince (22:11) is specifically named. Chapter 24 contains an account of the reign of Joash which is, in general, like that in II Kings 12:1-15 though there are many differences in detail. The same is true of the account of Amaziah's reign in Chapter 25. Chronicles adds more details about Amaziah's defeat of the Edomites, but in general quotes Kings verbatim. The discussion of Uzziah's (Azariah's) reign in Chapter 26 is much more complete than the corresponding II Kings 15:1-7, adding many touches to his biography. The same is true to a less extent of the discussion of the reign of Jotham in Chapter 27. The discussions of Ahaz in Chronicles and Kings vary distinctively. Both books regard him as an evil king, but tell different, somewhat conflicting stories about him. For instance, while Chronicles says that he was defeated by Israel, Kings denies this fact. Both say that he introduced pagan practices into Israelite religion but differ as to what these practices were. Chapters 29-32 include a lengthy description of Hezekiah which goes far beyond what II Kings has to say, for these chapters describe in great detail Hezekiah's reform of religion. Basically, both books agree that Hezekiah was, on the whole, a good and faithful king, but Chronicles does much more to emphasize what he did for the cult. Chapter 33 contains a discussion of the reigns of Manasseh and Amon. Although certain materials are added, Chronicles concurs with Kings that these men were despicably evil. The two books also agree concerning their assessment of Josiah. While Kings mentions his destruction of the shrine of Bethel, Chronicles concentrates upon the way in which passover was celebrated by him. In the final chapter (36) Chronicles contains a somewhat abbreviated account of the reigns of the last four kings: Jehoahaz, Jehoiakim, Jehoiachin, and Zedekiah. While II Kings ends with Jehoichin in exile and Jerusalem in ruins, however, Chronicles concludes with the edict of Cyrus according to which the Jews were allowed to return to their homeland. These same words are repeated at the beginning of the book of Ezra.

Suggested Readings

CHAPTER I: *Some Problems of Interpretation*

In order to study the Bible *in depth* one needs a shelf of reference works which ought to include:

SEVERAL DIFFERENT TRANSLATIONS

Among the best modern ones are:

The Anchor Bible. Garden City, New York: Doubleday and Company, 1964.—In process.

The Jerusalem Bible, ed. Alexander Jones. Garden City New York: Doubleday and Company, 1966.

The New English Bible with Apocrypha. Oxford: Oxford University Press, 1970.

The Holy Bible, Revised Standard Version. New York: Thomas Nelson and Sons, 1952.

The Torah: The Five Books of Moses. Philadelphia: Jewish Publication Society of America, 1963.

A CONCORDANCE

The standard concordance for the Revised Standard Version is:

Nelson's Complete Concordance of the Revised Standard Version, compiled by J. W. Ellison. New York: Thomas Nelson and Sons, 1957. For those who can use either Greek or Hebrew, the following will be of great value, for it provides Hebrew and Greek equivalents:

Youngs, Analytical Concordance to the Bible. Twenty-second American edition, revised by W. B. Stevenson, New York: Funk and Wagnall, 1955.

AN ATLAS OF THE BIBLE

Two very useful atlases are:

May, Herbert, G., *Oxford Bible Atlas.* Oxford: Oxford University Press, 1964.

Wright, G. Ernest and Floyd V. Filson, eds. *The Westminster Historical Atlas to the Bible*, rev. ed. Philadelphia: Westminster Press, 1956

A ONE-VOLUME COMMENTARY

Black, M. and H. H. Rowley, eds., *Peake's Commentary on the Bible*, rev. ed. New York: Thomas Nelson and Sons, 1962.
Perhaps the best.

Harrelson, Walter, *Interpreting the Old Testament.* New York: Holt, Rinehart and Winston, 1964.
This is not *exactly* a commentary but may be used as such.

Orchard, B. E. F. Sutcliffe and R. Russell, eds., *A Catholic Commentary on Holy Scripture.* Edinburgh: Thomas Nelson and Sons, 1953. A good, conservative commentary.

A DICTIONARY OF THE BIBLE

Buttrick, George, *et al*, eds., *The Interpreters Bible Dictionary*. 4 Vols. New York: Abingdon Press, 1962.

The most up-to-date and complete.

Miller, Madeline S. and J. Lance Miller, *et al*, ed., *Harper's Bible Dictionary*. New York. Harper and Brothers, 1952.

The best one-volume dictionary.

AN INTRODUCTION TO THE OLD TESTAMENT

Among the better introductions which pursue higher criticism in some detail are:

Anderson, George W., *A Critical Introduction to the Old Testament*. London: Gerald Duckworth and Company, 1959.

Eissfeldt, Otto. *The Old Testament, An Introduction*. Translated by Peter R. Ackroyd. New York: Harper and Row, 1965.

Weiser, Artur, *The Old Testament: Its Foundation and Development*. Translated by D. M. Barton. New York: Association Press, 1961.

CHAPTER II: *Interpreting the Bible: Some Classical Considerations*

THE QUESTION OF TEXT

Jeffery, Arthur, "Text and Ancient Versions of the Old Testament," *The Interpreter's Bible*. New York: Abingdon Press, 1952. I, 46-62.

Roberts, Bleddyn J., *The Old Testament Text and Versions: The Hebrew Texts in Transmission and the History of Ancient Versions*. Cardiff: University of Wales Press, 1951.

THE QUESTION OF CANON

Filson, Floyd, *Which Books Belong in the Bible?* Philadelphia: Westminster Press, 1957.

Jeffery, Arthur, "The Canon of the Old Testament," *The Interpreter's Bible*. New York: Abingdon Press, 1952. I, 32-45.

Zeitlin, Solomon, *An Historical Study of the Canonization of the Hebrew Scriptures*. Philadelphia: Jewish Publication Society of America, 1933.

MYTH AND HISTORY

Buber, Martin, *I and Thou*. Translated by Ronald Gregor Smith, 2nd ed. New York: Charles Scribner's Sons, 1958.

Bultmann, Rudolph, *Jesus Christ and Mythology*. New York: Charles Scribner's Sons, 1958.

Child's Brevard S., *Myth and Reality in the Old Testament*. (Studies in Biblical Theology No. 27). London: S.C.M. Press, 1960.

Dentan, Robert C. (ed.), *The Idea of History in the Ancient Near East*. New Haven: Yale University Press, 1955.

Eliade, Mircea, *Cosmos and History*. Translated by Willard R. Trask. New York: Harper and Row, 1954.

Frankfort, Henri, *et al*, *Before Philosophy*. Baltimore: Penguin Books, 1949.

Gaster, Theodore H., *Thespis: Ritual, Myth, and Drama in the Ancient Near East*. New York: Harper and Row, 1950.

CHAPTER III: *The Geography of the Land of Israel*

Besides the atlases listed above, the following may be of use:

Aharoni, Yohanan, *The Land of the Bible: A Historical Geography.* Translated by A. F. Rainey. Philadelphia: Westminster Press, 1967.

Baley, Denis, *Geographical Companion to the Bible.* London: Lutterworth Press, 1963.

———, *The Geography of the Bible.* New York: Harper and Brothers, 1957.

Pearlman, Moshe and Y. Yanni, *Historical Sites in Israel.* New York: Simon and Schuster, Inc., 1969.

CHAPTER IV: *A Brief History of Israel*

SOME GENERAL WORKS

Albright, William F., *From the Stone Age to Christianity*, 2nd ed. Baltimore: Johns Hopkins Press, 1946.

———, *The Archaeology of Palestine*, rev. ed., Baltimore: Penguin Books, 1961.

Bright, John, *A History of Israel.* Philadelphia: Westminster Press, 1959.

De Vaux, Roland, *Ancient Israel: Its Life and Institutions.* Translated by J. McHugh. New York: McGraw-Hill Book Company, 1961.

Gray, John, *Archaeology and the Old Testament World.* New York: Thomas Nelson and Sons, 1962.

Kenyon, Kathleen, *Archaeology in the Holy Land*, 3rd ed. New York: Praeger Publishers, 1970.

Noth, Martin, *The History of Israel.* Translated by S. Godman, revised by P. R. Ackroyd. 2nd ed. New York Harper and Row, 1960.

Pritchard, James (ed.), *Ancient Near Eastern Texts Relating to the Old Testament,* 3rd ed. Princeton: Princeton University Press, 1969.

Orlinsky, Harry M., *Ancient Israel.* Ithaca, N. Y.: Cornell University Press, 1964.

Wright, G. Ernest, *Biblical Archaeology*, 2nd ed. Philadelphia: Westminster Press, 1962.

BEFORE THE HEBREWS

Anati, Emmanuel, *Palestine Before the Hebrews: From the Earliest Arrival of Man to the Conquest of Canaan.* New York: Alfred Knof, 1963.

Frankfort, Henri, et al, *Before Philosophy.* Baltimore: Penguin Books, 1951.

Gardiner, Sir Alan, *Egypt of the Pharaohs.* New York: Oxford University Press, 1966.

Gray, John, *The Canaanites.* New York: Praeger Publishers, 1964.

Gurney, O. R., *The Hittites*, rev. ed. Baltimore: Penguin Books, 1961.

Kramer, Samuel, *The Sumerians: Their History, Culture, and Character.* Chicago: University of Chicago Press, 1963.

Mendenhall, George E., "Mari," *The Biblical Archaeologist Reader*, 2. Garden City, New York: Doubleday and Company, 1964.

THE AGE OF THE PATRIARCHS

Glueck, Nelson, *Rivers in the Desert: A History of the Negeb.* New York: Farrar, Straus, and Cudahy, 1959. Ch. iii.

Gordon, Cyrus H., "Biblical Customs and the Nuzu Tablets," *The Biblical Archaeologist Reader, 1.* Garden City, New York: Doubleday and Company, 1964, pp. 21-33.

Hunt, Ignatius, *The World of the Patriarchs.* Englewood Cliffs, N. J.: Prentice-Hall, 1967.

Woolley, Sir Leonard, *Ur of the Chaldees.* Baltimore: Penguin Books, 1950.

ISRAEL IN EGYPT

Buber, Martin, *Moses: The Revelation and the Covenant.* New York: Harper and Row, 1958.

Meek, Theopile, *Hebrew Origins*, rev. ed. New York: Harper and Brothers, 1950.

Mendenhall, George E., *Law and Covenant in Israel and the Ancient Near East.* Pittsburgh: Biblical Colloquim, 1955.

Rad, Gerhard von, *Moses.* London: Lutterworth Press, 1960.

Rowley, Harold H., *From Joseph to Joshua.* London: The British Academy, 1950.

Williams, Jay G., *Ten Words of Freedom, An Introduction to the Faith of Israel.* Philadelphia: Fortress Press, 1971.

THE CONQUEST OF THE PROMISED LAND

Ginsberg, H. L., "Ugaritic Studies and the Bible," *The Biblical Archaeologist Reader, 2.* Garden City, N. Y.: Doubleday and Company, 1964, pp. 34-50.

Gray, John, *The Legacy of Canaan*, 2nd ed. Leiden: E. J. Brill, 1965.

Kenyon, Kathleen, *Digging Up Jericho.* New York: Frederick A. Praeger, 1957.

Kauffman, Yehezekel, *The Biblical Account of the Conquest.* Translated by M. Dagut. Jerusalem: Magnes Press, 1955.

Pritchard, James, *Gideon, Where the Sun Stood Still: The Discovery of a Biblical City.* Princeton: Princeton University Press, 1962.

Rad, Gerhard von, *Old Testament Theology.* Translated by G. M. Stalker. New York: Harper and Row, 1962. I, 15-35.

IN THE TIME OF THE JUDGES

Buber, Martin, *The Prophetic Faith.* Translated by C. Witton-Davis. New York: The Macmillan Company, 1949. Pp. 1-30.

Harrelson, Walter, *From Fertility Cult to Worship.* Garden City, N. Y.: Doubleday and Company, 1970.

Palmer, A. Smythe, *The Samson Saga.* London: Sir Isaac Pitman and Sons, 1913.

Wright, G. Ernest, *Shechem, the Biography of a City.* New York: McGraw-Hill, 1965.

THE RISE OF THE KINGSHIP

James, Fleming, *Personalities in the Old Testament.* New York: Charles Scribner's Sons, 1939. Pp. 96-165.

Maly, Eugene H., *The World of David and Solomon.* Englewood Cliffs, N. J.: Prentice-Hall, 1965.

Wright, G. Ernest, *et al.*, "The Significance of the Temple in the Ancient Near East," *The Biblical Archaeologist Reader, 1.* Garden City, New York: Doubleday and Company, 1961. Pp. 145-200.

THE DIVIDED KINGDOMS

James, Fleming, *Personalities in the Old Testament.* New York: Charles Scribner's Sons, 1939. Pp. 162-181.

Mazar, Benjamin, "The Aramean Empire and Its Relation with Israel," *Biblical Archaeologist Reader*, 2. Garden City, New York: Doubleday and Company, 1964, Pp. 127-151.

JUDAH STANDS ALONE

Albright, William F., *From the Stone Age to Christianity*, 2nd ed. Baltimore: Johns Hopkins Press, 1946, Pp. 273-333.

Bright, John, *Jeremiah.* (The Anchor Bible) New York: Doubleday and Company, 1965.

Oppenheim, A. Leo, *Ancient Mesopotamia: Portrait of a Dead Civilization.* Chicago: University of Chicago Press, 1968.

Parrot, Andre, *Babylon and the Old Testament.* Translated by B. E. Hooke. New York: Philosophical Library, 1958.

———, *Nineveh and the Old Testament.* Translated by S. H. Hooke and Beatrice. Chester Springs, Pa.: Dufour, 1968.

EXILE AND RESTORATION

Ackroyd, Peter R., *Exile and Restoration.* Philadelphia: Westminster Press, 1968.

Ghirshman, R., *Iran.* Baltimore: Penguin Books, 1954.

Olmstead, A. T., *The History of the Persian Empire.* Chicago: University of Chicago Press, 1948.

Snaith, Norman, *The Jews from Cyrus to Herod.* New York: Abingdon Press, 1956.

THE END OF THE OLD TESTAMENT PERIOD

Bickermann, Elias, *From Ezra to the Last of the Maccabees.* New York: Schocken Books, 1962.

Tcherifover, Victor, *Hellenistic Civilization and the Jews.* Translated by S. Applebaum. Philadelphia: Jewish Publication Society, 1959.

CHAPTER V: *The Torah, An Introduction*

Alt, Albrecht, *Essays on Old Testament History and Religion.* Translated by R. A. Wilson. Garden City, N. Y.: Doubleday and Company, 1967.

Kaufmann, Yezekel, *The Religion of Israel.* Translated and abridged by Moshe Greenberg, Chicago: University of Chicago Press, 1960, Pp. 153-211.

Koch, Klaus, *The Growth of the Biblical Tradition: The Form-Critical Method.* New York: Charles Scribner's Sons, 1969.

Nielsen, Eduard, *Oral Tradition* (Studies in Biblical Theology, No. 11). London: S.C.M. Press, 1961.

North, Christopher R., "Pentateuchal Criticism," *The Old Testament and Modern Study*, ed. H. H. Rowley, Oxford: Clarendon Press, 1951, Pp. 48-83.

Simpson, Cuthbert A., "The Growth of the Hexateuch," *The Interpreter's Bible.* New York: Abingdon Press, 1952. I, 185-200.

CHAPTER VI: *Genesis: Introduction and Analysis*

Gunkel, Hermann, *The Legends of Genesis, The Biblical Sagas and History.* Translated by W. H. Carruth. New York: Schocken Books, 1964.

Hooke, S. H., *In the Beginning.* New York: Oxford University Press, 1947.

Rad, Gerhard von, *Genesis* (The Old Testament Library). Translated by J. H. Marks. Philadelphia: Westminster Press, 1961.

Speiser, E. A., Genesis (The Anchor Bible). New York: Doubleday and Co., 1964.

CHAPTER VII: *Exodus: Introduction and Analysis*

Buber, Martin, *Moses, The Revelation and the Covenant.* New York: Harper and Row, 1958.

Finegan, Jack, *Let My People Go: A Journey Through Exodus.* New York: Harper and Row, 1963.

Meek, Theopile, *Hebrew Origins*, rev. ed. New York: Harper and Brothers, 1950.

Noth, Martin, *Exodus, A Commentary* (Old Testament Library). Translated by J. S. Bowden. Philadelphia: Westminster Press, 1962.

Rad, Gerhard von, *Moses* (World Christian Books). London: Lutterworth Press, 1960.

Williams, Jay G., *Ten Words of Freedom.* Philadelphia: Fortress Press, 1971.

CHAPTER VIII: *Leviticus: Introduction and Analysis*

Micklem, Nathaniel, "Introduction and Exegesis to the Book of Leviticus," *The Interpreter's Bible*. New York: Abingdon Press, 1952. II, 3-134.

Noth, Martin, *Leviticus, A Commentary* (Old Testament Library). Translated by J. E. Anderson. Philadelphia: Westminster Press, 1965.

CHAPTER IX: *Numbers: Introduction and Analysis*

Marsh, John, "Introduction and Exegesis to Numbers," *The Interpreter's Bible.* New York: Abingdon Press, 1952. II, 137-308.

Noth, Martin, *Numbers, A Commentary* (Old Testament Library). Translated by James D. Martin. Philadelphia: Westminster Press, 1969.

CHAPTER X: *Deuteronomy: Introduction and Analysis*

Rad, Gerhard von, *Deuteronomy, A Commentary* (Old Testament Library). Translated by Dorothea Barton. Philadelphia: Westminster Press, 1966.

———, *Studies in Deuteronomy* (Studies in Biblical Theology, No. 9). London: S.C.M. Press, 1953.

Wright, G. Ernest, "Introduction and Exegesis to Deuteronomy," *The Interpreter's Bible.* New York: Abingdon Press, 1952. II, 311-537.

CHAPTER XI: *The Prophets, A General Introduction*

Buber, Martin, *The Prophetic Faith.* Translated by C. Witton-Davies. New York: Macmillan Company, 1949.

Fosbroke, Hughell E. W., "The Prophetic Literature," *The Interpreter's Bible.* New York: Abingdon Press, 1952. I, 201-211.

Heschel, Abraham J., *The Prophets.* New York: Harper and Row, 1963.

Lindblom, Johannes, *Prophecy in Ancient Israel.* Oxford: Basil Blackwell, 1962.

Mowinckel, Sigmund, *He That Cometh.* Translated by G. W. Anderson. New York: Abingdon Press, 1956.

Rad, Gerhard von, *Old Testament Theology.* Translated by D. M. G. Stalker. New York: Harper and Row, 1965. Vol. II.

Scott, R. B. Y., *The Relevance of the Prophets.* New York: the Macmillan Co., 1944.

CHAPTER XII: *Joshua: Introduction and Analysis*

Bright, John, "Introduction and Exegesis to Joshua," *The Interpreter's Bible.* New York: Abingdon Press, 1953. II, 540-673.

Kaufmann, Yehezkel. *The Biblical Account of the Conquest of Palestine.* Translated by M. Dagut. Jerusalem: Magnes Press, 1955.

CHAPTER XIII: *Judges: Introduction and Analysis*

Moore, G. F., *International Critical Commentary: A Critical and Exegetical Commentary on Judges.* New York: Scribner, 1895.

Myers, Jacob M. "Introduction and Exegesis to Judges," *The Interpreter's Bible.* New York: Abingdon Press, 1953. II, 677-826.

CHAPTER XIV: *Samuel I and II: Introduction and Analysis*

Caird, George B. "Introduction and Exegesis to I-II Samuel," *The Interpreter's Bible.* New York: Abingdon Press, 1953. II, 855-1176.

Hertzberg, H. W. *The Books of Samuel* (Old Testament Library). Translated by J. S. Bowden. Philadelphia: Westminster Press, 1964.

CHAPTER XV: *Kings I and II: Introduction and Analysis*

Gray, John. *I and II Kings* (Old Testament Library). Philadelphia: Westminster Press, 1963.

Snaith, Norman. "Introduction and Exegesis to I-II Kings," *The Interpreter's Bible.* New York: Abingdon Press, 1954. III, 3-338.

CHAPTER XVI: *Isaiah: Introduction and Analysis*

Blank, Sheldon M. *The Prophetic Faith in Israel.* New York: Harper and Row, 1958.

Kissane, Edward J. *The Book of Isaiah*, 2nd ed. 2 Vols. Dublin: Browne and Nolan, 1960.

Knight, George A. F. *Deutero-Isaiah.* Nashville: Abingdon Press, 1965.

McKenzie, John L. *Second Isaiah* (The Anchor Bible). Garden City, N. Y.: Doubleday and Company, 1968.

Muilenberg, James. "Introduction and Exegesis to Isaiah 40-66," *The Interpreter's Bible.* New York: Abingdon Press, 1956. V, 381-773.

North, Christopher. *The Suffering Servant in Deutero-Isaiah, an Historical and Critical Study.* London. Oxford University Press, 1964.

Scott, R. B. Y. "Introduction and Exegesis to Isaiah 1-39," *The Interpreter's Bible*. New York: Abingdon Press, 1956. V, 151-381.

CHAPTER XVII: *Jeremiah: Introduction and Analysis*

Bright, John. *Jeremiah* (The Anchor Bible). New York: Doubleday and Company, 1965.

Hyatt, J. P. "Introduction and Exegesis to the Book of Jeremiah," *The Interpreter's Bible*. New York: Abingdon Press, 1956. V, 777-1142.

Skinner, John. *Prophecy and Religion*. New York: Cambridge University Press, 1922.

CHAPTER XVIII: *Ezekiel: Introduction and Analysis*

Ackroyd, Peter R. *Exile and Restoration* (The Old Testament Library). Philadelphia: Westminster Press, 1968.

May, Herbert G. "Introduction and Exegesis to the Book of Ezekiel," *The Interpreter's Bible*. New York: Abingdon Press, 1956. VI, 41-338.

Rowley, Harold H. *The Book of Ezekiel in Modern Study*. Manchester: Manchester University Press and John Rylands Library, 1953.

CHAPTER XIX: *The Minor Prophets: Hosea, Joel, Amos, Obadiah, Jonah,Micah, Nahum, Habakkuk, Zephamiah, Haggai, Zechariah, Malachi*

Besides the various introductions and exegeses to these books found in Volume 6 of *The Interpreter's Bible*, the following may be of use:

Cohen, A. *The Twelve Prophets* (Soncino Bible). London: Soncino Press, 1948.

Kapelrud, Arvid S. *Central Ideas in Amos*. Oslo: H. Aschenhoug, 1956.

Morgenstern, Julian. *Amos Studies I-III*. Cincinatti: Hebrew Union College Press, 1941.

Snaith, Norman. *Amos, Hosea and Micah*. Oslo: H. Aschenhoug, 1956.

CHAPTER XXI: *The Book of Job: Introduction and Analysis*

Jung, Carl G. *Answer to Job*. Translated by R. F. C. Hull. London: Routledge and Kegan Paul, 1954.

Pope, Marvin H. *Job* (The Anchor Bible). Garden City, N. Y.: Doubleday and Company, 1965.

Terrien, Samuel. *Job, Poet of Existence*. Indianapolis: Bobbs-Merrill, 1958.

CHAPTER XXII: *Psalms: Introduction and Analysis*

Dahood, Mitchell. *Psalms I (1-50)* (The Anchor Bible). Garden City, N. Y.: Doubleday and Company, 1966.

———. *Psalms II (51-100)* The Anchor Bible). Garden City, N. Y.: Doubleday and Company, 1968.

———. *Psalms III (101-150)* (The Anchor Bible). Garden City, N. Y.: Doubleday and Company, 1970.

Kissane, Edward J. *The Book of Psalms*, 2 Vols. Dublin: Browne and Nolan, 1952, 1954.

McCullough, W. Stewart and William R. Taylor. "Introduction and Exegesis to the Psalms," *The Interpreter's Bible*. New York: Abingdon Press, 1955. IV, 3-763.

Mowinckel, Sigmund. *The Psalms in Israel's Worship*, 2 Vols. Translated by D. R. Ap-Thomas. Oxford: Basil Blackwell, 1962.

Pfeiffer, Robert H. *Introduction to the Old Testament*. New York: Harper and Row, 1941. Pp. 619-644.

Weiser, Artur, *The Psalms, A Commentary* (The Old Testament Library). Philadelphia: Westminster Press, 1962.

CHAPTER XXIII: *The Book of Proverbs: Introduction and Analysis*

Fritsch, Charles T. "Introduction and Exegesis to the Book of Proverbs," *The Interpreter's Bible*. New York: Abingdon Press, 1955. IV, 767-957.

Noth, Martin and D. Winton Thomas, eds. *Wisdom in Israel and the Ancient Near East* (Supplements to Vetus Testamentus, III). Leiden: E. J. Brill, 1955.

Rankin, O. S. *Israel's Wisdom Literature*. Edinburgh: T. & T. Clark, 1936.

Scott, R. B. Y. *Proverbs and Ecclesiastes* (The Anchor Bible). Garden City, N. Y.: Doubleday and Company, 1965.

CHAPTER XXIV: *The Megillot: Ruth, Song of Songs, Lamentations, Ecclesiastes, Esther*

Beside the introductions and exegeses to these books found in *The Interpreter's Bible*, Volumes 2, 3, 5, and 6, the following may be of interest:

Gaster, Theodore. *Purim and Hanukkah in Custom and Tradition*. New York: Abelard-Schuman, 1950.

Gordis, Robert: *Koheleth, the Man and His World*. New York: Jewish Theological Seminary, 1951.

Gottwald, Norman K. *Studies in the Book of Lamentations* (Studies in Biblical Theology, No. 14). London: S. C. M. Press, 1954.

Schauss, Hayyim. *Guide to Jewish Holy Days, History and Observances*. Translated by Samuel Jaffe. New York: Shocken Books, 1962.

CHAPTER XXV: *Daniel*

Jeffrey, Arthur. "Introduction and Exegeses to Daniel," *The Interpreter's Bible*. New York: Abingdon Press, 1956. VI, 341-549.

Porteous, Norman W. *Daniel* (Old Testament Library). Philadelphia: Westminster Press, 1965.

Rowley, Harold H. *The Relevance of Apocalyptic*, 2nd ed. London: Lutterworth Press, 1947.

Russell, D. S. *The Method and Message of Jewish Apocalyptic* (Old Testament Library). Philadelphia: Westminster Press, 1964.

CHAPTER XXVI: *Ezra and Nehemiah: Introduction and Analysis*

Ackroyd, Peter R. *Exile and Restoration* (Old Testament Library). Philadelphia: Westminster Press, 1968.

Bowman, R. A. "Introduction and Exegeses to Ezra and Nehemiah," *The Interpreter's Bible*. New York: Abingdon Press, 1954. III, 551-819.

CHAPTER XXVII: *Chronicles I and II: Introduction and Analysis*

Elmslie, W. A. L. "Introduction and Exegesis to 1-2 Chronicles," *The Interpreter's Bible*. New York: Abingdon Press, 1954. III, 341-548.

Myers, Jacob M. *Chronicles I and II*, 2 Volumes (The Anchor Bible). Garden City, N. Y.: Doubleday and Company., 1965.

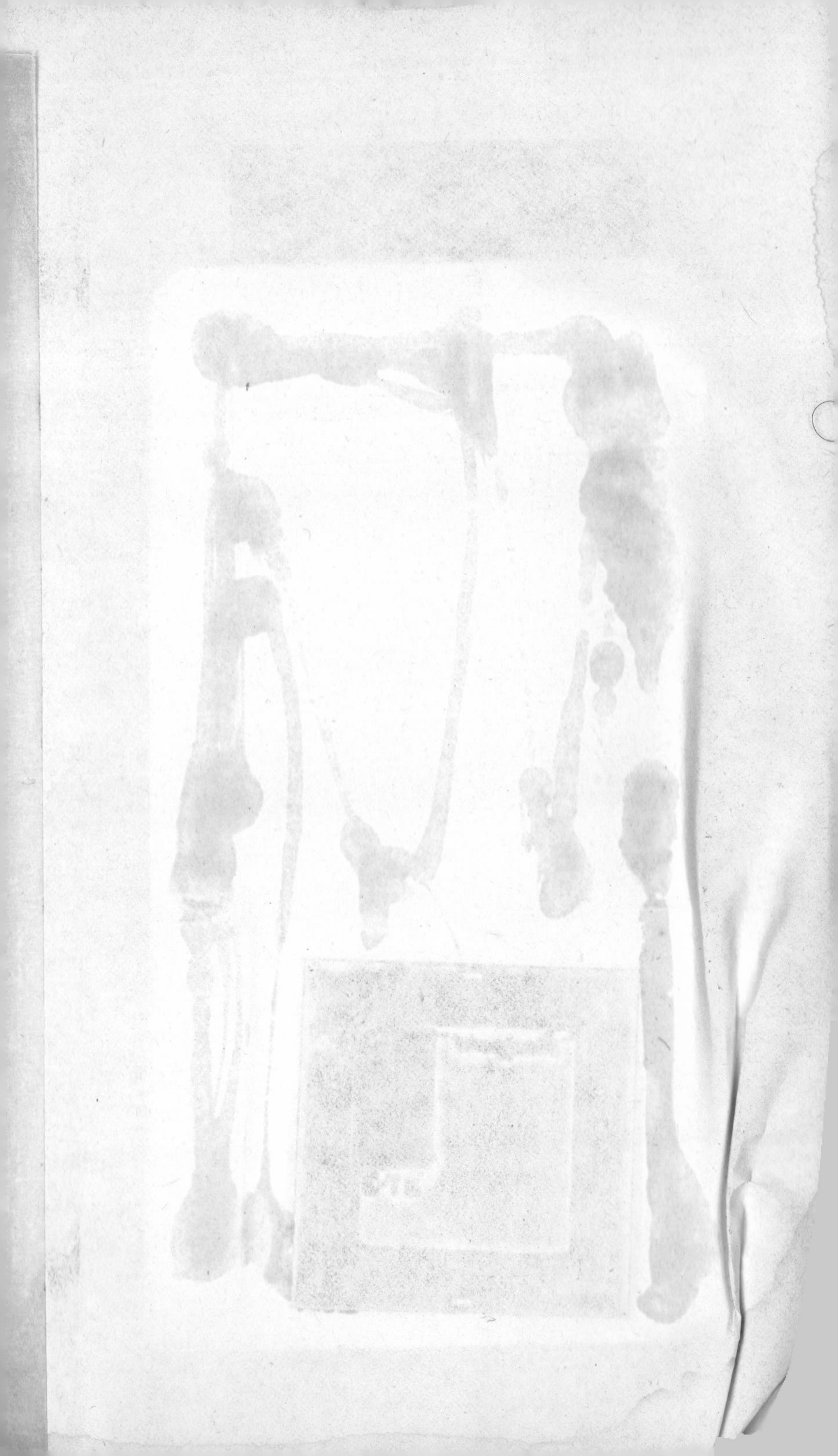